AF361509

METAPHYSICAL
DISPUTATION I

EARLY MODERN
CATHOLIC SOURCES

Volume 2

FRANCISCO SUÁREZ

METAPHYSICAL DISPUTATION I

ON THE NATURE OF FIRST PHILOSOPHY OR METAPHYSICS

Translated and annotated,
with corrected Latin text,
by SHANE DUARTE

THE CATHOLIC UNIVERSITY
OF AMERICA PRESS
Washington, D.C.

Copyright © 2021

The Catholic University of America Press

All rights reserved

The paper used in this publication meets the minimum

requirements of American National Standards for

Information Science—Permanence of Paper for Printed Library

Materials, ANSI z39.48—1984.

∞

Cataloging-in-Publication Data available from

the Library of Congress

ISBN 978-0-8132-3402-1

In memoriam patris

José Hermínio de Magalhães Duarte

(1933–2017)

CONTENTS

ACKNOWLEDGMENTS

I would like to take this opportunity to thank a number of people who have helped me during the course of my project to translate Metaphysical Disputations I–IV. My thanks to Sydney Penner for providing me with a scan of the first edition of Suárez's *Metaphysical Disputations* (*DM*). For feedback on various parts of the entire translation, I would like to thank Sydney Penner, Brian Embry, and Lukáš Novák. For providing me with funds to travel to Groningen for the conference "Varieties of Unity in Early Modern Philosophy" (April 12–13, 2019), organized by Brian Embry and Marleen Rozemond, my thanks go to the University of Notre Dame's Institute for Scholarship in the Liberal Arts. For their reading of *DM* 1, I would like to thank the graduate students in Christopher Shields's fall 2017 seminar on Suárez's *Disputations*. I would also like to express my thanks to Christopher Shields for his generous advice, kind encouragement, and expert feedback on various aspects of this project. Finally, my deepest gratitude goes to my wife, the brilliant Michelle Karnes, for her unfailing and kind support and encouragement during the many years of this project.

INTRODUCTION

Francisco Suárez (1548–1617) was one of the most important philosophers and theologians of Iberian Scholasticism, an intellectual movement tracing its origins to the Dominican thinkers Francisco de Vi-
toria (1486–1546), Domingo de Soto (1494–1560), and Melchior Cano
(1509–60) at the University of Salamanca.[1] Although Suárez spent most
of his academic career as a professor of theology, he is best known today for his *Metaphysical Disputations* (1597) and for his contributions
to moral, legal, and political theory. His influence extended beyond the
Roman Catholic world of which he was a part and into the Protestant
universities of seventeenth-century Europe. The precise extent of his
influence on the early modern philosophers most studied today—for
example, René Descartes (1596–1650)—still remains to be determined,
but there is no doubt that he was frequently cited in the philosophy
textbooks on which many such thinkers were educated.

1. Life and Works

Francisco Suárez was born January 5, 1548 to a prosperous family in
Granada. He was one of eight children. His mother, Antonia Vázquez
de Utiel, was sister to the famous Jesuit cardinal Francisco de Toledo
(1532–96). Suárez's early twentieth-century biographer Raoul de Scorraille, SJ, affirms that Suárez was "of altogether Christian and Spanish
blood" (*d'un sang tout chrétien et tout espagnol*),[2] but in fact the cardinal

---

1. For a discussion of this intellectual movement, see Thomas Izbicki and Matthias
Kaufmann, "The School of Salamanca," in *The Stanford Encyclopedia of Philosophy*, ed. Ed-
ward Zalta (March 2019), https://plato.stanford.edu/entries/school-salamanca/.

2. Raoul de Scorraille, *François Suárez de la Compagnie de Jésus* (Paris: P. Lethielleux,
1912–13), 1:4.

and his sister had Jewish ancestors, and according to one inquisitor, several of their forebears were burned at the stake.[3]

In 1561, after early schooling in rhetoric and grammar, Francisco was sent, aged thirteen, to study canon law at the University of Salamanca. He did not distinguish himself in his studies, and in June of 1564 his request to join the recently founded Society of Jesus was denied for want of talent and concerns over his health.[4] After an appeal to the Jesuit provincial of Castile in Valladolid, however, he was admitted to the Society as an "indifferent," which is to say that the question of whether he would be a priest or a lay brother of the order was left unresolved, to be decided later by appeal to the aptitudes he evinced during his novitiate.[5] As it turned out, Suárez was ordained in March of 1572, at the age of twenty-four.[6]

In Salamanca, Suárez studied philosophy from 1564 to 1566, and then theology from 1566 to 1570. During this time, he clearly impressed his teachers and superiors, since in 1570 he was chosen to represent the Jesuit college at the university in a "Grand Act," a kind of public disputation reserved for the most promising students, taking place over the course of two sessions in a single day.[7] Suárez's performance generated some controversy, since he chose to defend, among various theological theses, the doctrine of the Immaculate Conception, that is to say, the view that the Virgin Mary was born without the stain of original sin.[8] He is said to have drawn a large crowd and acquitted himself admirably.[9]

From 1571 to 1574, Suárez taught philosophy in Segovia. Since he taught only theology after this period, it was likely during these years

---

3. Robert Aleksander Maryks, *The Jesuit Order as a Synagogue of Jews: Jesuits of Jewish Ancestry and Purity-of-Blood Laws in the Early Society of Jesus* (Leiden & Boston: Brill, 2010), 104.

4. Scorraille, *François Suárez*, 1:43.

5. Scorraille, *François Suárez*, 1:44–47.

6. Scorraille, *François Suárez*, 1:133.

7. Scorraille, *François Suárez*, 1:110–13.

8. Theologians variously defined the doctrine and debated its status as a revealed truth up until December 8, 1854, when Pius IX, in the Constitution *Ineffabilis Deus*, defined it once and for all and required belief in it by all Roman Catholics. Although some version of the doctrine was widely accepted for centuries, some theologians nonetheless continued to hold that Christ alone was without original sin, including many Dominicans, in part because this was thought to have been the view of Thomas Aquinas.

9. Scorraille, *François Suárez*, 1:113–15.

that he wrote the lectures on metaphysics that he would later revise and work up into his *Metaphysical Disputations*.[10] It may also have been during this time that he wrote several commentaries on various of Aristotle's works, including *De generatione et corruptione* and the *Posterior Analytics*.[11] In the two academic years beginning in September 1574, he taught theology first at Valladolid and then at Segovia and Ávila. In September of 1576, he returned to Valladolid as a professor of theology. In 1580 he was called to Rome, to teach theology at the Jesuits' most prestigious college, the Collegio Romano. Here, however, Suárez's health (which had never been very good to begin with) took a turn for the worse, aggravated, apparently, by the Roman climate.[12] In 1585 he was accordingly sent back to Spain, where he assumed the post of Professor of Theology at the University of Alcalá. There he replaced Gabriel Vázquez (1549–1604), who in turn replaced Suárez at the Collegio Romano.

It was while at Alcalá that Suárez's first works were published. By this time, the *Summa theologiae* (*ST*) of Thomas Aquinas (1225–74) was well on its way to displacing the *Sentences* of Peter Lombard (ca. 1100–1160) as the textual focus of many theology courses in the Roman Catholic world.[13] Most of Suárez's published works are explicitly offered as commentaries on some part of Aquinas's *Summa theologiae*, although

10. In the proem to the *Metaphysical Disputations*, after noting the usefulness of metaphysics or "natural wisdom" for supernatural theology, Suárez tells the reader that the *Disputations* is the product of reviewing and enriching "what I had labored on and publicly dictated about this natural wisdom many years ago as a young man."

11. See Salvador Castellote, "Transcripción y notas del manuscrito inédito suareciano 'De Generatione et Corruptione,'" in *Francisco Suárez: "Der ist der Mann," Apéndice Francisco Suárez*, De generatione et corruptione: *Homenaje al Prof. Salvador Castellote*, 435–682 (Valencia: Facultad de Teología San Vicente Ferrer, 2004). No commentary by Suárez on the *Posterior Analytics* has been recognized as such today. However, at *DM* 1.4.18, Suárez states that he has discussed a particular question regarding the habit of principles in *Post. An.* II. Moreover, in the posthumously published first edition of Suárez's *De angelis* (1620) one finds, after an "Authoris Vita" ("Life of the Author"), a section entitled "Libri editi iam in lucem, edendique propediem" ("Books already published, and very soon to be published") listing various of Suárez's works. Item 24 reads: "*Commentaria in logicam, aliosque Aristotelis libros. Tomus unicus edendus*" ("Commentaries on the logic and other books of Aristotle. One volume, to be published"). I have been unable to locate any such published volume.

12. Scorraille, *François Suárez*, 1:177–79.

13. See Jacob Schmutz, "From Theology to Philosophy: The Changing Status of the *Summa Theologiae*, 1500–2000," in *Aquinas's* Summa Theologiae: *A Critical Guide*, ed. Jeffrey Hause, 221–41 (Cambridge: Cambridge University Press, 2018).

these writings are much less directly tied to the text of the *Summa* than
(say) the famous commentary of Cardinal Cajetan (1469–1534) is.[14] Indeed, in respect of scope, Suárez's commentaries typically go beyond
what is found in the corresponding parts of the *Summa*. In any case,
Suárez's first published work, which appeared in 1590, is offered as a
commentary on *ST* III, qq. 1–26.[15] It is commonly referred to as *De
verbo incarnato* (*On the Incarnate Word*) or *De incarnatione* (*On the
Incarnation*). While at Alcalá, Suárez also published, in 1592, a similar
commentary on *ST* III, qq. 27–59, commonly referred to as *De mysteriis
vitae Christi* (*On the Mysteries of the Life of Christ*).

Suárez left Alcalá for the University of Salamanca in the fall of 1593,
again on account of his health, which seems to have been adversely af-
fected by various tensions and conflicts with Gabriel Vázquez, who had
returned to Alcalá from the Collegio Romano in 1591.[16] In 1595, while
at Salamanca, Suárez published *De sacramentis* (*On the Sacraments*),
a commentary on and an elaboration of issues discussed in *ST* III,
qq. 60–83. The following year, Philip II of Spain (1527–98), then also
Philip I of Portugal, requested of the Jesuits that Suárez be given the
principal chair of theology at the University of Coimbra. Suárez was
reluctant to take the post, in part because he had come to Salamanca in
the expectation of entering into the final phase of his career, one chiefly
devoted to writing. Accordingly, he traveled to Toledo to ask the king
in person that he be excused from the appointment, on grounds of
poor health. The petition was successful, and the man whose planned
retirement had prompted Philip to request Suárez as a replacement,
the Portuguese Dominican António de São Domingos (ca. 1531–96),
was ordered to remain at his post, at least temporarily. However, Father António died in late 1596, and soon thereafter Philip once again
asked—rather more insistently this time—that Suárez take the position
in Coimbra. Suárez evidently felt that he had no choice but to accept.[17]

14. Cajetan's commentary is printed together with the *Summa* in Thomas Aquinas,
Sancti Thomae Aquinatis opera omnia (Leonina), ts. 4–12 (Romae: Ex Typographia Polyglotta, S. C. De Propaganda Fide, 1888–1906).

15. Information regarding the first editions of Suárez's works can be found in this volume's bibliography.

16. For more on his conflict at Alcalá with Vázquez, see Scorraille, *François Suárez*,
1:283–314.

17. Scorraille, *François Suárez*, 1:335–42.

He taught at Coimbra from 1597 until his retirement from teaching in July 1615. He died September 25, 1617, in Lisbon.

The same year that saw Suárez's move to Portugal also witnessed the publication, in two volumes, of his *Metaphysical Disputations*, in Salamanca. Most of the works Suárez published during his lifetime appeared while he was a professor of theology at Coimbra. In 1599, he published, in a single volume, several shorter works devoted to the *De auxiliis* controversy between Dominicans and Jesuits, a controversy centered on the question of how human freedom is to be reconciled with divine grace, foreknowledge, providence, and predestination.[18] In 1602, he published a work commonly known as *De poenitentia* (*On Penance*), which serves as a commentary on *ST* III, qq. 84–90, and is a continuation of his discussion of the sacraments, covering the sacraments of penance (or confession) and extreme unction (or the annointing of the sick), as well as related matters. In 1603, there appeared *De censuris* (*On Censures*), which is conceived as a kind of addition to *ST* III, censures having an important connection to the sacrament of penance. In 1606, he published *De Deo uno et trino* (*On God, One and Triune*), which serves as a commentary on, and as an elaboration of issues discussed in, *ST* I, qq. 1–43. In 1608 and 1609 he published the first two parts of his *De virtute et statu religionis* (*On the Virtue and State of Religion*). The third and fourth parts of this work would be published posthumously, in 1624 and 1625, under the supervision of Suárez's literary executor, Baltasar Álvares (1560–1630). Together, these volumes treat of religion in two distinct, though importantly connected, senses of the term: in one sense, as a virtue common to all Christians, inclining them to certain actions, and in another sense, as a state or manner of life peculiar to those who are properly called religious (e.g., monks and friars), a state "in which some faithful are gathered in order to worship God in a more perfect way" (*in quo aliqui fideles congregantur ad perfectiori modo colendum Deum*).[19] To the extent that the work discusses the virtue of religion, it is offered as a commentary

---

18. For an introduction to the *De auxiliis* controversy, see R. J. Matava, *Divine Causality and Human Free Choice: Domingo Báñez, Physical Premotion and the Controversy de Auxuliis Revisited* (Leiden & Boston: Brill, 2016), ch. 1.

19. Francisco Suárez, *R. P. Francisci Suarez, E Societate Jesu, Opera Omnia*, 28 vols. in 30 (Parisiis: Apud Ludovicum Vivès, 1856–78), 13:8b.

on *ST* II-II, qq. 81–100, and insofar as it discusses the state of religion, it is conceived as a commentary on *ST* II-II, qq. 183–89.[20]

In 1612, Suárez published *De legibus, ac de Deo legislatore* (*On the Laws, and on God the Lawgiver*), commonly referred to simply as *De legibus*. Presented as a commentary on *ST* I-II, qq. 90–108, *De legibus* exercised a significant influence over later natural law theorists such as Hugo Grotius (1583–1645). Over the course of its ten books, Suárez deals with law in general, divine or eternal law, natural law, the law of nations (*ius gentium*), civil or positive law, canon law, the interpretation, abrogation and emendation of human laws, unwritten law or custom, laws conferring privileges, the Mosaic or old divine law, and the new divine law.

Also bearing on political theory is Suárez's *Defensio fidei catholicae adversus anglicanae sectae errores* (*Defense of the Catholic Faith against the Errors of the Anglican Sect*), written in part at the behest of the papal nuncio in Madrid, Decio Caraffa (1556–1626), and published in 1613.[21] It presents a reply to arguments in favor of the Oath of Allegiance (1606), which required English Catholics in particular to affirm and acknowledge, among other things, that the pope had no authority to depose James I or absolve his subjects of their obligations of obedience to him. In this work, Suárez presents, as he does in *De legibus*, an account of the origin and nature of civil authority that is opposed to the absolute rights of monarchs. He also goes so far as to argue, in bk. VI, ch. 4, that in certain conditions citizens can legitimately have recourse to tyrannicide. The work was publicly burned in London and Paris.

Suárez's *Defensio fidei* was the last of his major writings to appear in his lifetime. A significant number of his works, however, were published posthumously, for the most part under the supervision of his

---

20. See Francisco Suárez, *Opera Omnia*, 13:2: "Est ergo religio totius huius operis scopus et obiectum. Sed quia duos hoc nomen *religio* praecipuos habet significatus; alterum, quo exprimit virtutem quamdam omnibus Christianis communem, alterum, quo peculiarem significat statum eorum qui proprie religiosi appellantur, duas etiam [first edition: enim] praecipuas partes totum hoc opus continebit, quarum una virtutis, altera status cognitionem comprehendat. Quamvis enim D. Thomas 2. 2, a quaest. 81 usque ad 100, de virtute religionis disputaverit, et postea, multis interiectis, a quaest. 183, et praesertim in 186 et sequentibus, de statu disseruerit, nihilominus virtus et status religionis ita mutuo nexu copulantur, ut ad unius exactam cognitionem alterius notitita requiri videatur."

21. Scorraille, *François Suárez*, 2:172.

literary executor, Baltasar Álvares. In addition to the third and fourth parts of *De virtute et statu religionis*, mentioned above, there appeared in 1619 the first and third parts of *De gratia* (*On Grace*). The second part would be published only in 1651. Together, *De gratia*'s three parts correspond to *ST* I-II, qq. 109–114. Moreover, in 1620, *De angelis* (*On the Angels*) was published, covering *ST* I, qq. 50–64, and in 1621 there appeared a volume containing both *De opere sex dierum* (*On the Work of Six Days*), corresponding to *ST* I, qq. 65–74, and *De anima* (*On the Soul*), corresponding to *ST* I, qq. 75–89.[22] Also in 1621, Álvares arranged to have published Suárez's *De fide, spe, et caritate* (*On Faith, Hope, and Charity*), corresponding to *ST* II-II, qq. 1–46. Moreover, in 1628 a volume was published containing five treatises, *De ultimo fine hominis, ac beatitudine* (*On the Ultimate End of the Human Being, and on Beatitude*), *De voluntario, & involuntario* (*On the Voluntary and Involuntary*), *De humanorum actuum bonitate, & malitia* (*On the Goodness and Wickedness of Human Acts*), *De passionibus, & habitibus* (*On Passions and Habits*), and *De vitiis, atque peccatis* (*On Vices and Sins*). Together, these works correspond to Aquinas's *ST* I-II, qq. 1–89. In 1655, another work of Suárez's dealing with the *De auxiliis* controversy was published, entitled *De vera intelligentia auxilii efficacis eiusque concordia cum libero arbitrio* (*On the True Understanding of Efficacious Aid and Its Agreement with Free Choice*). Finally, worth mentioning here as well is Suárez's *De immunitate ecclesiastica a Venetis violata* (*Regarding the Ecclesiastical Immunity Violated by the Venetians*), dealing with the limits of papal jurisdiction and a conflict between the Republic of Venice and the papacy. This work was only published for the first time in 1859, and then only in part. It moved Pope Paul V (1552–1621) to characterize Suárez as an "eminent and pious" theologian, from which arose Suárez's honorific, *Doctor eximius ac pius*.[23]

---

22. As regards *ST* I, qq. 44–49, in the proem of *De angelis* Suárez explains that he has covered this material in his *Metaphysical Disputations*, Disputation XX, *De prima causa efficiente, primaque eius actione, quae est creatio* ("On the First Efficient Cause, and His First Action, Which Is Creation"). See Francisco Suárez, *Opera Omnia*, 2:xii.

23. Scorraille, *François Suárez*, 2:126–27.

2. The *Metaphysical Disputations* (*DM*) and Its Place in the History of Metaphysics

Suárez's *Metaphysical Disputations* is often said to be the first systematic work of scholastic first philosophy not to take the form of a commentary on Aristotle's *Metaphysics*.[24] This claim stands in need of some qualification, however. For starters, in 1587, the Dominican Diego Mas (1553–1608) published his *Metaphysica disputatio de ente et eius proprietatibus* (*Metaphysical Disputation on Being and Its Properties*), and in 1597—the same year in which Suárez's *Metaphysical Disputations* appeared—the Augustinian Hermit Diego de Zúñiga (1536–98) published his *Philosophiae prima pars, qua perfecte et eleganter quatuor scientiae metaphysica, dialectica, rhetorica et physica declarantur* (*First Part of Philosophy, by which the four sciences of Metaphysics, Dialectic, Rhetoric, and Physics are completely and elegantly explained*).[25] Moreover, Jacob Schmutz has claimed that many unpublished metaphysical treatises written by Spanish Jesuits in the 1570s did not follow the traditional order of exposition.[26] Nevertheless, if we confine ourselves to published works, it remains the case that Suárez's *Metaphysical Disputations* is in some sense unprecedented, since it far outstrips the metaphysical treatises of Mas and de Zúñiga in size and scope.[27] It's also worth noting that it was much more popular, going through at least ten further editions during its author's lifetime, in Venice (1599, 1605, 1610), Mainz (1600, 1605,

---

24. See, for example, Oliva Blanchette, "Suárez and the Latent Essentialism of Heidegger's Fundamental Ontology," *The Review of Metaphysics* 53, no. 1 (1999): 3.

25. See Jordán Gallego Salvadores, "El maestro Diego Mas y su tratado de Metafísica," *Analecta sacra tarraconensia* 43, no. 1 (1970): 3–92; Jordán Gallego Salvadores, "La aparición de las primeras metafísicas sistemáticas en la España del XVI: Diego Mas (1587), Francisco Suárez y Diego de Zuñiga (1597)," *Escritos del Vedat* 3 (1973): 91–162; Juan José Gallego Salvadores, "El dominico valenciano Diego Mas y la primera metafísica sistemática," in *Francisco Suárez, "Der ist der Mann,"* 211–23. Information on the first editions of these works by Mas and de Zúñiga can be found in the bibliography of this volume.

26. Jacob Schmutz, "Science divine et métaphysique chez Francisco Suárez," in *Francisco Suárez, "Der ist der Mann,"* 347–48n1.

27. The same should be said of Suárez's *DM* in comparison with the *Tractatus de transcendentibus* (*Treatise on the Transcendentals*) of Crisostomo Javelli (ca. 1470–ca. 1538), first published in 1555, in: Giovanni Crisostomo Javelli, *Epitome Chrysostomi Iavelli Canapitii, In universam Aristotelis Philosophiam, tam naturalem, quam transnaturalem* (Venetiis: apud Ioannem Mariam Bonellum, 1555).

1614), Paris (1605), Cologne (1608, 1614), and Geneva (1614)[28]—this as compared to two further posthumous editions for Mas's *Metaphysica disputatio* (Cologne, 1616 and 1623) and (possibly) one additional posthumous edition for de Zúñiga's *Philosophiae prima pars*.[29]

The number of editions printed in Suárez's lifetime testifies to the influence of, and interest in, the *Metaphysical Disputations*, as does the fact that its author is frequently cited in popular philosophy textbooks like the *Cursus Philosophicus* of John of St. Thomas (born João Poinsot, 1589–1644) or those produced at the University of Alcalá by the Discalced Carmelites, collectively known as the *Complutenses*. (The *Cursus Philosophicus* cites Suárez 167 times,[30] and the *Complutenses'* logic textbook, first published in 1624, mentions him by name more than 100 times.[31]) Nor was Suárez's influence confined to Roman Catholic thinkers; it extended to Reformed and Lutheran thinkers as well.[32] Still, it is worth sounding a note of caution when discussing Suárez's importance for the subsequent development of particular views and doctrines. Our understanding of Suárez's position in, and importance for, the subsequent history of metaphysics arguably still has a long way to go. For one thing, the amount of scholarly attention given to his metaphysical doctrines lags well behind that given to the metaphysical systems of

28. Information on all of these editions save the 1614 Geneva edition (which is listed in WorldCat) can be found in this volume's bibliography, under "Editions of Suárez's *Disputationes Metaphysicae* cited in the Notes on the Latin Text."

29. See Jordán Gallego Salvadores, "La aparición de las primeras metafísicas sistemáticas," 100–101, notes 9 and 11.

30. As noted by John Doyle in his introduction to Francisco Suárez, *On Real Relations (Disputatio Metaphysica XLVII)*, trans. John P. Doyle (Milwaukee: Marquette University Press, 2006), 12n8. See John of St. Thomas, *Ioannis a Sancto Thoma O.P. Cursus Philosophicus Thomisticus*, ed., Beatus Reiser (Taurini: Marietti, 1930–37), 3:492–95.

31. Collegium Complutense Sancti Cyrilli, *Artium Cursus sive Disputationes in Aristotelis Dialecticam, et Philosophiam naturalem* (Compluti: apud Ioannem de Orduña, 1624).

32. See Karl Eschweiler, "Die Philosophie der spanischen Spätscholastik auf den deutschen Universitäten des siebzehnten Jahrhunderts," in *Spanische Forschungen der Görresgesellschaft, 1. Reihe: Gesammelte Aufsätze zur Kulturgeschichte Spaniens*, ed. Heinrich Finke and Johannes Vincke, 251–325 (Münster: Aschendorff, 1928); Francisco Baciero, "La influencia de Suárez en las universidades alemanas del siglo XVII: El caso de Leibniz," in *Filosofía hispánica y diálogo intercultural*, ed. Roberto Albares Albares, Antonio Heredia Soriano and Ricardo Piñero Moral, 397–412 (Salamanca: Gustavo Bueno, 2000); Marco Lamanna, "Tra Fonseca e Suárez: L'ingresso della nozione di *ens reale* nella *Schulmetaphysik*," in *Francisco Suárez and his Legacy: The Impact of Suárezian Metaphysics and Epistemology on Modern Philosophy*, ed. Marco Sgarbi, 141–168 (Milano: Vita e Pensiero, 2010).

Descartes, Spinoza (1632–77), and Leibniz (1646–1716) (for example), especially in the English-speaking world. The reasons for this are various, but evident factors include the sheer size of the *Disputations* (which is many times longer than Descartes's *Meditations* with its seven sets of Objections and Replies) and the lack of a complete translation into any modern language save Spanish.[33] What's more, when one considers Suárez's fame and the greater scholarly attention he has received, as compared with that given to contemporary and near-contemporary scholastic thinkers such as Francisco de Toledo, Jacopo Zabarella (1533–89), and Pedro da Fonseca (1528–99), one naturally wonders whether a resulting distortion of perspective has been partly responsible for the fact that some scholars have seen in Suárez's metaphysical thought key turning-points along the road leading to the better understood metaphysical systems of later thinkers, including (among others) those of Christian Wolff (1679–1754) and Immanuel Kant (1724–1804).[34]

33. Much of the secondary literature on Suárez also has a regrettable tendency toward hagiography at the expense of careful analysis of his views and arguments.

34. Many scholars have discerned Suárez's influence at work in the thought of later philosophers. In keeping with the topic of this volume, however, I here confine myself to calling the reader's attention to works that deal with the issue of Suárez's influence on how the science of metaphysics itself is conceived. (It is worth noting, however, that this literature tends often to focus also on Suárez's discussion of the nature of being in *DM* 2.) On this issue, see: Étienne Gilson, *Being and Some Philosophers*, 2nd ed. (Toronto: Pontifical Institute of Mediaeval Studies, 1952), 96–120; José Hellín, "Existencialismo escolástico suareciano: I. La existencia, constitutivo del ente," *Pensamiento* 12, no. 46 (1956): 157–78; José Hellín, "Existencialismo escolástico suareciano: II. La existencia es lo principal en el ente," *Pensamiento* 13, no. 49 (1957): 21–38; John P. Doyle, "Suárez on the Reality of the Possibles," *The Modern Schoolman* 45, no. 1 (1968): 29–48; John P. Doyle, "Heidegger and Scholastic Metaphysics," *The Modern Schoolman* 49, no. 3 (1972): 201–20; Jean-Luc Marion, *Sur la théologie blanche de Descartes: Analogie, création des verités éternelles et fondement* (Paris: PUF, 1981); Jean-François Courtine, *Suárez et le système de la métaphysique* (Paris: PUF, 1990); Ludger Honnefelder, *Scientia transcendens: Die formale Bestimmung der Seiendheit und Realität in der Metafysik des Mittelalters und der Neuzeit* (Hamburg: Felix Meiner, 1990); Jorge J. E. Gracia, "Suárez's Conception of Metaphysics: A Step in the Direction of Mentalism?" *American Catholic Philosophical Quarterly* 65, no. 3 (1991): 287–309; Franco Volpi, "Suárez et le problème de la métaphysique," *Revue de métaphysique et de morale* 98, no. 3 (1993): 395–411; Norman J. Wells, "*Esse Cognitum* and Suárez Revisited," *American Catholic Philosophical Quarterly* 67, no. 3 (1993): 339–48; Olivier Boulnois, *Être et représentation: Une généalogie de la métaphysique moderne à l'époque de Duns Scot (XIIIe–XIV siècle)* (Paris: PUF, 1999); Jean-Paul Coujou, "Introduction," in *Suárez et la refondation de la métaphysique comme ontologie: étude et traduction de l'«Index détaillé de la Métaphysique d'Aristote» de F. Suárez*, trans. Jean-Paul Coujou, *1–*67 (Louvain-la-Neuve & Louvain, Paris: Éditions de l'Institut supérieur de philosophie & Éditions Peeters, 1999); Rolf Darge, "«Ens in quantum ens»: Die Erklärung des Subjekts der Metaphysik bei F. Suarez," *Recherches de théologie et*

Of course, these observations in no way count against taking Suárez's metaphysics seriously as an object of study. There is no doubt that the *Metaphysical Disputations* is a major and influential milestone in the history of metaphysics. Not only does Suárez's *Disputations* systematically address a vast array of major metaphysical questions, often at great length, it also typically supplies its reader with a learned survey of different opinions on these questions. Indeed, according to one scholar, in the *Disputations* Suárez cites 247 different authors across 7,718 citations.[35] Suárez's erudition, in other words, is impressive, and no doubt the surveys he provides of his predecessors' views and arguments go a long way towards accounting for the popularity of the *Disputations* in the seventeenth century and beyond: the work is, among other things, a sort of compendium of scholastic views and arguments on a vast array of metaphysical issues.[36]

3. The Genesis and Structure of the *Metaphysical Disputations*

At the very beginning of the *Metaphysical Disputations*, in a note to the reader entitled "Reason for, and Survey of, the Entire Work" (*Ratio et Discursus Totius Operis, Ad Lectorem*), Suárez asserts that it is impossible to become a fully-formed theologian without first becoming versed in metaphysics. For this reason, he explains, he has always thought it advisable, before publishing any theological commentaries, to write the

---

de philosophie médiévales 66, no. 2 (1999): 335–61; José Pereira, *Suárez: Between Scholasticism and Modernity* (Milwaukee: Marquette University Press, 2006) 27, 137–39, 201–11; Victor Salas, "Francisco Suárez: End of the Scholastic ἐπιστήμη?" in *Francisco Suárez and His Legacy*, 9–28; Marco Sgarbi, "Francisco Suárez and Christian Wolff: A Missed Intellectual Legacy," in *Francisco Suárez and his Legacy*, 227–41; Rolf Darge, "Suárez on the Subject of Metaphysics," in *A Companion to Francisco Suárez*, ed. Victor M. Salas and Robert L. Fastiggi, 91–123 (Leiden & Boston: Brill, 2015); Costantino Esposito, "Introduzione," in Francisco Suárez, *Disputationi Metafisiche I–III*, 2nd. ed., introduced and translated by Costantino Esposito, 7–39 (Firenze & Milano: Giunta Editore S.p.A. & Bompiani, 2017).

35. Jesús Iturrioz, *Estudios sobre la metafísica de Francisco Suárez, S.J.* (Madrid: Estudios Onienses, 1949), 58–65.

36. For more on Suárez's place in the history of metaphysics, see Martin Grabmann, "Die Disputationes metaphysicae des Franz Suarez in ihrer methodischen Eigenart und Fortwirkung," in *P. Franz Suarez S.J.: Gedenkblätter zu seinem dreihundertjährigen Todestag (25. September 1917): Beiträge zur Philosophie des P. Suarez*, ed. Karl Six, 29–73 (Innsbruck: Tyrolia, 1917).

work now in the reader's hands. After noting that, despite this conviction of his, he could not defer the publication of certain theological commentaries on the third part of Aquinas's *Summa* (for reasons he leaves unspecified here),[37] he explains that he has since become even more convinced that "divine and supernatural theology" requires or presupposes "this human and natural" theology, that is, metaphysics. Elaborating on all this later, in the work's proem, Suárez asserts that in the treatment of divine mysteries there is frequently occasion to discuss metaphysical questions, and that without an understanding of the relevant metaphysical doctrines it is well-nigh impossible to treat of divine mysteries adequately. For this reason, he adds, in his theological works he was often compelled "either to mix together inferior [i.e., metaphysical] questions with divine and supernatural matters, which is unwelcome and of little use to readers, or at least (in order to avoid this same inconvenience) briefly to present my opinions regarding such matters and require, as it were, a bare faith in them from my readers." This last expedient, he goes on to observe, could reasonably have seemed inappropriate to his reader, given the fact that metaphysical principles and doctrines "so cohere with theological conclusions and reasonings that, if knowledge and perfect cognition of the former is taken away, it is necessary that knowledge of the latter be exceedingly weakened." According to Suárez, in other words, to simply demand of the reader of a theological work that he or she accept certain metaphysical claims on faith is inconsistent with the aim of providing genuinely scientific theological knowledge. For this reason, and persuaded by the urgings of others, he explains, he has decided to interrupt the progress of his theological writings in order to write the *Metaphysical Disputations*.

In the earlier note to the reader, Suárez also explains that it would be virtually impossible to observe a suitable method if, "after the fashion of expositors," he were to deal with all metaphysical questions "as they presented themselves incidentally and, as it were, by chance in the text" of Aristotle's *Metaphysics*. Accordingly, he says, he has judged it "easier and more useful if all the things that could be investigated and examined regarding the entire object of this wisdom were sought

37. By this time, Suárez had already published his *De incarnatione* (1592) and his *De mysteriis vitae Christii* (1595).

out and placed before the eyes of the reader" in a manner consistent with the order of teaching. And in fact, for those familiar with Aristotle's *Metaphysics*, even a cursory survey of the *Disputations'* table of contents reveals the extent to which Suárez departs from the order of exposition set by Aristotle's work.[38]

The *Metaphysical Disputations* was originally published in two volumes, each divided into twenty-seven disputations, making for a total of fifty-four disputations. The following is an outline of the work's structure and contents:

A. The nature of metaphysics (*DM* 1)

B. Being, its properties, and its causes (*DM* 2–27)

    I. The essence of real being, the adequate object of metaphysics (*DM* 2)

    II. The properties or passions of being (*DM* 3–11)

        1. The properties of being in general (*DM* 3)

        2. Unity (*DM* 4–6)

            a. Transcendental unity in general (*DM* 4)

            b. Individual unity and its principle (*DM* 5)

            c. Formal and universal unity (*DM* 6)

        3. The various kinds of distinction (*DM* 7)

        4. Truth (*DM* 8)

        5. Falsity (*DM* 9)

        6. Goodness (*DM* 10)

        7. Evil (*DM* 11)

    III. The causes of being (*DM* 12–27)

        1. The causes of being in general (*DM* 12)

        2. The material cause (*DM* 13–14)

            a. The material cause of substance (*DM* 13)

            b. The material cause of accidents (*DM* 14)

---

38. For a discussion of the larger intellectual context in which the *Metaphysical Disputations* appeared and the factors motivating the composition of it and other metaphysical treatises by members of the Jesuit order, see Charles H. Lohr, "Jesuit Aristotelianism and Sixteenth-Century Metaphysics," in *Paradosis: Studies in Memory of Edwin A. Quain*, 203–20 (New York: Fordham University Press, 1976); Charles H. Lohr, "Metaphysics," in *The Cambridge History of Renaissance Philosophy*, ed. Charles B. Schmitt, Quentin Skinner, Eckhard Kessler, and Jill Kraye, 535–638 (Cambridge: Cambridge University Press, 1988).

4. Disputation I: The Nature of Metaphysics

Although the First Disputation has been the object of some scholarly
attention, most of this attention has focused on Suárez's identification,
in section 1, of first philosophy's adequate object, which is in some

respects a fairly straightforward matter. By contrast, regarding (say) Suárez's appeal to the notion of a "formal *ratio* under which" (*ratio formalis sub qua*) in section 2, during the course of arguing that metaphysics does not consider all things according to their proper natures or *rationes*, relatively little has been said. One is left to wonder about the precise nature of a "formal *ratio* under which." Indeed, the fact of the matter is that the scholarly literature leaves untreated some parts of the First Disputation that most call out for explanation and critical appraisal.

In the hopes of partly making good this lack, I have, in the remainder of this introduction, aimed to offer a rather detailed survey of Suárez's discussions in *DM* 1. More attention is paid to sections 2 through 4 of *DM* 1 (relative to their length), since these pose the greatest interpretive challenges; the treatments of sections 1, 5, and 6 are brief by comparison. I can't boast of having made everything clear, of course. There are parts of *DM* 1 where one wishes Suárez had been more explicit, particularly in section 4's discussion of the role that metaphysics plays vis-à-vis the objects of the other sciences. But calling attention to these issues will perhaps lead others to find answers where I have not. In any case, it is my hope that the following discussion and the accompanying translation will lead to substantially more research into Suárez's conception of metaphysics.

Section 1: Identifying the adequate object
or subject of metaphysics

Suárez classifies metaphysics or first philosophy as a natural science (*scientia naturalis*) (*DM* 1.2.17). In so classifying it, he in no way means to identify it with a branch of physics or natural philosophy. Rather, "natural" is here contrasted with "supernatural," so that in this sense of the expression mathematics also counts as a natural science, whereas sacred or supernatural theology, based on divine revelation, does not. Suárez further classifies metaphysics as a real science (*scientia realis*), since it is about things (*res*) or real beings (*DM* 1.2.13). The implicit contrast here is with a rational science (*scientia rationalis*) such as logic, which is not about any thing or real being, but is commonly thought to deal with objective second intentions (e.g., genus, species, subject, predicate, antecedent, consequent), which are beings of reason or items existing only objectively in the mind as objects of thought. Suárez also classifies metaphysics as a theoretical or speculative science (*scientia speculativa*) (*DM* 1.2.13), since it has the contemplation of truth as its highest end, unlike the practical and productive sciences, whose truths are ordered to some further goal (i.e., action or production). In none of this is Suárez in any way unusual.

On the Aristotelian conception of a theoretical science, a science like physics or metaphysics is a special kind of knowledge or cognition. As such, it is something that exists in the knower's soul or intellect: it is a "habit" (*habitus*, ἕξις) of the human intellect and an intellectual virtue, acquired through certain acts or operations performed by the intellective faculty. Viewed in terms of its content, on the other hand, a speculative science is conceived to be composed of demonstrations connected in such a way that the conclusions of some demonstrations serve as premises in others. These demonstrations are themselves composed of categorical propositions in which some predicate is affirmed to belong necessarily to some subject. The notion of a demonstration (*demonstratio*, ἀπόδειξις) is crucial here: strictly speaking, science (*scientia*, ἐπιστήμη), according to Aristotle, is cognition *of* the conclusion of a demonstration, and it is the kind of cognition that one has by virtue of possessing a demonstration (*Post. An.* I, ch. 2, 71b17–19). The indemonstrable premises on which all of a science's conclusions ultimately depend, which are deemed explanatory of these same conclusions, are called *principles* of that science, and cognition of them is not called "science," but "understanding" (*intellectus*, νοῦς). Such a principle is cognized *per se* through a grasp of the immediate and necessary connection that obtains between its subject and predicate.

On the Aristotelian conception of a speculative science, every such science has an adequate subject (*subiectum adaequatum*) or adequate object (*obiectum adaequatum*), which is what that science is primarily about and that in relation to which all other things discussed in the science are considered. Indeed, according to Aristotle, the speculative sciences are defined and individuated by appeal to their adequate objects, so that each receives its essential character and unity from its object. The adequate subject of a science, moreover, is typically a genus, or something general, and the various species of this genus can likewise count as subjects—though not *adequate* subjects—of the same science. The term "object" is used in this context because a science is a kind of knowledge or cognition, and cognition invariably has its object, namely, that which is cognized by means of it. The term "subject" is likewise used here because the conclusions of a science are all categorical propositions in which some necessary property or characteristic—a so-called "proper passion" (*propria passio*)—is predicated of an object. In other words, a science's objects appear as subjects in its conclusions.[39]

Aristotelians were more or less unanimous in holding that natural or mobile being (*ens naturale vel mobile*)—that is, material substance—is the adequate object of physics or natural philosophy, and that the adequate object of mathematics is quantity, which, in the Aristotelian scheme of the categories, is not a substance, but an accident. They also commonly held that the two species of quantity, discrete and continuous, serve as the adequate objects of arithmetic and geometry, respectively. The physicist, therefore, will demonstrate various conclusions about natural beings as such, for example, that motion is a proper passion of mobile or natural being.[40] In addition, the physicist will demonstrate conclusions about the various species of natural being (about plants and animals, for example), all of which can also be termed objects or subjects of natural philosophy, although (to repeat) no such species of natural being will count as the *adequate* object or subject of physics. Particular species of natural being are instead conceived to fall under natural philosophy's adequate object or subject.

Although Aristotelians were more or less unanimous in holding that natural or mobile being is the adequate object of physics, and quantity the adequate object of mathematics, there was considerably less agreement about the adequate object of metaphysics, in part because Aristotle's own pronouncements on this issue are not altogether clear.[41]

39. See Collegium Complutense Sancti Cyrilli, *Artium Cursus sive Disputationes in Aristotelis Dialecticam*, p. 100a (disp. 1, q. 2, n. 8).

40. See Domingo de Soto, *Super octo libros Physicorum Aristotelis Commentaria* (Salmanticae: ex Officina Ildefonsi à Terranova & Neyla, 1582), fol. 37va (bk. 3, ch. 1), and John of St. Thomas, *Cursus Philosophicus Thomisticus*, 2:9a (p. 1, q. 1, art. 1).

41. Scholars still debate the question of what Aristotle took the subject of metaphysics to

To be sure, commentaries on Aristotle's works, whether line-by-line commentaries, question commentaries, or combinations of both, standardly began by asking what the adequate object of the relevant science is. But in the case of metaphysics, the answers given to this question by different thinkers differed to a much greater extent than they did in the case of other sciences.

When considering what the adequate object of metaphysics is, it is important to bear in mind that, for Aristotle, not everything discussed in a science falls under its subject or adequate object. There are at least two reasons for this. First, according to Aristotle, scientific knowledge of a thing requires a cognition of its principles and causes,[42] and these principles and causes need not fall under the adequate object of the relevant science. For example, mobile being, the adequate object of physics or natural philosophy, is none other than material substance, and, according to Aristotelians, scientific knowledge of any material

----

be. See, for example: Paul Natorp, "Thema und Disposition der aristotelische Metaphysik," *Philosophische Monatshefte* 24 (1888): 37–65, 540–74; Werner Jaeger, *Aristotle: Fundamentals of the History of his Development*, 2nd ed., trans. Richard Robinson (Oxford: Oxford University Press, 1948); Augustin Mansion, "L'objet de la science philosophique suprême d'après Aristote, Métaphysique, E, 1," in *Mélange de philosophie grecque offerts à Mgr. Diès par ses élèves, ses collègues et ses amis*, 151–68 (Paris: Vrin, 1956); Philip Merlan, *From Platonism to Neoplatonism*, 2nd ed. (The Hague: Martinus Nijhoff, 1960); Günther Patzig, "Theology and Ontology in Aristotle's *Metaphysics*," in *Articles on Aristotle, Vol. 3: Metaphysics*, ed. J. Barnes, M. Schofield, and R. Sorabji, 33–49 (London: Duckworth, 1979); Vianney Décarie, *L'objet de la métaphysique selon Aristote* (Paris & Montréal: Vrin & L'Institut d'Études Médiévales, 1961); Giovanni Reale, *The Concept of First Philosophy and the Unity of the Metaphysics of Aristotle*, trans. John Catan (Albany: SUNY Press, 1979); Leo Elders, "Aristote et l'objet de la métaphysique," *Revue philosophique de Louvain* 60 (1962): 165–83; Joseph Owens, *The Doctrine of Being in the Aristotelian Metaphysics*, 3rd ed. (Toronto: The Pontifical Institute of Mediaeval Studies, 1978); Walter Leszl, *Aristotle's Conception of Ontology* (Padua: Editrice Antenore, 1975); Gérard Verbeke, "La physique d'Aristote est-elle une ontologie?" *Pensamiento* 35, nos. 138–39 (1979): 171–93; Philip Merlan, "On the Terms 'Metaphysics' and 'Being-*qua*-Being,'" *The Monist* 52, no. 2 (1986): 174–94; Michael Frede, "The Unity of General and Special Metaphysics: Aristotle's Conception of Metaphysics," in Michael Frede, *Essays in Ancient Philosophy*, 81–95 (Minneapolis: University of Minneapolis Press, 1987); Jacques Follon, "Le concept de philosophie première dans la «Métaphysique» d'Aristote," *Revue philosophique de Louvain* 90, no. 88 (1992): 387–421; Kyle Fraser, "Demonstrative Science and the Science of Being *qua* Being," *Oxford Studies in Ancient Philosophy* 22 (2002): 43–82; Shane Duarte, "Aristotle's Theology and its Relation to the Science of Being *qua* Being," *Apeiron* 40, no. 3 (2007): 267–318; Christopher Shields, "Being *qua* Being," in *The Oxford Handbook of Aristotle*, ed. Christopher Shields, 343–71 (Oxford: Oxford University Press, 2012).

42. Aristotle, *Phys.* I, ch. 1, 184a10–16.

substance requires a cognition of its form or formal cause, which is not itself a mobile being or material substance. Similarly, according to Aristotelians, quantitative unity is a principle of number or discrete quantity, the adequate object of arithmetic, but it is not itself a discrete quantity. (One, according to Aristotle, is not a number, although it is a principle of number.)[43] A second reason why not everything discussed in a science falls under its adequate object has to do with the fact that, as mentioned, Aristotle holds that the practitioner of a given science demonstrates that certain properties or characteristics necessarily belong to her science's object: on his view these properties or proper passions themselves do not (at least standardly) fall under that science's adequate object. For example, equality and inequality are often held to be proper passions of quantity,[44] but in the Aristotelian scheme of the categories, neither is a quantity, but rather a relation. The fact that something is discussed in a science, then, does not guarantee that it is, or falls under, the adequate object of that science. Accordingly, although Aristotle himself devoted considerable space to a discussion of God and the unmoved movers in *Metaphysics* XII, a faithful Aristotelian might nonetheless hold that God neither is, nor falls under, the adequate object of metaphysics, and that God is instead discussed by Aristotle in the *Metaphysics* as the first principle and cause of first philosophy's object (e.g., finite being in general). Indeed, as Suárez himself points out, this view, or a version of it, is sometimes attributed to Thomas Aquinas (*DM* 1.1.18).[45]

What, then, is the adequate object of metaphysics, according to Suárez? His answer to this question is: real being or being *qua* being. This is the conclusion he draws after considering and rejecting six other opinions regarding first philosophy's adequate object. The first two, according to Suárez, saddle metaphysics with an adequate object of excessive scope, while the last four restrict this scope overly much. According to the first, the adequate object of metaphysics is being taken in the most abstract possible sense, so that it includes *per se* beings (God

43. Aristotle, *Metaph.* XIV, ch. 1, 1088a4–6.
44. See Aristotle, *Cat.* 6, 6a26–35.
45. See Thomas Aquinas's commentary on Boethius's *De Trinitate*, q. 5, art. 4, in: *Sancti Thomae de Aquino opera omnia* (Rome & Paris: Commissio Leonina & Les Éditions du Cerf, 1992), t. 50, pp. 153–54.

and beings located in the categories), *per accidens* beings (i.e., aggregates of two or more *per se* beings), and beings of reason. The second opinion differs from the first only in excluding beings of reason from the adequate object of metaphysics. Against the first opinion, Suárez argues that the adequate object of a science must be formally one in some way—that is, must be some one nature, quiddity, or *ratio*—and that beings of reason are beings only in name and therefore do not agree with real beings in the nature or *ratio* of being. This conclusion, Suárez points out, is perfectly compatible with the fact that the metaphysician does indeed discuss beings of reason (as he himself does in *DM* 54), since (again) not everything discussed in a science falls under its adequate object. In fact, beings of reason are discussed by the metaphysician, in part, so that they can be distinguished from real beings, and this in order to make clear what has genuine entity and reality and what does not. Against both the first and second opinions, moreover, Suárez argues that a *per accidens* being, as such, is not a being, but an aggregate of two or more real beings. It does not, therefore, have a proper definition,[46] nor, consequently, any proper passions that might be demonstrated of it. But the adequate subject of a science, as well as anything falling under that subject, must have both.

The third opinion considered by Suárez is the most restrictive: it takes God alone to be the adequate object of metaphysics. This position is rejected, in part, on the grounds that no natural science affords cognition of God as he is in himself; a natural science can only provide us with a cognition of God on the basis of creatures, his effects, which necessarily involves cognizing him under some concept common to him and created beings. To be sure, Suárez grants, "it is a great excellence for a science to have God for an object to which alone it is directed *per se* and primarily," but this "surpasses the natural powers of the human intellect and those of a science which can be acquired through those powers" (*DM* 1.1.12). The fourth opinion is that immaterial substance, understood so as to include both God and the intelli-

---

46. See Aristotle, *Metaph.* VII, ch. 4, 1029b22–1030a17. See also Francisco Suárez, *Opera Omnia*, 25:xxxii; Francisco Suárez, *A Commentary on Aristotle's* Metaphysics, *or "A Most Ample Index to the* Metaphysics *of Aristotle,"* trans. John P. Doyle (Milwaukee: Marquette University Press, 2005), 124.

gences (or angels), is the adequate object of metaphysics. In response to the arguments offered in support of this position, Suárez grants that they succeed in showing that immaterial substance, as such, is a proper object of metaphysics, or (in other words) that metaphysics alone, of all the theoretical natural sciences, investigates immaterial substances as such. But Suárez argues that there are, in addition, certain *rationes* or natures—for example, the *ratio* of substance—that are independent of matter in the sense that they can exist without it (even if they are sometimes found joined to it), and that such natures therefore transcend the domains of the physicist and the mathematician, falling to be investigated instead by the metaphysician.

According to the fifth opinion that Suárez considers, the adequate object of metaphysics is being divided into the ten categories. This view is distinguished into two versions, depending on whether immaterial substances and their accidents are taken to belong to the categories. If so, then the opinion amounts to the view that finite being serves as the adequate object of metaphysics, God alone being excluded from this object, although God, according to this opinion, will still be considered in metaphysics insofar as he is the first cause of its adequate object. Those who exclude immaterial substances and their accidents from the categories hold that only material substances and their accidents fall under the object of metaphysics. Thomas Aquinas is occasionally affirmed to be a supporter of this version on the grounds that he sometimes "teaches that God and the intelligences are considered by the metaphysician as principles and causes of her object, not as parts of it" (*DM* 1.1.18). Suárez rejects this view as well, in part because God is, he says, naturally knowable, from which it follows that he can fall under the object of a natural science, and this science must be metaphysics, since there is no higher natural science. Suárez also appeals to the fact that Aristotle himself says that metaphysics is superior to physics by virtue of its consideration of primary (or spiritual) substance (*Metaph.* IV, ch. 3, 1005a33–b1): Aristotle, he explains, cannot have been motivated to say this merely because metaphysics considers spiritual substances as principles, for physics, too, considers spiritual substances as principles (i.e., principles of motion), as can be gathered from

Phys. VIII. As regards Thomas Aquinas, he never teaches the opposite, Suárez insists. He merely claims that in this science we *first* reach God under the aspect of a principle.

According to the sixth opinion considered by Suárez, the adequate object of metaphysics is substance insofar as it abstracts from, or includes under itself, both material and immaterial, finite and infinite substance. This view is rejected, in part, on the grounds that it fails to recognize that there is a single nature of being, common to substance and accident, with which "some science can concern itself, explaining its *ratio* and unity, and demonstrating some attributes of it" (*DM* 1.1.23). This science, Suárez claims, can be none other than metaphysics. Nor does the analogy of being stand in the way of this, he adds, for although being is said analogically of substances and accidents, it is nevertheless one and common in relation to these, as shall be argued in *DM* 2, "On the Essential *Ratio*, or the Concept of Being."

Having rejected these six opinions regarding the adequate object of metaphysics, refuting the arguments offered on their behalf, Suárez states his own opinion: the adequate object of first philosophy, he affirms, is real being. This, he claims, is Aristotle's opinion, as well as the opinion of Thomas Aquinas, Alexander of Hales (ca. 1185–1245),[47] John Duns Scotus (1265/6–1308), Albert the Great (ca. 1200–1280), and Alexander of Aphrodisias (fl. early 3rd c. CE). It is also said to have been endorsed by Averroes, Avicenna (ca. 970–1037), Paul Soncinas (d. 1494), and Giles of Rome (ca. 1247–1316). In proof of this opinion, Suárez cites the arguments that he has offered against the other opinions, for it has been shown, he says, that the adequate object of this science must include God and the other immaterial substances, and not only these substances. It has also been shown that it must include real accidents, but not *per accidens* beings or beings of reason. Only real being, as such, fits the bill.

Suárez poses and answers the question, "What is real being?" only

---

47. Suárez attributes this opinion to Alexander of Hales on the basis of a commentary on Aristotle's *Metaphysics* that was falsely attributed to Alexander. The commentary in question, *In duodecim Aristotelis Metaphysicae libros dilucidissima expositio*, was in fact authored by Alexander of Alexandria (also known as Alexander Bonini) (ca. 1268–1314).

in the Second Disputation.[48] Here in the First Disputation, immediately after affirming that real being is the adequate object of metaphysics, Suárez entertains an objection to his conclusion. Against this view, he notes, it might be objected that the adequate object of a science must have properties that can be demonstrated of it, as well as principles and causes by appeal to which such properties are demonstrated, but that being cannot have such properties, principles, and causes. It cannot have properties because the subject of which properties are demonstrated cannot belong to the essence of those properties, whereas being pertains to the essence of every being and, therefore, to the essence of every mode or property of any given being. And being cannot have principles and causes, since if it did, there would have to be principles and causes of *every* being, "since what agrees with the superior insofar as it is such must agree with everything contained under it" (*DM* 1.1.27). God, however, has no principle or cause.

With respect to properties of being, Suárez replies that, in fact, being does have properties, although he grants that these properties, unlike other properties, are only rationally or conceptually distinct from their subject. This is an issue to which he will return in *DM* 3, the disputation devoted to the passions of being in general. As regards causes and principles, Suárez addresses the issue first by making a distinction between complex and simple principles. Complex principles, which are propositions, serve as the premises in a science's demonstrations. They are also termed "principles of cognition." Principles of this sort, he explains, are not wanting in metaphysics. In fact, one of the main functions of metaphysics is to establish the first of all complex principles, through which other principles, including the principles of the other sciences, can in some way be demonstrated. The other kind of principle, which is simple, is the principle or cause signified by the middle term in a demonstration. It amounts to an explanation of why the predicate holds of the subject in a demonstration's conclusion. Such principles, Suárez continues, are of two sorts: some are true causes that are in some way really distinct from their effects, while others are

---

48. The meaning and significance of Suárez's reply to this question are a matter of some controversy. I defer discussion of this issue to the introduction to my translation of *DM* 2. Many of the works cited in n. 34 bear on this issue, however.

explanatory of things from which they are only conceptually distinguished. Moreover, simple principles of the former sort are not absolutely necessary for constructing demonstrations, Suárez claims. For one can demonstrate attributes of God not merely *a posteriori*, from effects, but also *a priori*, by inferring one attribute from another—for example, immortality from immateriality, or being a free agent from being intelligent—though of course God's attributes are only conceptually distinguished from God himself and each other. Much the same goes for being, Suárez explains: although being as such does not have simple principles in the first of the two senses identified, nevertheless, it has some ground or explanation (*ratio*) of its properties. "Therefore," he concludes, "some science can concern itself with" being insofar as it is being, and this science is "none other than metaphysics" (*DM* 1.1.29).

Section 2: Whether metaphysics deals with all
things according to their proper *rationes*

The conclusion that real being is the adequate object of metaphysics is not without its problems, however. For it might be thought to imply that metaphysics investigates every particular kind of being, just as natural philosophy, which has natural or mobile being for its adequate object, investigates every species of natural being. The problem with this, of course, is that if metaphysics studies every kind of being, mathematics and natural philosophy turn out to be superfluous or, at best, mere parts of metaphysics. Suárez rejects both of these claims, as do most scholastic philosophers.

The question posed by Suárez in section 2 of *DM* 1 is whether metaphysics treats of all beings according to their proper "*rationes*." A *ratio* (plural: *rationes*), in the sense relevant here, is an essence or nature, or an element in the essence or nature of a thing, conceived as an object of cognition.[49] Thus, Suárez speaks of "the *ratio* or quiddity of being

---

49. See Johannes Micraelius, *Lexicon Philosophicum Terminorum Philosophis Usitatorum* (Jenae: impensis Jeremiae Mamphrasii, 1653), col. 949: "*Ratio* Metaphysicis est ipsa Essentia in respectu ad cognitionem nostram, Graece λόγος τῆς οὐσίας"; and Stéphane Chauvin, *Lexicon Philosophicum* (Leovardiae: Excudit Franciscus Halma, 1713), p. 556a: "Ratio Metaphysicis idem est quod essentia, seu id quo aliquid tale est, ipsum esse rei."

as such" (*rationem seu quidditatem entis ut sic*) (*DM* 2.1.8).[50] A thing's proper *ratio*, moreover, is the *ratio* proper or peculiar to it. Accordingly, to ask whether metaphysics deals with all things according to their proper *rationes* is to ask whether metaphysics treats of (say) horses insofar as they are horses (i.e., whether it treats of horses "as such"), and similarly for every genus, subaltern species, and lowest species of being. If not, does it investigate only being and its proper passions? Or does it perhaps consider certain genera and species of being, but not others?

Suárez attributes the view that metaphysics investigates all things and their properties, down to the lowest species, to both Giles of Rome and Antonio Bernardi della Mirandola (1503–65), the latter of whom is said to have held that all the sciences are merely parts of a single science that is by custom distinguished into several in order to facilitate learning. Suárez's own view is that metaphysics deals with some genera and species of being, but not with others. For starters, it deals with God, the genus of created spirits or angels, and (to the extent possible for a natural science) the various species of angel. Common to these is the fact that they are substances treated of in no other natural theoretical science. Physics deals with material substance and its species, while mathematics deals with an accident, quantity. But in addition to God, finite spiritual substance, and the species of finite spiritual substance, Suárez holds, there are certain other *rationes* or natures that fall to be investigated by metaphysics and by no other science, and these are those natures which do not depend for their existence on, and are not defined by appeal to, matter, even if they are sometimes found together with matter. These include, beside the *ratio* of being itself, the nature or *ratio* of substance, the nature or *ratio* of quality, as well as any nature or *ratio* that is found in, or is common to, both material and immaterial things.

The question that presents itself at this point is this: on what principle does Suárez rely here? Granted that various natures fail to be investigated in physics and mathematics, it is hardly surprising that Suárez should want to assign their treatment to the last of the three

---

50. In my translation of *DM* 1, I have rendered the Latin "*ratio*" in various ways. For a discussion of this, see "Remarks on the Latin Text and English Translation," immediately following this introduction.

main branches of speculative science identified by Aristotle, that is, to metaphysics. But the Aristotelian conception of a theoretical science requires that there be some community of nature among the particular things dealt with in a science. What is needed at this point, then, is some such *ratio* which can both serve as the source of first philosophy's unity and ground its distinction from the other main natural theoretical sciences, physics and mathematics.

In this context Suárez invokes the notion of a "formal *ratio* under which" (*ratio formalis sub qua*). This is a notion whose origins are ill understood, although it is sometimes said to be a mere clarification of Thomas Aquinas's distinction between the formal and material objects of a power or habit. Those who so characterize it, Suárez included, commonly make a point of citing Cardinal Cajetan (or Tommaso de Vio), the great Thomist theologian and philosopher, when introducing it, however.[51] In fact, Gabriel Vázquez, who rejects both the notion itself and its alleged origin in the thought of Thomas Aquinas, regards it as a Cajetanian innovation.[52]

As Cajetan describes it, the notion of a "formal *ratio* under which" is motivated in part by problems that were sometimes thought to affect the Aristotelian way of individuating and distinguishing the soul's powers and habits. In *De anima* II, ch. 4, 415a14–22, Aristotle famously claims that the powers of the soul are individuated by appeal to their (proper) objects—for example, taste by appeal to flavor, smell by appeal to odor, etc. Habits of the soul, including the various theoretical sciences, were commonly thought to be individuated in the same way. The basic idea is that a power or habit is judged to be one because its object is one, while a particular power or habit is judged to be specifically (or generically) different from another power or habit because the object of the former is specifically (or generically) different from the object of the latter. Here, of course, it is necessary that the object of the relevant power or habit be properly specified, for absent the proper specification, the unity of the power or habit, as well as its distinction

---

51. See *DM* 44.11.64.

52. See Gabriel Vázquez, *Commentariorum, ac Disputationum in primam partem S. Thomae Tomus Primus* (Compluti: Ex officina Ioannis Gratiani, apud viduam, 1598), pp. 37–8 (disp. 7, ch. 3).

from other powers or habits, will go undetected and unexplained. For example, although we commonly speak of seeing a human being, a donkey, a stone, etc., the object by appeal to which vision is individuated is none of these, but instead something they all have in common, that is, color. This point is commonly made by appeal to the distinction, familiar from Thomas Aquinas, between the formal and material objects of a power or habit.[53] As it is explained by Antonio de Olivera (or Antonio de la Madre de Dios, 1583–1637), the author of the popular seventeenth-century *Complutense* textbook of Aristotelian logic, the object of a habit or power

is twofold, or, to speak more properly, there are two parts of the entire object, one material and the other formal. The material object or part is that which is reached or considered in a science not *per se*, but by virtue of the formal object. But the formal object or part is that which is reached or considered by such a science *per se* or by virtue of itself. An example of each is seen in the case of the potency of sight, the entire object of which is the colored thing, in which the material part or object is body, since it is not seen *per se*, but by virtue of its color. But color is the formal part or object, since it is perceived by the potency of sight *per se* and by virtue of itself.[54]

As de Olivera explains, the formal object or *ratio* of a given power is that by virtue of which something other than that object is reached or grasped (*attingitur*) by that power, while it is itself reached or grasped by that power by virtue of itself.[55] Thus, vision reaches cats, dogs, and trees by virtue of their color, while vision reaches color by virtue of itself.

---

53. See, e.g., Thomas Aquinas, *ST* I, q. 1, art. 3, in: *Sancti Thomae Aquinatis opera omnia* (Leonina), t. 4, p. 12a.

54. Collegium Complutense Sancti Cyrilli, *Artium Cursus sive Disputationes in Aristotelis Dialecticam*, p. 100a–b (disp. 1, q. 2, n. 8): "Hoc autem obiectum duplex est: vel, ut proprius loquamur, eiusdem integri obiecti duae sunt partes; alia materialis, & alia formalis. Obiectum, seu pars materialis est id, quod non per se, sed ratione obiecti formalis attingitur, seu consideratur in scientia: obiectum vero seu pars formalis est id, quod per se, seu ratione sui attingitur, seu consideratur a tali scientia. Utriusque exemplum cernitur in potentia visiva, cuius obiectum integrum est coloratum; in quo pars materialis, seu obiectum materiale est corpus: quia non per se, sed ratione coloris videtur: color vero est pars, seu obiectum formale; quia per se, & ratione sui percipitur a potentia visiva."

55. See John of St. Thomas, *Cursus Philosophicus Thomisticus*, 1:260a (p. 2, q. 1, art. 3): "And that formality or *ratio* or determination through the mediation of which something is reached by some habit or potency is called the formal object." (*Et dicitur formale obiectum illa formalitas seu ratio vel determinatio, mediante qua aliquid habet attingi ab aliquo habitu vel potentia.*)

Even with this distinction between material and formal objects in place, however, the Aristotelian view regarding the individuation of the soul's powers and habits was still sometimes thought to be problematic. For, as de Olivera explains it, from this view

it seems necessarily to follow that the unity of a potency or habit must be as great as the unity of its object, and that consequently there cannot be specifically one potency or habit directed at an object that is generically one. But this, it is clear, is plainly false, both because many potencies are directed at an object that is generically one, such as sight in relation to color, and in fact one only analogically, as is clear regarding the intellect and the will in relation to being. And also it seems absurd to multiply habits according to the specific multiplication of the object, so that there is one science of the human being and another science of the horse, etc. [...] Therefore, the specific distinction, or unity, of a science, habit, or potency cannot be taken from the entity of the object.[56]

The worry articulated here assumes that, where a power or habit is specifically one or indivisible into lower species, its object must likewise be specifically one or indivisible into lower species. This, however, is problematic, for everyone agreed in thinking that vision (for example) is formally indivisible, even though its proper object, color, manifestly is not, since it is rather a genus divisible into species (yellow, blue, white, etc.). Likewise, no one held that scientific knowledge of the lion and scientific knowledge of the horse constitute specifically distinct sciences, or that geometry is subdivided into a science of the triangle, a science of the square, etc.

As de Olivera puts it, it seems to follow from this that the specific unity and distinction of a science (or power) "cannot be taken from the entity" of its object—that is, cannot be taken from its object considered as a thing (*res*) or being (*ens*). For, so considered, the object is

56. Collegium Complutense Sancti Cyrilli, *Artium Cursus sive Disputationes in Aristotelis Dialecticam*, p. 750a–b (disp. 19, q. 4, n. 35): "Ex quo necessario sequi videtur tantam debere esse unitatem potentiae, vel habitus; quanta fuerit unitas obiecti: & per consequens circa obiectum unum generice, non posse versari potentiam, aut habitum specifice unum. Quod tamen plane constat esse falsum. Tum quia plures potentiae versantur circa obiectum generice unum, ut visus respectu coloris; imo unum tantum analogice, ut patet de intellectu, & voluntate respectu entis. Tum etiam quia absurdum videtur multiplicare habitus iuxta specificam multiplicationem obiecti; ita ut alia sit scientia de homine; alia de equo &c. [...] Ergo ab entitate obiecti sumi non potest specifica distinctio, aut unitas, scientiae, habitus, vel potentiae."

not formally indivisible; it is rather divisible into lower species. What is needed is a different way of considering and classifying the object of specifically one science or power, a way according to which that object *is* formally indivisible.

This is what Cajetan offers in both his commentary on Thomas Aquinas's *Summa theologiae* I, q. 1, art. 3, and in his commentary on Aristotle's *Posterior Analytics* I, chs. 27–29.[57] In both texts, Cajetan distinguishes two ways in which the object of a habit or power can be conceived: either as a thing (*ut res*) or as an object (*ut obiectum*).[58] He is quite explicit that conceiving any object in these two ways amounts to locating it in two different genera. For example, color, which is the proper object of vision, can either be located in the genus of affective quality (*qualitas passibilis*), which is one of the four species of quality that Aristotle distinguishes in chapter 8 of the *Categories* (9a28ff.), or it can be located in the genus of the sensible (*sensibile*), which is itself divided into the visible, the audible, the olfactible, the tangible, and the gustable.[59] Likewise, continuous quantity, the adequate object of geometry, can either be located in the category of quantity, or it can be located somewhere under the genus of the knowable (*scibile, speculabile*).[60] It seems clear that what Cajetan is proposing here is a distinc-

---

57. Several ways of dividing Aristotle's *Posterior Analytics* into chapters were current in the early modern period. In the division used by Cajetan, these three chapters formed a single one, ch. 22. In the two different divisions used by Toletus and Zabarella, these three chapters are together labeled ch. 23.

58. Tommaso de Vio, in Thomas Aquinas, *Sancti Thomae Aquinatis opera omnia* (Leonina), t. 4, p. 12a: "Ad evidentiam huius rationis, nota duplicem esse rationem formalem obiecti in scientia: alteram obiecti ut *res*, alteram obiecti ut *obiectum*." Tommaso de Vio, *In Posteriorum analeticorum libros* (Venetiis: Impensis nobilis viri Luceantonii de giunta florentini, die 9 Julii 1519), fol. 76rb: "Et propterea oportet distinguendo dicere quod ratio formalis subiecti potest dupliciter accipi. Uno modo ut res est […]. Alio modo ut obiectum est."

59. Tommaso de Vio, *Sancti Thomae Aquinatis opera omnia* (Leonina), t. 4, p. 12a–b: "obiectum sensus est in duobus generibus, scilicet sub *passibili qualitate* et sub *sensibili*. Aliae namque sunt differentiae et species passibilis qualitatis, et aliae sensibilis. Illius enim sunt species color, sonus, odor, etc.: istius vero species sunt visibile, audibile, odorabile." Tommaso de Vio, *In Posteriorum analeticorum libros*, fol. 76va: "obiecta sensuum duplex genus ingrediuntur, scilicet sensibile & passibilem qualitatem: ut tales res sunt, puta odor, sapor, color, etc. sub passibili qualitate essentialiter continentur. Ut sensibiles vero denominantur, sic sub sensibili continentur."

60. Tommaso de Vio, *Sancti Thomae Aquinatis opera omnia* (Leonina), t. 4, p. 12b: "obiectum scientiae est in genere entis et in genere speculabilis, ita quod haec duo genera aliis et aliis differentiis propriis dividuntur in proprias species." Tommaso de Vio, *In Poster-*

tion between two different ways of conceiving the object of a power or habit: as it is in itself (as a *res*) or in relation to some power or habit (as an *obiectum*).

In his commentary on Aristotle's *Posterior Analytics* I, chs. 27–29, Cajetan is clear in his view that the specific unity of a power or habit is to be determined by appeal to its object considered as an *object*, and not by appeal to its object considered as a *thing*.[61] As regards the individuation of the senses, this gives Cajetan the result he seeks, since although he (like everyone else) takes color, sound, odor, etc. to be subaltern species—that is, to be divisible into lower species—he also holds that the corresponding species of *sensibile* (the visible, the audible, the olfactible, etc.) are not. Vision and the visible, hearing and the audible, etc., are each formally indivisible.[62]

---

iorum analeticorum libros, fol. 76va: "res obiectae scientiae duplex quoque genus ingrediuntur, scilicet, scibile & genus proprium secundum quod tales res sunt."

61. Tommaso de Vio, *In Posteriorum analeticorum libros*, fol. 76rb: "Si vero consideretur ut hoc genus, scilicet, scibile ingreditur, sic una formaliter et simpliciter est: ita quod, ut exemplariter dicatur, si numerus consideretur in eo quod numerus, sic (ut dictum est) numerus non est unus formaliter simpliciter, eo quod divisibilis est formaliter, et consequenter (ut sic) non stat unitatem specificam arithmeticae. Dictum enim est iam, quod genus subiectum debet esse unum simpliciter, si scientia est una simpliciter. Aliter cum scientia secetur sicut et res subiecta, ut dicitur in tertio de anima: scientia non esset una simpliciter subiecto formaliter diviso. Si vero consideretur numerus ut genus scibilis ingreditur, sic unius speciei specialissimae est, et consequenter unum formaliter, et consequenter ut sic unitatem dat specificam arithmeticae. [...] Dicimus igitur secundum S. Tho. doctrinam, quod scientiae secantur quemadmodum et res, non ut res, sed ut scibiles, et quod secundum unitatem genericam rerum ut scibiles sunt sumitur unitas generica scientiarum, et secundum unitatem specificam sumitur specifica."

62. Tommaso de Vio, *In Posteriorum analeticorum libros*, fol. 76va: "omne enim per se primo sensibile a sensu exteriori (de tali enim loquimur) est qualitas passibilis et e converso: omnis passibilis qualitas est sensibilis etc. Species autem eorum specialissimae non ita convertibiliter se convertuuntur: sed in una specie sensibilis multae species passibilis qualitatis clauduntur: unde species sensibilis cum speciebus subalternis passibilis qualitatis convertuntur. Dividitur enim sensibile in visibile, audibile, odorabile, etc. tanquam in species specialissimas, quorum nullum cum specialissimis passibilis qualitatis, sed subalternis, convertitur, odorabile cum odore, audibile cum sono etc. Cernimus ergo in sensuum obiectis propriis unitatem formalem, inquantum sensibilia sunt, et divisibilitatem formalem ut res sunt. Supponamus quoque pro nunc (quod et verum est) quod sensus proprii sint species specialissimae, & quod tam distinctionem quam unitatem formalem sumant ex obiectis, et videbimus quod cum sensus sensibile (ut sic) per se respicit, et per proprias differentias sensibilis distinguantur specifice obiecta ipsorum sensuum, non inquantum res, sed inquantum obiecta, id est, sensibilia sunt, unient, et distinguent eos, ita quod odor inquantum est species athoma in genere sensibilis olfactum specifice distinguit ab auditu, quem sonus inquantum alteram speciem sensibilis ingreditur in specie reponit, et sic de aliis."

It is worth observing that Cajetan's approach to the individuation of the senses is liable to appear question-begging. After all, his aim is to individuate sight or vision, a power of the soul, by appeal to its object. But in designating the visible as the object of sight he would seem also to be individuating the object by appeal to the power. For what is the visible but that which admits of being apprehended by sight? Whether Cajetan himself recognized the potential circularity here is unclear, but others certainly did. Suárez, for one, addresses this concern by granting that if being visible (*esse visibile*) is understood as a mere extrinsic denomination taken from vision, then there is indeed a begging of the question: the unity of the object is derived from the unity of the potency, and the unity of the potency is derived from the unity of the object. However, he continues, when we speak of being visible here, this is not what we mean. What we mean, rather, is some intrinsic *ratio* or nature common to the species of color, "by reason of which they can constitute, as it were, one specific object"—for example, some one manner, shared by all colors, of affecting (*immutare*) the faculty of sight (*DM* 44.11.64).

As regards the individuation of the sciences, Cajetan explains that the object of a science has *two* formal *rationes*: a "formal *ratio* which" (*ratio formalis quae*) and a "formal *ratio* under which" (*ratio formalis sub qua*). The former kind of *ratio*, he explains, is of the object as a thing (*ut res*), and it formally constitutes the object in a particular sort of real being (*in tali esse reali* or *esse rei*). It is also said to be that from which the passions of the science's subject flow. The "formal *ratio* which" of a science's object is, therefore, none other than its essence or quiddity. The "formal *ratio* under which," on the other hand, is of the object as an object (*ut obiectum*), and it formally constitutes the object in a particular sort of knowable being or being of a knowable object (*in tali esse scibili* or *esse scibilis*). With respect to the three main divisions of natural speculative science, the "formal *ratio* which" of the object of metaphysics is said to be entity (*entitas*), the "formal *ratio* which" of the object of mathematics is said to be quantity, and the "formal *ratio* which" of the object of physics is said to be mobility (*mobilitas*).[63]

---

63. Tommaso de Vio, *Sancti Thomae Aquinatis opera omnia* (Leonina), t. 4, p. 12a: "III. Ad evidentiam huius rationis, nota duplicem esse rationem formalem obiecti in scientia:

Moreover, according to Cajetan, what constitutes each such object or essence in a particular sort of knowable being or being of a knowable object—that is, its "formal *ratio* under which"—is its *abstraction*, that is, its degree of abstraction or independence from matter. For different things or essences are knowable in different ways and to different degrees depending on their relation to matter.[64] Suárez, for his part, will speak of how all the things falling under the subject of a given science belong to, or participate in, the same *ratio* of knowable object (*ratio scibilis*).[65]

The classic text for this way of distinguishing the objects of the theoretical sciences, in terms of their relation to matter, is Aristotle's *Metaphysics* VI, ch. 1, 1025b25–1026a21. Here Aristotle claims that physics deals with an object that is mobile and separate neither with respect to

---

alteram obiecti ut *res*, alteram obiecti ut *obiectum*; vel alteram obiecti ut *quae*, alteram ut *sub qua*. Ratio formalis obiecti ut res, seu *quae*, est ratio rei obiectae quae primo terminat actum illius habitus, et ex qua fluunt passiones illius subiecti, et quae est medium in prima demonstratione; ut entitas in metaphysica, quantitas in mathematica, et mobilitas in naturali. Ratio autem formalis obiecti ut obiectum, vel *sub qua*, est immaterialitas talis, seu talis modus abstrahendi et definiendi: puta sine omni materia in metaphysica, cum materia intelligibili tantum in mathematica, et cum materia sensibili, non tamen hac, in naturali. IV. Necessitas autem, qualitas et distinctio harum rationum sumenda est ex distinctione duorum generum, in quibus oportet locare obiectum scientiae. Oportet enim quod formaliter sit talis *res*, taliter *scibilis*. Et ideo oportet quod habeat et rationem formalem constituentem formaliter ipsam in tali esse reali, et rationem formalem constituentem formaliter ipsam in tali esse scibili; ut sic reponatur et in genere rerum et in genere scibilium."

64. Tommaso de Vio, *In Posteriorum analeticorum libros*, fol. 76va: "Manifestum quoque est, quod et ens formaliter per modos, et differentias diversificatur, et quod scibile propriis differentiis dividitur. Et de diversitate quidem entis non oportet aliud dicere, quia clara est, et fit per praedicamenta, & eorum differentias, et per actum et potentiam etc. Diffinitionem autem scibilis (licet in sexto metaphysicae facilius persuaderemus) tamen tangamus et nunc, dicentes, quod cum scibile immateriale et immobile sonet, eo quod obiectum immateriale oportet esse: quia substantia in intellectu est: et impossibile aliter se habere: quia scire non contingit nisi huiusmodi: quia ex immaterialitate. ergo propter potentiam intellectivam et ex immobilitate propter habitum scientificum constat scibile ut sic. Et propriae differentiae alicuius sunt quae illud genus ut sic non solum dividunt sed diversificant. scibile optime dividitur per diversimode habere immaterialitatem et immobilitatem in subalterna et specialissima: ut fecit Aristo. 6. metaphysicae ut secetur scibile in universale abstractum a materia et motu secundum esse et rationem: et abstractum secundum rationem et non secundum esse et abstractum non secundum esse nec secundum rationem tanquam in genera distinguentia tres partes philosophiae, scilicet, metaphysicam et mathematicam et naturalem."

65. See *DM* 1.2.22: "It is not necessary that a science which considers a universal *ratio* descend in particular to all the things which are contained under that *ratio*, but only that it descend in particular to those things which participate in the same *ratio* of knowable object or in the same abstraction [*ad ea quae eandem rationem scibilis, seu eandem abstractionem participant*]."

existence nor according to reason from matter, which is to say that the objects of physics depend on matter both for their existence and for their being known (since they must be defined by appeal to matter). He also claims that the objects of metaphysics are immobile and depend on matter in neither of these ways. As regards the object of mathematics, the claim in this text is that it is immobile and can be defined without appeal to matter, even if it depends on matter for its existence. For this reason, it was often said to abstract from matter according to reason (*secundum rationem*), but not with respect to being or existence (*secundum esse*). The case of mathematics is complicated somewhat, however, by a distinction that Aristotle elsewhere draws between sensible and intelligible matter (*Metaph.* VII, ch. 11, 1036a26–37a5, and VIII, ch. 6, 1045a33–35), the suggestion in these other texts being that although sensible matter does not enter into the definition of a mathematical object, intelligible matter does.

The corresponding scholastic analysis sometimes took its start with Aristotle's claim in *Posterior Analytics* I, ch. 2, that an object of scientific knowledge cannot be otherwise, that is, must be necessary (71b15–16). Granted that matter is the ultimate source of contingency and mutability, this requirement was then taken to imply that the object of a speculative science must be constituted through some sort of abstraction from matter.[66] According to de Olivera, moreover, three kinds of abstraction are commonly distinguished, corresponding to the three types of matter from which abstraction can be made: singular, sensible, and intelligible. Physics, the object of which is constituted through the lowest grade of abstraction, abstracts from singular matter alone: it considers flesh and bones in general, not this flesh and these bones.[67]

66. See the passage from Cajetan quoted in n. 64 above. See also Collegium Conimbricense, *In octo libros Physicorum Aristotelis Stagiritae* (Lugduni: Sumptibus Ioannis Baptistae Buysson, 1594), 1:7–8 (proem, q. 1, art. 3), and Collegium Complutense Sancti Cyrilli, *Artium Cursus sive Disputationes in Aristotelis Dialecticam,* p. 758b (disp. 19, q. 4, n. 47).

67. Collegium Complutense Sancti Cyrilli, *Artium Cursus sive Disputationes in Aristotelis Dialecticam,* pp. 758b–59a (disp. 19, q. 4, n. 47): "Est autem triplex gradus huius abstractionis formalis, ut ex Arist. 6. Metaph. tex. 2. docet Sanctus Doct. opus citato, & admittunt communiter Doctores, iuxta triplicem materiam, a qua potest aliqua res abstrahi, scilicet singularem, sensibilem, & intelligibilem. Materia singularis dicitur in praesenti, quidquid pertinet ad singularitatem rerum sensibilium; ut hae carnes, & haec ossa, haec albedo, &c. Unde illa scientia abstrahit a materia singulari tantum, quae considerat res sensibiles, verbi gratia hominem, cum materia sensibili communi, nempe carne, & ossibus: non tamen

As regards sensible matter, de Olivera explains, a science is said to abstract from such matter as well when it considers its object without regard for the qualities perceived by the senses (e.g., sound, cold, odor, and the like). This is precisely what mathematics does, since it treats of quantity "not caring whether the line is hot or the surface white, or the body hard, etc."[68] However, the mathematical sciences, de Olivera explains, do not abstract from intelligible matter—that is, from "corporeal substance itself or prime matter," which is "called intelligible because it can be perceived only by the intellect"—since they "do not consider quantity without the material substance in which it exists and on which it depends for the cognition of itself."[69] Finally, metaphysics abstracts both according to reason and with respect to existence even from intelligible matter, since it treats of things which do not depend for their existence on prime matter, either because they are incapable of existing in matter (e.g., God and the angels) or because they *can* exist without matter (e.g., substance, quality, act and potency, one and many, etc.).[70]

---

considerat singulariter hanc carnem, & haec ossa. Et huiusmodi est Philosophia naturalis. Quae consequenter habet infimum gradum abstractionis formalis: siquidem haec ad minus requiritur in obiecto, ut de illo possit esse scientia." See Aristotle, *Metaph.* VII, ch. 10, 1035a14–b3.

68. Collegium Complutense Sancti Cyrilli, *Artium Cursus sive Disputationes in Aristotelis Dialecticam*, p. 759a (disp. 19, q. 4, n. 47): "Materia sensibilis dicuntur omnes qualitates, quae sensibus percipiuntur, ut color, frigus, sonus, odor, & similes. Unde illae scientiae abstrahunt a materia sensibili, quae considerant suum obiectum sine istis qualitatibus. Et huiusmodi sunt Mathematicae, quae agunt de quantitate, non curando: an linea sit calida; superficies alba; aut corpus durum, &c."

69. Collegium Complutense Sancti Cyrilli, *Artium Cursus sive Disputationes in Aristotelis Dialecticam*, p. 759a (disp. 19, q. 4, n. 47): "Non tamen abstrahunt a materia intelligibili: quia non considerant quantitatem absque substantia materiali, cui inest, & a qua in sui cognitione dependet. Et ideo obtinent secundum locum, seu gradum abstractionis. Tandem materia intelligibilis est ipsa substantia corporea, seu materia prima: quae dicitur intelligibilis: quia solo intellectu percipi potest."

70. Collegium Complutense Sancti Cyrilli, *Artium Cursus sive Disputationes in Aristotelis Dialecticam*, p. 759a–b (disp. 19, q. 4, n. 47): "Unde illae scientiae abstrahunt a materia intelligibili, quae tractant de rebus, quae sine materia prima esse possunt; vel quia nunquam in materia, ut Deus, & Angeli; vel quia in quibusdam sunt in materia in quibusdam vero non: & ideo secundum se non dependent ab illa, ut substantia, & qualitas; actus, & potentia; unum, & multa, &c. Et huiusmodi est Metaphysica, quae propterea Theologia naturalis, & prima Philosophia nuncupatur: obtinetque supremum gradum abstractionis inter scientias naturales." See Suárez, *DM* 44.11.68: "est sententia valde communis, hanc unitatem obiecti in scientiis sumendam esse ex gradu abstractionis; et ita solet distingui triplex scientia ex triplici abstractione a materia, vel individua tantum, et non omnino a materia sensibili, vel a materia sensibili, et non ab intelligibili, vel ab omnibus. Quae divisio antiqua est: eam

Cajetan's version of the distinction between various modes of abstraction from matter adds a couple of refinements that allow him to arrive at his intended result, namely, a formally indivisible "formal *ratio under which*" for the object of each lowest species of natural theoretical science. For example, since mathematics is divided into arithmetic and geometry, Cajetan subdistinguishes that which is abstracted from matter according to reason, but not with respect to existence, into that which is abstracted from the continuous, "which is a certain kind of matter," and that which is not.[71] However, not everyone shared the view that the distinction between different degrees of independence from matter suffices for the division of theoretical science into lowest species. Some held that it could only yield the division of theoretical science into metaphysics, physics, and mathematics, the last two of which (if not all three) were commonly thought to be subdivisible into specifically different sciences. Indeed, Suárez reports that there is a great diversity of opinion on this issue (*DM* 44.11.68). For his part, de Olivera concedes that the "unity or distinction of a science, both generic and specific, is taken neither from the material object, nor from the formal object *in esse rei*, that is, from the *ratio formalis quae*, but from the object *in esse scibilis*, that is, from the *ratio formalis sub qua*."[72] But he also holds that only the *generic* unity and distinction of the speculative sciences is to be derived from different objects' various degrees of abstraction from matter.[73] In other words, de Olivera holds that there is

---

vero copiose tractant moderni scriptores in principio Phys. et Metaphys." (Francisco Suárez, *Opera Omnia*, 26:715a.)

71. Tommaso de Vio, *In Posteriorum analeticorum libros*, fol. 76va: "Dividitur siquidem abstractum a materia secundum rationem in abstractum a continuo quod materia quaedam est: et non abstractum ab eo etc. et haec sunt specialissima et constituunt arithmeticam et geometriam." The Conimbricenses likewise distinguish between two kinds of abstraction found in the mathematical sciences in order to distinguish arithmetic and geometry. See Collegium Conimbricense, *In octo libros Physicorum Aristotelis Stagiritae*, 1:9 (proem, q. 1, art. 4).

72. Collegium Complutense Sancti Cyrilli, *Artium Cursus sive Disputationes in Aristotelis Dialecticam*, p. 762a (disp. 19, q. 4, n. 52): "Unitas, aut distinctio scientiae, tam generica, quam specifica, neque sumitur ab obiecto materiali, neque ab obiecto formali in esse rei, seu a ratione formali *quae*, sed ab obiecto in esse scibilis, seu a ratione formali *sub qua*."

73. Collegium Complutense Sancti Cyrilli, *Artium Cursus sive Disputationes in Aristotelis Dialecticam*, p. 763a–b: "Ratio *sub qua*, a qua sumitur unitas, & distinctio generica scientiarum, accipienda est ex abstractione a materia: ac proinde illae scientiae erunt eiusdem generis, quae habuerint eandem abstractionem; illae vero diversi generis, quae diversas sortiuntur abstractiones."

more to the *ratio formalis sub qua* of a science's object than its degree of independence or abstraction from matter. The *specific* unity or distinction of two theoretical sciences belonging to the same genus, on his view, is to be derived from elsewhere, and in particular from the specific unity or distinction of the scientific principles within one and the same grade of abstraction.[74]

Be that as it may, Suárez invokes the notion of a "formal *ratio* under which" in the course of arguing that metaphysics "does not consider all the proper *rationes* or quiddities of beings in particular, or insofar as they are such, but only those which are contained under its proper abstraction" (*DM* 1.2.13). He states that this is the view of Aristotle and others who have written about first philosophy, for, he explains, they all "distinguish a threefold abstraction in real and speculative sciences" (*DM* 1.2.13). To be sure, he notes, physics, mathematics, and metaphysics all agree in some abstraction, since they all consider things in a universal way. But they differ as regards their abstraction from matter, for physics abstracts from singulars, but not from sensible matter— that is, the matter of sensible accidents—since it rather appeals to such matter in its reasonings. Mathematics, on the other hand, does abstract according to reason from sensible matter, "but not from intelligible matter, since quantity, however much it is abstracted, cannot be conceived except as a corporeal and material thing" (*DM* 1.2.13). As regards metaphysics, it abstracts from both sensible and intelligible matter, and not merely according to reason, but with respect to existence as well, "since the *rationes* of being that it considers are in reality found without matter," so that matter does not figure in their objective concepts (*DM* 1.2.13). After then noting, regarding this way of distinguishing theoretical sciences, that "so far no more suitable basis for distinguishing these sciences has been found," Suárez asserts that, "in any case, this one seems fitting enough" (*DM* 1.2.13). For,

---

74. Collegium Complutense Sancti Cyrilli, *Artium Cursus sive Disputationes in Aristotelis Dialecticam*, p. 764a (disp. 19, q. 4, n. 55): "Ratio *sub qua*, ex qua sumitur unitas, vel distinctio specifica scientiarum, petenda est ex unitate, vel distinctione specifica principiorum intra idem genus scibilis, seu intra eandem abstractionem. Tunc autem principia erunt eiusdem speciei in esse scibilis; quando vel unum derivatur ex alio, vel ambo ex alterutro intra eandem abstractionem. Tunc vero erunt specie distincta in esse scibilis; quando neque derivantur ex aliis, neque ex alterutris."

since these sciences are about things themselves, and are most of all speculative, and therefore employ abstraction in order to constitute a knowable
object about which demonstrations can be made, the knowable object as such
is rightly understood to be varied in accordance with diverse modes of abstraction. And therefore, this abstraction, insofar as it has a foundation in the
object itself, is usually called the "formal *ratio* under which" of such an object
in its character as a knowable [object] [*in ratione scibilis*] (*DM* 1.2.13).

The "foundation in the object itself" of which Suárez speaks here is of
course the relevant essence's aptitude to being abstracted from matter
by means of the mental operation of formal abstraction.[75] It is, in other
words, an essence's degree of independence from matter, which is also
sometimes termed its "abstraction" from matter. This, Suárez says, is
usually called "the formal *ratio* under which" of a science's object. As it
is varied, so is the knowable object (*obiectum scibile*) varied. And this
knowable object, Suárez makes clear, is that by appeal to which the various theoretical sciences are individuated and distinguished from each
other. For he adds that, "since things are more perfectly intelligible the
more they abstract from matter," and "cognition is more certain to the
extent that it is of a more immaterial, and consequently more abstract,
object, it follows that *the variety of both knowable objects and sciences
is rightly conceived in terms of diverse grades of abstraction or immateriality*" (*DM* 1.2.13, my emphasis). Suárez then states that on the basis
of "this received doctrine" regarding the distinction of the theoretical
sciences, the claim that metaphysics does not consider all things according to their proper *rationes* "is easily understood and proved, since
a science does not transgress the limits of its formal object, or the limits
of its object's 'formal *ratio* under which,' but it considers whatever is
contained under it" (*DM* 1.2.13).

Suárez, then, appeals to the notion of a "formal *ratio* under which"
in arguing for the claim that metaphysics does not consider all things
according to their proper *rationes*. Still, both the appeal and the claim
itself raise questions. As regards the claim, we are left to wonder how
it is to be reconciled with Suárez's conclusion in *DM* 1.1 that real being
is the adequate object of metaphysics. Cajetan's claim that the "formal

---

75. On formal abstraction, see Collegium Complutense Sancti Cyrilli, *Artium Cursus
sive Disputationes in Aristotelis Dialecticam*, pp. 757b–58b (disp. 19, q. 4, n. 46).

ratio which" of first philosophy's object is entity (*entitas*) might lead us to think that *DM* 1.1 is devoted to identifying the "formal *ratio* which" of first philosophy's object, and that *DM* 1.2 is devoted to identifying the "formal *ratio* under which" of this same object. One possible problem with this suggestion is that, unlike sound and the audible (or flavor and the gustable, etc.), real being and that which abstracts from matter with respect to existence are not extensionally equivalent: the objects of both mathematics and physics are real beings, but they do not abstract from matter with respect to existence. Accordingly, *DM* 1.2's conclusion regarding "the formal *ratio* under which" of first philosophy's object seems to be a qualification and limitation of *DM* 1.1's conclusion regarding the adequate object of metaphysics, and not merely an attempt to offer a new characterization of precisely the *same* object.

It is not clear, then, how the main conclusions of *DM* 1.1 and *DM* 1.2 are to be reconciled, or how they might be seen as successive stages in a single coherent effort to determine first philosophy's essential character by appeal to its object.[76] But it is perhaps worth noting that Suárez is not unique in this respect, for he was not alone in holding both that the adequate subject of metaphysics is real being (or being *qua* being) and that metaphysics treats only of things that abstract from matter with respect to existence. For example, Paul Soncinas—whom Suárez cites more than one hundred and fifty times in the course of his

---

76. For a discussion of this issue, see Marco Forlivesi, "Impure Ontology: The Nature of Metaphysics and Its Object in Francisco Suárez's Texts," *Quaestio* 5 (2005): 559–86. As Forlivesi points out, n39, Hans Seigfried, *Wahrheit und Metaphysik bei Suarez* (Bonn: Bouvier, 1967), 85–88 and 168–69nn20–21, claims that Suárez in *DM* 1.1 determines that real being is the material object of metaphysics and in *DM* 1.2 determines that being (*ens*) abstracted from matter according to *esse* is the formal object of metaphysics. I agree with Forlivesi that this seems mistaken. The material object of a science is generally understood to be something that is considered in a science, not *per se*, but by reason of its coincidence with the science's formal object, and real being is surely not considered in this way by the metaphysician, according to Suárez. Daniel Heider, "The Unity of Suárez's Metaphysics," *Medioevo* 34 (2009): 475–505, also claims that in *DM* 1.1 Suárez's aim is to identify the material object of metaphysics. It is not clear to me, however, that Heider is using the expression "material object" here in the traditional sense. Rolf Darge, "Suárez on the Subject of Metaphysics," discusses Suárez's appeal to abstraction from matter according to *esse* (105–9), but he does not raise the issue of *DM* 1.2's compatibility with *DM* 1.1. Jorge Uscatescu Barrón, "El concepto de metafísica en Suárez: su objeto y dominio," *Pensamiento* 51, no. 200 (1995): 215–236, asserts that the criterion of abstraction from matter according to *esse* "undermines the proper generality of metaphysics" (229).

Metaphysical Disputations—also holds that "being insofar as it is being, or being common to God and creatures, is the adequate subject of metaphysics."[77] And he too maintains both that the "generic distinction of the speculative sciences is taken from the distinction of the formal *ratio* of the object insofar as it is an object," and that "what admits of being contemplated through every sort of abstraction from matter is the object of metaphysics."[78]

As regards Suárez's appeal to the notion of a "formal *ratio* under which," what is most striking about it, perhaps, is the fact that, unlike Cajetan and others, Suárez does not invoke it in order to establish that metaphysics is specifically one science or indivisible into specifically different sciences. Both Cajetan and de Olivera explicitly characterize the distinction between the "formal *ratio* which" and the "formal *ratio* under which" of a science's object as motivated by the need to furnish specifically one habit with an object that is likewise specifically one or formally indivisible, although they disagree on the question of whether an object's "formal *ratio* under which" is determined entirely by its degree of independence from matter. By contrast, Suárez, as we shall see, seeks to establish the specific unity of metaphysics by arguing that the parts of first philosophy which might be thought specifically distinct are so closely interconnected that they cannot plausibly be regarded as specifically different sciences. What exactly we are to make of all this is unclear. But it seems unlikely that Suárez was the only scholastic philosopher to employ a technical notion for a purpose other than that for which it was originally devised.

In any case, having argued that metaphysics does not investigate every *ratio* of every being, but only those *rationes* which are contained

77. Paul Soncinas, *Pauli Soncinatis Ordinis Praedicatorum Quaestiones Metaphysicales acutissimae* (Lugdunum: apud Carolum Presnot, 1579), p. 15a (bk. 4, q. 10): "ens inquantum ens, sive ens commune Deo et creaturis, est adaequatum subiectum metaphysicae."

78. Paul Soncinas, *Quaestiones Metaphysicales acutissimae*, p. 103b (bk. 6, q. 8): "Secunda conclusio. Generica distinctio scientiarum speculativarum sumitur ex distinctione formalis rationis obiecti, in quantum est obiectum, & non ex ratione formali quae attingitur in obiecto. Ista conclusio habetur a philosopho in hoc sexto libro. Ex cuius doctrina sic arguitur. Speculabile per omnimodam abstractionem a materia, est obiectum metaphysicae. Speculabile per abstractionem a materia sensibili, & non a materia intelligibili, est obiectum mathematicarum. Speculabile per abstractionem a materia sensibili particulari & non communi, est obiectum naturalis philosophiae, ut dicitur in textu."

under its abstraction, Suárez goes on to mention some of the *rationes* that first philosophy does investigate. The enumeration in some respects sets the agenda for the remainder of the work, although not every *ratio* mentioned here receives an extensive discussion in the disputations that follow. The first two *rationes* that Suárez mentions are the *ratio* of substance and the *ratio* of accident. Each of these, he explains, is knowable, can have proper and adequate attributes, and is not the concern of either physics or mathematics. What's more, knowledge of both is necessary for perfect science. Suárez also mentions the *rationes* of created and uncreated being, the *rationes* of finite and infinite substance, the *rationes* of absolute and relative accident, the *ratio* of quality, the *ratio* of action, the *ratio* of operation, and the *ratio* of dependence (*DM* 1.2.15). *Rationes* that can be found only in immaterial beings include the *ratio* of immaterial substance, the *ratio* of first or uncreated substance, the *ratio* of created spirit (or angel), and the proper *rationes* of all species of created spirit (*DM* 1.2.16). In addition to these, Suárez notes, various *rationes* of cause pertain to metaphysics, including the common *ratio* of cause and effect, "for in God, who is supremely immaterial, the *ratio* of cause is found, and in the angels the *ratio* of effect, and to all created beings, insofar as they are finite beings, it is common and essential that they emanate from some cause" (*DM* 1.2.17). What's more, some genus of operation or causality pertains to all created beings, whether material or immaterial. Suárez also explains that the *rationes* of efficient, final, and exemplar cause abstract from matter with respect to existence, since all three are found in God. As regards the material and formal causes, although insofar as they are causes of substance in particular they evidently do not abstract from matter with respect to existence, nevertheless, "they too are separated from matter insofar as they abstract from substances and accidents according to their common *rationes*" (*DM* 1.2.17). In other words, since material causality is exercised not only by matter in relation to the composite substance, but also by any substance (whether material or immaterial) in relation to accidents, there is a common *ratio* of material cause that abstracts from matter with respect to existence. The same is true, *mutatis mutandis*, of formal causality. What's more, Suárez notes, it pertains to metaphysics to investigate the first *rationes* of causing that are found in the first cause, God. Accordingly, the metaphysician will investigate God as the first efficient and ultimate final cause (*DM* 1.2.17).

In the course of discussing what *rationes* pertain to metaphysics, Suárez also considers several that, one might think, should be assigned to metaphysics, but that, for various reasons, he assigns instead to another science. For example, the *rationes* of the living and the intelligent are found in both material and immaterial things and therefore should, by rights, fall to metaphysics. However, Suárez observes that since such *rationes* cannot be cognized by us except by appeal to the diverse grades of soul, "nothing about them can suitably be said here aside from what is said in the science of the soul" (*DM* 1.2.15). Moreover, even though he has assigned the *ratio* of created spirit to metaphysics, Suárez notes that he will say little (*perpauca*) about these intelligences in this work, since "it pertains to the perfection of a science to consider its subject wholly and completely," and when it comes to the angels, supernatural theology is in a much better position than metaphysics is to treat of them in as complete a fashion as possible (*DM* 1.2.20). A similar consideration applies to God, Suárez notes, "although, since more things can naturally be cognized about God than about the intelligences, and since natural cognition of him is more necessary to the perfection of" metaphysics, Suárez will have some things (*nonnulla*) to say about God in the *Metaphysical Disputations* (*DM* 1.2.20). Finally, in this context Suárez also considers the case of the rational soul. The treatment of this soul might be thought to pertain to metaphysics, he explains, since it is an immaterial substance, abstracts from matter with respect to existence, and has operations which are likewise independent of matter (*DM* 1.2.19). Suárez argues that, nonetheless, "the consideration of this soul is to be left to the final and most perfect part of natural philosophy," in part because the human being, as such, is a physical being, and it pertains to the same science to consider both a whole and its essential parts (*DM* 1.2.20). Moreover, even if some plausibly argue that it pertains to the metaphysician to consider the state of the separated soul, and its mode of operation in that state, nevertheless, these things are more appropriately considered in natural philosophy, since (once again) it pertains to the perfection of a science to consider its subject wholly and completely. What's more, the consideration of the soul and its states, "when divided into parts and handed down in diverse sciences, generates prolixity and confusion" (*DM* 1.2.20).

Although Suárez holds that metaphysics does not treat of all things according to their proper *rationes*, it is important to note that he nonetheless also maintains that its treatment of its own objects requires some consideration of matter and material things. As regards *rationes* that are not found without matter, Suárez explains, metaphysics deals with them to the extent necessary for "teaching the general divisions of being into the ten highest genera, and other similar ones, so as to prescribe the proper objects of the other sciences" (*DM* 1.2.26). This function of prescribing the proper objects of the other sciences, Suárez explains, can evidently pertain to no other science. But he also asserts that the handing down of these divisions is required in order for metaphysics to treat properly of its own objects. For the common *ratio* of being, he explains, is analogical, and therefore distinct cognition of it requires that one distinguish the modes by which it is contracted to the various categories of being, some of which (e.g., quantity and situation) are never found without matter. Moreover, metaphysics cannot reach its more specific *rationes* unless it first separates and distinguishes them from others that fall outside its abstraction, which of course it cannot do unless it cognizes these other *rationes*. Finally, Suárez observes that certain *rationes* common to material and immaterial things even belong to material things as such, and that metaphysics must accordingly consider these material things, at least to some extent. In this context, he explicitly mentions "being composed from act and potency, and the mode of this composition," and the fact that material substance "is a kind of being that is *per se* one" (*DM* 1.2.27). First philosophy's consideration of the *rationes* of potency and act, then, will require consideration of matter and form (which are related as potency and act), and its consideration of unity, one of the attributes of being, will require consideration of the material substance's unity in particular. Suárez, therefore, concludes that metaphysics "considers certain generic grades that reach matter, but not by setting aside its abstraction," and that it "only indirectly reaches their proper *rationes* in relation to its proper abstraction—namely, so as to make clear how common and transcendental predicates are found in them, and how other grades or genera

that truly and really abstract from all matter are distinguished from
them" (*DM* 1.2.28).

Section 3: Whether metaphysics is divided
into specifically different sciences

In section 3 of *DM* 1 Suárez addresses the question of whether metaphysics is formally one and indivisible. It might be thought, he observes, that metaphysics is only generically one, as mathematics is, on
the grounds that the abstraction through which its object is constituted
admits of being distinguished into several kinds. For, on the one hand,
there is the "necessary" abstraction that characterizes those *rationes*
which can never be found in matter—for example, the *ratio* of created spirit. On the other, there is the merely "permissive" abstraction
that characterizes *rationes* which *can* be found in matter, but need not
be—for example, the *ratio* of substance. The difference between these
two abstractions, Suárez explains, might seem "sufficient to vary the
knowable object as such specifically, and consequently sufficient to vary
the science specifically as well" (*DM* 1.3.2). Moreover, regarding those
rationes which are never found in matter, one might argue "that the
abstraction of God—who is altogether pure act and abstracts even from
metaphysical composition—is very different from the abstraction of
the other intelligences" (*DM* 1.3.2). Accordingly, Suárez explains, one
might distinguish three specifically different sciences under a generic
unity of metaphysics: one that investigates being as being and at most
descends to the ten highest genera of being, a second that treats of created intelligences, and a third that treats of God alone.

A second argument considered by Suárez focuses on metaphysics
conceived as a habit of the intellect (*DM* 1.3.3–6). A partial account of
the argument runs as follows. If metaphysics is specifically one science,
it can only be so in respect of the judicative habit left in the mind as a
result of its acts. In other words, if metaphysics is specifically one science, this is because the habit of metaphysics, existing in the intellect
of the knower, is specifically one quality. But, it is alleged, the habit of
metaphysics cannot be specifically one. For the habit is either simple
in its entity, or it is a composite quality. But that it cannot be simple is

proved in two ways. First, the habit of metaphysics inclines or disposes its possessor to various judgments regarding the most diverse things, and this is something that a single simple quality cannot do. Second, the habit of metaphysics is first acquired by means of a single act or judgment regarding one object, for example, the judgment that every being is true. By means of other acts or judgments it is subsequently extended to other, very different conclusions. But this extension can occur only through the addition of some reality or entity to the habit, since the habit's scope is increased. Therefore, the resulting habit of metaphysics cannot be a simple quality, but must be composite. However, if the habit is composite in this way, it cannot be specifically one. For what is first acquired in a habit by an act of one species is specifically distinct from what is later acquired in that habit by an act of another species, and one quality of a single species cannot be composed from two specifically distinct qualities.

Suárez's own view is that metaphysics is specifically one science, unlike mathematics. Regarding the second argument for the merely generic unity of metaphysics, he claims that the challenge it poses is in fact "general and of the same nature in the case of all sciences and almost all acquired habits, namely, whether they are simple qualities or are instead composite according to the extension they have relative to their objects" (*DM* 1.3.7). That is, Suárez thinks that this argument, if successful, would undermine the specific unity of any science. For this reason, he does not undertake to reply to it here in *DM* 1.3. His own view, as he makes clear both in this section (*DM* 1.3.12) and at much greater length in section 11 of *DM* 44 ("On habits"), is that *no* science is specifically one habit. A science is invariably composed of many partial habits. The specific unity of a science cannot, therefore, be based on that science's being specifically one habit or quality.[79]

As regards the first argument for the merely generic unity of metaphysics, Suárez will pronounce it dealt with after he gives his own positive arguments for first philosophy's specific unity. The first of these (see *DM* 1.3.9) appeals to authority, primarily Aristotle's, although it would perhaps be better to speak here of an assortment of considerations, the

---

79. See John P. Doyle, "Suárez on the Unity of a Scientific Habit," *The American Catholic Philosophical Quarterly* 65, no. 3 (1991): 309–31.

interrelations of which are not always clear. In any case, Suárez begins
by asserting that Aristotle always speaks of metaphysics as specifically
one science, and he points to a feature of Aristotle's discussion of first
philosophy that has often puzzled readers of the *Metaphysics*: the fact
that Aristotle, to all appearances, variously characterizes one and the
same science as theology, divine science, first philosophy, the universal science, and wisdom. The first three names, Suárez explains, are
given to metaphysics insofar as it treats of God and the intelligences;
the fourth, "universal science," is applied to it insofar as it treats of being *qua* being, its primary attributes, and its principles; and the fifth,
"wisdom," is assigned to it insofar as it investigates all these things and
also first principles and the first causes of things. Aristotle, then, clearly indicates that specifically one and the same science deals with all
these things, Suárez says. He also observes that in *Metaph.* IV, chs. 2
and 3, VII, ch. 1, and XII, Aristotle asserts both that being is the adequate object of this science and that the principal part of this object
is substance, either substance without qualification or immaterial and
primary substance.[80] In fact, in bk. XII, Aristotle hands down cognition
of God and the intelligences, holding that this cognition "is the principal part of this doctrine, to which the other parts are in some way
ordered" (*DM* 1.3.9).[81] Suárez's point here is that Aristotle in this way
indicates that both the treatment of being in general and the treatment
of immaterial substance in particular belong to one and the same science. After then asserting that according to Thomas Aquinas in *ST* I-II,
q. 57, art. 2, natural wisdom or metaphysics is one, while the habits of
the other sciences are many,[82] Suárez, relying on the identification of
metaphysics and wisdom, invokes the conception of wisdom as having
among its tasks both the consideration of the highest causes and the
confirmation of the first principles common to all the sciences. Granted
this, he says, neither that part of metaphysics which treats of God, nor
that part which treats of being as such, can be termed wisdom, for the
former does not treat of first principles, and the latter does not treat of

---

80. See Aristotle, *Metaph.* IV, ch. 2, 1003a33–b19, ch. 3, 1005a19–b8, VII, ch. 1 (in its
entirety), and XII, ch. 1, 1069a18–26.

81. See Aristotle, *Metaph.* VII, ch. 11, 1037a10–17.

82. Thomas Aquinas, *Sancti Thomae Aquinatis opera omnia* (Leonina), t. 6, p. 365b.

the highest causes. "It must, therefore, be the case," Suárez concludes, "that one and the same science embraces all these things" (*DM* 1.3.9).[83]

In his second argument for the specific unity of metaphysics (*DM* 1.3.10), Suárez asserts that there is no sufficient foundation to suppose that there are several sciences of metaphysics in the way that there are several sciences of mathematics. Besides, he continues, the things dealt with in metaphysics are so interconnected that they cannot be attributed to diverse sciences, especially since they all agree in the same *ratio* of knowable object (*in eadem ratione scibilis*) by virtue of participating in the same abstraction. Perhaps recognizing that this last claim seems to beg the question against his opponents, who distinguish three abstractions in metaphysics, Suárez concedes that God and the angels, "considered in themselves" (*secundum se consideratae*), "seem to be constituted in some higher grade and order." However, he adds, insofar as they fall under our consideration (*prout in nostram considerationem cadunt*), they cannot be separated from a consideration of the transcendental attributes, *one*, *true*, and *good*, which, as attributes of being as such, are investigated in the context of the treatment of being in general. Suárez's claim, in other words, is that the part of metaphysics which treats of God and the angels is inseparable from the part of metaphysics which treats of being insofar as it is being; these parts cannot constitute distinct sciences. In justification of this claim, he explains that the cognition of God and the angels afforded by metaphysics involves cognition of all the predicates in them, including common and transcendental predicates. In this respect, first philosophy's treatment of God and other separate substances differs from natural philosophy's treatment of material substance, since natural philosophy does not consider the common and transcendental predicates that are in material substance, "but supposes them cognized by a higher science" (*DM* 1.3.10). This, however, is something that the science of God and the intelligences cannot do, he explains, since it is itself the highest of all the natural sciences. Accordingly, it must include whatever is necessary for the perfect cognition of immaterial substances. "Therefore," Suárez concludes, "the same science that treats of these special objects"—namely, God

83. See *DM* 1.5.15.

and the intelligences—"at the same time considers all the predicates that are common to them and other things." In other words, the natural science that treats of God and the intelligences must likewise treat of being as such and its properties, *one, true,* and *good.*

It is in the immediate wake of this last argument that Suárez announces that the first argument for the merely generic unity of metaphysics has been dealt with (*DM* 1.3.11). It has been shown, he says, how (*quo modo*) the difference between necessary and permissive abstraction from matter does not vary the specific *ratio* of knowable object (*specificam rationem obiecti scibilis*). By way of explanation, he cites the connection that he has just argued for between immaterial substances and transcendental predicates, suggesting again that this connection is somehow due to our cognitive situation. He also alleges that all these things belong to "the same order of doctrine and certainty" (*DM* 1.3.11). It is not, however, evident that either of these points serves to explain why or how the difference between necessary and permissive abstraction fails to vary the *ratio* of knowable object. To be sure, the inseparability of first philosophy's treatment of immaterial substances from its treatment of being in general may establish that immaterial substances, on the one hand, and being and its properties, on the other, do, as a matter of fact, fall under the same abstraction or under the same specific *ratio* of knowable object. But it is difficult to see here an attempt to address or dismantle that argument for first philosophy's mere generic unity which is based (in part) on the difference between necessary and permissive abstraction. It is perhaps worth remembering, however, that the notion of a "formal *ratio* under which" is formulated in the service of classifying objects in a manner that is in some sense relativized to our cognitive faculties. Accordingly, the implied contrast between two ways of considering God and the angels—in themselves, on the one hand, and insofar as they fall under our consideration, on the other—might be taken to suggest the view that, even if immaterial substances abstract from matter in a way different from that in which *rationes* common to material and immaterial things do, still, this difference cannot, given our cognitive situation, make for a difference of knowable object and thus give rise to a specific difference between scientific knowledge of being *qua* being, on the one hand, and scientific knowledge of God and the angels, on the other.[84] The suggestion, in other words, is that the difference between these two kinds of abstraction or degrees of independence from matter does not give rise to, or correspond to, two different ways in which the human intellect abstracts the relevant *rationes* from matter. The difference between them is, as a result, irrelevant to the human cognitive situation. This might explain why Suárez goes on to say—apparently with the intention of offering a third explanation for why the difference between necessary and permissive abstraction from matter fails to vary the knowable object—that this difference "is only according to diverse concepts of reason" (*solum est secundum diversos conceptus rationis*). The suggestion seems to be that a mere distinction of reason is somehow at work here. Therefore, Suárez says, the difference between these kinds of abstraction does not alone "suffice *per se* for constituting a diverse science, unless another, greater ground of distinction presents itself" (*DM* 1.3.11). This interpretation, however, is admittedly speculative.[85]

84. It is perhaps worth noting here that according to Suárez the human being's natural cognition of God "does not reach God as he is in himself, but insofar as he can be made manifest from creatures by the natural light of the intellect" (*DM* 1.1.11). For this reason, when the human being cognizes God by natural means, "the *ratio* under which he is reached is always common to him and other, created things" (*DM* 1.1.11). It is also worth noting that according to Suárez created spiritual substances are naturally cognized by us "very imperfectly, at most in accordance with certain common *rationes* and negative concepts, but not in accordance with their proper and specific differences" (*DM* 1.2.16).

85. See Marco Forlivesi, "Impure Ontology: The Nature of Metaphysics and Its Object in Francisco Suárez's Texts," 574–76; Daniel Heider, "The Unity of Suárez's Metaphysics," 488; Daniel Heider, "The Nature of Suárez's Metaphysics: *Disputationes Metaphysicae* and Their Main Systematic Strains," *Studia Neoaristotelica* 6, no. 1 (2009): 106. The claim that the difference between necessary and permissive abstraction is only according to diverse concepts of reason finds no echo in either Francisco de Araujo (1580–1664) or Blasius a Conceptione (1603–94), both of whom address the argument for the mere generic unity of metaphysics based on diverse forms of abstraction. See Blasius a Conceptione, *Metaphysica in Tres Libros Divisa* (Lutetiae Parisiorum: Sumptibus Dionysii Thierry, 1640), p. 26 (disp. 1, q. 3, n. 52), and Francisco de Araujo, *Commentariorum in Universam Aristotelis Metaphysicam Tomus Primus* (Brugis et Salmanticae: Ex Officinis Typographicis Ioannis Baptistae Varesii & Antoniae Ramirez viduae, 1617), pp. 108b–109b (bk. 1, q. 5, art. 2).

Section 4: The end, utility, and
functions of metaphysics

A science, like most things, is defined in the Aristotelian system by specifying its proximate genus and difference. The proximate genus of metaphysics is the genus of speculative or theoretical science, and the difference by which metaphysics is essentially distinguished from physics and mathematics is taken from its object. Metaphysics, then, is defined by Suárez as the speculative science of being, which treats of both being in general and those beings which abstract from matter with respect to existence.

Suárez accordingly opens section 4 of *DM* 1 by announcing that the object and essence of metaphysics have been explained, and that something must now be said about its causes. The material cause of metaphysics, he begins, is simply the subject in which it exists, that is, the intellect. It is itself a form (i.e., an accidental form) and thus has no other formal cause. As an acquired habit, moreover, it is acquired as all such habits are, that is, by certain acts or operations, which serve as its efficient cause. As regards first philosophy's final cause or end, Suárez first identifies that end which it has in common with all speculative sciences. Like all such sciences, he notes, its end is the contemplation of truth for its own sake. Its proper or distinctive end, on the other hand, is "to make clear the nature, properties, and causes of being as being, and the nature, properties, and causes of its parts, insofar as they abstract from matter with respect to existence" (*DM* 1.4.3).

By far the largest part of *DM* 1.4 is devoted to the task of discussing first philosophy's "usefulness" (*utilitas*) and "functions" (*munera*). Suárez identifies two respects in which first philosophy is useful or necessary as well as three functions that it performs. He does not explicitly address the question of how a function and an end or final cause differ, although he evidently thinks that they are closely connected, and that a thing's function can be inferred from its final cause. However, it is also clear that Suárez wants to be able to assert that metaphysics is useful for various things without asserting that it is ordered to them as a means is ordered to an end, since that would imply that metaphysical cognition is not for its own sake (*propter se*), but for the sake of these other things, which would in turn imply that it is inferior in worth to these other things.[86]

Suárez states that the first necessity or utility (*prima necessitas seu utilitas*) of metaphysics is "to perfect the intellect in itself" and "to cognize the most perfect things and *rationes* of things" (*DM* 1.4.4). These are not, on his view, distinct or independent. For Suárez, like all Aristotelians, understands scientific cognition to be a perfection of the intellect. What's more, he holds that metaphysics perfects the intellect in itself (*secundum se*) precisely by virtue of the fact that it is cognition of the most perfect things and *rationes* of things. For the objects of natural philosophy and mathematics, unlike first philosophy's objects, do not abstract altogether from matter, and from this it follows, according to Suárez, that the former two sciences do not perfect the intellect in itself. Rather, they perfect the intellect "insofar as it uses the senses and concerns itself with sensible things" (physics) or "insofar as it abstracts in some way from the experience of the external senses, although with a dependence on imagination or phantasy" (mathematics) (*DM* 1.4.4). Metaphysics, by contrast, "illuminates the intellect in itself," by abstracting from the senses and imagination and considering "spiritual and divine things, and *rationes* and principles common to all things, and the general attributes of beings, which are considered by no inferior science" (*DM* 1.4.4).

Suárez goes on to state that metaphysics is, in the second place, "very useful" (*valde utilis*) for perfectly acquiring the other sciences. He cites Aristotle as the source of this claim,[87] and he explains that, according to the ancient philosopher, other sciences serve metaphysics, while it itself is set over them, although it does not exercise a practical rule or dominion (*imperium practicum*) over them—such a rule pertains rather to prudence or the moral sciences[88]—but instead provides speculative direction or guidance (*directio speculativa*) to them. Moreover, Suárez claims that Aristotle holds metaphysics to be so related to the other sciences for two reasons: first, because "it deals with the most excellent things, with the first causes of things, and with the ultimate

---

86. See *DM* 1.4.6 and Aristotle, *Nicomachean Ethics* I, ch. 1.
87. Aristotle, *Metaph.* I, ch. 2, 982a14–19, and *Metaph.* III, ch. 2, 996b10–13.
88. See Aristotle, *Nicomachean Ethics* I, ch. 2.

end and highest good" (*DM* 1.4.5), and second, because "metaphysics alone concerns itself with the first principles of the other sciences" (*DM* 1.4.5). Regarding the latter point, Suárez explains that in the *Posterior Analytics* Aristotle distinguishes between two kinds of principle.[89] Some of a science's principles are proper, and these "are made clear in each of the sciences" (*DM* 1.4.5). Others are common to all the sciences, since all sciences make use of them, at least to the extent required by their subject matter and insofar as their proper principles depend on them. Regarding these common principles, on which all sciences "depend to the greatest degree" (*DM* 1.4.5), Suárez states that cognition and consideration of them can pertain only to metaphysics, since such a principle is composed from the most abstract and universal terms. Moreover, the claim that metaphysics is very useful for perfectly acquiring the other sciences can be proved in two ways, Suárez explains: first, by argument, for this science considers the highest *rationes*, the most universal properties, the proper *rationes* of essence and existence, as well as the various modes of distinction to be found in things, and perfect cognition of particular things cannot be had without a distinct cognition of these. This usefulness of metaphysics can also be shown, second, by appeal to experience, for other sciences frequently make use of its principles in their demonstrations and arguments. For this reason, it often happens that one makes mistakes in other sciences through an ignorance of metaphysics.

The remainder of *DM* 1.4 is devoted to a more detailed explanation of first philosophy's usefulness for perfectly acquiring the other sciences. It is divided into three parts, each devoted to a function performed by metaphysics vis-à-vis the other sciences. In the first (*DM* 1.4.9–14), Suárez considers the claim that metaphysics shows that the objects of the particular sciences exist and what they are. In the second (*DM* 1.4.15–27), he explains how metaphysics confirms and defends first principles. In the third (*DM* 1.4.28–34), he argues that metaphysics is not concerned to hand down or teach the so-called "instruments of knowledge" (*instrumenta sciendi*)—definition, division, and argumentation—since this is rather the function of logic or dialectic, although

---

89. Aristotle, *Post. An.* I, ch. 10, 76a37ff.

he also argues that the science of metaphysics perfects these to a great degree insofar as they have a foundation in things.

Suárez begins his discussion of the first function by noting that metaphysics is commonly thought to prescribe or fix the objects of the other sciences and, if necessary, demonstrate that they exist. This view is attributed to Averroes.[90] It is also said to receive support from Aristotle's claim in *Post. An.* I, ch. 10, that a science does not prove, but rather assumes, both that its subject exists and what it is.[91] For since the essence and existence of a science's subject are not always known *per se*, but often require explanation and proof, a special science must rely on some higher science in this regard, and this higher science can only be metaphysics, since it pertains to metaphysics to consider the *rationes* of essence and existence.

In the remainder of the discussion, Suárez entertains several objections to this view, concedes various points, and then endeavors to explain how metaphysics is concerned with the objects of the other sciences. The first objection begins by challenging the notion that metaphysics demonstrates the existence of another science's subject. A science does not require the actual existence of its subject, it alleges, nor can the actual existence of its subject be demonstrated, at least when this subject is a created being. For existence does not necessarily belong to created beings, and what admits of being demonstrated and scientifically known is necessary. Therefore, any science of created objects abstracts from their actual existence. Moreover, if to this objection one replies that metaphysics merely proves, but does not demonstrate, that the object of another science actually exists (which does not presuppose the necessary existence of that object), then the proof in question must be *a posteriori*, from effects. But this sort of proof, the objection alleges, "seems rather to pertain to the natural philosopher, who philosophizes from sensible effects" (*DM* 1.4.9). Moreover, if it is alleged that metaphysics merely demonstrates that it is *possible* for the object of another science to exist, this too is something which does not admit of

90. See Averroes, *Averrois Cordubensis commentum magnum super libro De celo & mundo Aristotelis*, ed. R. Arnzen, G. Endress, and F. Carmody (Leuven, Belgium: Peeters, 2003), 2:490–91 (bk. 3, text 4).

91. Aristotle, *Post. An.* I, ch. 10, 76b3–6.

being demonstrated. For there is no middle term through which this might be done, "just as it also cannot be demonstrated, of a science's subject, what it is, because there is no middle term through which the essence of each thing agrees with it; rather, the essence agrees with it immediately and *per se*" (*DM* 1.4.9).

In response to the first part of this objection, Suárez concedes that metaphysics does not demonstrate the actual existence of any other science's subject (*DM* 1.4.10). He also concedes that, except for scientific knowledge of God, whose existence is necessary, a science abstracts from the actual existence of its subject. Indeed, speaking *per se*, a science does not even assume that its subject actually exists. Suárez also notes, however, that the actual existence of a science's subject might well be necessary if *we* are to acquire the science, "since we receive science from things themselves" (*DM* 1.4.10).[92]

Much the same view is found in de Olivera and Antonio Rubio (1548–1615), the author of a two-volume commentary on Aristotle's logic.[93] At the beginning of the *Posterior Analytics*, Aristotle affirms that "all teaching and all intellectual learning come from already existing knowledge" (71a1–2). By way of explanation, he says:

It is necessary to be already aware of things in two ways: of some things it is necessary to believe already that they are [ὅτι ἔστι], of some one must grasp what the thing said is [τί τὸ λεγόμενόν ἐστι], and of others both—e.g., of the fact that everything is either affirmed or denied truly, one must believe that it is; of the triangle, that it signifies *this*; and of the unit both (both what it signifies and that it is).[94]

---

92. The view that a theoretical science abstracts from the actual existence of any creature goes back at least to John Duns Scotus (1265/66–1308). See Allan Wolter, *The Transcendentals and Their Function in the Metaphysics of Duns Scotus* (Washington, D.C.: The Catholic University of America Press, 1946), 65–71. The significance of Suárez's endorsement of it, however, is matter of some controversy. This is an issue to which I shall return in the introduction to my translation of *DM* 2.

93. Antonio Rubio, *Commentarii in Universam Aristotelis Dialecticam*, 2 vols. (Compluti: Ex Officina Iusti Sanchez Crespo, 1603). This two-volume work, which sometimes goes under the title *Logica Mexicana*, should not be confused with the abbreviated version of it that also goes under this title. The earliest edition of the latter that I have been able to identify is *Logica Mexicana, hoc est, commentarii breviores et maxime perspicui in universam Aristotelis dialecticam* (Lugduni: Apud Ioannem Pillohotte, 1611).

94. Aristotle, *Post. An.*, 71a12–16, in *The Complete Works of Aristotle: The Revised Oxford Translation*, ed. J. Barnes (Princeton: Princeton University Press, 1984), 1:114.

De Olivera and Rubio see in this text a doctrine about what things must be cognized or assumed before the work of demonstration can begin. Both hold that the subject of a science is that about which one must assume or cognize beforehand both that it is and what it is. In other words, they take Aristotle to be of the view that, before one can demonstrate, of a given subject, that it has this or that proper passion, one must assume or cognize both what the subject is and that it exists. The clear implication is that a science proves neither. Moreover, both take Aristotle to be of the view that the passions demonstrated of a subject are the things about which one must cognize beforehand what they are (or what they signify). That these passions are or exist is shown when one demonstrates that they belong to their subjects, since they exist only as attributes of their subjects (i.e., for them *esse* is *inesse*). Further, de Olivera and Rubio interpret Aristotle as holding that complex principles are the things about which one must assume or know beforehand that they are—that is, that they are the case.

De Olivera and Rubio deny, however, that Aristotle is to be taken as affirming that a science necessarily involves cognition of the actual existence of either its subject or the passions demonstrated of it. In support of this denial, Rubio argues that a proposition like "the human being is a rational animal" or "the human being is capable of laughter" is true even if there are no human beings and never have been any human beings.[95] He also appeals, as Suárez does, to the fact that existence does not pertain to the essence of any created being, that is, to the fact that a creature's existence is not necessary: since science is of the necessary, or of what does not admit of being otherwise, it follows that a science must abstract from the actual existence of its subject.[96] Moreover, since de Olivera and Rubio deny that a science assumes the actual existence of its subject, they interpret Aristotle's claim regarding the prerequisites of demonstration as involving a claim about the essence and *possible* existence of the relevant subject. That is, Rubio takes Aristotle to be saying, not that one must cognize or assume beforehand

95. Antonio Rubio, *Commentarii in Universam Aristotelis Dialecticam*, vol. 2, col. 295 (bk. 1, q. 2). See Collegium Complutense Sancti Cyrilli, *Artium Cursus sive Disputationes in Aristotelis Dialecticam*, p. 686b (disp. 17, q. 2, n. 24).

96. Antonio Rubio, *Commentarii in Universam Aristotelis Dialecticam*, vol. 2, col. 295 (bk. 1, q. 2).

that the subject of a science actually exists, but that one must cognize or assume that the subject "has a true essence, to which actual existence can belong" (*veram habere essentiam, cui potest actualis existentia convenire*).[97] De Olivera, for his part, speaks of cognizing beforehand that the subject has the aptitude to exist (*esse in aptitudine*).[98]

Since a science, according to Suárez, does not assume that its object actually exists, one naturally wonders whether metaphysics, in his opinion, demonstrates that it is possible for the object of another science to exist. As mentioned, the objection considered by Suárez specifically anticipates and addresses the suggestion that metaphysics demonstrates that the subject of another science has existence in potency or aptitude. Against this suggestion, it claims that, for want of an appropriate middle term, this cannot be done, "just as it also cannot be demonstrated, of a science's subject, what it is, because there is no middle term through which the essence of each thing agrees with it; rather, the essence agrees with it immediately and *per se*" (*DM* 1.4.9). Motivating this second claim is the thought that there is no cause or explanation of the fact that (say) a human being is a rational animal. That is, while the essence of the human being is explanatory, more or less immediately, of her proper passions (e.g., being capable of instruction, being liable to wonder, being capable of laughter), there would seem to be nothing that explains the fact that she is a rational animal. Being a rational animal agrees *per se* and immediately with the human being.

Unfortunately, Suárez never explicitly addresses the claim that one cannot demonstrate that it is possible for some thing to exist. Rather, he notes that a thing's essence and existence cannot be demonstrated of it through a proper intrinsic middle term, that is, by appeal to its formal or material cause, and this no doubt because, if a thing has material and formal causes, its essence is itself constituted from these causes. Very shortly after this, however, he notes that a thing can sometimes be shown to exist through extrinsic causes, "such as the final and efficient," and that this is done especially through primary and universal causes,

---

97. Antonio Rubio, *Commentarii in Universam Aristotelis Dialecticam*, vol. 2, col. 297 (bk. 1, q. 2).

98. Collegium Complutense Sancti Cyrilli, *Artium Cursus sive Disputationes in Aristotelis Dialecticam*, p. 686b (disp. 17, q. 2, n. 24).

which are the concern of metaphysics (*DM* 1.4.11). "For instance," he says, "we can show that angels exist because they are necessary to the perfection of the universe and are of such a nature that it is not impossible for them to be made by God" (*DM* 1.4.11). This is interesting, in part, because later in this section, while discussing how metaphysics can be said to demonstrate principles, including the principles of the other sciences—which, it should be noted, include the definition of a science's subject—Suárez asserts that "from a final cause it can be shown that the human being is a rational animal, because she can be made in order to cognize and love God" (*DM* 1.4.22).[99] He later claims, in other words, that a thing's essence *can* be demonstrated of it, by using as a middle term one of its extrinsic causes, and in particular, an extrinsic cause of the sort that metaphysics investigates. Suárez, moreover, explicitly states that such a demonstration abstracts from actual existence. Unfortunately, it is not at all clear how, or even whether, this claim bears on the question of whether one can demonstrate that it is possible for some thing to exist.

Be that as it may, after granting that one cannot demonstrate the actual existence of a science's object, Suárez goes on to explain how metaphysics can be said to show that the objects of the other sciences

99. Antonio Rubio gives this very argument in the course of commenting on *Post. An.* II, chs. 8–10, which chapters are devoted to the question of whether it is possible to demonstrate a thing's essence. See his *Commentarii in Universam Aristotelis Dialecticam*, vol. 2, col. 697 (bk. 2, ch. 8): "The whatness and definition of the human being is rational animal, or to be constituted from a body and a rational soul, and the two such parts are called the same cause, since the whatness is composed from them. And the other cause, that is, the extrinsic one, will be the adequate and proper end for the sake of which she is constituted, namely, beatitude, through which [the whatness] will be able to be demonstrated in this way: whatever is constituted for beatitude (that is, in order to enjoy God) is a rational animal, for only the nature which participates in reason or intellect is capable of beatitude. But the human being is constituted for beatitude. Therefore, [the human being] is a rational animal. Behold, the whatness of the human being is demonstrated *a priori* through the end as through an extrinsic cause, though a proper, adequate, and prior cause." (*Quod quid est homo, eiusque definitio est animal rationale, vel esse ex corpore, & rationali anima constitutum, & eiusmodi duae partes dicuntur causa eadem, quia ex eisdem constat quod quid est: causa autem alia, hoc est, extrinseca erit finis adaequatus, & proprius, cuius rei gratia conditus est, nempe beatitudo, per quam sic poterit demonstrari: quidquid est conditum ad beatitudinem [hoc est ut Deo perfruatur] est animal rationale, nam sola natura, quae rationem, vel intellectum participat, capax beatitudinis est; sed homo est conditus ad beatitudinem, ergo est animal rationale. Ecce quod quid est hominis demonstratum a priori per finem tanquam per causam extrinsecam, propriam tamen, adaequatam, & priorem.*)

exist and what they are. Here, I take it that Suárez has in mind some sort of proof that falls short of a demonstration, one that carries no implication of necessary existence. Metaphysics can be said to show that the objects of the other sciences exist, he explains, only "because it supplies principles to show in what grade of beings such objects are located, and what quiddity they have" (*DM* 1.4.10). In other words, Suárez claims that metaphysics can be said to show that the objects of the other sciences exist insofar as it provides the means to show *what* these objects are. And it does so, he explains, in the first place, "by making clear the very *ratio* of being and the *ratio* of essence or quiddity, and in what they consist, and second, by distinguishing the various grades of beings under which all the objects of the sciences are contained" (*DM* 1.4.10). That is, metaphysics helps to show that the objects of the other sciences exist by explaining both what a being is and what an essence is, and also by distinguishing various grades of beings. Suárez elsewhere claims, moreover, that, when it comes to distinguishing grades of beings, metaphysics has the advantage over other sciences by virtue of the fact that it expressly treats of the various kinds of distinction between things (*DM* 1.4.32).[100] He will also later claim that metaphysical cognition of "the various grades and modes of essences" enables one to know which parts of a thing figure in its definition, and which method of definition is to be used for different kinds of thing, "for example, in the case of a substance or accident, and in the case of a simple thing or a composite one" (*DM* 1.4.32).

Having argued that metaphysics shows what the objects of the other sciences are, he explains why metaphysics can, for this reason, be said to show that the objects of the other sciences exist:

> although the object of a science cannot *a priori* and in itself be demonstrated to exist through a proper intrinsic middle term, nor can what it is, nevertheless, with respect to us it can be shown from signs or effects, by making clear, first, what is required for the *ratio* of being, and in what the *ratio* of essence consists, and what connection it can have with such signs or effects—all of which cannot accurately be shown except through this doctrine's principles. (*DM* 1.4.32)

---

100. Suárez devotes *DM* 7 to elaborating his theory of distinctions.

In response, no doubt, to the objection's claim that the natural philosopher is better suited to proving, *a posteriori* and from effects, that the object of a science exists, in this passage Suárez claims that metaphysics is uniquely suited to showing what the objects of the other sciences are, and that they exist, not only because it explains what a being is, what an essence is, and what grades of being there are, but also because it explains what connection a thing's essence can have with certain observed signs and effects. Suárez doesn't specify what it is that enables the metaphysician to explain this connection between an essence and these signs or effects, but he may have in mind the fact that she investigates various *rationes* of cause and effect. An understanding of this connection would seem to be required for an *a posteriori* proof of some thing's existence. It may also enable one to infer a thing's essence on the basis of its properties. The upshot of all this, perhaps, is that although metaphysics does not *demonstrate* that the object of another science actually exists, it can be said to *prove* or *show* its existence and essence insofar as it provides the means to define the object and indicate its connection to various observed signs and effects.

Suárez considers several more objections to this conception of the role that metaphysics plays with respect to the objects of the other sciences. Against the objection that the subjects of the other sciences transcend its abstraction, he reminds us that metaphysics reaches objects lying outside its abstraction insofar as this is necessary to explain its own *rationes* and hand down various general divisions of being (*DM* 1.4.12). Moreover, even if there are objects dealt with in the other sciences that it never considers, still, it provides principles and clarifies terms "which other sciences can use to assume or prove their objects, to whatever extent necessary" (*DM* 1.4.12). Another objection alleges that it cannot be the case that other sciences depend on metaphysics in order to get their objects from it, since if this were so, they could not be learned before metaphysics is learned, which is false and contrary to experience. In response, Suárez asserts that, "if the order of doctrine is considered in itself"—that is, setting aside our mode of cognition and the constraints it imposes upon us with respect to the acquisition of the sciences—metaphysics is indeed prior to the other speculative sciences, and this not just because of the role it plays in determining the objects of the other sciences, but also because of two further functions that metaphysics performs—those, namely, which Suárez will go on to discuss in the remainder of *DM* 1.4 (*DM* 1.4.13). However, "because of our mode of cognition," he explains, we acquire the science of metaphysics last, and this in part because things which abstract from matter with respect to existence are only discovered by us through motion, one of their effects (*DM* 1.4.13).

The second function that renders metaphysics useful for perfectly acquiring the other sciences is that of confirming or corroborating (*confirmare*) and defending (*defendere*) first principles. Suárez is explicit in his view that metaphysics performs this function not only with respect to the most universal principles that are in some way proper to it, but also with respect to the first principles of the other sciences (*DM* 1.4.27). Aristotle and Thomas Aquinas are both cited in support of this claim about first philosophy's role vis-à-vis the first principles of other sciences. Suárez also argues that some of the ways in which metaphysics proves first principles can be used to prove other sciences' principles.

Suárez begins his discussion of this function much as he began his discussion of the first function, by canvassing objections to it. Informing his discussion here is a conception of first principles as immediate propositions. An immediate proposition is commonly characterized as one that has no middle term through which it might be demonstrated using a demonstration *propter quid,* which is the sort of demonstration that yields science (*scientia,* ἐπιστήμη) strictly so-called. Such a proposition is frequently said to be known *per se* or through itself (*per se nota*), although it would be more precise to say that an immediate proposition is *suited* to being known *per se* or through itself, and this by virtue of the fact that its truth admits, in principle, of being grasped merely through an adequate apprehension of its terms (its subject and predicate). For example, the proposition that every human being is a rational animal is said to be known *per se* or through itself because the adequate apprehension of its terms involves recognizing that to be a human being just *is* to be a rational animal, or that *rational animal* is the essence of the human being. So-called mediate propositions, on the other hand, are demonstrable propositions. They are not known *per se* or through themselves, thanks to a mere apprehension of their terms, but *per aliud* or through something else. For one can be said to know them, in the strict sense (i.e., in the way required for science), only if one possesses a *propter quid* demonstration of them from suitable premises. Explaining the distinction between mediate and immediate propositions, de Olivera avails himself of the following analogy, which, he says, is drawn from Albert the Great:

Just as the sun is visible by itself [*per se*], since by nature it has in itself ingrafted light, whereas other bodies, which participate in light from the sun, are not visible by themselves, but by means of something else [*per aliud*], so also, among intelligibles, some are known by themselves [*per se*] and from themselves [*ex se*], for instance, immediate propositions, whereas others are known through something else [*per aliud*], by which they are, as it were, illuminated, for instance, mediate propositions.[101]

Of course, when de Olivera speaks here of knowing (*noscere*) propositions either *per se* or *per aliud* he is using the term "know" in a fairly strict sense. When an Aristotelian says that some proposition is known *per se*, and not *per aliud*, she is not thereby denying that someone might first cognize or come to be convinced of that proposition by means of (say) an *a posteriori* argument, from effects. However, she will in this case deny that the cognition afforded by such an argument rises to the level of understanding (*intellectus*, νοῦς), which is the kind of cognition that a scientific expert has of the first principles of her science.

This basic picture is complicated somewhat, however, by a distinction that Aristotelians make between two kinds of proposition that are known *per se*. Some of these are *per se* known in themselves, but not in relation to us (*per se nota secundum se, non vero quoad nos*), while others are *per se* known both in themselves and in relation to us (*per se nota secundum se, & quoad nos*). An example of the latter is the proposition that the human being is a rational animal. Being a rational animal is the very essence of the human being. What's more, *we* can

---

101. Collegium Complutense Sancti Cyrilli, *Artium Cursus sive Disputationes in Aristotelis Dialecticam*, p. 701a (disp. 18, q. 1, n. 6): "Sicut enim Sol quia in se habet a natura insitam lucem, est visibilis per se ipsum; alia vero corpora, quae lucem a sole participant sunt non per se ipsa, sed per aliud visibilia: sic inter intelligibilia, alia sunt ex se, & per se nota, ut propositiones immediatae; alia vero noscuntur per aliud, a quo quasi illuminantur, ut propositiones mediatae."

grasp that it is the very essence of the human being. Therefore, this proposition admits of being known *per se* by us, and so counts as *per se* known both in itself and in relation to us. As an example of the former sort of proposition, on the other hand, de Olivera cites the proposition that God exists. This proposition is said to be known *per se* in itself because, as a matter of fact, existence belongs to the divine essence and therefore agrees immediately with God. However, since we, at least in this life, cannot grasp the essence of God, the proposition is said to be *per se* known in itself, but not by us or in relation to us.[102] Accordingly, in this life, we can cognize that God exists only *per aliud*, and in particular, through or from his effects. Other propositions of the former sort, de Olivera tells us, are those in which a so-called first or primary passion (*prima passio*) is predicated of its subject, for such a passion or property agrees immediately with its subject. However, according to de Olivera, such a proposition is not immediate in relation to us, but is rather mediate and demonstrable for us:

Since between a first passion and the subject itself there is nothing in reality that mediates, through which it might be proved, such a proposition is in itself immediate and indemonstrable, and it is as a consequence *per se* known in itself. [...] But in relation to us it can be said not to be known *per se* or immediate, since through the intellect we distinguish the definition of the subject from the subject itself, and we take the definition as a middle term in order to demonstrate such a passion of it.[103]

Antonio Rubio asserts in his commentary that the capacity for instruction (*capacitas disciplinae*) is a primary passion of the human being, and that it emanates immediately (*proxime*) from the human essence. He also claims that this passion is demonstrated of the human being using the definition of the human being as a middle term. Subsequent passions (e.g., the capacity for wonder, risibility) are demonstrated of

---

102. See *DM* 1.5.32.

103. Collegium Complutense Sancti Cyrilli, *Artium Cursus sive Disputationes in Aristotelis Dialecticam*, p. 701b (disp. 18, q. 1, n. 7): "Huiusmodi etiam est propositio, in qua prima passio praedicatur de subiecto. Cum enim inter primam passionem: & ipsum subiectum nihil in rei veritate mediet, per quod probetur, talis propositio est secundum se immediata, & indemonstrabilis; & per consequens per se nota secundum se. [...] Quoad nos tamen dici potest, non esse per se notam, aut immediatam: quia per intellectum distinguimus diffinitionem subiecti ab ipso, eamque assumimus ut medium ad talem passionem de illo demonstrandam."

the human being using prior passions as middle terms.[104] This is entirely in keeping with what de Olivera says in the passage just quoted: notwithstanding the immediate agreement that obtains between the capacity for instruction and the human being, we treat the proposition that the human being is capable of instruction as a mediate and demonstrable proposition, since we distinguish—by means of a distinction of reason, it seems—the human being from her essence and use her essence or definition as a middle term linking the demonstration's minor term (i.e., the subject, *human being*) and its major term (i.e., the predicate, *capable of instruction*).

The first objection that Suárez considers against the view that metaphysics confirms and defends first principles insists that such principles are known *per se* and without reasoning (*sine discursu*). Moreover, since metaphysics is "essentially a science in all of its parts," the objection alleges, it "can in none of them be concerned with anything except by reasoning" (*DM* 1.4.15). Accordingly, it can be concerned only with conclusions and mediate propositions and can perform no function in respect of first principles. The second objection rests on the distinction between understanding, which has first principles as its object, and science, which is an effect of demonstration and takes the conclusions of demonstrations as its object. Every science, or scientific habit, it insists, is distinct from understanding, or the habit of principles. It also appeals to the view that the assent to first principles afforded by understanding involves greater evidence and certainty than a science's assent to conclusions does. From this it follows, the objection alleges, that "metaphysics cannot confirm first principles, or add some force to the assent to them, unless it assumes the function of the habit of first principles" (*DM* 1.4.15). But metaphysics, the objection asserts, cannot assume the function of the habit of principles, since this would erase the distinction between understanding and wisdom (i.e., metaphysics), contrary to what Aristotle asserts in *Nicomachean Ethics* VI, ch. 3 (1139b15–17). The third objection asserts that if metaphysics confirms and defends first principles it can conceivably do so only in one of two ways, neither of which is in fact possible for it. For either it performs

104. Antonio Rubio, *Commentarii in Universam Aristotelis Dialecticam*, vol. 2, cols. 709–10 (bk. 2, ch. 9, q. unica).

this function by explaining the terms from which first principles are composed, or it performs this function by somehow demonstrating first principles. But clarifying terms is not the function of a science, since knowledge of terms requires the mere apprehension of simples, whereas a scientific habit has to do with judgments. As regards the suggestion that metaphysics is concerned to demonstrate first principles, this too is impossible. For if it is to demonstrate a first principle, it must use either an *a priori* demonstration (i.e., a *propter quid* demonstration) or an *a posteriori* demonstration (i.e., a demonstration *quia*). But it cannot use an *a priori* demonstration, since first principles are immediate propositions. Moreover, if a first principle that is not immediate in relation to us is at issue—of which sort is the proposition in which a first passion is predicated of its subject—it is not the function of metaphysics to demonstrate such principles, "but each science in its own subject matter demonstrates those which pertain to it" (*DM* 1.4.15). Further, it cannot be the case that metaphysics proves first principles using *a posteriori* demonstrations, for the kind of cognition that such a demonstration yields—mere science *a posteriori* or science of the fact (*scientia quia*)—is inferior to, and distinct from, the perfect scientific knowledge of metaphysics. Moreover, there is no reason why such a way of demonstrating first principles should be proper to metaphysics.

In response to the first and second objections, Suárez concedes that the function of metaphysics with regard to first principles "is not to elicit that evident and certain assent which the intellect, led by the natural light, bestows without any reasoning on first principles when they are sufficiently set forth" (*DM* 1.4.16). Rather, it pertains to this science to confirm and defend first principles through some sort of reasoning. However, Suárez also denies that the habit of principles adds "some evidence or certainty to that assent to principles which can be had by nature alone" (*DM* 1.4.19). He claims, in other words, that when we first grasp the truth of a first principle by means of an adequate apprehension of its terms, our assent at that point involves no less evidence and certainty than it does later, after we have acquired the habit of principles (which takes time). What the habit of principles adds to our initial grasp of a principle is not evidence and certainty in our assent to principles, but "a facility and readiness in the use of that evidence and certainty" (*facilitatem & promptitudinem in exercenda illa evidentia & certitudine*) (*DM* 1.4.19). What it adds, in other words, is a readiness to actually affirm the principle in an act of judgment.[105] In this respect, Suárez goes on to explain, metaphysics differs from the habit of principles, for unlike the habit of principles it *does* add certainty and evidence, "since it produces assent to the same truth in a new way and by a new means" (*DM* 1.4.19). Suárez hastens to add, however, that this increase "is not intensive, but extensive" (*DM* 1.4.19). By this he seems to mean that metaphysics does not actually increase our degree of conviction or confidence in the truth of first principles when it confirms and defends them by reasoning, but that it instead provides an additional basis for assenting to first principles. Suárez gives two reasons for the negative conclusion. First, metaphysics does not increase the evidence or certainty of the assent involved in the habit of principles, for "metaphysics in no way operates on that assent," but rather "furnishes a new mode of assent by means of an act that is assuredly distinct" (*DM* 1.4.19). Second, the assent of metaphysics is in fact "not more certain or evident than the assent of the habit of principles," since it itself invariably depends on, and therefore cannot have a greater evidence and certainty than, an assent to first principles that are known to us *per se* (*DM* 1.4.19).

In response to the third objection, Suárez asserts that metaphysics confirms and defends first principles in both of the ways explicitly targeted in that objection: it both demonstrates first principles and explains the terms from which they are composed. Regarding the latter task, Suárez observes that metaphysics teaches what many things are, thereby clarifying the *rationes* of numerous terms that compose first principles—for example, "being," "substance," "accident," "whole," "part," "act," and "potency." To be sure, he says, although there is nothing about essences themselves that requires that they be cognized

---

105. Speaking of the habit of principles, Suárez states, approvingly, that Thomas Aquinas "judges that this habit is not in itself natural, but natural with respect to a sort of beginning, since, namely, the acts through which it is acquired are not had through reasoning, but flow forth immediately from the very light of nature, although in the beginning and before the habit they do not emanate with such great readiness and facility as they do after the habit has been acquired" (*DM* 1.4.18). Of course, the acts through which the habit of principles is acquired are acts of judgment.

through demonstration, nevertheless, in relation to us, what a thing is can often be demonstrated, "especially by using a division constituted from opposed members, and by demonstrating what a thing is not (which is frequently better known by us) and thence concluding what it is" (*DM* 1.4.20). Further, Suárez explains that metaphysics is in this way especially useful for confirming and defending the most universal first principles, that is, those constituted from "very abstract terms, that is, from terms that signify things or *rationes* of things which can exist without matter" (*DM* 1.4.20). The degree to which metaphysics confirms the particular principles of the other sciences by clarifying their terms is rather more limited, he says, since metaphysics is concerned with such terms only in one of the two ways explained earlier, namely, "insofar as is necessary for teaching its own definitions, and for explaining its own terms, or insofar as general *rationes*, and especially transcendental ones, are included in them" (*DM* 1.4.20).

The second way metaphysics confirms and defends first principles is by demonstrating them. Suárez distinguishes between two kinds of demonstration, or two ways of demonstrating, that metaphysics employs to corroborate first principles. The second of these is by deduction to the impossible (*per deductionem ad impossibile*), through which all other principles are in some sense proved by appeal to "the most general principle proper to this doctrine," namely, the proposition that "it is impossible to affirm and deny the same thing of the same thing at the same time" (*impossibile est de eodem simul idem affirmare et negare*) (*DM* 1.4.25). Suárez does not speak much of this principle and its use here in *DM* 1, since he discusses it at some length in *DM* 3.3.

The other way metaphysics employs demonstration to confirm and defend first principles is by demonstrating them *a priori*. Against the objection that this is impossible, since a first principle is an immediate proposition, Suárez grants that it is not possible to demonstrate a first principle by using an intrinsic formal or material cause as a middle term. However, it is sometimes open to the metaphysician to use an extrinsic cause as a middle term, whether a final, efficient, or exemplar cause. For since metaphysics treats of first causes and God himself—"who, just as he is the first truth, is a cause of every truth, at least an extrinsic cause"—it can at least demonstrate first principles through the universal cause (*DM* 1.4.21). Suárez, however, concedes that this cannot be done for the most universal principles that are composed from terms common to God and creatures. For the fact that God is without an efficient cause makes it impossible that any such principle should rest on, and admit of being demonstrated through, an efficient cause. These principles include, Suárez says, the proposition that any given thing either is or is not (*quodlibet est vel non est*), as well as the proposition that it is impossible to affirm and deny something of the same thing at the same time. The truth of such a principle, Suárez holds, is not dependent on an efficient cause. Moreover, for this reason it also follows that such a principle cannot be demonstrated by appeal to a final cause, since a final cause is present only where production (*effectio*) is, and "therefore those things which abstract from the efficient cause also abstract from an end" (*DM* 1.4.21). Suárez further notes that one might hold that principles common only to creatures cannot be demonstrated through an efficient or final cause on the grounds that such principles "abstract from actual existence and consequently from efficiency" (*DM* 1.4.21). Moreover, one might think that it is also impossible to demonstrate such principles by using an exemplar cause as a middle term, for "what abstracts from an efficient cause also abstracts from an exemplar cause," since an exemplar serves as a model for what an efficient cause aims to bring about (*DM* 1.4.21). However, Suárez replies that although principles common only to creatures abstract from actual efficiency, they do not abstract "from possible efficiency, and consequently they do not abstract altogether from the efficient, exemplar, and final cause" (*DM* 1.4.22). It is at this point that Suárez cites the earlier-mentioned demonstration regarding the essence of the human being, which purports to prove that the human being is a rational animal by appeal to the fact that "she can be made in order to cognize and love God" (*DM* 1.4.22). He further speaks of proving "that every whole is greater than its part because it can in this way be made by God, but not otherwise," and also of proving that the human being is a rational animal "because she is so represented in the divine idea, for the human being would not have such a real essence unless she had such an exemplar in God" (*DM* 1.4.22).

Suárez, however, grants that these ways of demonstrating are not all applicable to every first principle. For there are propositions that do not have a final cause, for example, the proposition that three and four make seven, or the principle that any given thing either is or is not. However, the essences and properties of things, he says, have a final cause "through which they can be demonstrated, if such a final cause is otherwise known *per se,* or can be shown through another, better known principle" (*DM* 1.4.23). Suárez nonetheless also cautions that this genus of proof often "exceeds the power of the human intellect's natural light" (*DM* 1.4.24). For one thing, the divine exemplars cannot be used as a means to cognize some truth unless they are seen in their very selves, which, he says, is something that metaphysics does not enable us to do. At best, metaphysics can show *a posteriori,* by appeal to things themselves, that God has these or those exemplars. Much the same is true of God considered as the first efficient cause: metaphysics does not afford a cognition of "the power of God in itself" (*DM* 1.4.24), although we can investigate God's power by considering what he has actually made, so as to demonstrate what it can do in other cases (*quid in aliis facere possit*). Likewise, Suárez says, from God's perfection and efficiency we can investigate the end and perfection of his works, and from this we can infer what natures he has assigned to things.

Near the end of his discussion of how metaphysics confirms and defends first principles, Suárez mentions yet another way in which it does this: by considering the natural light of the intellect and tracing it back "to the source from which it emanates, namely, the divine light itself" (*DM* 1.4.25). For, he says, we can in this way infer that first principles are true, "since they are immediately and *per se* shown to be true by means of the natural light itself" (*DM* 1.4.25). For when this light thus assents to a principle it cannot be deceived or err, given that "it is a participation of the divine light that is perfect in its own genus and order" (*DM* 1.4.25).

The third function that renders metaphysics useful for perfectly acquiring the other sciences, according to Suárez, concerns the so-called instruments of knowledge (*instrumenta sciendi*), that is, definition, division, and argumentation. There are some people, he explains, who claim that it pertains to metaphysics to hand down these instruments. Although they grant that the dialectician teaches one how to define, divide, and reason, they nonetheless hold that the dialectician is not equipped to explain these instruments "from proper principles and give their reason" (*DM* 1.4.28), this being a task that falls to the metaphysician instead. After all, definition serves to make a thing's essence clear, and it pertains to the metaphysician to explain the *ratio* of essence. Moreover, division—by which we divide (for example) the genus *animal* into its species[106]—serves to make the distinctions between things clear, and it is the metaphysician who treats of the various kinds of distinction. As for argumentation, with respect to its form, its entire force depends on one of two principles that are proper to the science of metaphysics, namely, the principle that things which are the same as a third thing are the same as each other, and the principle that the same thing cannot be affirmed and denied of the same thing at the same time. Therefore, even if the dialectician teaches *that* these instruments are to be used in the acquisition of scientific knowledge, it still pertains to the metaphysician to make clear "their first roots and causes" (*DM* 1.4.28).

Suárez rejects this view, although he grants that cognition of the instruments of knowledge is greatly perfected (*plurimum perfici*) by the science of metaphysics. It is, he says, the proper function of dialectic to hand down or teach the method of knowing (*sciendi modus*), which it does precisely by teaching the instruments of knowledge and demonstrating their power and properties. Nor is it true that the dialectician explains these instruments only in a superficial way (*perfunctorie*) and without explaining why they must have the features they do. Indeed, Suárez says, it is clear from experience that dialectic hands down not only rules for rightly defining and arguing, but also "demonstrates *a priori* why a correct definition and argumentation require such characteristics and properties, and the like" (*DM* 1.4.30). For if dialectic did not demonstrate these things, but rather left it to metaphysics to explain why definition and demonstration must have the characteristics they have, it would not suffice for the acquisition of real science, and

---

106. The division of a genus into its species is an example of so-called "potential" division. Another example of potential division is the division of an analogical into its analogates. See Collegium Complutense Sancti Cyrilli, *Artium Cursus sive Disputationes in Aristotelis Dialecticam*, p. 10a–b (*Praeambula de modis sciendi*).

one would have to learn metaphysics as well before going on to learn the other theoretical real sciences. And this "is plainly false and against the thought and practice of all" (*DM* 1.4.30). Dialectic would not suffice by itself for acquiring the sciences because genuine science requires knowing that one knows, and "one cannot know that one's cognition is true science unless one knows that one's reasoning is a true demonstration" (*DM* 1.4.30), and this in turn presupposes that one knows what a genuine demonstration is and why it must have the features that it has. What's more, Aristotle explicitly indicates that dialectic must be acquired before the other sciences, including metaphysics, when he says "that it is absurd to seek at the same time a science and that science's method" (*Metaph.* II, ch. 3, 995a13–14).

As mentioned, however, Suárez grants that cognition of the instruments of knowledge is greatly perfected by metaphysics. These instruments, he explains, "are properly and formally found in the thoughts of the mind, or in the internal acts of the intellect" (*DM* 1.4.29). However, such acts or operations must be in some way proportioned to things themselves if they are to be true. Accordingly, the instruments of knowledge must be founded on things themselves. Therefore, although the arguments alleged in favor of the view that metaphysics hands down the instruments of knowledge do not succeed in their aim, they do point to ways in which metaphysics is useful for perfecting one's grasp of these instruments. For although it is not the job of metaphysics to hand down the art of defining, nevertheless, the science of metaphysics "greatly contributes to the perfect method of defining" (*DM* 1.4.32), since, aside from handing down the *ratio* of essence in general, it also makes clear, in a manner consistent with its abstraction, the various grades and modes of essences, and a cognition of these grades and modes is especially useful for knowing "which parts the definitions of things must be constituted from, or which method of definition must be adhered to in the case of diverse things" (*DM* 1.4.32). A similar consideration applies in the case of division, for division is based on the distinction and opposition of things, and it pertains to metaphysics to treat of the various modes of distinction. Metaphysics is useful also when it comes to argumentation or demonstration, and this with respect to both the matter and form of demonstration. It helps with respect to the matter of demonstration insofar as it distinguishes and separates "the *rationes* of almost all beings" and explains what a thing is in its essence, what properties are, what a thing is, and what a mode is. And it helps with respect to the form of demonstration insofar as it treats of the principles on which the correct forms of argumentation depend.

Section 5: Metaphysics as the most
perfect science and true wisdom

Suárez has thus far explained the essence of metaphysics, its causes, and its usefulness or effect. At the beginning of section 5 he announces that its attributes remain to be discussed.

Suárez's first principal conclusion in this section is that metaphysics is the most perfect of all the speculative sciences. That this science is speculative is clear from the fact that its end is the cognition of truth for its own sake. Moreover, it was argued in *DM* 1.1 that this science's object is the noblest, both on account of its supreme abstraction and on account of the noblest beings that it embraces, and since every science has its nobility from its object, it follows that metaphysics is the most excellent of all the sciences (*omnium praestantissima*) (*DM* 1.5.2). Further, although someone might think that metaphysics is practical as well as speculative, since it affords perfect natural knowledge of God, and correct judgments regarding action depend on cognition of the divine being, this is not in fact the case. For metaphysics considers God as the ultimate end and highest good only speculatively, without determining how God is the end of the human being in particular, or what the human being must do in order to reach him (*DM* 1.5.3–5).

Suárez's second principal conclusion in section 5 is that metaphysics is not only a science, but also natural wisdom (*naturalis sapientia*) (*DM* 1.5.6). This conclusion, he tells us, is proved by Aristotle in *Metaphysics* I and III, partly by appeal to the assumption that there is in fact a particular intellectual virtue called wisdom, which is to be distinguished from several other intellectual states that sometimes also go under the name "wisdom," including one that arises from the complete acquisition of all the sciences (*DM* 1.5.7). Aristotle's argument for the conclusion, Suárez explains, begins with the identification of six characteristics of wisdom, some of which are proper to wisdom while others are common to it and the remaining speculative sciences, although these common characteristics are possessed by wisdom to an eminent degree. The argument then proceeds by showing that metaphysics has all six characteristics in the way required for wisdom.

The first such characteristic concerns wisdom's scope. Wisdom, Suárez explains, "is concerned with all things, and is the science of all things, insofar as this is possible" (*DM* 1.5.8). The second characteristic is that of being concerned with "things that are more difficult and more remote from the senses" (*DM* 1.5.9). The third characteristic of wisdom is that it is the most certain natural cognition (*certissima cognitio*), which involves clarity and evidence, "since natural certainty [...] arises from evidence and is commensurate with it" (*DM* 1.5.10). The fourth characteristic is that of being more suited to teaching and to identifying the causes of things (*aptior ad docendum, causasque rerum tradendas*), since teaching involves identifying the causes of things, and wisdom is supposed to reach "the higher and more universal causes" (*causas altiores et universaliores*) (*DM* 1.5.11). The fifth characteristic is that of being the science which is most of all desired for its own sake (*DM* 1.5.12). The sixth and final characteristic of wisdom is that of ruling "over the other sciences" (*DM* 1.5.13).

The remainder of section 5 (*DM* 1.5.14–53) is given over to the task of proving that metaphysics possesses these six characteristics of wisdom. A number of related issues are discussed along the way. Thus, in his discussion of the first characteristic—the characteristic of being concerned with all things to the extent that this is possible for us—Suárez identifies three different ways in which metaphysics treats of all things (*DM* 1.5.14) and then goes on to consider whether all three ways are necessary for wisdom (*DM* 1.5.15). The first way metaphysics considers all things is "confusedly and in a general way" (*confuse et in communi*), insofar as it treats of the most common *rationes* and the most universal principles. To the extent allowed by our intellect's limited perfection, metaphysics also considers all things more particularly and according to more specific *rationes*, or at least all things which abstract from matter with respect to existence, and it also considers material things to some extent as well. Finally, metaphysics considers all things inasmuch as it treats of all things, "not in themselves, but in their causes" (*DM* 1.5.14), since it investigates the most universal causes, including God. As regards the question of whether all three ways are necessary for wisdom, Suárez argues that indeed they are.

Regarding the second characteristic, that of dealing with the most difficult things, Suárez observes that Aristotle's argument for first philosophy's possession of this feature appeals to the fact that metaphysics "treats of things that are maximally universal and most remote from sense" (*DM* 1.5.16), the implication being that the most universal things are the most difficult for us to cognize. This leads Suárez to consider the question of how, therefore, one ought to make sense of a pronouncement near the beginning of the *Physics* (184a16–26) which seems to imply the opposite view, that is, the view that we more easily cognize a thing the more universal it is (*DM* 1.5.17–21). Suárez's reconciliation of the two passages alleges that in these two texts Aristotle is speaking of different kinds of cognition.

The third characteristic of wisdom, that it is most certain cognition, provides the occasion for a lengthy discussion of whether, and how, metaphysics is in fact the most certain of the sciences (*DM* 1.5.22–33). Suárez argues that the part of metaphysics which treats of being, its principles, and its properties is more certain than that part of it which treats of special *rationes* of beings, and that the former part is also the most certain of all doctrines. This, he further argues, is a sufficient basis upon which to assign the property of being most certain to metaphysics "absolutely and without qualification, for whenever a comparison is made between habits, this should be done according to what is best and greatest in them, as is gathered from *Topics* III, ch. 2 [117b36–39]" (*DM* 1.5.23). This conclusion holds of metaphysics insofar as it includes its principles. On the other hand, Suárez grants that metaphysics, understood as cognition of demonstrated conclusions alone, is less certain than cognition of the principles from which these same conclusions are demonstrated (*DM* 1.5.30). Nonetheless, he also insists that the former is nobler than the latter, since it reaches God and the intelligences, about which nothing is known *per se*, through understanding (*DM* 1.5.32). Moreover, he further judges it "plausible" (*probabilis*) that the conclusions of metaphysics are more certain than the principles of the other sciences, at least insofar as the latter "are cognized by us, for," he says, "you will hardly find" a principle of one of the other sciences "that is of the sort to become known to us, solely on the basis of a cognition of terms, with as much certainty as it can be when it is made manifest from the principles of metaphysics" (*DM* 1.5.33).

The fourth characteristic of wisdom, that it is most of all suited to teaching, prompts a consideration of several questions (*DM* 1.5.34–42), including: (i) Why is this characteristic affirmed of metaphysics on the grounds that it identifies the causes of things? Don't other sciences also identify and discuss the causes of things? (ii) How can metaphysics deal with causes, if being as such does not have a cause? (iii) Does metaphysics demonstrate through all the genera of cause, or only though some? To the first question, Suárez replies that metaphysics is most suited to teaching because, unlike the other theoretical sciences, it considers the first causes and principles of things, from which it follows that metaphysics "teaches fully and exactly, by itself alone and without the assistance of another science, all the things that fall under its object, whereas other sciences depend in many respects on it in order to be able to hand down an exact cognition of causes" (*DM* 1.5.36). To the second question, Suárez replies by repeating his earlier claim that an attribute can be demonstrated of a subject by means of a middle term that is only conceptually distinct from the attribute (see *DM* 1.1.29). This is how we demonstrate of God that he is a perfect being by appeal to the fact that he is a necessary being (*DM* 1.5.38). To the third question, Suárez replies that metaphysics makes use of formal, final, and efficient causes in its demonstrations, and also the material cause, although not matter, properly so-called. He also states that metaphysics sometimes uses the exemplar cause, but never the divine exemplars, which cannot be seen in this life (*DM* 1.5.39–42).

Regarding the fifth characteristic of wisdom, that it is the science most of all desired for its own sake, Suárez has little to add here, since it has already been shown that metaphysics is the most perfect of the speculative sciences (*DM* 1.5.43).

Finally, consideration of the sixth characteristic of wisdom, that it rules the other sciences, prompts Suárez to consider the question of whether metaphysics is inferior to moral science or prudence, as well as the question of whether first philosophy's dominion over the other theoretical sciences involves their subalternation to it (*DM* 1.5.44–52). He answers both questions in the negative.

Section 6: The human being's desire
for metaphysical cognition

In the final section of *DM* 1, Suárez takes up the question of whether the human being desires metaphysics above all other sciences by means of a natural appetite. Addressing this question, he explains, will give him the opportunity to clarify some of Aristotle's remarks in *Metaph.* I, chs. 1–2, as well as further highlight the worth or dignity of first philosophy, which, he notes, is the human being's "highest natural perfection" (*DM* 1.6.1).

According to Suárez, Aristotle argues for an affirmative answer to this question by taking as his most important premise the "axiom" (*axioma*) that the human being naturally desires to know. Accordingly, Suárez begins with an explanation of this axiom's key terms (*DM* 1.6.3–6). Focusing first on the notion of desire or appetite, he says that the common distinction between two kinds of appetite—innate (*innatus*) and elicitive (*elicitivus*)—must be assumed. The former, he explains, is only improperly and metaphorically called appetite, since it "is properly nothing other than a natural propensity which each thing has to some good" (*DM* 1.6.3). In a passive potency, this propensity or inclination is simply the potency's capacity for, and proportion to, its perfection, while in an active potency it is simply the natural faculty for acting itself. An elicitive appetite, on the other hand, is properly called an appetite. Two things are distinguished in the case of such an appetite: (i) the faculty of appetition, which is either sensitive or rational (rational appetite being none other than the will) and (ii) the act of appetition itself. The latter is also called "elicited appetite." The former faculty is innate in the sense that it is given by nature, Suárez explains, but unlike an innate appetite it is elicitive of actual appetition and is for this reason distinguished from purely innate and metaphorical appetite.

With respect to the terms "natural" and "naturally," Suárez focuses on two senses in which something can be called natural. In the first sense, what is given by nature itself and is not brought about by a proper action is called natural. In this sense, both innate appetite and elicitive appetite are natural, but an appetition or elicited appetite is not. In the second sense, what comes about necessarily as a result of an intrinsic propensity of nature is called natural, even if it is not, strictly speaking, given by nature but is rather produced by the thing that desires. Hunger, thirst, and all such sensitive appetites are natural in this sense, but not all of the will's appetitions are, "since the will is free" (*DM* 1.6.4). Suárez further explains that the necessity found in appetite is of two kinds, necessity with respect to exercise and necessity with respect to specification. The former kind of necessity is present when a vital appetite necessarily elicits an act of appetition. It is found in sensitive appetite, but not in the will, at least not in this life. Necessity of specification is present in the will when, although the will does not exercise its act of appetition necessarily, nevertheless, when it does exercise such an act, it necessarily aims at some particular object. In this case, the act is said to be necessary with respect to species, but not with respect to exercise. Moreover, an act that is thus necessary is not in every respect free. It is in this way, Suárez notes, that we seek the good in general.

As regards the terms "knowledge" (*scientia*) and "know" (*scire*), Suárez explains that it can be taken either generally for any sort of cognition of the truth, or more specifically for the certain and evident cognition of a thing through its causes. Taken in the latter sense, we can speak indefinitely of knowledge or distributively of all the sciences (*scientiae*), as well as individually of some particular science.

As regards the axiom that the human being naturally desires to know, then, Suárez next explains that Aristotle understands this claim to concern knowledge generally, and not any particular kind of knowledge. He also explains that the claim is to be understood as one about all human beings. He then notes that Aristotle's commentators disagree on the issue of whether he means merely to assert that human beings have an innate appetite for knowledge, or also an elicited appetite. Suárez himself argues that Aristotle intends to assert that we have both.

In support of this conclusion he cites an argument of Thomas Aquinas which takes as a premise the claim that each thing naturally seeks or has an appetite for (*appetit*) its perfection, operation, and happiness. Knowing (*scientia*) generally is related to the human being as a perfection and operation, Suárez notes, while the knowing or contemplation made possible by one's possession of metaphysical knowledge is that in which the natural happiness of the human being consists. Moreover, he claims, the human being does not merely have a natural inclination for her own perfection, operation, and happiness; she has an elicited appetite for them as well. It follows that the human being seeks knowledge by means of an elicited appetite.

Suárez notes that Aristotle himself confirms his axiom by appeal to the human being's love of the senses, and especially sight. On Suárez's account of the argument, we prefer sight to the other senses, according to Aristotle, because it is the most useful for knowledge. Moreover, the fact that we love sight above the other senses for this reason shows that our love of knowledge is greater than our love of sight and the other senses. For where we love *A* for the sake of *B*, *B* is loved to a greater degree than *A*, and this in accordance with the principle that that on account of which each thing is *X* is *X* to a greater degree.

Regarding the question of how we can be said naturally to desire knowledge by means of an elicited appetite, Suárez observes that one cannot plausibly claim that a human being will always experience a desire for knowledge whenever she thinks of it, or that she is incapable of spurning knowledge, since both claims are manifestly contrary to experience. It follows that the elicited appetite for knowledge is not altogether necessary either in respect of exercise or in respect of specification. Rather, Suárez says, the elicited appetite for knowledge is only *in some way* necessary with respect to specification (*DM* 1.6.13). For a human being, he explains, can fail to want knowledge by means of an efficacious desire to obtain it "only on account of extrinsic causes or obstacles which are conjoined accidentally to knowledge," such as the difficulty involved in the pursuit of knowledge, or the fact that its pursuit prevents one from obtaining other things that one needs or has an appetite for. Indeed, he explains, it is on account of difficulty that "those with a rather uncultivated intelligence seem to desire knowledge less" (*DM* 1.6.13). Nevertheless, Suárez claims, knowledge "cannot be displeasing *per se*," and so, impediments aside, it is loved with a kind of necessity, at least in respect of specification.

Suárez goes on to say that this elicited appetite for knowledge, which can only be an act of the will, is "most of all for the speculative sciences, which are sought only for the sake of cognizing truth" (*DM* 1.6.15). Aristotle makes this clear, he says, when in the first chapter of the *Metaphysics* he distinguishes between sense, memory, experience, art, and knowledge, and then goes on to distinguish between knowledge that is sought for the sake of utility and knowledge that is sought for its own sake. Suárez's analysis of Aristotle's discussion of these forms of cognition goes into great detail (*DM* 1.6.16–31), touching even on the question of whether flies have memory (*DM* 1.6.18) and the "great controversy" (*magna controversia*) over apine hearing (*DM* 1.6.20). His aim throughout is to show how the more widely shared forms of cognition are ordered as means to the less widely shared forms of cognition, and this because such an ordering is invariably taken, among Aristotelians, to be indicative of the relative worth of the things ordered: where *A* is ordered as a means to *B*, *B* is better than *A*. Thus, in discussing Aristotle's distinction between the practical and speculative sciences, Suárez stresses the fact that the practical sciences are "directed to the advantages and conveniences of life, while the speculative are directed only to the cognition of truth" (*DM* 1.6.31). The clear implication is that the former serve as means to the latter. Indeed, so *final* is the contemplation of truth made possible by the speculative sciences that, "although the greatest pleasure ensues from this contemplation, nevertheless, according to the right and best order of nature, it is not sought for the sake of pleasure, but for its own sake" (*DM* 1.6.31). It follows that the speculative sciences are superior to the practical sciences. From this it follows, in turn, that the former are "preferred" (*praeferri*) to the latter (*DM* 1.6.31). The same conclusion, Suárez notes, is established by appeal to the fact that the contemplation of the truth is the best thing in the human being and to the fact that this contemplation is more excellent the more it concerns things that are higher and not ordained to an operation.

From here it is a short step to the principal conclusion that Suárez, following Aristotle, has been aiming at, namely, the conclusion "that metaphysics is most desirable (*maxime appetibilem*) to the human being insofar as she is a human being" (*DM* 1.6.34). For, Suárez explains, if "among all the sciences, the speculative sciences are most of all desired," metaphysics, "which is supreme among them, will certainly be of itself the most desirable" (*DM* 1.6.34). Moreover, he adds, the greatest natural appetite of the human being is for her own natural happiness, and this, as Aristotle explains in *Nicomachean Ethics* X, chs. 7–8, consists in the perfect attainment of wisdom. For the natural happiness of the human being "is found in the contemplation of God and the separate substances, and this contemplation is the proper act and chief end of this science" (*DM* 1.6.34).

REMARKS ON THE LATIN TEXT AND THE ENGLISH TRANSLATION

My starting-point in the preparation of the Latin text that appears in this edition was an electronic version of the First Disputation prepared by Michael Renemann and Salvador Castellote.[1] This version is based on a scan of the Latin text that appears together with the Spanish translation of Sergio Rábade et al. The latter text, moreover, is substantially the same as the one that appears in volumes 25 and 26 of the Vivès edition of Suárez's works (although the authors of the Spanish translation do sometimes change the Latin text—without drawing attention to that fact—by appeal to early editions). A comparison of Renemann and Castellote's text with the text of the first edition of the *Disputationes Metaphysicae*, however, revealed that the former contained a number of errors and omissions, some minor, but some quite significant. To name but a few of the more significant errors: in a passage where the first edition reads "*externos*" ("external"), the edition of Rábade et al. reads "*internos*" ("internal"). In another, where the former reads "*in his non expectatur maior evidentia*" ("with respect to these, a greater evidence is not expected"), the latter reads "*in his expectatur maior evidentia*" ("with respect to these, a greater evidence is expected"). And in a third, where the former reads "*quia nulla est sufficiens ratio ad fingendum illum*" ("because there is no sufficient reason to suppose it"), the latter reads nothing at all, but rather omits these words altogether. I accordingly decided to revise Renemann and Castellote's text in the light of what I found printed in the first edition. Where these differed, I also

1. Renemann and Castellote have since made a number of corrections to their text of *DM* 1, partly as a result of my suggestions. See "Francisco Suárez, *Disputationes Metaphysicae*," prepared by Michael Renemann and Salvador Castellote, last updated June 12, 2020, http://homepage.ruhr-uni-bochum.de/Michael.Renemann/suarez/index.html.

consulted (in part simply out of curiosity) fifteen other early printed editions, produced between 1599 and 1751. The result is a Latin text which substantially reproduces that of the first edition, annotated so as to mark the passages where it differs from the Vivès text. In the notes on the Latin text I also give any alternative readings found in the other editions that I have consulted. A sense of the accuracy of these early editions, judged by the standard of fidelity to the first edition, can be gathered from these notes. By far the most accurate editions are the Venice editions of 1599 and 1605.

The Vivès edition also does some violence to the text as found in the earlier editions, both by ignoring some of the early editions' marginalia, and by taking other marginalia and re-positioning them at the beginning of paragraphs. The situation of these marginal notes in the earlier editions makes more sense. I have accordingly supplied missing marginalia and restored others to their original positions, though without indicating that I have done so in particular instances. It's worth noting that these notes, as they appear in the Vivès edition, are sometimes thought to have been the work of Charles Berton (1825–66), editor of volumes 25 and 26 of the Vivès edition. They are not. They appear in the first edition of the *Disputations* (which was published twenty years before Suárez's death) as well as in the fifteen other early editions that I've consulted. There is plenty of reason to think that they came from Suárez's own hand. And of course, they were known to early readers of the *Metaphysical Disputations*.

For ease of reference, I have retained the numbering of paragraphs found in the Vivès edition, which differs in spots from that of the first edition. I have also inserted into the Latin text bracketed page numbers that reproduce the paginations of both the first edition and the Vivès edition. The numbers appearing in square brackets—for example, "[38a]"—refer to the pagination of the first edition, while the letters "a" and "b" immediately following these numbers refer to the first and second columns (respectively) appearing on that page. The numbers appearing in angled brackets—for example, "⟨64a⟩"—refer to the pagination of the Vivès edition, and the letters that appear there refer (again) to columns.

Most of the notes on the English translation of *DM* 1 serve to clarify, or bring additional specificity to, Suárez's references to other authors. These notes are an important tool for the reader, in part because Suárez's ways of citing other authors frequently differ from our own. This is often the case with his references to Aristotle's works, since the chapter divisions of these works in Suárez's day often differ from the ones that we are familiar with. (There were even different and competing chapter divisions current at the time.) Accordingly, if Suárez refers to (say) *Posterior Analytics* I, ch. 7, but my note refers to *Posterior Analytics* I, ch. 9, 76a15–25, the reader should not assume that I am endeavoring to correct Suárez's citation. I am rather re-casting it so as to bring it into line with our modern editions of Aristotle's works. (Any corrections I make to Suárez's citations are explicitly identified as corrections.) The reader will also see that Suárez often refers to a numbered text in a particular book of (say) Aristotle's *Metaphysics*. This was a common way of citing a passage in Aristotle and is based on a division of books into numbered texts, which is a division that existed alongside their division into chapters. This division into numbered texts is not reproduced in recent translations of Aristotle's works, or even in recent editions of medieval Latin translations of them.

Other notes on Suárez's citations refer the reader to various editions of works by other authors. A complete list of these editions will be found in the bibliography. I do not always refer the reader to a recent edition of such a work, or to a recent reproduction of some early modern edition. My choice of which edition to cite has been guided, for the most part, by considerations of reliability and availability. Having looked through a good number of scans of early modern editions, I have found that they vary significantly in quality and reliability. Scans of most of the editions I have used are available for download from various sites, such as the HathiTrust Digital Library (https://www.hathitrust.org), the Internet Archive (https://archive.org), the Bavarian State Library (https://www.bsb-muenchen.de), the Post-Reformation Digital Library (http://www.prdl.org/index.php), and Google Books (https://books.google.com).

I have aimed for some measure of consistency in my rendering of key Latin words. The following are worth noting:

cognitio	cognition
cognoscere	to cognize
dicere	to signify$_d$ (in some contexts)
ens	being
esse	existence$_e$, being$_e$, to exist$_e$ (in some contexts)
existentia	existence
existere	to exist
innotescere	to become known$_n$
noscere	to know$_n$
notitia	knowledge$_n$
notus, -a, -um	known$_n$
ratio	reason, argument; account$_r$, aspect$_r$, basis$_r$, character$_r$, concept$_r$, conception$_r$, consideration$_r$, ground$_r$, method$_r$, nature$_r$, notion$_r$
res	thing$_r$
scientia	knowledge, science
scire	to know
significare	to signify

Those familiar with Latin know that it is frequently necessary to supply the English word "thing" when rendering Latin terms—for example, *album*, "white thing." This can be problematic in the context of scholastic philosophy, where *res*, "thing," is a technical term. In order to spare the reader the need to look repeatedly over at the Latin text, I have, by means of a subscript "r," indicated where "thing" renders *res*.

As regards the Latin word *ratio*, it is not always possible or desirable to use one and the same English word to render it, even across instances where it is employed in one and the same sense—for example, to mean something like *nature* or *essence*. (To do so leads to some rather strange-sounding expressions and can also lead to confusion—for example, if one were to render *ratio* in *ratio formalis* as "concept.") Therefore, since I have used various terms to render *ratio*, I have clearly indicated to the reader when one of these terms is being so used, again by means of a subscript "r." In many instances, readers should feel free to replace one of these terms with another, according as they see fit (e.g., "character$_r$" with "nature$_r$," or vice versa).

Finally, I have used subscript letters to mark various other distinctions—for example, between *ens* and *esse* (both of which can often be rendered "being"), and between *scientia* and *notitia* (both of which can often be rendered "knowledge").

Please note: I give one form of the word corresponding to the abbreviation, normally the nominative form, unless the case of the word can be inferred from the abbreviation. But of course in many instances Suárez would have the reader understand the word to be in some case other than the nominative. E.g., when citing a text, 'cap.' should be understood to mean 'capite.'

1.	primus (in some instances)
2.	secundus (in some instances)
3.	tertius (in some instances)
Aegid.	Aegidius (Romanus)
Albert.	Albertus (Magnus)
Alens.	(Alexander) Alensis
Alpharab.	Alpharabius
Aphrod.	(Alexander) Aphrodisiensis
Arist.	Aristoteles
Aristot.	Aristoteles
Aristotel.	Aristoteles
art.	articulus
artic.	articulus
Averr.	Averroes
Avicen.	Avicenna
c.	caput
ca.	caput
Caiet.	Caietanus
cap.	caput
capi.	capite

capit.	capite
Cicer.	Cicero
comm.	commentarium
Comm.	Commentator
contra Gent.	Summa contra Gentiles
Corinth.	Ad Corinthios
D.	Divus
1. 2	prima secundae (referring to the *Summa Theologiae*)
2. 2	secunda secundae (referring to the *Summa Theologiae*)
de anim.	de anima
de evers. singul. certam.	De eversione singularis certaminis
de Finib.	De finibus (bonorum et malorum)
de hist. anim.	De historia animalium
de histor. animal.	De historia animalium
de Repub.	De republica
de sapien.	De sapiente
de sensu & sensib.	De sensu & sensibilibus
dialog.	dialogus
Div.	Divus
Ethi.	Ethica
Ethic.	Ethica
Ethicor.	Ethicorum
Euclid.	Euclides
Iavell.	Iavellus
in 2. d. 3	*In Sent.* II, distinctio 3
lect.	lectio
li.	liber
lib.	liber
libr.	libro
Metaph.	Metaphysica
Metaphys.	Metaphysica
Officior.	(Libri) Officiorum

p.	pars
Paraphr.	Paraphrasis
part.	parte
Periherm.	Perihermenias
Physi.	Physica
Physic.	Physica
Physicor.	Physicorum
Politicor.	Politicorum
Poster.	(Analytica) Posteriora
Posterior.	(Analytica) Posteriora
Prior.	(Analytica) Priora
Problem.	Problemata
Psal.	Psalmus
q.	quaestio
quaest.	quaestio
quaestio.	quaestione
sect.	sectio
sectio.	sectione
sequen.	sequens
Soncin.	Soncinas
tex.	textus
text.	textus
Themist.	Themistius
Tho.	Thomas
Thom.	Thomas
Topic.	Topica
tract.	tractatus
Tusc.	(Libri) Tusculanarum (Disputationum)
ult.	ultimus
v. g.	verbi gratia

ENGLISH ABBREVIATIONS

a. Abbreviations for titles of works and books:

Cor.	Corinthians
DM	*Disputationes Metaphysicae* (*Metaphysical Disputations*)
DM 1.2.3	Metaphysical Disputation 1, section 2, paragraph 3
De Int.	*De Interpretatione* (*On Interpretation*)
Hist. An.	*History of Animals*
Metaph.	*Metaphysics*
Nic. Eth.	*Nicomachean Ethics*
Phys.	*Physics*
Pol.	*Politics*
Post. An.	*Posterior Analytics*
Pr. An.	*Prior Analytics*
Sent.	*Sentences*
ST	*Summa Theologiae*
Top.	*Topics*

b. Other abbreviations:

ad 1	reply to objection 1
art.	article
bk.	book
ch. / chs.	chapter / chapters
col. / cols.	column / columns
d.	distinction
fol. / fols.	folio / folios

lect.	lesson or lecture
p. / pp.	page / pages
pt.	part
q.	question
r	recto
resp.	reply
t. / ts.	volume / volumes
v	verso
vol. / vols.	volume / volumes

LATIN TEXT AND ENGLISH TRANSLATION

RATIO ET DISCURSUS TOTIUS
OPERIS AD LECTOREM.

Quemadmodum fieri nequit, ut quis Theologus perfectus evadat, nisi firma prius Metaphysicae iecerit fundamenta: ita intellexi semper, operae pretium fuisse, ut antequam Theologica scriberem Commentaria (quae partim iam in lucem prodiere, partim collaboro, ut quam primum, Deo favente, compleantur) opus hoc, quod nunc, Christiane Lector, tibi offero, diligenter elaboratum praemitterem. Verum iustas ob causas lucubrationes in tertiam D. Thomae partem differre non potui, easque primum omnium praelo mandare oportuit. In dies tamen luce clarius intuebar, quam illa divina ac supernaturalis Theologia hanc humanam & naturalem desideraret, ac requireret: adeo ut non dubitaverim illud inchoatum opus paulisper intermittere, quo huic doctrinae metaphysicae suum quasi locum, ac sedem darem, vel potius restituerem. Et quanvis in eo opere elaborando diutius immoratus fuerim, quam initio putaveram, & quam multorum expostulatio, qui Commentaria illa in tertiam partem, vel (si sperari potest) in universam D. Thomae Summam, perfecta desiderant, tamen suscepti laboris nunquam me poenitere potuit, confidoque, lectorem sententiam meam, vel ipso adductum experimento, comprobaturum.

Ita vero in hoc opere Philosophum ago, ut semper tamen prae oculis habeam, nostram philosophiam debere Christianam esse, ac divinae Theologiae ministram. Quem mihi scopum praefixi, non solum in quaestionibus pertractandis, sed multo magis in sententiis, seu opinionibus seligendis, in eas propendens, quae pietati, ac doctrinae revelatae sub-

REASON FOR, AND SURVEY OF, THE ENTIRE WORK, TO THE READER.

Just as it is impossible to become a fully-formed theologian unless one has first laid secure foundations with metaphysics, so have I always understood it to be worthwhile, before I write theological commentaries (which have, in part, already seen the light of day, and which, in part, I still labor on, so that, with God's favor, they might be completed as soon as possible), to dispatch in advance this work, diligently wrought, that I now offer you, Christian reader. But for good reasons, I was not able to put off my studies on the third part of St. Thomas's Summa, *and it was necessary to commit them to the press first of all. Nevertheless, day by day I saw more clearly than the sun that this divine and supernatural theology called for and required this human and natural one, to the point where I did not hesitate to interrupt that work, already begun, for a short time, so that I might give, or rather restore, to this metaphysical doctrine its place and seat, as it were. And although I have lingered in preparing this work longer than I initially thought, and than was demanded by many who wanted me to complete the commentaries on that third part—or even (if it could be hoped for) on the whole of St. Thomas's* Summa—*nevertheless, I have been unable to regret the labor I have undertaken, and I trust that the reader, even if induced only by his own experience, will approve of my decision.*

But in this work I act the part of the philosopher in such a way that I yet always keep in mind that our philosophy must be Christian and a servant of divine theology. And I have made this my aim not only in dealing with questions, but much more in choosing views or opinions, inclining to those which seem more to serve piety and revealed doctrine. For this rea-

servire magis viderentur. Eamque ob causam, philosophico cursu non-nunquam intermisso, ad quaedam Theologica diverto, non tam ut illis examinandis, aut accurate explicandis immorer (quod esset abs re, de qua nunc ago) quam ut veluti digito indicem lectori, quanam ratione principia Metaphysicae, sint ad Theologicas veritates confirmandas referenda, & accommodanda. Fateor me in divinis perfectionibus, quae attributa vocant, contemplandis immoratum fuisse diutius, quam alicui fortasse praesens institutum exigere videretur: at compulit me rerum in primis dignitas, & altitudo, deinde quod mihi nunquam visus sum luminis naturalis, atque adeo nec Metaphysicae, limites transilire.

Et quoniam judicavi semper magnam, ad res intelligendas ac penetrandas, in eis convenienti methodo inquirendis, & indicandis[1] vim positam esse, quam observare, vix, aut ne vix quidem possem, si, Expositorum more, quaestiones omnes, prout obiter, & veluti casu circa textum Philosophi occurrunt, pertractarem: idcirco expeditius & utilius fore censui, servato doctrinae ordine, ea omnia inquirere, & ante oculos Lectoris proponere, quae de toto huius sapientiae objecto investigari, & desiderari poterant. Illud vero objectum, quodnam sit, explanat prima huius operis disputatio, simulque in ea praefamur dignitatem, utilitatem, & caetera, quae in prooemiis scientiarum scriptores praemittere consueverunt. Deinde in priori Tomo eiusdem objecti amplissima, & universalissima ratio, quae[2] videlicet appellatur ens, eiusque proprietates, & causae diligenter expenduntur. Et in hac causarum contemplatione latius, quam fieri soleat, immoratus sum, quod & perdifficilem illam, & ad omnem Philosophiam, & Theologiam utilissimam esse existimaverim. In Tomo autem altero inferiores eiusdem obiecti rationes prosecuti sumus, initio sumpto ab illa Entis divisione in creatum, & creatorem, *utpote quae prior est, & entis quidditati vicinior, & ad huius doctrinae decursum aptior: qui subinde procedit per contentas sub his partitiones, ad usque genera omnia, & gradus entis, qui intra huius scientiae terminos, seu limites continentur.*

---

1. Reading "*indicandis*" here with C_2, S, V_1, and V_2. The following read "*iudicandis*": C_1, G_2, M_1, M_2, M_3, M_4, P_1, P_2, V_3, V_4, V_5, and Vivès.

2. Reading "*quae*" here with V_2. The following read "*qua*": C_1, C_2, G_2, M_1, M_2, M_3, M_4, P_1, P_2, S (I think), V_1, V_3, V_4, V_5, and Vivès.

son, I sometimes interrupt the course of the philosophical discussion and turn to theological matters, not so much in order to dwell on an examination or careful explanation of them (which would be foreign to my purpose here), but in order that I might indicate to the reader, as if by my finger, in what way the principles of metaphysics are to be adduced and applied in order to corroborate theological truths. I confess that, in the view of some, perhaps, I have lingered in the consideration of those divine perfections which are called attributes longer than my present purpose would seem to require. But, in the first place, the importance and loftiness of the subject matter compelled me to do this, and second, I never seemed to transgress the limits of the natural light, nor, therefore, the limits of metaphysics.

And since I have always judged that a great capacity for understanding and penetrating into things lies in investigating and revealing them according to a suitable method, which I could barely—or not even barely—follow if, after the fashion of expositors, I dealt with all questions as they presented themselves incidentally and, as it were, by chance in the text of the Philosopher, for this reason I judged that it would be easier and more useful if all the things that could be investigated and examined regarding the entire object of this wisdom were sought out and placed before the eyes of the reader in a way that conformed to the order of teaching. And the first disputation of this work explains what that object is, and in it we discuss at the same time the worth and usefulness of metaphysics and the other points that writers normally set out beforehand in their introductions to the sciences. Then, in the first volume, I carefully consider the same object's most extensive and universal nature, (which is called being), its properties, and its causes. And I have dwelt on this consideration of causes longer than is usual because I judged it both very difficult and most useful for all of philosophy and theology. In the second volume, I have discussed the inferior natures, of the same object, beginning with that division of being into creator and created, inasmuch as it is prior, and closer to the quiddity of being, and better suited to the course of this teaching, which course proceeds from there through the divisions contained under these, right on to all the genera and grades of being which are contained within the bounds or limits of this science.

Quia tamen erunt permulti, qui doctrinam hanc universam Aristotelis libris applicatam habere cupient, tum ut melius percipiant, quibus tanti Philosophi principiis nitatur, tum ut eius usus ad ipsum Aristotelem intelligendum facilior sit, ac utilior: hac etiam in re lectori inservire studui, indice, quem toti operi praescripsimus,[3] a nobis elaborato, quo, si attente legatur, facillime (ni fallor) poterunt omnia, quae Aristoteles in libris Metaphysicae pertractavit, & comprehendi, & memoria retineri: rursusque prae manibus haberi quaestiones omnes, quae inter illos libros exponendos excitari solent.

Demum benignum lectorem admonendum duximus, unum quidem opus hoc esse, nec eius disputationes fuisse ab uno volumine seiungendas, nisi aliqua nos ratio coegisset. Nam, in primis ne mole sua nonnihil afferret molestiae, in duo volumina illud divisimus: deinde vero, ut, quoad fieri posset, nostrorum laborum studiosis debitum officium praestaremus, hoc prius emisimus statim ac e praelo prodiit, quanvis aliud eo iam processerit, ut existimem, non prius hanc partem perlectam fore, quam illa fuerit in lucem edita. Utinam utraque, & caetera, quae molimur, in magnam Dei Optimi Maximi gloriam, & Ecclesiae Catholicae utilitatem cedant. Vale.

3. Reading "*quem toti operi praescripsimus,*" here with S, V_1, and V_2. The following omit these words: C_1, C_2, G_2, M_1, M_2, M_3, M_4, P_1, P_2, V_3, V_4, V_5, and Vivès.

But since there will be many who want this entire teaching connected to the books of Aristotle, both in order that they might see on which principles of so great a philosopher it relies, and in order that its use for understanding Aristotle himself might be easier and more profitable, in this respect also I have tried to be of service to the reader, and this by means of an index which I have prefixed to the entire work, prepared by me, by means of which, when attentively read, the reader will most easily (if I am not mistaken) comprehend and retain in memory all the things which Aristotle has dealt with in the books of the Metaphysics; *and in addition, he shall have in his hands all the questions that are wont to be raised in expounding these books.*[1]

Finally, we think that the reader should be advised that this is indeed one work, and that its disputations would not have been separated into more than one volume if some reason had not compelled us. For, in the first place, we have divided it into two volumes so that its weight not prove troublesome. And second, we sent out this volume as soon as it came from the press in order that we might discharge, to the extent possible, the duty owed to those who are eager for our labors, although the other volume has so far progressed that, I reckon, this first part will not have been completely read before the other is published. May both volumes, and the others that we are planning, redound to the greater glory of God, the Best and Greatest, and to the advantage of the Catholic Church. Farewell.

1. This is the so-called "*Index locupletissimus in Metaphysicam Aristotelis.*" For the Latin text, see Francisco Suárez, *R. P. Francisci Suarez, E Societate Jesu, Opera Omnia*, 28 vols. in 30 (Parisiis: Apud Ludovicum Vivès, 1856–78), 25:i–lxvi. For an English translation, see Francisco Suárez, *A Commentary on Aristotle's* Metaphysics, *or "A Most Ample Index to the* Metaphysics *of Aristotle,"* trans. John P. Doyle (Milwaukee: Marquette University Press, 2005).

⟨1a⟩

DISPUTATIONES METAPHYSICAE

UNIVERSAM

DOCTRINAM DUODECIM

LIBRORUM ARISTOTELIS

COMPREHENDENTES.

Autore R. P. Francisco Suarez e Societate JESU.

METAPHYSICAL DISPUTATIONS

CONTAINING THE
ENTIRE DOCTRINE OF
ARISTOTLE'S
TWELVE BOOKS.

*By the Reverend Father Francisco Suárez,
of the Society of JESUS.*

PROOEMIUM.

Divina & supernaturalis Theologia, quanquam divino lumine principi-
isque a Deo revelatis nitatur, quia vero humano discursu & ratiocinati-
one perficitur, veritatibus etiam naturae lumine notis iuvatur, eisque ad
suos discursus perficiendos, & divinas veritates illustrandas, tanquam
ministris, & quasi instrumentis utitur. Inter omnes autem naturales
scientias, ea quae prima omnium est, & nomen primae Philosophiae
obtinuit, sacrae ac supernaturali Theologiae praecipue ministrat. Tum
quia ad divinarum rerum cognitionem inter omnes proxime accedit:
tum etiam quia ea naturalia principia explicat atque confirmat, quae
res universas comprehendunt, omnemque doctrinam quodammodo
fulciunt atque sustentant. Hanc igitur ob causam, quanvis gravioribus
Sacrae Theologiae commentationibus, ac disputationibus pertractandis, & in lucem emittendis sim distentus, earum cursum paululum intermittere, vel potius remittere sum coactus, ut quae de hac naturali
sapientia ante plures annos iuvenis elaboraveram, & publice dictav-
eram, saltem succisivis temporibus recognoscerem & locupletarem, ut
in publicam utilitatem omnibus communicari possent. Cum enim inter
disputandum de divinis mysteriis haec Metaphysica dogmata occur-
rerent, sine quorum cognitione & intelligentia vix, aut ne vix quidem,
possunt altiora illa mysteria pro di[1b]gnitate tractari, cogebar saepe,
aut divinis & supernaturalibus rebus inferiores quaestiones admiscere,
quod legentibus ingratum est & parum utile: aut certe, ut hoc incom-
modum vitarem, in huiusmodi rebus sententiam meam breviter proponere, & quasi nudam fidem in eis a legentibus postulare. Quod &
mihi quidem molestum, & illis etiam importunum videri merito potu-
isset. Ita enim haec principia & veritates Metaphysicae cum Theologicis

PROEM.

Although divine and supernatural theology depends on the divine light and on principles revealed by God, nevertheless, since it is perfected by human reasoning and rational discourse, it is also assisted by truths known$_n$ by the light of nature, and it employs these as servants and instruments in order to perfect its reasonings and illuminate divine truths. But among all the natural sciences, that which is first of all, and has acquired the name of first philosophy, especially serves sacred and supernatural theology, both because, of all these sciences, it most nearly approaches cognition of divine things$_r$, and also because it explains and confirms those natural principles which embrace all things$_r$ and in a certain way support and sustain every doctrine. For this reason, therefore, although I have been busy meditating over, and publishing, more important commentaries and disputations of sacred theology, I have been forced briefly to leave off, or rather slow, their progress, in order that I might, at least in my spare time, review and enrich what I had labored on and publicly dictated about this natural wisdom many years ago as a young man, in order that it might be communicated to all for the public benefit. For since, when dealing with divine mysteries, there is occasion to discuss these metaphysical doctrines, without cognition and understanding of which those higher mysteries can scarcely be dealt with in a worthy fashion (or not even scarcely), I was often compelled either to mix together inferior questions with divine and supernatural matters, which is unwelcome and of little use to readers, or at least (in order to avoid this same inconvenience) briefly to present my opinions regarding such matters and require, as it were, a bare faith in them from my readers. This was indeed troublesome to me and

conclusionibus ac discursibus cohae⟨1b⟩rent, ut si illorum scientia ac perfecta cognitio auferatur, horum etiam scientiam nimium labefactari necesse sit. His igitur rationibus & multorum rogatu inductus hoc opus praescribere decrevi, in quo Metaphysicas omnes disputationes ea doctrinae methodo complecterer, quae ad rerum ipsarum comprehensionem & ad brevitatem aptior sit: revelataeque sapientiae inserviat magis. Quapropter necessarium non erit in plures libros opus hoc distribuere seu partiri, nam brevi disputationum numero, ea omnia, quae huius doctrinae sunt propria, quaeve subiecto eius sub ea ratione, qua in ipsa consideratur, conveniunt, comprehendi & exhauriri possunt: quae vero ad puram Philosophiam aut Dialecticam pertinent (in quibus alii Metaphysici scriptores prolixe immorantur) ut aliena a praesenti doctrina, quoad fieri possit, resecabimus. Prius vero quam de materia huic doctrinae subiecta dicere incipiam, de ipsamet sapientia seu Metaphysica, eiusque obiecto, utilitate, necessitate, attributisque illius atque muneribus, Deo auspice, disserere aggrediar.

could rightly have seemed inappropriate to them. For these metaphysical principles and truths so cohere with theological conclusions and reasonings that, if knowledge and perfect cognition of the former is taken away, it is necessary that knowledge of the latter be exceedingly weakened. Persuaded, therefore, by these considerations and by the requests of many, I decided to write this work beforehand, so as to include in it all metaphysical disputations by that method of instruction which better serves revealed wisdom and is more suited to brevity and to the comprehension of things, themselves. For this reason, it will not be necessary to divide or apportion this work into many books, for by means of a small number of disputations we shall be able to cover and exhaustively consider all those things which are proper to this doctrine, or which agree with its subject under that aspect, in respect of which it is considered in the same doctrine. But to the extent possible, we shall set aside as foreign to the present teaching those things which pertain to pure philosophy or dialectic (on which other metaphysical writers have dwelt at length). But before I begin to speak of the subject matter of this doctrine, I will, under the guidance of God, begin by discussing this same wisdom or metaphysics, as well as its object, utility, necessity, attributes, and functions.

DISPUTATIO I.[4]

DE NATURA PRIMAE PHILOSOPHIAE,

SEU METAPHYSICAE.

Varia Meta-physicae nomina. Ut a nomine, ut par est, sumatur exordium, varia sunt nomina, partim ab Aristotele, partim ab aliis autoribus, huic doctrinae imposita. Primo enim appellata est *sapientia* 1. Metaph. cap. 2. quoniam de primis rerum causis, & supremis ac difficillimis rebus, & quodammodo de universis entibus disputat. Nec refert quod 1. Metaphys. *prudentia* appelletur, id enim cognomen non proprie, sed per analogiam quandam illi accommodatum est: quia sicut in practicis prudentia, ita in speculativis haec sapientia maxime expetenda est. Deinde dicitur absolute & quasi per antonomasiam *Phi⟨2a⟩losophia* 4. libr. Metaphys. text. 5. ubi etiam text. 4. & libr. 6. text. 3. *Prima Philosophia* nominatur: est enim *Philosophia*, studium sapientiae: hoc autem studium intra naturae ordinem in hac scientia acquirenda maxime adhibetur, cum ipsa sapientia sit & in divinarum rerum cognitione versetur. Hinc rursus, *naturalis Theologia* vocatur ex libr. 6. Metaphys. capit. 1. & libr. 11. capit. 6. quoniam de Deo ac divinis rebus sermonem habet, quantum ex naturali lumine haberi potest: ex quo etiam *Metaphysica* nominata est, quod nomen non tam ab Aristotele, quam ab eius interpretibus habuit: sumptum vero est ex inscriptione, quam Aristoteles suis Metaphysicae libris praescripsit, videlicet, Τῶν μετὰ τὰ φυσικὰ, id est, de his rebus quae scientias seu res naturales consequuntur. Abstrahit enim haec scientia a sensibilibus,

---

4. Regarding my procedure for establishing the Latin text that appears here, see "Remarks on the Latin Text and English Translation," pp. xci–xcii.

DISPUTATION I.

ON THE NATURE OF FIRST PHILOSOPHY

OR METAPHYSICS.

To take our start, as is fitting, from the name: various names are im- posed on this doctrine, partly by Aristotle, partly by other authors. For in the first place it is called *wisdom* in *Metaph.* I, ch. 2,[2] since it deals with the first causes of things_r, the highest and most difficult things_r, and in a certain way all beings. Nor does it matter that it is called *prudence* in *Metaph.* I,[3] since this name is applied to it not properly, but by a certain analogy, for just as prudence is most of all to be sought in practical matters, so is wisdom most of all to be sought in speculative matters. Second, it is called *philosophy* absolutely and, as it were, by antonomasia in *Metaph.* IV, text 5,[4] and also in text 4.[5] And in *Metaph.* VI, text 3,[6] it is named *first philosophy.* For *philosophy* is zeal for wisdom, and this zeal within the order of nature is most of all directed to the acquisition of this science, since this science is wisdom itself and

2. Aristotle, *Metaph.* I, ch. 2, 982a6.

3. Aristotle, *Metaph.* I, ch. 2, 982b24.

4. Aristotle, *Metaph.* IV, ch. 2, 1004a34, b1. According to the *Latinitatis Medii Aevi Lexicon Bohemorum* (Prague: Academia, 1977–), "*per antonomasiam*" means "*per excellentiam*" (κατ' ἐξοχήν), i.e., "*par excellence.*" See the entry for "*antonomasia.*" In the *Dictionary of Medieval Latin from British Sources* (Oxford: pub. for the British Academy by Oxford University Press, 1975–2013), one of the meanings given for "*antonomasia*" is: "(use of general term in) special sense."

5. Aristotle's *Metaph.* IV, text 4, is *Metaph.* IV, ch. 2, 1004a1–34. It's not clear to me that Aristotle uses the terms "philosophy" or "philosopher" to refer to metaphysics in this text. But see 1004a3 and 1004a6.

6. Aristotle, *Metaph.* VI, ch. 1, 1026a24.

seu materialibus rebus (quae Physicae dicuntur, quoniam in eis naturalis Philosophia versatur) & res divinas & a[5] materia separatas, & communes rationes entis, quae absque materia existere possunt, contemplatur: & ideo *Metaphysica* dicta est, quasi post Physicam, seu ultra physicam constituta: post (inquam) non dignitate, aut naturae ordine: sed acquisitionis, generationis, seu inventionis: vel, si ex parte obiecti illud intelligamus, res de quibus haec scientia tractat, dicuntur esse post Physica seu naturalia entia, quia eorum ordinem superant, & in altiori rerum gradu constitutae sunt. Ex quo tandem appellata est haec scientia, aliarum *princeps & domina*, 6. Metaph. cap. 1. & libr. 11. cap. 6. quod dignitate antecellat, & omnium principia aliquo modo stabiliat & confirmet. Haec autem universa nomina ex obiecto, seu materia circa quam haec doctrina versatur, sumpta sunt, ut ex eorum rationibus & interpretationibus facile constare potest. Solent enim a sapientibus unicuique rei nomina imponi, spectata prius cuiusque natura & dignitate, ut Plato in Cratilo docuit, uniuscuiusque autem scientiae natura & dignitas ex obiecto potissimum pendet, & ideo primum omnium inquirendum nobis est huius doctrinae obiectum, seu subiectum, quo cognito constabit facile, quae sint huius sapientiae munera, quae necessitas vel utilitas, & quanta dignitas.

5. Reading "a" here with C_1, C_2, G_2, M_1, M_2, M_3, M_4, P_1, P_2, S, V_1, V_2, V_3, and V_4. The following omit "a": V_5 and Vivès.

is concerned with the cognition of things_r divine. Hence it is in addition called *natural theology* in conformity with *Metaph.* VI, ch. 1, and *Metaph.* XI, ch. 6,[7] since it discusses God and matters divine insofar as this can be done by means of the natural light. For this reason it is also named *metaphysics*, which name it has received not so much from Aristotle as from his interpreters, for it is taken from the title that Aristotle prefixed to his books of *Metaphysics*, namely: τῶν μετὰ τὰ φυσικὰ, that is, concerning those things_r which come after natural things_r or after the natural sciences. For this science abstracts from sensible or material things_r (which are called physical, since natural philosophy is concerned with them) and considers things_r that are divine and separated from matter, as well as the common natures_r of being that are capable of existing without matter. And therefore it was called *metaphysics*, as if constituted after physics or following physics—"after," I say, not in respect of dignity, or in the order of nature, but in the order of acquisition, generation, or discovery. Or, if we understand "after" in connection with the object, the things_r of which this science treats are said to be after physical or natural beings because they are above the order of physical or natural beings and are constituted in a higher grade of things_r. For this reason, finally, this science is called *the chief and mistress* of the rest in *Metaph.* VI, ch. 1, and *Metaph.* XI, ch. 6,[8] since it is superior in dignity and in some way fixes and confirms the principles of all the sciences. But all these names have been taken from the object or subject matter with which this doctrine is concerned, as can easily be established from their accounts_r and explanations. For the wise usually impose names on each thing_r after having first considered

7. Aristotle, *Metaph.* VI, ch. 1, 1026a19, and *Metaph.* XI, ch. 7, 1064b3.

8. The text labeled *Metaph.* XI, ch. 6, by Suárez is our *Metaph.* XI, ch. 7. The words *"princeps"* (here translated "chief") and *"domina"* (here rendered "mistress") do not appear in *Metaph.* VI, ch. 1, or in *Metaph.* XI, ch. 7, in the so-called *Translatio media* of the *Metaphysics* or in the Latin translations made by William of Moerbeke, John Argyropoulos, Basilios Bessarion, and Pedro Fonseca. However, the Greek words "ἀρχικωτάτη καὶ ἡγεμονικωτάτη," which occur at *Metaph.* III, ch. 2, 996b10, are rendered *"princeps ... atque domina"* and *"princeps ac domina"* in the translations of John Argyropoulos and Pedro Fonseca, respectively. See Aristotle, *Aristotelis Stagiritae De Prima Philosophia seu Metaphysicorum Libri XII, Ioanne Argyropylo Byzantino interprete* (Parisiis: Apud Thomam Richardum, 1548), fol. 16v, and Pedro da Fonseca, *Commentariorum in libros Metaphysicorum Aristotelis tomus primus* (Coloniae: Sumptibus Lazari Zetzneri Bibliopolae, 1615), col. 568.

its nature and dignity, as Plato teaches in *Cratylus*.[9] But the nature and dignity of each science depend chiefly on its object, and therefore the first of all things that must be investigated by us is the object or subject of this doctrine: once this is cognized, it will easily be established what the functions of this wisdom are, what its necessity or utility is, and how great its dignity is.

9. Plato, *Cratylus*, 390d and passim.

 # Sectio I.

Quod sit Metaphysicae obiectum.

———

1. Variae sunt de hac re sententiae, quae sigillatim ac breviter sunt annotandae & exa⟨2b⟩minandae, ut intelligamus exacte, de quibus rebus in discursu huius doctrinae nobis disserendum sit, ita ut neque illius fines transgrediamur, neque aliquid intra eos contentum relinquamus intactum.

Prima & secunda opiniones exponuntur.

2. Prima igitur sententia est, ens abstractissime sumptum, quatenus sub se complectitur non solum universa entia realia tam per se, quam per accidens, sed etiam rationis entia, esse obiectum adaequatum huius scientiae. Quae opinio suadetur primo, quia ens sic sumptum potest esse obiectum adaequatum alicuius scientiae: ergo maxime huius, quae est omnium abstractissima. Antecedens patet, tum quia ens in tota illa amplitudine intellectui obiicitur: ergo & potest obiici uni scientiae, est enim eadem ratio: tum etiam quia sicut intellectus illa omnia intelligit, ita haec scientia de omnibus illis disserit, nempe de entibus rationis, & realibus: & de entibus per se & per accidens: ergo, si propter illam causam continentur sub obiecto intellectus, propter similem contineri debent sub obiecto adaequato huius scientiae: ergo ens prout obiicitur huic scientiae, sumi debet sub ea abstractione & latitudine, qua haec omnia directe comprehendat: & eodem modo sumenda erunt communia attributa, de quibus haec scientia tractat, qualia sunt unitas, multitudo, veritas, & similia. Unde argumentor secundo, quia ad perfectionem & amplitudinem huius scientiae pertinet ut haec omnia separet ac distinguat, & de universis doceat, quicquid certa cognitione de his sciri potest: nam hoc maxime pertinet ad rationem sapientiae: ergo haec omnia entia secundum communes rationes suas directe continentur sub obiecto adaequato huius scientiae. Tertio, nam, si quid impediret

What the Object of Metaphysics Is.

———

1. On this matter, there are various opinions, which are severally and briefly to be taken note of and examined in order that we might accurately understand what things_r_ are to be discussed by us in the course of this doctrine, so that we neither exceed its boundaries nor leave untouched something that is contained within them.

The first and second opinions are expounded.

2. The first opinion, then, is that the adequate object of this science is being taken in the most abstract way, insofar as it embraces under itself not only all real beings, *per se* as well as *per accidens*, but beings of reason as well. This opinion is urged, first, because being, so taken, can be the adequate object of some science. Therefore, most especially the object of this science, which is the most abstract of all the sciences. The antecedent is evident, both because being according to that entire wide extent is the object of the intellect; therefore, it can also be the object of a single science, since the basis_r_ is the same; and also because, just as the intellect understands all those things, so does this science treat of all those things, namely, beings of reason and real beings, both *per se* and *per accidens*; therefore, if for that reason they are contained under the object of the intellect, for a similar reason they must be contained under the adequate object of this science. Therefore, being, insofar as it is the object of this science, should be taken in that abstraction and breadth according to which it directly comprehends all these things, and the common attributes with which this science deals (such as unity, multitude, truth, and the like) will have to be taken in the same way. Hence I argue, second, because it pertains to the perfection and fullness of this science that it separate and distinguish all these things, and that it teach, concerning all of them, whatever can be known about them

quominus ens sic sumptum posset esse obiectum, maxime quia non est univocum: sed hoc non refert, satis enim est quod sit analogum: alias nec commune esse posset accidentibus realibus, & substantiis creatis, ac increatae: ens autem quatenus analogum est, etiam rationis entia complectitur, ut ex 4. Metaph. text. 2. sumi potest: ubi Aristoteles privationes, negationes, seu non entia subiicit analogiae entis, quatenus intelligibilia sunt: ergo ens sic analogum esse potest adaequatum obiectum huius scientiae, eo vel maxime quod omnia illa comprehenduntur sub abstractione adaequata huius scientiae, quae est ab omni materia sensibili & intelli⟨3a⟩gibili: nam omnes illae rationes entium possunt absque huiusmodi materia reperiri. Tandem in ipsismet proprietatibus quae de ente in communi demonstrantur in hac scientia, ita includuntur entia rationis, ut sine his illae intelligi non possint, ut postea videbimus: ergo necesse est ut haec scientia de illis disputet.

3. Nec satis est si quis dicat disserere quidem hanc scientiam de his entibus, non tamen per se & ex in[3a]stituto ut de obiecto, sed obiter, & dum aliud agit, vel ad melius explicanda sua obiecta, vel quia horum cognitio facile comparatur ex obiecti cognitione: hoc (inquam) satis non est, quia rationes factae plus probare videntur: alioqui idem posset dici de accidentibus, imo & de substantiis creatis. Praesertim quia huiusmodi entia rationis & similia, sunt per se scibilia, multaque de illis naturaliter cognoscuntur & demonstrantur: nulla est autem alia scientia, ad quam hoc per se pertineat. Licet enim nonnulli hoc tribuant Dialecticae, tamen neque in universum dici hoc potest de omnibus entibus rationis, sed ad summum de quibusdam respectibus qui consequuntur operationes intellectus: nec de eis per se inquirit Dialecticus, quomodo rationem entis & proprietates eius participent, sed solum obiter ea attingit, quantum ad explicandas conceptiones intellectus, & denominationes ab eis provenientes necessarium est.

by certain cognition, for this pertains most of all to the nature$_r$ of wisdom. Therefore, all these beings according to their common natures$_r$ are directly contained under the adequate object of this science. Third, because if something prevented being so taken from being able to be the object of this science, it would most of all be because it is not univocal. But this does not matter, for it is sufficient that it be analogical; otherwise, neither could it be common to real accidents and created and uncreated substances. But being, insofar as it is analogical, also embraces beings of reason, as can be gathered from *Metaph.* IV, text 2, where Aristotle places privations, negations or non-beings under the analogy of being, insofar as they are intelligible.[10] Therefore, being that is in this way analogical can be the adequate object of this science, especially given that all those things are comprehended under the adequate abstraction of this science, which abstraction is from all sensible and intelligible matter, for all those natures$_r$ of beings can be found without such matter. Finally, beings of reason are so included in those very properties that are demonstrated of being in general that without the former the latter cannot be understood, as we shall see later.[11] Therefore, it is necessary that this science discuss them.

3. Nor is it sufficient if someone should say that this science does indeed deal with these beings, but not *per se* and by design as with an object, but in passing and while it does something else, either so as to better explain its objects, or because cognition of them is easily obtained from cognition of its object. This, I say, is not sufficient, because the arguments made seem to prove more; otherwise, the same could be said of accidents—and, in fact, of created substances as well. And this especially because such beings of reason and the like are knowable *per se*, and many things are naturally cognized and demonstrated about them, and there is no other science to which this pertains *per se*. For although some attribute this task to dialectic, nevertheless, this cannot be said generally of all beings of reason, but at most of certain relations that are consequent upon the operations of the intellect. Nor does the dialectician *per se* inquire, with respect to these, how they participate in the nature$_r$ of being and its properties, but he touches on these things

---

10. Aristotle, *Metaph.* IV, ch. 2, 1003b5–10.
11. See *DM* 3.1.

4. Secunda opinio esse potest, obiectum huius scientiae esse ens reale in tota sua latitudine, ita ut directe non comprehendat entia rationis, quia entitatem & realitatem non habent, complectatur vero non solum entia per se, sed etiam entia per accidens, quia etiam haec realia sunt, vereque participant rationem entis & passiones eius: & de his urgentius procedunt rationes factae in confirmationem superioris opinionis. Et potest confirmari, quia aliquae scientiae particulares habent entia per accidens pro obiectis: sed obiectum huius scientiae directe complectitur omnia obiecta particularium scientiarum: ergo.

Refutantur duae primae opiniones.

5. Hae vero duae opiniones manifeste repugnant Aristoteli 6. Metaph. Nam in primis, quod ad entia per accidens attinet, quatenus talia sunt, sub scientiam cadere non possunt, ut ibidem Aristot. probat tex. 4. appellatur enim hic ens per accidens, non in ratione effectus, sed in ratione entis, id est, non ⟨3b⟩ quod ex accidente seu contingenter & praeter intentionem agentis efficitur, sed quod in se vere unum non est, sed quoddam aggregatum ex multis: de qua distinctione dicemus plura inferius agentes de unitate. Cum ergo hoc ens per accidens non sit unum, sed aggregatio multorum, nec definitionem propriam habere potest, nec passiones reales quae de illo demonstrentur, & ideo sub scientiam non cadit. Quod si tale ens consideretur quatenus aliquo modo unum est, eiusque unitas aliquo modo est in re, iam non consideratur tale ens ut omnino per accidens, sed ut aliquo modo comprehensum sub latitudine entis per se, quanvis fortasse in illa imperfectum aliquem gradum teneat: sunt enim varii modi entis per se, & per accidens, ut suo loco declarabimus, de unitate tractantes. Propterea enim dixi, sermonem esse de ente per accidens quatenus tale est: nam illud ut sic non est ens, sed entia, & ideo directe non comprehenditur sub obiecto unius scientiae, sed plurium, ad quas pertinere possunt entia per se, ex quibus tale ens per accidens constat, ut D. Thom. notavit dicto lib. 6. Metaph. lect. 4. Si autem illa unitas non sit in re, sed tantum in appre-

only in passing, insofar as this is necessary in order to explain the conceptions of the intellect and the denominations arising from them.

4. The second opinion can be that the object of this science is real being according to its entire extent, so that it does not directly comprehend beings of reason, since beings of reason do not have entity and reality, although it does embrace, not only *per se* beings, but also *per accidens* beings, for the latter too are real and truly participate in the nature᷊ of being and its passions. And regarding these, the arguments made in confirmation of the previous opinion are more compelling. And this can be confirmed, because some particular sciences have *per accidens* beings as their objects. But the object of this science directly embraces all the objects of the particular sciences. Therefore.

The first two opinions are refuted.

5. But these two opinions are clearly in conflict with Aristotle, *Metaph*. VI. For, in the first place, with respect to *per accidens* beings, insofar as they are such, they cannot fall under a science, as Aristotle proves in the same place, text 4,[12] for a thing is here called a *per accidens* being not insofar as it is an effect, but insofar as it is a being, that is, not because it is effected accidentally or contingently and beyond the intention of the agent, but because in itself it is not truly one, but a sort of aggregate of many things. (Concerning this distinction we shall have more to say below when treating of unity.[13]) Since, therefore, this *per accidens* being is not one thing, but an aggregation of many, it can have neither a proper definition nor real passions that might be demonstrated of it, and therefore it does not fall under a science. But if such a being should be considered insofar as it is in some way one, and its unity in some way real, in that case such a being is not considered insofar as it is altogether *per accidens*, but insofar as it is in some way comprehended under the extension of *per se* being, although perhaps in that extension it has some imperfect grade, for there are various modes of *per se* being and *per accidens* being, as we shall make clear in its proper place, while treating

12. Aristotle, *Metaph*. VI, ch. 2, 1026b2–b24.
13. See *DM* 4.3.

hensione vel conceptione, tale ens ut sic non vere dicetur reale: unde eadem erit de illo ratio quae de caeteris entibus rationis. Haec autem excludun[3b]tur a consideratione directa huius scientiae ab eodem Arist. lib. 6. Metaph. in fine, ut ibidem omnes interpretes notarunt. Et ratio est, quia talia neque vere sunt entia, sed fere nomine tantum, neque cum entibus realibus conveniunt in eodem conceptu entis, sed solum per quandam imperfectam analogiam proportionalitatis, ut infra videbimus: obiectum autem adaequatum scientiae requirit unitatem aliquam obiectivam.

6. Unde non refert quod aliquando Aristoteles analogiam entis declaraverit prout se extendit ad haec entia, quia ibi non assignabat huius scientiae obiectum, sed explicabat vocis significationem ad aequivocationem tollendam. Postea vero in proprio loco docuit, ens non esse obiectum secundum totam illam analogiam, quae magis in unitate vocis, quam obiecti consistit. Et propter hoc etiam non est similis ratio de accidentibus realibus: nam illa revera sunt entia, & sub unitate conceptus obiectivi entis aliquo modo comprehenduntur, ut postea videbimus. Neque necesse est omnia quae aliquo modo con⟨4a⟩siderantur in scientia, directe contineri sub adaequato obiecto eius, nam multa considerantur obiter per quandam analogiam, seu reductionem, vel ut eorum cognitione obiectum ipsum magis illustretur, vel quia, cognito obiecto, per analogiam ad illud caetera cognoscuntur, & fortasse aliter cognosci non possunt. Item proprietates subiecti quae de ipso demonstrantur, non est necesse directe contineri sub ipso obiecto, saltem secundum omnia quae includunt. Sic igitur, quanvis·

Entia rationis quare excludantur ab obiecto huius scientiae.

haec scientia multa consideret de entibus rationis, nihilominus merito excluduntur ab obiecto per se & directe intento (nisi quis velit de nomine contendere) propter utramque causam dictam. Nam in primis entia rationis considerantur aliquo modo in hac scientia, non tamen

of unity.[14] It is for this reason that I said that the discussion is about *per accidens* being insofar as it is such, for as such it is not a being, but beings, and it is therefore not directly comprehended under the object of a single science, but under the objects of several sciences, to which the *per se* beings of which such a *per accidens* being is composed can pertain, as St. Thomas notes in lect. 4 of the mentioned book VI of the *Metaphysics*.[15] If, however, that unity does not exist$_e$ in reality, but only in apprehension or conception, such a being, as such, will not truly be called real, for which reason the same argument will apply to it as applies to other beings of reason. But these are excluded from the direct consideration of this science by the same Aristotle, *Metaph.* VI, near the end,[16] as all interpreters have noted in the same place. And the reason is that such beings are not truly beings, but beings in name only, nor do they agree with real beings in the same concept of being, but only through a certain imperfect analogy of proportionality, as we shall see below.[17] But the adequate object of a science requires some objective unity.

6. For this reason it does not matter that Aristotle sometimes explains the analogy of being insofar as it extends to these beings, since there he is not assigning the object of this science, but explaining the signification of the word in order to remove an equivocation. However, later he teaches in its proper place that being is not the object of this science according to the whole of that analogy, which consists more in a unity of word than of object. And for this reason also a similar argument does not apply to real accidents, for these really are beings and are in some way comprehended under the unity of the objective concept of being, as we shall see later.[18] Nor is it necessary that all the things which are in some way considered in a science be contained directly under its adequate object, for many things are considered in passing by a certain analogy or reduction, or insofar as the object itself is made clearer through cognition of them, or because, when the object has been cog-

14. See *DM* 4.3.

15. See Thomas Aquinas, *In duodecim libros metaphysicorum Aristotelis expositio* (Turin & Rome: Marietti, 1950), pp. 311–12 (bk. VI, lect. 4, n. 1243). It's not clear to me that Aquinas here makes the point Suárez attributes to him. See also Aquinas, *In duodecim libros metaphysicorum Aristotelis expositio*, pp. 301–3 (ns. 1171–89).

16. Aristotle, *Metaph.* VI, ch. 4.

17. See *DM* 54.1.9–10.

18. See *DM* 2.2.

per se, sed propter quandam proportionalitatem, quam habent cum entibus realibus, & ut ab eis distinguantur, & ut melius & clarius concipiatur quid habeat in entibus entitatem & realitatem, quid vero non habeat nisi solam speciem eius. Unde (ut sic dicam) magis considerantur haec rationis entia ut cognoscantur non esse entia, quam ut eorum scientia vel cognitio acquiratur. Deinde considerantur ad declarandas proprietates entis realis, & obiecti huius scientiae, quae a nobis non satis concipiuntur & explicantur nisi per huiusmodi entia rationis: ita enim agit haec scientia aliquo modo de genere & specie ad explicandas rerum unitates, & sic de aliis, ut sumitur ex 4. Metaph. cap. 1. & 2. & ex lib. 6. & 7. ex discursuque materiae id magis constabit. Deinde saepe tractatur de his entibus ratione alicuius realis fundamenti quod habent in rebus, vel certe quia fundamentum ipsum non potest satis cognosci, neque eius realitas a nobis declarari, nisi prius explicemus, quaenam denominationes rationis ibi misceantur.

Solvuntur fundamenta praecedentium opinionum. 7. Argumenta igitur praecedentium opinionum probant quidem, huiusmodi entia considerari in hac scientia, non vero quod sint partes directe contentae sub obiecto eius. Imo, ut ego existimo, ad nullam scientiam per se & primario pertinent, quia, cum non sint entia, sed potius defectus entium, non sunt per se scibilia, sed quatenus deficiunt a vera ratione entium quae per se consideratur, vel quatenus aliquo modo illam comitari videntur. Priori modo agit Philosophus de caecitate, & de tene[4a]bris, ac vacuo, quatenus sunt defectus privationesque visus, lucis, ac realis ⟨4b⟩ loci. Posteriori modo tractant multi

nized, the others are cognized by analogy with it, and perhaps cannot be cognized otherwise. Further, it is not necessary that the properties of a subject which are demonstrated of it be contained directly under the same object, at least with respect to all they include.[19] Accordingly, although this science considers many things about beings of reason, nevertheless, they are rightly excluded from its *per se* and directly intended object (unless someone should want to argue over a name) for the two reasons mentioned. For, in the first place, beings of reason are in some way considered in this science, though not *per se*, but on account of a certain proportionality that they have with real beings, both in order that they might be distinguished from real beings and in order to better and more clearly conceive what, among beings, has entity and reality and what does not, but only the appearance of it.[20] For this reason, these beings of reason are considered (so to speak), not so much in order that science or cognition of them might be acquired, but rather in order that they might be cognized *not* to be beings. Second, they are considered in order to make clear the properties of real being, or the properties of this science's object, which are not sufficiently conceived and explained by us except by means of such beings of reason.[21] For thus does this science treat in some way of genus and species in order to explain the unities of things_r (and similarly regarding other [properties of being]), as is gathered from *Metaph.* IV, chs. 1 and 2, and from *Metaph.* VI and VII, and this will be clearer from our discussion of this subject.[22] Finally, one often treats of these beings because of some real foundation that they have in things_r, or at least because the foundation itself cannot be sufficiently cognized, nor its reality made clear by us, unless we first explain which denominations of reason are there mixed in.

Why beings of reason are excluded from the object of this science.

7. The arguments for the preceding opinions, then, do indeed prove that such beings are considered in this science, but not that they are parts directly contained under its object. In fact, in my opinion, they pertain *per se* and primarily to no science, given that, since they are not

The foundations of the preceding opinions are refuted.

19. See *DM* 3.1.

20. *DM* 54 is devoted to beings of reason.

21. See *DM* 3.1.

22. It's not clear what texts, in particular, Suárez has in mind here. Here are some possibilities: Aristotle, *Metaph.* IV, ch. 1, 1003a21–22, *Metaph.* IV, ch. 2, 1003b22ff, *Metaph.* VI, ch. 1, 1026a31–32, *Metaph.* VII, chs. 13–16.

de relationibus seu denominationibus rationis. Dialecticus in quantum ad illum pertinet dirigere & ordinare reales conceptus mentis, a quibus denominationes rationis sumuntur, & in quibus hae relationes rationis fundantur: a Philosopho vero etiam considerantur, vel considerari possunt, quatenus ipse & per se proprie speculatur operationes intellectus, non solum directas, sed etiam reflexas, & obiecta earum. In hac vero scientia considerantur ob rationes iam dictas.

Tertia opinio exponitur.

8. Praetermissis ergo his sententiis, quae nimium amplificabant huius scientiae obiectum, sunt plures aliae, quae nimium illud coarctant. Tertia itaque opinio, & per extremum opposita, solum supremum ens reale (Deum videlicet) facit obiectum huius scientiae adaequatum. *Albert.* Hanc opinionem refert Albertus in principio Metaphysicae ex Alpharabio, libro de divisione scientiarum, potestque tribui Averroi 1. Physicorum, commento ultimo: reprehendit enim Avicennam, eo quod dixerit, ad primum Philosophum pertinere demonstrare primum principium esse: at (obiicit Averroes) nulla scientia demonstrat suum subiectum[6] esse: Deus autem seu primum principium est obiectum totius Philosophiae. Aristoteles etiam lib. 1. Metaphysicae, in principio ait, hanc scientiam contemplari primam rerum causam, & ideo esse maxime Divinam, quare ut vidimus, *Theologiam* illam appellat: Theologia autem nihil aliud est, quam scientia de Deo: erit ergo Deus huius scientiae obiectum: nam ex obiecto accipit scientia suam dignitatem & praestantiam, eaque attributa vel nomina quibus talis dignitas indicatur: sed

Alpharab.
Averroes.
Avicenna.

Aristoteles.

6. Reading "subiectum" here with C_1, C_2, G_2, M_1, M_2, M_3, M_4, S, V_1, V_2, V_3, V_4, and V_5. The following read "obiectum": P_1, P_2, and Vivès.

beings, but rather defects of beings, they are not *per se* knowable, but are knowable insofar as they fall short of those true natures$_r$ of beings which are considered *per se*, or insofar as they seem in some way to accompany those natures$_r$. It is in the first way that the philosopher treats of blindness, darkness, and the vacuum, insofar as they are defects and privations of sight, light, and real place.[23] It is in the second way that many treat of relations or denominations of reason—[for example,] the dialectician, insofar as it pertains to her to arrange and order the real concepts of the mind, from which denominations of reason are taken, and on which these relations of reason are founded. But they are also considered, or can be considered, by the philosopher, insofar as she too *per se* and properly investigates the operations of the intellect, not only the direct operations, but also the reflex ones, and their objects. But in this science they are considered for the reasons already mentioned.

The third opinion is expounded.

8. With these opinions that excessively extend the object of this science set aside, there are several others that restrict it overly much. The third opinion, then, and the one at the opposite extreme, makes only the supreme real being (I mean God) the adequate object of this science. Albert reports this opinion at the beginning of his *Metaphysics*,[24] *Albert.* from Al-Farabi, *On the Division of the Sciences*,[25] and it can be attribut- *Al-Farabi.* ed to Averroes, *Phys.* I, final comment.[26] For Averroes reproaches Avi- *Averroes.* cenna for saying that it pertains to the first philosopher to demonstrate *Avicenna.* that the first principle exists$_e$.[27] However, (Averroes objects) no science

23. Scholastic Aristotelians commonly referred to Aristotle as "the philosopher." But Suárez commonly refers to physics or natural philosophy simply as "philosophy," and therefore to the physicist simply as "the philosopher."

24. Albert the Great, *Metaphysica*, bk. I, tract. 1, ch. 2, in: Albert the Great, *Alberti Magni opera omnia* (Münster: Aschendorff, 1960), vol. 16, pt. 1, pp. 3–4. Albert makes no explicit mention of Al-Farabi here.

25. See Al-Farabi, *Catálogo de las Ciencias*, ed Ángel Gonzalez Palencia, 2nd ed. (Madrid: Consejo Superior de Investigaciones Científicas, 1953), pp. 163–66. It's not clear that Al-Farabi endorses the conception of metaphysics that Suárez attributes to him.

26. Averroes, *Aristotelis opera cum Averrois Commentariis* (Venetiis: apud Junctas, 1562), vol. 4, fol. 47E–I, commenting on 192a34–b4.

27. See, e.g., Avicenna, *Liber de philosophia prima, sive scientia divina I–IV*, ed. S. Van Riet (Louvain & Leiden: Peeters & Brill, 1977), pp. 4–5.

praestantissimum obiectum est Deus: ergo hoc debet esse obiectum praestantissimae ac dignissimae scientiae.

Occurritur obiectioni.   9. Neque satisfaciet qui respondeat Deum esse praecipuum huius scientiae obiectum, idque satis esse ad illam scientiae dignitatem & appellationem, licet obiectum adaequatum non sit. Contra hoc enim urgetur argumentum. Primo, quia nobilius & excellentius est habere Deum pro obiecto adaequato, quam solum pro principali: est autem haec scientia nobilissima omnium, quae possunt naturali intellectus lumine acquiri: ergo Deus est adaequatum obiectum eius. Primum antecedens probatur, quia Deus secundum propriam rationem quid no⟨5a⟩bilius est, quam esse possit quaelibet ratio communis Deo & creaturis, ut per se constat, quia Deus secundum propriam rationem est ens infinite perfectum: omnis autem alia ratio abstractior, ex se non dicit, neque requirit infinitam perfectionem: sed illa scientia quae habet pro obiecto adaequato Deum, immediate & per se primo tendit in ipsum secundum propriam rationem eius: illa vero scientia, quae solum respicit Deum ut principale obiectum, ad summum potest per se primo versari circa aliquam rationem entis communem Deo & creaturis: ergo illa prior scientia erit longe nobilior: quia nobilitas scientiae sumitur ex illo obiecto, in quod per se primo tendit. Quod etiam potest exemplis declarari & confirmari, quia divinus intellectus nobilissimus omnium est, & ideo solum Deum habet pro adaequato obiecto, ni[4b]hilque aliud attingit, nisi in quantum in ipsomet Deo, seu per ipsum manifestatur. Similiter visio beata nobilior est, habens Deum pro adaequato obiecto, quam si immediate attingeret Deum, & aliquid aliud sub aliqua ratione communi. Et denique propter hanc causam Theologia supernaturalis censetur habere pro adaequato obiecto solum Deum ut supernaturaliter revelatum: ergo eadem ratione Deus, ut naturali lu-

demonstrates that its subject exists$_e$, and God or the first principle is the object of the whole of philosophy. Aristotle also, at the beginning of *Metaph.* I, says that this science considers the first cause of things$_r$,[28] and is therefore most divine,[29] for which reason, as we have seen, he calls it theology. But theology is nothing other than the science of God. God, therefore, will be the object of this science. For it is from its object that a science receives its worth and excellence, as well as the attributes or names by which such worth is revealed. But the most excellent object is God. Therefore, this must be the object of the most excellent and most worthy science.

Aristotle.

9. It will not be satisfactory to reply that God is the foremost object of this science, and that this suffices for the worth and name of the science,[30] even if God is not its adequate object. For against this an argument is urged. First, because it is nobler and more excellent to have God as an adequate object than it is to have him only as a principal object. But this science is the noblest of all those which can be acquired by the natural light of the intellect. Therefore, God is its adequate object. The first antecedent is proved because God, according to his proper nature$_r$, is something nobler than any nature$_r$ common to God and creatures can be, as is clear *per se*, since God, according to his proper nature$_r$, is an infinitely perfect being, while every other more abstract nature$_r$ does not of itself signify$_d$ or require infinite perfection. But that science which has God for its adequate object is immediately and *per se* and primarily directed to God according to his proper nature$_r$, whereas that science which merely regards God as its principal object can at most *per se* and primarily concern itself with some nature$_r$ of being common to God and creatures. Therefore, the former science will be far nobler, since the nobility of a science is drawn from that object to which it is *per se* and primarily directed. This can also be made clear and confirmed by examples, since the divine intellect is the noblest of all intellects and therefore has God alone for its adequate object, and it reaches nothing else except insofar as it is manifested in God himself or through him. Likewise, the beatific vision is nobler in having God for its adequate object than

An objection is met.

<hr>

28. Aristotle, *Metaph.* I, ch. 1, 981b28.
29. Aristotle, *Metaph.* I, ch. 3, 983a4–11.
30. Sc. the name "theology."

mine intellectus nostri cognoscibilis, erit adaequatum obiectum huius naturalis Theologiae. Quin potius argumentari possumus, Deum non posse esse principale obiectum huius scientiae, si non est adaequatum, quia Deus & creatura non possunt convenire sub aliqua communi ratione obiecti scibilis: ergo, vel Deus dicendus est adaequatum obiectum huius scientiae, vel omnino excludendus ab obiecto illius. Antecedens patet primo, quia Deus est obiectum intelligibile longe alterius rationis & eminentioris, quam sit omne obiectum creatum, magisque distat Deus ab obiecto quovis creato, in abstractione & immaterialitate, quam distent omnia entia creata secundum proprias rationes suas: sed non possunt omnia obiecta creata convenire secundum proprias rationes sub uno adaequato obiecto huius scientiae: ergo multo minus poterunt convenire Deus & alia entia creata. Deinde, quia commune obiectum est prius natura iis quae sub ipso continentur, quia est superius ipsis, & cum eis non convertitur subsistendi consequentia: sed nihil potest esse prius natura Deo: ergo non potest esse obiectum principale contentum sub aliquo communi: erit ergo adaequatum. ⟨5b⟩

Solvitur
obiectio.

10. Quod si obiicias, scientiam hanc non de solo Deo, sed de multis aliis rebus disserere: Respondent, alia non tractari in hac scientia per se, seu propter se, sed quatenus ad Dei cognitionem conferre possunt. Et ita Aristoteles in 12. lib. Metaphysicae concludit scientiam de Deo, omnia vero quae in superioribus libris tradit, ad illum ultimum tanquam ad conclusionem praecipue intentam referuntur. Unde D. Tho. 1. 2. q. 56. art. 2. & Caietanus ibi, dicunt, hanc scientiam versari circa id quod est ultimum respectu totius cognitionis, & iudicare de omnibus principiis per resolutionem ad primas causas, quod Caietanus interpretatur de prima, seu altissima causa, quae eminenter continet primas rationes causandi, quae & universales sunt, & ad perfectionem simpliciter pertinent, ut sunt finis, efficiens, exemplar: nam materia & forma universales non sunt, & imperfectionem includunt.

it would be if it immediately reached God and something else under some common nature$_r$. And finally, it is for this reason that supernatural theology is judged to have God alone, as supernaturally revealed, for its adequate object. Therefore, for the same reason, God, insofar as he is cognizable by the natural light of our intellect, will be the adequate object of this natural theology. In fact, we can argue that God cannot be the principal object of this science if he is not its adequate object, because God and a creature cannot agree under some common concept$_r$ of knowable object. Therefore, either God must be called the adequate object of this science, or he is to be excluded altogether from its object. The antecedent is clear, first, because God is an intelligible object of a far different and far more eminent nature$_r$ than is every created object, and God is more distant from any created object, in abstraction and immateriality, than all created beings are from each other according to their proper natures$_r$. But according to their proper natures$_r$ all created objects cannot agree under the single adequate object of this science. Therefore, much less can God and other, created beings agree. Second, because a common object is prior by nature to those things which are contained under it, since it is superior to them and is not converted with them by an inference of subsistence.[31] But nothing can be prior by nature to God. Therefore, God cannot be the principal object contained under some common object. Therefore, he will be the adequate object.

10. But if you object that this science is not about God alone, but treats of many other things$_r$, they reply that other things are not dealt with in this science *per se* or on their own account, but insofar as they can contribute to the cognition of God. And thus Aristotle concludes the science of God in *Metaph.* XII, and all the things that he teaches in earlier books are referred to that end as to the conclusion chiefly intended.[32] For this reason, St. Thomas, *ST* I-II, q. 56, art. 2,[33] and Cajetan in the same place[34] say that this science is concerned with that

An objection is refuted.

Aristotle.

St. Thomas.

Cajetan.

---

31. See John Buridan, *Summulae de Dialectica*, trans. Gyula Klima (New Haven: Yale University Press, 2001), pp. 215–16.

32. See Aristotle, *Metaph.* VII, ch. 11, 1037a10–14.

33. The reference is in fact to *ST* I-II, q. 57, art. 2. See Thomas Aquinas, *Sancti Thomae Aquinatis opera omnia*, t. 6 (Romae: Ex Typographia Polyglotta, S. C. De Propaganda Fide, 1891), p. 365.

34. Thomas Aquinas, *Sancti Thomae Aquinatis opera omni*, t. 6, p. 366b.

Reiicitur tertia opinio.

11. Nihilominus haec sententia probanda non est, repugnat enim Aristoteli, & reliquis fere Philosophis, & interpretibus eius, ut videbimus: repugnat etiam ipsi (ut sic dicam) experientiae, & doctrinae, quae in hac scientia tradi solet, & ad eius perfectionem & complementum necessaria censetur: nam in ea multa continentur & docentur, quae per se sunt necessaria ad alias res cognoscendas praeter Deum, & ad perfectionem intellectus humani, quatenus in huiusmodi rebus, vel in rationibus ac principiis communibus cognoscendis versari potest, & ad Deum cognoscendum, vel nihil, vel parum conducunt, neque ex modo aut ratione talis scientiae ad hoc referuntur, quidquid sit de intentione scientis. Ratio denique a priori est, quia [5a] haec scientia, cum discursu naturali procedat, non attingit Deum prout in se est, sed quantum ex creaturis manifestari potest lumine naturali intellectus humani, & ideo nulla esse potest scientia naturalis quae ipsum attingat, & respiciat ut adaequatum obiectum, quia ratio, sub qua attingitur, semper communis est aliis rebus creatis. Unde constat recte dictum esse, tractando fundamentum superioris sententiae, Deum contineri sub obiecto huius scientiae ut primum ac praecipuum obiectum, non tamen ut adaequatum.

12. Ad instantias vero seu replicas respondetur. Ad primam quidem fatemur esse ma⟨6a⟩gnam excellentiam scientiae, habere Deum pro obiecto, in quod solum per se ac primario tendat, & per illud in reliqua, dicimus tamen, hanc perfectionem superare naturales vires in-

which is ultimate in relation to all cognition, and that it makes judgments about all principles through a resolution to first causes, and this Cajetan interprets as being about the first or highest cause, which eminently contains the first causalities,[35] which are both universal and pertain without qualification to perfection, such as the end, the efficient cause, and the exemplar cause. For matter and form are not universal and involve imperfection.

The third opinion is rejected.

11. Nevertheless, this opinion is not to be approved, since it contradicts Aristotle and almost all other philosophers and interpreters of him, as we shall see. It is also in conflict, so to speak, with experience itself and with the doctrine that is normally handed down in this science and judged to be necessary for its perfection and completeness. For in this science many things are included and taught which are *per se* necessary for the cognition of things$_r$ other than God, and for the perfection of the human intellect, insofar as it can concern itself with the cognition of such things$_r$, or with the cognition of common natures$_r$ and principles, and these things conduce not at all or very little to the cognition of God, nor are they referred to this in accordance with such a science's mode or method$_r$, whatever may be the case regarding the intention of the knower. Finally, an argument *a priori* is: because this science, since it proceeds by natural reasoning, does not reach God as he is in himself, but insofar as he can be made manifest from creatures by the natural light of the human intellect, and therefore, there can be no natural science which reaches and considers him as an adequate object, since the nature$_r$ under which he is reached is always common to him and other, created things$_r$. For this reason, it is clear that it was rightly said, in treating of the foundation of the previous opinion, that God is contained under the object of this science as its first and foremost object, but not as its adequate object.

12. I reply to the counter-arguments or rejoinders. To the first,[36] we

---

35. I sometimes use the word "causality" to render "*ratio causandi.*" See the title of *DM* 23.4: "Quid sit vel in quo consistat ratio causandi seu causalitas causae finalis."
36. See *DM* 1.1.9 above.

genii humani, & scientiae quae per illas acquiri potest: & ideo, quanvis haec scientia sit nobilissima intra suum ordinem, non propterea illi tribuenda est tanta perfectio. Neque in hoc est comparanda cum intellectu divino, ac visione beata, imo nec cum Theologia supernaturali, quae sub altiori lumine, & ex altioribus principiis procedit. Quanquam nec de supernaturali Theologia constet solum Deum esse obiectum adaequatum illius: multi enim censent, non Deum, sed ens revelatum, esse obiectum adaequatum illius doctrinae: quia divina revelatio, quae est ratio formalis sub qua illius obiecti, aeque cadere potest in Deum & res alias, quod attinet ad vim & rationem cognoscendi, quanvis in ratione finis, & in excellentia rei revelatae Deus omnia superet, & ideo dici soleat vel principale obiectum, vel simpliciter obiectum, practice & in ordine ad mores res considerando. Sed de hoc alias.

Deus an cum creaturis in ratione obiecti possit convenire.   13. Ad ultimum respondetur, non repugnare, Deum ut cognitum per creaturas convenire cum illis in aliqua ratione communi obiecti: nam, licet in suo esse, & secundum se magis distet a creatura qualibet, quam ipsae inter se, tamen secundum ea, quae de ipso manifestari possunt scientia naturali, & iuxta rationem & modum quo manifestari possunt ex creaturis maior proportio & convenientia inveniri potest inter Deum & creaturas, quam inter aliquas creaturas inter se. Neque ad huiusmodi obiectum adaequatum constituendum, quod Deum sub se comprehendat, necesse est dari aliquid, vel aliquam rationem entis, quae sit prior natura Deo, sed satis est ut detur secundum abstractionem vel considerationem intellectus, quod non repugnat, ut infra ostendemus, tractando de conceptu entis. Sicut enim intelligi potest convenientia aliqua vel similitudo imperfecta inter Deum & creaturas in ratione entis, substantiae, vel spiritus, ita possunt dari aliqui conceptus secundum rationem priores Deo in universalitate praedicationis: haec autem non est prioritas naturae, nec ratione causalitatis, ut per se constat, nec ratione independentiae seu prioritatis in subsistendo: nam

grant that it is a great excellence for a science to have God for an object to which alone it is directed *per se* and primarily, being directed to the remaining things through that. But we say that this perfection surpasses the natural powers of the human intellect and those of a science which can be acquired through those powers. And therefore, although this science is the noblest within its order, it is not for this reason to be assigned so great a perfection. Nor in this respect is it to be compared to the divine intellect and the beatific vision, nor, in fact, to supernatural theology, which proceeds under a higher light and from higher principles. Although neither is it clear that God alone is the adequate object of supernatural theology, for many judge that not God, but revealed being, is the adequate object of that doctrine, since divine revelation, which is the "formal aspect_r under which" of supernatural theology's object, can apply equally to God and other things_r when it comes to the capacity and ground_r of cognizing, although in respect of the concept_r of end and the excellence of the thing_r revealed, God surpasses all things and is therefore normally called either the principal object or the object without qualification of supernatural theology, considering the matter practically or in relation to custom. But this is discussed elsewhere.

13. To the last counter-argument,[37] it is replied that it is not impossible that God, as cognized by means of creatures, should agree with them in some common concept_r of object, for although in his being_e and as he is in himself he is more distant from any creature than any creature is from any other, nevertheless, with respect to those things which can be made manifest about him by natural science, and according to the method_r and mode in which they can be made manifest from creatures, a greater proportion and agreement can be found between God and creatures than among some creatures. Nor, in order to constitute an adequate object of the sort that will comprehend God under itself, is it necessary that there be something or some nature_r of being that is prior by nature to God. Rather, it is enough that there be [something or some nature_r that is prior to God] according to the abstraction or consideration of the intellect, and this is not impossible, as we will show below when treating of the concept of being.[38] For just as some

Whether God can agree with creatures in the concept_r of an object.

37. See *DM* 1.1.10 above.
38. See *DM* 2.1–3.

omnis ratio, quantumvis abstrahatur, communis Deo, & creaturis, ita comparatur ad Deum, ut existe⟨6b⟩re non possit in rerum natura nisi in ipsomet Deo, vel dependenter a Deo, & ideo non potest esse prior natura ipsomet Deo.

Refutatur quarta opinio.

14. Atque ex dictis contra praecedentem sententiam facile excluduntur duae aliae parum certe probabiles. Quarta ergo opinio sit, sub-[5b]stantiam aut ens immateriale, prout in se includit solum Deum & intelligentias, esse adaequatum obiectum huius scientiae. Quae opinio solet tribui Commentatori 1. Physic. com. ult. Sed ibi solum dicit, intelligentias per se pertinere ad obiectum huius scientiae, non vero esse adaequatum obiectum. Potest autem haec opinio suaderi ex discursu seu partitione scientiarum: omissis enim scientiis rationalibus, quae potius sunt artes quaedam, & de vocibus seu conceptibus tractant, & scientiis Mathematicis, quae non agunt de substantia, sed de sola quantitate; inter scientias, quae agunt de substantiis, Philosophia tractat de omnibus substantiis generabilibus,[7] & corruptibilibus, & de substantiis etiam corporeis incorruptibilibus, & de substantia etiam composita ex materia, & immateriali forma, qualis est homo: & de ipsa etiam forma immateriali, anima scilicet rationali, ac denique de quinque gradibus seu ordinibus materialium substantiarum, scilicet simplicium corporum, mistorum inanimatorum, vegetabilium tantum, sentientium tantum, & rationalium, & de omnibus proprietatibus eorum. Nihil ergo sciendum superest in rebus praeter immateriales substantias; illae ergo complent obiectum adaequatum huius scientiae. Qui totus discursus primo confirmari potest duplici testimonio Aristotelis. Unum est 4.

Commentator.

Aristotelis duo testimonia pro hac sententia afferuntur.

---

7. Reading "generabilibus" here with C$_1$, C$_2$, G$_2$, M$_1$, M$_2$, M$_3$, P$_1$, P$_2$, S, and V$_3$. The following read "generalibus": M$_4$, V$_1$, V$_2$, V$_4$, V$_5$, and Vivès.

agreement or imperfect similarity can be understood between God and creatures in respect of the nature_r of being, substance, or spirit, so too can there be some concepts that are, according to reason, prior to God in universality of predication. But this is not a priority of nature, nor a priority by reason of causality, as is *per se* clear, nor is it a priority by reason of independence or by reason of priority in subsisting, for every nature_r that is common to God and creatures, however much it is abstracted, is related to God in such a way that it cannot exist in the nature of things_r except in God himself or dependently on God, and therefore it cannot be prior by nature to God himself.

The fourth opinion is refuted.

14. And on the basis of what has been said against the preceding view, two other assuredly implausible opinions are easily ruled out. Let the fourth opinion be, then, that immaterial substance or being, insofar as this includes in itself only God and the intelligences, is the adequate object of this science. This opinion is usually attributed to the Commentator, *Phys.* I, final comment.[39] However, there he only says that the intelligences pertain *per se* to the object of this science, not that they are its adequate object. But this opinion can be urged by appeal to a survey or division of the sciences, for—setting aside the rational sciences, which are rather certain arts and treat of words or concepts, as well as the mathematical sciences, which do not treat of substance but only of quantity—among the sciences that deal with substances, philosophy deals with all substances that are generable and corruptible, and corporeal incorruptible substances, and substance composed from matter and immaterial form, of which sort is the human being, and also immaterial form itself, namely, the rational soul, and finally, the five grades or orders of material substances, namely, simple bodies, mixed inanimate bodies, merely vegetative bodies, merely sensitive bodies, and rational material substances, as well as all their properties. Therefore, nothing remains to be known among things_r except for immaterial substances. Therefore, they fully supply the adequate object of

The Commentator.

---

39. Averroes, *Aristotelis opera cum Averrois Commentariis*, vol. 4, fol. 47E–I (in comment 83).

Metaphy. tex. 4. ubi dicit, tot esse partes Philosophiae, quot substantiae. Unde, sicut duplex est substantia, materialis scilicet & immaterialis, ita duplex est scientia, quae de substantiis philosophatur: unde concludit, illam esse primam philosophiam, quae primam substantiam, id est immaterialem, contemplatur. Alterum testimonium est 6. Metaph. tex. 3. ubi Aristot. ait, si non essent substantiae secundum esse abstrahentes a materia, naturalem Philosophiam fore primam, neque praeter illam fore aliam scientiam necessariam: ergo tota ratio obiectiva huius scientiae, quae illam suo modo constituit, & ab aliis distinguit, est substantia immaterialis: haec ergo est adaequatum ob⟨7a⟩iectum eius. Secundo confirmatur, quia communiter distinguuntur Philosophia naturalis, Mathematica, & Metaphysica, ex abstractione obiectorum: nam Physica considerat res materia sensibili constantes: Mathematica abstrahit ab illa materia secundum rationem, non autem secundum esse, & ideo dicitur non abstrahere a materia intelligibili: Metaphysica vero abstrahit a materia, tam sensibili, quam ab intelligibili, non solum secundum rationem, sed etiam secundum esse: sed sola substantia immaterialis abstrahit a materia secundum esse: ergo illa est obiectum adaequatum huius scientiae.

15. Haec vero sententia, ut dixi, non habet maiorem probabilitatem, quam praecedens: unde nullus est gravis autor qui illam defendat: nam in toto discursu facto diminute procedit. Probat quidem recte ille discursus substantias immateriales maxime pertinere ad obiectum huius scientiae. Probat etiam, ex rebus subsistentibus in rerum natura nullas alias cadere per se & secundum proprias rationes sub obiectum huius scientiae praeter substantias immateriales, ut paulo inferius contra AEgidium dicemus. Non tamen probat, nec recte concludit, substantiam immaterialem ut sic esse obiectum adaequatum huius scientiae, quia in ipsa immateriali substantia considerari possunt aliae rationes, seu conceptus obiectivi universaliores, & communiores, de quibus secundum adaequatam rationem potest aliqua scien[6a]tia tradi, nam his rationibus respondent propria principia & proprietates: nulla autem alia scientia praeter Metaphysicam has rationes contemplatur: igitur

this science. And this entire survey can be confirmed, in the first place, by two testimonies from Aristotle. One is *Metaph.* IV, text 4, where he says that there are as many parts of philosophy as there are substances.[40] For this reason, just as substance is twofold, namely material and immaterial, so is the science that philosophizes about substance twofold. Hence he concludes that first philosophy is that which considers primary, that is, immaterial, substance. The other testimony is *Metaph.* VI, text 3, where Aristotle says that, if there were no substances that abstract from matter with respect to existence$_e$, natural philosophy would be first,[41] nor would any other science aside from it be necessary. Therefore, this science's entire objective character$_r$, which constitutes it in its own way and distinguishes it from others, is immaterial substance. Therefore, this is its adequate object. And the survey is confirmed, in the second place, because natural philosophy, mathematics, and metaphysics are commonly distinguished by appeal to their objects' abstraction. For physics considers things$_r$ composed from sensible matter. Mathematics abstracts from that matter according to reason, but not with respect to existence$_e$, and therefore is said not to abstract from intelligible matter. But metaphysics abstracts from both sensible and intelligible matter, not only according to reason, but also with respect to existence$_e$, and only immaterial substance abstracts from matter with respect to existence$_e$. Therefore, immaterial substance is the adequate object of this science.

15. As I've said, however, this opinion is not more probable than the last one. This is why there is no serious author who defends it, for in the whole of the mentioned survey it proceeds defectively. To be sure, that survey rightly proves that immaterial substances most especially pertain to the object of this science. It also proves that, among things$_r$ subsisting in reality, no others fall *per se* and according to their proper natures$_r$ under the object of this science aside from immaterial substances, as we shall soon say against Giles of Rome.[42] Nevertheless, it neither proves nor rightly concludes that immaterial substance as such is the adequate object of this science, for in immaterial substance itself one can consider other, more universal and common natures$_r$ or

Two testimonies of Aristotle in favor of this view are adduced.

40. Aristotle, *Metaph.* IV, ch. 2, 1004a2–3.
41. Aristotle, *Metaph.* VI, ch. 1, 1026a27–29.
42. See *DM* 1.2.2.

adaequatum Metaphysicae obiectum sub aliqua universaliori ratione designandum est. Quanvis ergo discursui, & inductioni factae concedamus, omnes res materiales secundum eas rationes, in quibus cum immaterialibus non conveniunt, sufficienter sciri per alias scientias a Metaphysica distinctas, non recte concluditur immaterialem substantiam ut sic esse obiectum huius scientiae adaequatum: quia adhuc supersunt rationes utrisque rebus seu substantiis communes, in quibus propriae demonstrationes fieri possunt.

16. Et ideo ex testimoniis etiam Aristotelis nihil in contrarium colligi potest: ipse enim, ut statim videbimus, saepe assignat huic scientiae universalius obiectum, quam sit substantia im⟨7b⟩materialis. In priori autem loco citato solum dicit, substantias materiales & immateriales secundum proprias rationes suas ad diversas scientias pertinere, & eam scientiam, quae substantias immateriales contemplatur, priorem esse natura & dignitate: utrumque autem verissimum est, etiam si substantia immaterialis ut sic non sit adaequatum obiectum talis scientiae, sed aliquo modo proprium, in quantum a sola hac scientia consideratur, tam secundum immediatam rationem suam, quam secundum omnem rationem superiorem in illa inclusam, atque etiam secundum omnem rationem inferiorem seu partem subiectivam, quae sub tali ratione considerari possit. In posteriori autem loco conditionalis illa (*Si non esset alia substantia superior praeter materiales, naturalis Philosophia esset prima, neque esset alia scientia necessaria*) verissima est, non quia substantia immaterialis sit adaequatum obiectum primae Philosophiae: sed quia, hac substantia ablata, auferretur tam proprium, quam adaequatum obiectum primae Philosophiae, quia non solum auferretur immaterialis substantia, sed etiam omnes rationes entis vel substantiae communes rebus immaterialibus & materialibus, &, data illa hypothesi, sicut nulla essent entia immaterialia, ita nullae etiam essent rationes entium abstrahentes a materia secundum esse, & ideo non esset necessaria alia scientia distincta. Ex quo etiam constat, secundam confirma-

objective concepts, of which, according to their adequate nature_r, some science can be handed down. For proper principles and properties correspond to these natures_r. But no other science aside from metaphysics considers these natures_r. Therefore, the adequate object of metaphysics must be designated under some more universal nature_r. Therefore, although we concede to the survey or induction that was made that all material things_r, according to those natures_r in respect of which they do not agree with immaterial things, are sufficiently known by other sciences distinct from metaphysics, it is not rightly concluded that immaterial substance as such is the adequate object of this science, since there still remain natures_r common to both kinds of thing_r or substance, regarding which proper demonstrations can be made.

16. And therefore, neither can anything to the contrary be inferred from the testimonies of Aristotle, for he himself, as we shall see presently, often assigns to this science an object that is more universal than immaterial substance. In the first of the cited texts, he only says that, with respect to their proper natures_r, material and immaterial substances pertain to diverse sciences, and that that science which considers immaterial substances is prior by nature and in dignity. And both of these claims are most true, even if immaterial substance as such is not the adequate object of this science, but in some way its proper object, inasmuch as it is considered only by this science, both according to its immediate nature_r and according to every superior nature_r that is included in it, and also according to every inferior nature_r or subjective part that can be considered under such a nature_r. In the second passage, that conditional proposition ("If there were no other higher substance aside from material ones, natural philosophy would be first, and no other science would be necessary") is most true, not because immaterial substance is the adequate object of first philosophy, but because, absent this kind of substance, both the proper and the adequate object of first philosophy would be taken away. For not only would immaterial substance be taken away, so also would all the natures_r of being or substance that are common to material and immaterial things_r. And given that hypothesis, just as there would be no immaterial beings, so also there would be no natures_r of beings that abstract from matter with

Quid sit abstrahere a materia secundum esse.

tionem non recte concludere, quia non solum substantia immaterialis ut sic, sed etiam omnis ratio entis abstractior vel superior illa, abstrahit a materia sensibili, & intelligibili secundum esse: nihil enim aliud est abstrahere a materia secundum esse, quam quod possit in rerum natura vere ac realiter existere absque materia: hoc autem verum est non tantum de substantia immateriali ut sic, sed etiam de quacunque ratione superiori, quae cum sufficienter existere possit in substantia ipsa immateriali, constat posse etiam in rebus existere sine materia.

Obiectio.

17. Dices, esto hoc verum sit, diverso tamen modo convenire hoc abstractionis genus substantiae immateriali ut sic, & rationibus superioribus: nam substantiae seu enti immateriali convenit per se, positive ac necessario, quia nec communis ratio immaterialis substantiae, neque aliquid sub illa contentum potest in materia existere, at vero rationes communiores, ut sunt ratio entis, substantiae, accidentis, & similes, solum permissive (ut ⟨8a⟩ sic dicam) & quasi per aliud, participant illam abstra[6b]ctionem: possunt enim existere absque materia ratione unius partis illis subiectae, non tamen eis repugnat esse in materia, ratione alterius partis.

Solutio.

Respondetur, hoc nihil obstare quominus rationes illae sub obiecto huius scientiae contineantur, sufficienterque illius abstractionem participent, quia hoc ipso quod rationes illae possunt sine materia existere, nequeunt ad inferiorem Philosophiam, vel scientiam pertinere, ut per se notum est. Neque etiam requirunt aliam scientiam praeter hanc: vel enim esset prior quam Metaphysica, quod non est asserendum, cum Metaphysica sit prima Philosophia, ut ex Aristotele vidimus, & cum nullum sit nobilius obiectum scibile quam sit substantia immaterialis ut Deum comprehendit: Vel esset scientia aliqua posterior, & inferior, & hoc etiam dici non potest, tum quia scientia, quae contemplatur substantias immateriales secundum proprias rationes, potest multo magis contemplari rationes alias, quae in eis sunt, licet sint communes aliis rebus inferioribus; tum etiam quia scientia humana, & naturalis vix potest attingere substantias immateriales, nisi incipiendo a rationibus quae communes sint illis substantiis, & aliis rebus. Quocirca ad obiectum huius scientiae satis est quod in conceptu obiectivo suo materiam non includat, neque sensibilem, neque intelligibilem. Quod

respect to existence$_e$,[43] and so no other distinct science would be necessary. And from this it is also clear that the second confirmation does not rightly draw its conclusion, for not only immaterial substance as such, but also every nature$_r$ of being more abstract or higher than it, abstracts from sensible and intelligible matter with respect to existence$_e$. For to abstract from matter with respect to existence$_e$ is nothing other than to be able to exist in the nature of things$_r$ truly and really without matter, and this is true not only of immaterial substance as such, but also of any superior nature$_r$, which, since it can sufficiently exist in immaterial substance itself, can clearly also exist in things$_r$ without matter.

17. You will say that, even if this is true, nevertheless, it is in different ways that this genus of abstraction agrees with immaterial substance as such and with superior natures$_r$. For it agrees *per se*, positively, and necessarily with immaterial substance or being, since neither the common nature$_r$ of immaterial substance nor something contained under it can exist in matter. However, more common natures$_r$, such as the nature$_r$ of being, the nature$_r$ of substance, the nature$_r$ of accident, and the like, only permissively (so to speak) and through something else, as it were, participate in that abstraction, for they can exist without matter by reason of one of the parts subjected to them, but it is not impossible for them to be in matter by reason of the other part. I reply that this by no means prevents those natures$_r$ from being contained under the object of this science, or from sufficiently participating in its abstraction, since, by virtue of the very fact that those natures$_r$ can exist without matter, they cannot pertain to an inferior philosophy or science, as is known$_n$ *per se*. Nor do they require another science aside from this one, for either it would be prior to metaphysics, which is not to be asserted, since metaphysics is first philosophy, as we see from Aristotle, and since there is no knowable object nobler than immaterial substance, insofar as this includes God; or it would be some posterior and inferior science, and this also cannot be said, both because the science that considers immaterial substances according to their proper natures$_r$ is much more capable of considering other natures$_r$ that are in them, even though they are common to other inferior things$_r$ as well, and also because human

---

43. The expression "that abstract from matter with respect to existence$_e$" qualifies "natures$_r$ of beings," and not just "beings."

vero includat etiam aliquid repugnans materiae, hoc potest pertinere ad maiorem quandam excellentiam vel proprietatem obiecti, non tamen adaequatum obiectum constituit. Atque ad hanc & praecedentem sententiam reduci potest ea, quam Avicenna attingit in principio suae Metaphysicae, eorum scilicet, qui dicebam primam vel primas rerum causas esse obiectum adaequatum huius scientiae. Quae opinio ita absolute sumpta per se improbabilis est: qualiter autem causarum cognitio ad hanc scientiam pertineat, dicetur sect. sequente.

Avicenna.

Quinta opinio proponitur, & confutatur.

18. Quinta opinio, quae a fortiori etiam manet ex dictis improbata, est omnino diversa a duabus praecedentibus, iuxta diversos sensus illius: dicit enim ens divisum in decem praedicamenta esse adaequatum obiectum huius scientiae: dupliciter autem potest concipi hoc ens iuxta diversas opiniones. Primo supponendo immateriales substantias finitas, & accidentia earum in praedicamentis collocari, ⟨8b⟩ & hoc modo obiectum erit ens finitum, solumque excludetur Deus a ratione obiecti, quanvis non omnino excludatur a consideratione huius scientiae, saltem quatenus causa prima est obiecti eius, & hoc modo defendit hanc opinionem Flandria 1. Metaph. q. 1. Alter sensus esse potest, si supponamus, iuxta aliorum opinionem, substantias omnes immateriales in nullo praedicamento collocari: hoc enim supposito, omnes illae ab huiusmodi obiecto excludentur, si statuamus illud esse solum ens in decem praedicamenta divisum. Quod hi autores sic ex Aristotele colligunt: nam, postquam ille in lib. 4. Metaphysicae ens constituit obiectum huius scientiae, statim illud in lib. 5. divisit in decem praedicamenta. Addunt etiam D. Thomae testimonium, qui interdum docet, Deum & intelligentias considera[7a]ri a Metaphysico ut principia & causas sui obiecti non ut partes eius. Afferunt etiam nonnullas coniecturas, quae partim, tractando tertiam opinionem, solutae sunt: illae enim rationes, quibus

Flandria.

Aristoteles.

D. Thom.

and natural science can hardly reach immaterial substances except by beginning with natures_r that are common to those substances and other things_r. For this reason, for the object of this science, it is enough that it not include matter, either sensible or intelligible, in its objective concept. But that it should also include something incompatible with matter—this can pertain to a certain greater excellence or property of the object, although it does not constitute the adequate object. And to this opinion and the preceding one can be reduced that opinion which Avicenna touches on at the beginning of his *Metaphysics*, namely, the opinion of those who said that the first cause, or first causes, of things_r are the adequate object of this science.[44] This opinion, taken absolutely in this way, is *per se* implausible. But how a cognition of causes pertains to this science will be discussed in the next section.

Avicenna.

The fifth opinion is expounded and refuted.

18. The fifth opinion, which is *a fortiori* disproved by the things that have been said, is, according to its diverse senses, altogether different from the two previous ones. For it states that being divided into the ten categories is the adequate object of this science. But this being can be conceived in two ways, in accordance with different opinions. First, by supposing that finite immaterial substances and their accidents are located in the categories. And in this way the object will be finite being, and only God will be excluded from the concept_r of the object, although he is not altogether excluded from the consideration of this science, at least insofar as he is the first cause of its object. And in this way does Dominic of Flanders defend the opinion, *Metaph.* I, q. 1.[45] There can be another sense, if we suppose, in accordance with the opinion of others, that no immaterial substances are located in a category, for on this supposition, all immaterial substances will be excluded from such an object if we decide that this object is only being divided into the ten categories. These authors infer this from Aristotle in the following way: because after he establishes being as the object

Dominic of Flanders.

Aristotle.

---

44. See Avicenna, *Liber de philosophia prima, sive scientia divina I–IV*, pp. 4–9.

45. Dominic of Flanders, *In Duodecim Libros Metaphysicae Aristotelis* (Coloniae Agrippinae: Typis Arnoldi Kempensis, 1621), pp. 11a–13b (q. 1, art. 8).

probari videbatur, non posse Deum esse principale obiectum huius scientiae, nisi sit adaequatum, usurpantur ab his autoribus ad probandum non posse ullo modo esse obiectum: sed illis iam responsum est. Alia autem earum pars solvetur examinando veram sententiam.

19. Haec itaque opinio in utroque sensu falsa est & improbabilis, & in primis omitto posteriorem sensum, qui supponit sententiam plane falsam, & ad rem praesentem valde impertinentem, scilicet, substantias immateriales finitas, & proprietates earum non collocari in praedicamentis: est enim hoc sine fundamento dictum, cum in rebus illis sint vera genera & differentiae, & convenientiae univocae cum inferioribus rebus, ut in sequentibus propriis locis ostendemus. Nihil etiam hoc refert ad obiectum scientiae assignandum, quid enim interest quod res sit, vel non sit in praedicamento, ut sub obiecto scientiae collocetur, necne? Deinde ob hanc etiam rationem sine[8] causa excluditur Deus ab hoc obiecto, iuxta priorem sensum, propterea quod in praedicamentis non collocetur: est enim id impertinens. Falsumque subinde est, hanc *Deus non* scientiam non agere de Deo ut de primario ac principali obiecto suo, *solum ut* sed tantum ut de principio extrinseco. Idemque de caeteris intelligenti- *causa obiecti* is dicendum est, ut aperte ⟨9a⟩ colligitur ex Aristotele 4. Metaphysicae *Metaphysicae,* tex. 7. ubi ait, Metaphysicam superare Philosophiam naturalem, quia *sed etiam ut* considerat primam substantiam, nimirum, ut praecipuum obiectum, *pars illius* nam ut extrinsecum principium etiam a Philosophia aliquo modo con- *praecipua* sideratur, ut ex 8. Physicorum patet. Praeterea, lib. 6. c. 1. dicit Aris- *ad hanc* toteles, quoniam praeter substantias naturales datur alia superior, dari *scientiam* etiam superiorem scientiam, quam sit Philosophia naturalis, quae de *pertinet.* illa consideret. Intelligit ergo considerare de illa ut de obiecto praecipuo. Idemque satis convincunt omnia argumenta in favorem tertiae &

---

8. Reading "sine" here with all of the early editions. Vivès reads "sina."

of this science in *Metaph.* IV,[46] he immediately divides it into the ten categories in book V.[47] They also add a testimony of St. Thomas, who on occasion teaches that God and the intelligences are considered by the metaphysician as principles and causes of her object, not as parts of it.[48] They also bring forth some conjectures, which have been refuted in part while dealing with the third opinion, for those arguments by which it seems to be proved that God cannot be the principal object of this science, unless he is its adequate object, are made use of by these authors to prove that God cannot in any way be an object. But to these we have already replied. The others will be refuted while examining the true view.

St. Thomas.

19. This opinion, then, is in both of its senses false and implausible, and first I dismiss the second sense, which assumes a view that is plainly false and very much irrelevant to the matter at hand, namely, that finite immaterial substances and their properties are not located in the categories. For this is asserted without foundation, since in those things$_r$ there are true genera and differences, as well as univocal agreements with inferior things$_r$, as we will show later in their proper places. Also, this matters not at all when it comes to assigning the object of a science, for, when it comes to locating a thing$_r$ under the object of a science, what difference does it make that it is or is not in a category? Moreover, for this same reason also God is excluded without cause from this object according to the first interpretation of this opinion, on the grounds that he is not located in the categories. For this is irrelevant. And hence it is false that this science does not deal with God as its primary and principal object, but only as an extrinsic principle. And the same must be said of the other intelligences, as is clearly gathered from Aristotle, *Metaph.* IV, text 7, where he says that metaphysics is superior to natural philosophy because it considers primary sub-

God pertains to metaphysics, not merely as the cause of its object, but also as this object's principal part.

---

46. Aristotle, *Metaph.* IV, ch. 1, 1003a21–22.

47. *Metaph.* V, ch. 7, 1017a22–30, does present Aristotle's division of being into the ten categories, but bk. V does not *begin* with this division, as the adverb "immediately" (*statim*) suggests. Suárez may have in mind *Metaph.* VI and VII instead, since Aristotle begins bk. VI (which is fairly short) by claiming that metaphysics deals with being *qua* being (1025b3–10) and then *opens* bk. VII with the division of being into the categories (1028a10–13).

48. See, for example, q. 5, art. 4, resp., of Aquinas's commentary on Boethius's *De Trinitate*, in: *Sancti Thomae de Aquino opera omnia* (Rome & Paris: Commissio Leonina & Les Éditions du Cerf, 1992), t. 50, pp. 153–54.

quartae opinionis adducta. Nam Deus est obiectum naturaliter scibile aliquo modo (idemque semper de caeteris intelligentiis dictum intelligatur) ergo potest cadere sub aliquam naturalem scientiam, non solum ut principium extrinsecum, sed etiam ut obiectum praecipuum: ergo haec dignitas pertinet ad hanc scientiam. Probatur consequentia, tum quia haec est omnium naturalium scientiarum prima & dignissima, quae non est sine causa hac excellentia privanda, tum etiam quia non potest altiori via & modo Deus naturaliter investigari, quam in hac scientia fiat. Unde confirmatur, quia haec scientia non solum considerat Deum sub praeciso respectu principii, sed postquam ad Deum pervenit, ipsumque sub dicta ratione principii invenit, eius naturam & attributa absolute inquirit, quantum potest naturali lumine, ut ex 12. libr. Metaphysicae constat: ergo absolute Deus cadit sub obiectum huius scientiae. Confirmatur secundo, quia haec scientia est perfectissima sapientia naturalis: ergo considerat de[9] rebus & causis primis & universalissimis, & de primis principiis generalissimis, quae Deum ipsum comprehendunt, ut: *Quodlibet est, vel non est,* & similibus: ergo necesse [7b] est ut sub obiecto suo Deum complectatur.

20. Nec Divus Thomas unquam oppositum docuit, sed solum hanc scientiam pervenire ad cognitionem Dei sub ratione principii: non tamen negat, eandem scientiam tractare de Deo ut de praecipuo obiecto, ut ex eisdem locis facile constare potest, & ex his quae infra dicemus. Quod autem Aristoteles diviserit ens in decem praedicamenta, nihil obstat, nam si illa divisio intelligatur de his quae directe tantum

---

9. Reading "de" here with all the early editions. Vivès reads "da."

stance[49]—as its special object, undoubtedly, since primary substance is also in some way considered as an extrinsic principle by philosophy, as is clear from *Phys.* VIII.[50] What's more, in *Metaph.* VI, ch. 1, Aristotle says that, since there is another, higher substance aside from natural substances, there will also be a science higher than natural philosophy that considers it.[51] He therefore understands that it will consider the higher substance as its special object. And all the arguments brought forth in support of the third and fourth opinions sufficiently prove the same thing. For God is an object that is naturally knowable in some way (and let the same always be understood to be asserted of the other intelligences). Therefore, he can fall under some natural science, not only as an extrinsic principle, but also as a special object. Therefore, this dignity pertains to this science. The consequence is proved, both because this is the first and most worthy of all the natural sciences, which is not to be deprived of this excellence without cause, and also because God cannot be naturally investigated in a way or by a method that is higher than that which is used in this science. And this is confirmed for the following reason: because this science not only considers God under the prescinded aspect of a principle, but, after it reaches God and discovers him under the mentioned aspect$_r$ of a principle, it inquires absolutely into his nature and attributes insofar as it can do so by the natural light, as is clear from *Metaph.* XII.[52] Therefore, God falls absolutely under the object of this science. This is confirmed, in the second place, because this science is the most perfect natural wisdom. Therefore, it considers things$_r$ and causes that are first and most universal, as well as the first most general principles, which apply to God himself, such as, "Any given thing is or is not," and the like. Therefore, it is necessary that God be contained under its object.

20. Nor does St. Thomas ever teach the opposite, but only that this science arrives at cognition of God under the aspect$_r$ of a principle. Yet he does not deny that the same science deals with God as with its foremost object, as can easily be established by appeal to the same pas-

---

49. Aristotle, *Metaph.* IV, ch. 3, 1005a33–b1.
50. See Aristotle, *Phys.* VIII, ch. 6.
51. Aristotle, *Metaph.* VI, ch. 1, 1026a10–32.
52. Aristotle, *Metaph.* XII, ch. 7, 1072b13–1073a13, and ch. 9.

in praedicamento collocantur, sic constat divisum eius non esse ens, prout est adaequatum obiectum huius scientiae, nam illud non solum complectitur entia, quae in praedi⟨9b⟩camentis directe collocantur, sed etiam alias rationes transcendentales & analogas, ut accidentis, formae, & similes, atque etiam differentias entium. Si autem sub ea divisione intelligantur ea quae ad illa capita revocantur, sic etiam Deus dici potest ad substantiam reduci: ens ergo, vel substantia, prout est huius scientiae obiectum, non excludit Deum aut intelligentias.

Proponitur sexta opinio, ferturque
de illa iudicium.

21. Sexta opinio, quae Buridani esse dicitur, est, obiectum adaequatum huius scientiae esse substantiam quatenus substantia est, id est, ut abstrahit a materiali & immateriali, finita & infinita. Quod enim hoc obiectum non possit esse contractius, probant satis ea quae contra tres proximas praecedentes opiniones dicta sunt. Quod autem neque abstractius esse possit, sumi potest ex Aristotele, 7. Metaphysicae, tex. 5. ubi post divisionem entis in substantiam & accidentia, cum dixisset solam substantiam esse simpliciter ens, ita concludit, *Quapropter nobis maxime & primum, & solum (ut ita dicam) de ente hoc pacto quidnam sit, speculandum est.* Quibus verbis solam substantiam videtur constituere huius doctrinae subiectum. Unde in lib. 12. in principio iterum sic scribit, *Speculatio de substantia est, siquidem substantiarum principia & causae quaeruntur.* Ex quibus locis ratio etiam desumitur, nam substantia & accidens ita comparantur, ut substantia propter se sit, accidens vero sit proprietas substantiae: ergo haec scientia tractat de substantia ut de subiecto, & de accidenti ut de proprietate subiecti: ergo subiectum adaequatum huius scientiae non abstractius constituendum est, quam sit substantia ut sic. Patet consequentia, quia nihil potest esse abstractius, nisi aliquid commune directe seu in recto ad substantiam & accidens: hoc autem assignandum non est, quia subiectum adaequa-

sages, and by appeal to the things that we shall say below. The fact that Aristotle divides being into the ten categories is no obstacle, for if that division is understood to concern only those things which are directly located in a category, in this way it is clear that the thing he divides is not being insofar as it is the adequate object of this science, for this includes not only beings that are placed directly in the categories, but also other transcendental and analogical concepts$_r$—such as those of accident, form, and the like—as well as the differences of beings. But if things that are reduced to those headings are understood under that division, in this way God too can be said to be reduced to substance. Therefore, being or substance, insofar as it is the object of this science, does not exclude God or the intelligences.

*The sixth opinion is set out, and
judgment is rendered on it.*

21. The sixth opinion, which is said to be Buridan's,[53] is that the adequate object of this science is substance insofar as it is substance, that is, insofar as it abstracts from material and immaterial, finite and infinite. For that this object cannot be more limited is sufficiently proved by the things that have been said against the last three opinions. But that it cannot be more abstract can be gathered from Aristotle, *Metaph.* VII, *Aristotle.* text 5, where, after dividing being into substance and accidents, and saying that only substance is without qualification a being, Aristotle concludes as follows: "For this reason, we must investigate chiefly and primarily and (so to speak) exclusively, regarding that which is in this way a being, what it is."[54] With these words he seems to establish substance alone as the subject of this doctrine. For this reason, in book XII, at the beginning, he again writes thus: "The inquiry is about substance, since the principles and causes of substances are being sought."[55] From these passages an argument is also derived, for substance and accident are so related that substance exists$_e$ on its own account, while an ac-

---

53. See Buridan's commentary on Aristotle's *Metaphysics*, bk. IV, q. 5, in: John Buridan, *In Metaphysicen Aristotelis Quaestiones argutissimae* (Parisiis: Impensis Iodici Badii Acensii, 1518), fols. 15vb–16va.

54. Aristotle, *Metaph.* VII, ch. 1, 1028b6–7.

55. Aristotle, *Metaph.* XII, ch. 1, 1069a18–19.

tum scientiae non est commune illi subiecto, de quo demonstrantur passiones, & passionibus ipsis, sed obiectum adaequatum est illud subiectum, de quo passiones demonstrantur, alias aeque caderent sub scientiam subiectum & proprietates quae de illo dicuntur: de ratione autem communi utrique (quae assignaretur ut obiectum adaequatum) nihil posset demonstrari, quod est valde absurdum. Igitur, cum substantia & accidens se habeant ut subiectum & proprietas, non est assignandum obiectum huius ⟨10a⟩ scientiae, quod sit abstractius utroque, & directe ac per se illis commune: erit ergo sola substantia ut sic, accidens enim esse non [8a] potest, ut per se notum est, sed considerabitur ab hac scientia ut adaequata affectio substantiae.

22. Potestque hoc exemplis declarari ac confirmari, nam scientia quae considerat de homine, & proprietates eius de illo demonstrat, non habet pro adaequato obiecto aliquid commune homini & proprietatibus eius, sed tantum ipsum hominem. Similiter Philosophia naturalis habet pro adaequato obiecto substantiam naturalem, de qua demonstrat proprietates, & non aliquid commune ipsi & proprietatibus eius. Ergo idem est in praesenti dicendum de substantia & accidenti ut sic. Quod si contra hanc sententiam obiicias, hanc scientiam considerare rationem entis ut sic, quae latius patet quam substantia, & de illa demonstrare proprietates latius etiam patentes, & communes accidentibus: responderi potest haec omnia esse analoga, & primo ac simpliciter cum substantia converti, & ideo perinde esse haec demonstrare de ente, ac de substantia: quia ens simpliciter dictum nihil aliud est, quam substantia, praesertim si verum est, enti ut sic non unum, sed plures conceptus obiectivos respondere.

cident is a property of substance. Therefore, this science deals with substance as its subject, and with accident as a property of its subject. Therefore, something more abstract than substance as such should not be established as the adequate subject of this science. The consequence is clear, since nothing can be more abstract except something common directly or *in recto* to substance and accident. But this is not to be designated the subject of this science, since the adequate subject of a science is not common to both that subject of which passions are demonstrated and the passions themselves; rather, the adequate object is that subject of which passions are demonstrated, otherwise the subject and the properties which are said of it would fall equally under the science, and of the nature$_r$ common to both (which would be designated the adequate object) nothing could be demonstrated, which is altogether absurd. Therefore, since substance and accident are related as subject and property, what is more abstract than either and is directly and *per se* common to both should not be assigned as the object of this science. Therefore, only substance as such will be the object of this science, for this object cannot be accident, as is known$_n$ *per se*; rather, accident will be considered by this science as an affection adequate to substance.

22. And this can be made clear and confirmed by examples, for the science that considers the human being and demonstrates her properties of her does not have something that is common to the human being and her properties as its adequate object, but only the human being herself. Likewise, natural philosophy has natural substance, of which it demonstrates properties, as its adequate object, and not something common to both natural substance and its properties. Therefore, the same should be said in the present case of substance and accident as such. But if you object against this opinion that this science considers the nature$_r$ of being as such, which extends further than substance, and demonstrates of it properties that also extend further and are common to accidents, it can be replied that all these things are analogical and are primarily and without qualification convertible with substance, and therefore, that to demonstrate these things of being and to demonstrate them of substance come to the same thing, for being, spoken of without qualification, is nothing other than substance, especially if it is true that not one objective concept, but several objective concepts, correspond to being as such.

23. Haec sententia habet nonnihil verisimilitudinis & apparentiae: & re vera qui negant conceptum obiectivum entis, satis consequenter hoc modo loquerentur, quia si nullus est communis conceptus obiectivus substantiae & accidenti, nihil reale abstractius concipitur, quod possit esse huius scientiae adaequatum obiectum. Nihilominus haec opinio simpliciter falsa est, & a mente Aristotelis aliena, quia, ut inferius ostendetur, simpliciter verius est dari conceptum obiectivum entis secundum rationem abstrahibilem a substantia & accidenti, circa quem per se & ut sic potest aliqua scientia versari, eius rationem & unitatem explicando, & nonnulla attributa de illo demonstrando; hoc autem fit in hac scientia, ut ex discursu eius constat, nec potest ad aliam pertinere, quia nulla est prior hac scientia, nullaque praeter illam considerat rationes entium quae abstrahunt a materia secundum esse: ratio autem obiectiva entis ut sic abstrahit a materia secundum esse, imo est prima & abstractissima omnium, ideoque ad primam scientiam seu Philosophiam pertinere debet. Non ergo potest ratio substantiae ut sic esse adaequata ratio obiecti huius ⟨10b⟩ scientiae, quia non continet sub se rationem entis ut sic, sed sub illa potius continetur: & sicut illa ratio est secundum conceptus & obiective diversa a ratione substantiae, & latius patet quam illa, ita universaliora, & abstractiora habet principia, & attributa, & ideo non potest commode ad illam revocari in ratione obiecti scibilis, quia, licet analoga sit, est tamen una & communis, non tantum in unitate vocis, sed etiam obiectivi conceptus, & abstractionis eius.

24. Ex quo etiam intelligitur, in discursu seu fundamento huius sententiae non recte procedi. Primo quidem, quia supponitur, accidens esse adaequatum attributum quod haec scientia de subiecto demonstrat: quod tamen falsum est, tum quia prius demonstrat de suo subiecto alia attributa universaliora, quam sit accidens ut sic: qualia sunt, *unum, verum, bonum,* tum etiam, quia nec de substantia ut sic demonstratur accidens ut adaequata passio: nam datur aliqua substantia, [8b] quae nullum potest habere accidens: unde, si illud esset adaequatum obiectum huius scientiae, quod est veluti subiectum adaequatum ac-

23. This opinion has some semblance of truth and plausibility, and really, those who deny the objective concept of being would speak in this way consistently enough, since if there is no objective concept common to substance and accident, no real and more abstract thing is conceived that could be the adequate object of this science. Nevertheless, this opinion is without qualification false and foreign to Aristotle's thought, for, as will be shown below,[56] it is without qualification truer that there is an objective concept of being in accordance with a notion_r abstractable from substance and accident, with which concept *per se* and as such some science can concern itself, explaining its nature_r and unity, and demonstrating some attributes of it. But that is done in this science, as is clear from a survey of it, nor can it pertain to another science, since there is no science prior to this one. And no science aside from this one considers the natures_r of beings which abstract from matter with respect to existence_e. And the objective character_r of being as such abstracts from matter with respect to existence_e; in fact, it is the first and most abstract of all natures_r and therefore must pertain to the first science or first philosophy. The nature_r of substance as such, therefore, cannot be the adequate nature_r of this science's object, since it does not contain under itself the nature_r of being as such, but is rather contained under it. And just as the latter nature_r is, according to concepts and objectively, diverse from the nature_r of substance, and extends further than it, so also does it have principles and attributes that are more universal and abstract. And therefore, as a knowable object, it cannot rightly be reduced to the nature_r of substance, since, even though it is analogical, it is nevertheless one and common, not only with a unity of name, but with the unity of both its objective concept and its abstraction.

24. From this it is also understood that the reasoning or foundation supporting this opinion does not proceed correctly. First, indeed, because it supposes that accident is an adequate attribute which this science demonstrates of its subject, which is, however, false, both because this science first demonstrates of its subject other attributes that are more universal than accident as such—of which sort are *one, true, good*—and also because accident is not demonstrated of substance as

---

56. See *DM* 2.2.

cidentis, non substantia ut sic, sed substantia finita, ponendum esset adaequatum obiectum huius scientiae, quod tamen falsum est, ut ostendimus. Unde e converso, si substantia ut sic ponitur adaequatum obiectum, assignandae sunt proprietates, quae de illa possint adaequate demonstrari, & conveniant omnibus substantiis: hae autem fortasse nullae sunt praeter eas quae enti ut ens est, communes sunt, ac per se primo conveniunt: nam substantia finita, & infinita, nullam communem & adaequatam passionem habere videntur praeter rationem subsistendi, & negationem inhaerendi quae illam intrinsece comitatur. Accedit, quod, licet omne accidens dicatur proprietas substantiae quatenus est affectio eius, non tamen semper ita est talis haec proprietas quae per se consequatur rationem substantiae, & ideo non semper consideratur ut proprietas, quae de substantia ut subiecto adaequato demonstretur, quia solum illae proprietates quae per se consequuntur rationem subiecti, hoc modo demonstrantur. Ac denique quanvis ipsum accidens aliquid substantiae sit, tamen in illo ut sic potest interdum aliquid veluti absolute considerari, & ideo aliquando potest aliqua scientia in solis accidentibus versari, ut Mathematica in quantitate.

Accidens esse potest subiectum alicuius scientiae.
25. Haec igitur scientia, quae univer⟨11a⟩salissima est, non considerat accidens solum ut proprietatem de substantia demonstrabilem, sed ut ipsum in se participat rationem & proprietates entis, quanvis illas semper participet in ordine ad substantiam. Quapropter non sunt similia exempla quae ibi adducuntur. Neque etiam verba Aristotelis repugnant his quae aliis locis ipse docuit ut statim videbimus: non enim intendit accidens excludere, sed substantiam ei praeferre, primumque ac principalem locum substantiae attribuere, ut D. Thomas recte exposuit, & ex eodem Aristotele sumitur, libr. 4. Metaph. tex. 20. & ex verbis eiusdem in praedicto loco lib. 7. si recte ponderentur: ait enim, *maxime & primum de substantia esse speculandum,* cum vero addit, *& solum,* subiungit illam limitationem (*ut ita dicam*) veluti significans il-

such as an adequate passion, since there is some substance that can have no accident. For this reason, if that which is the adequate subject of accident were the adequate object of this science, then not substance as such, but finite substance, would have to be supposed the adequate object of this science. This, however, is false, as we have shown.[57] For this reason, conversely, if substance as such is supposed the adequate object, then properties must be designated that can be adequately demonstrated of substance and agree with *all* substances. But these, perhaps, are none other than those which are common to, and *per se* and primarily agree with, being insofar as it is being, for finite and infinite substance seem to have no common and adequate passion other than subsistence and the negation of inherence, which intrinsically accompanies substance. Add to this the fact that, although every accident is called a property of substance inasmuch as it is an affection of it, nevertheless, this property is not always such as to follow *per se* the nature$_r$ of substance, and therefore, it is not always considered a property which is demonstrated of substance as its adequate subject, since only those properties which *per se* follow the nature$_r$ of a subject are demonstrated in this way. And finally, although accident itself is something belonging to substance, nevertheless, in accident as such something can sometimes be considered absolutely, as it were, and for this reason sometimes some science can concern itself with accidents alone, as mathematics concerns itself with quantity.

25. Therefore, this science, which is the most universal, does not consider accident only as a property demonstrable of substance, but insofar as it in itself participates in the nature$_r$ and properties of being, although it always participates in these in relation to substance. For this reason, the examples adduced in connection with this opinion are not similar.[58] Nor also do Aristotle's words conflict with the things that he himself teaches in other places, as we shall presently see, for he does not mean to exclude accident, but to give priority to substance over accident, and to attribute to substance the first and principal place, as

An accident can be the subject of some science.

57. See *DM* 1.1.18–20 above, where Suárez introduces and rejects the view that God forms no part of the subject of metaphysics.
58. See *DM* 1.1.22 above.

lud esse per exaggerationem dictum, quia simpliciter non de illa solum speculandum est: quodammodo tamen dici potest, illam solam esse contemplandam, quia illa solum propter se, accidentia vero fere tantum propter illam inquiruntur.

Diffinitur, quod sit Metaphysicae adaequatum obiectum.

26. Dicendum est ergo, ens in quantum ens reale esse obiectum adaequatum huius scientiae. Haec est sententia Aristotel. 4. Metaph. fere in principio, quam ibi D. Thom. Alensis, Scotus, Albert. Alex. Aphrod. & fere alii sequuntur, & Comment. ibi, & lib. 3. comm. 14. & lib. 12. comm. 1. [9a] Avicen. lib. 1. suae Metaph. c. 1. Soncin. 4. Metaphy. q. 10. AEgid. lib. 1. q. 5. & reliqui fere Scriptores. Probataque est haec assertio ex dictis hactenus contra reliquas sententias. Ostensum est enim, obiectum adaequatum huius scientiae debere comprehendere Deum, & alias substantias immateriales, non tamen solas illas. Item debere comprehendere non tantum substantias, sed etiam accidentia realia, non tamen entia rationis, & omnino per accidens: sed huiusmodi obiectum nullum aliud esse potest praeter ens ut sic: ergo illud est obiectum adaequatum.

St. Thomas rightly explains,[59] and as can be gathered from Aristotle himself in *Metaph.* IV, text 20,[60] and from his own words in the afore-mentioned place, book VII,[61] if they are carefully considered. For he says "we must investigate substance chiefly and primarily," and when he adds "exclusively," he subjoins this qualification: "so to speak," as if signifying that this is said by way of exaggeration, since, speaking without qualification, it is not only substance that must be investigated. In a certain way, however, it can be said that it alone is to be considered, since it alone is investigated on its own account, while accidents are investigated almost wholly on account of it.

What the adequate object of metaphysics is, is determined.

26. It must be said, therefore, that being insofar as it is real being is the adequate object of this science. This is the opinion of Aristotle in *Metaph.* IV, near the beginning,[62] which opinion St. Thomas,[63] Alexander of Hales,[64] John Duns Scotus,[65] Albert the Great,[66] Alexander of Aphrodisias,[67] and others follow there as well, and also the

Aristotle.
St. Thomas.
Alex. of Hales.
Scotus.
Albert.
Alex. of Aphrodisias.

59. Thomas Aquinas, *In duodecim libros metaphysicorum Aristotelis expositio*, p. 318 (bk. VII, lect. 1, n. 1262).

60. The reference is to *Metaph.* IV, ch. 5, 1009a30–38. But I suspect that "20" is a misprint and that "2" should be read instead. If so, the reference is to *Metaph.* IV, ch. 2, 1003a33–b22.

61. Aristotle, *Metaph.* VII, ch. 1, 1028b6–7.

62. Aristotle, *Metaph.* IV, ch. 1, 1003a21ff.

63. Thomas Aquinas, *In duodecim libros metaphysicorum Aristotelis expositio*, pp. 150–51 (bk. IV, lect. 1, ns. 529–31).

64. [Ps.-] Alexander of Hales [Alexander Bonini], *In duodecim Aristotelis Metaphysicae libros dilucidissima expositio* (Venetiis: apud Simonem Galignanum de Karera, 1572), fol. 75rb–75vb.

65. In his *Questions on the* Metaphysics *of Aristotle*, Scotus takes up the question of what the subject of metaphysics is, not in connection with *Metaph.* IV, but in connection with *Metaph.* I. See John Duns Scotus, *B. Ioannis Duns Scoti Opera Philosophica* (St. Bonaventure, N.Y.: The Franciscan Institute and St. Bonaventure University, 1997), 3:15–72. In his reference to Scotus here, therefore, Suárez likely has in mind a commentary on Aristotle's *Metaphysics* that is no longer thought to have been composed by Scotus, but by a disciple of his, Antonius Andreae (ca. 1280–ca. 1320/5). See John Duns Scotus, *Joannis Duns Scoti Doctoris Subtilis Ordinis Minorum Opera Omnia* (Parisiis: Apud Ludovicum Vivès, 1891), 5:648ff.

66. Albert the Great, *Metaphysica*, bk. IV, tract. 1, ch. 2, in: *Alberti Magni opera omnia*, vol. 16, pt. 1, pp. 162–63.

67. Alexander of Aphrodisias, *Commentaria in duodecim Aristotelis libros de Prima Philosophia* (Venetiis: Apud Hieronymum Scottum, 1561), pp. 81–82.

Dissolvitur
obiectio
contra
assertionem.

27. Sed, ut haec assertio amplius declaretur, occurrendum est obiectioni quae statim se se offert, nam ad constituendum aliquod obiectum scientiae necesse est ut habeat proprietates, quae de illo demonstrari possint, & principia ac causas per quas possint demonstrari: sed ens in quantum ens non potest habere ⟨11b⟩ huiusmodi proprietates, principia & causas: ergo. Maior constat, quia hoc est munus scientiae, demonstrare scilicet proprietates de subiecto suo, quas debet per causas demonstrare ut sit perfecta scientia, ut constat ex 1. Poster. Minor autem quoad priorem partem patet, quia ens in quantum ens ita abstractum includitur per se & essentialiter in omni ente, & in omni modo vel proprietate cuiuslibet entis: ergo non potest habere proprietatem ita adaequatam & propriam, quia subiectum non potest esse de essentia suae proprietatis. Quoad posteriorem autem partem probatur, quia ens in quantum ens complectitur Deum, qui est sine principio & sine causa: ergo ens in quantum ens non potest habere principia & causas, quia alioqui talia principia & causae deberent convenire omni enti, quia quod convenit superiori in quantum tale est, debet convenire omni contento sub illo. Et confirmatur, quia haec scientia est nobilissima: ergo debet habere obiectum nobilissimum: sed ens in quantum ens, est imperfectissimum obiectum, quia est communissimum, & in infimis etiam entibus includitur, multoque perfectius esset substantia, vel substantia spiritualis, vel Deus.

Commentator, there and in book III, comment 14, and in book XII, comment 1,[68] and Avicenna, in book I of his *Metaphysics*, ch. 1,[69] and Paul Soncinas, in *Metaph.* IV, q. 10,[70] and Giles of Rome, book I, q. 5,[71] and nearly all the remaining writers. And this claim is proved on the basis of what has been said thus far against the other opinions, for it has been shown that the adequate object of this science must include God and the other immaterial substances, but not only these. Further, that it must include not only substances, but also real accidents, though not beings of reason or beings that are altogether *per accidens*. But there can be no object of this sort other than being as such. Therefore, this is the adequate object.

The Commentator. Avicenna. Soncinas. Giles.

27. But in order to further explain this claim, an objection that immediately presents itself must be met, for, in order to establish some object of a science, it is necessary that it have properties which can be demonstrated of it, and also principles and causes through which they can be demonstrated. But being as being cannot have such properties, principles, and causes. Therefore. The major is clear, since this is the function of a science, namely, to demonstrate properties of its subject, properties which it must demonstrate through causes if it is to be a perfect science, as is clear from *Post. An.* I.[72] And the minor is clear with respect to its first part, since being as being, abstracted in this way, is included *per se* and essentially in every being and in every mode or property of any given being. Therefore, it cannot have a property thus adequate and proper, since a subject cannot belong to the essence of its property.[73] As regards the second part of the minor, moreover, this is proved because being as being includes God, who is without principle and without cause. Therefore, being as being cannot have principles

An objection against the assertion is refuted.

68. Averroes, *Aristotelis opera cum Averrois Commentariis*, vol. 8, fol. 64B–G, fol. 53C–F (commenting on *Metaph.* III, ch. 4, 999b24–1000a4), fol. 290H–L (commenting on *Metaph.* XII, ch. 1, 1069a18–19). I see no reference to the subject of metaphysics in the second of these three texts.

69. Avicenna, *Liber de philosophia prima, sive scientia divina I–IV*, pp. 4–9. See also pp. 12–13.

70. Paul Soncinas, *Pauli Soncinatis Ordinis Praedicatorum Quaestiones Metaphysicales acutissimae* (Lugdunum: apud Carolum Presnot, 1579), pp. 14b–16a.

71. Giles of Rome, *Metaphysicales Quaestiones Aureae Domini Aegidii Romani* (Venetiis: Apud Octavianum Scotum D. Ama Dei, 1552), fols. 2vb–3rb.

72. See Aristotle, *Post. An.* I, ch. 2, 71b9–12, and ch. 7, 75a39–75b2.

73. See *DM* 3.1.1.

28. Respondetur, negando priorem partem minoris, nam revera ens habet suas proprietates, si non re, saltem ratione distinctas, ut sunt unum, verum, bonum, quod ostendemus statim disput. tertia, ubi declarabimus an ens includatur intrinsece & per se in huiusmodi proprietatibus: & an illud principium, quod subiectum non sit de essentia proprietatis, limitandum sit, vel ad proprietates realiter distinctas, vel ad subiecta quae non dicunt rationes transcendentales, vel potius dicendum sit, has proprietates non esse omnino reales quantum ad id quod addunt supra ens, satisque esse quod ens non includatur in illis quantum ad id quod supra ens addunt, quod probabilius est, ut videbimus. Unde potest argumentum factum in contrarium retorqueri, quia plures proprietates quas demonstrat haec scientia, immediate non conveniunt nisi enti in quantum ens, & in eis explicandis magna ex parte versatur: ergo illud est adaequatum obiectum huius scientiae, quia illud est subiectum scientiae, de quo proprietates communiores[10] in scientia immediate & per se demonstrantur.

29. Ad posteriorem ⟨12a⟩ partem respondetur in primis duplicia principia posse in scientia requiri: quaedam dicuntur complexa seu composita, qualia sunt illa [9b] ex quibus demonstratio conficitur: alia sunt simplicia, quae significantur per terminos qui loco medii in demonstratione a priori sumuntur. Priora dicuntur principia cognitionis: posteriora autem, principia essendi. In hac ergo scientia non desunt principia complexa, imo, ut infra videbimus ad eam pertinet principia explicare, & confirmare, & primum omnium principiorum constituere,

---

10. Reading "communiores" here with all of the early editions. Vivès reads "communiore."

and causes, since otherwise such principles and causes would have to agree with every being, since what agrees with the superior insofar as it is such must agree with everything contained under it. And this is confirmed, because this science is the noblest. Therefore, it must have the noblest object. But being as being is the most imperfect object, since it is the most common, and is also included in the lowest beings, while substance, or spiritual substance, or God, would be much more perfect.

28. I reply by denying the first part of the minor, for being really *What* has its own properties that are distinct from it, if not in reality, then at *properties* least rationally, such as *one, true, good*, which is something that we will *metaphysics* soon show in the third disputation, where we shall make clear whether *of its object.* being is included intrinsically and *per se* in properties of this sort, and whether that principle—that a subject does not belong to the essence of its property—is to be restricted either to really distinct properties or to subjects that do not signify$_d$ transcendental concepts$_r$, or whether it should rather be said that these properties are not altogether real with respect to what they add to being, and that it is sufficient that being not be included in them with respect to what they add to being, which is more probable, as we shall see.[74] For this reason, the argument that was made can be turned to contrary effect, since several properties that this science demonstrates do not immediately agree with anything except being as being, and to a great extent it devotes itself to explaining these. Therefore, this is the adequate object of this science, since the subject of a science is that of which the more common properties are immediately and *per se* demonstrated in that science.

29. To the second part of the minor, I reply, first of all, that two *And what* types of principle can be required in a science. Certain principles are *principles* [*it* called complex or composite, and of this sort are those from which *uses*]. a demonstration is made. Other principles are simple, and these are signified by the middle terms in a demonstration *a priori*. The former are called principles of cognition, the latter principles of existence$_e$. In this science, then, complex principles are not lacking. In fact, as we shall see below, it pertains to this science to explain and confirm principles, and to establish the first of all principles, through which others

74. See *DM* 3.1.11.

per quod alia quodammodo demonstrentur. At vero principia incomplexa duplici modo intelligi possunt, primo quod sint verae causae secundum rem aliquo modo distinctae ab effectibus, vel proprietatibus quae per illas demonstrantur: & huiusmodi principia, vel causae non sunt simpliciter necessariae ad rationem obiecti, quia necessariae non sunt ad veras demonstrationes conficiendas, ut constat ex 1. Posteriorum. Deus enim est obiectum scibile, & de eo demonstrantur attributa, non solum a posteriori & ab effectibus, sed etiam a priori, unum ex alio colligendo, ut immortalitatem ex immaterialitate, & esse agens liberum, quia intelligens est. Alio modo dicitur principium seu causa id quod est ratio alterius secundum quod obiective concipiuntur, & distinguuntur: & hoc genus principii sufficit ut sit medium demonstrationis: nam sufficit ad reddendam veluti rationem formalem ob quam talis proprietas rei convenit. Quanvis ergo demus ens in quantum ens non habere causas proprie & in rigore sumptas priori modo: habet tamen rationem aliquam suarum proprietatum: & hoc modo etiam in Deo possunt huiusmodi rationes reperiri, nam ex Dei perfectione infinita reddimus causam cur unus tantum sit, & sic de aliis. Quocirca etiam hanc partem argumenti retorquere possumus, nam ens in quantum ens de se est obiectum scibile habens sufficientem rationem formalem, & principia sufficientia ut de eo demonstrentur proprietates: ergo circa illud versari potest aliqua scientia, quae non est alia praeter Metaphysicam. An vero ens in quantum ens habeat aliquo modo veras & reales causas, dicemus infra in disputatione de causis.

30. Ad confirmationem respondetur ex Divo Thoma, prima parte, quaestione quarta, articulo secundo ad tertium, quanvis ens ut praecise sumptum, & ratione distinctum, sit mi⟨12b⟩nus perfectum, quam gradus inferiores, qui includunt ipsum ens & aliquid aliud, tamen simpliciter ens seu ipsum esse secundum quod in re reperitur cum tanta perfectione quam habere potest in ratione essendi, esse quid perfectissimum. Scientia ergo haec quanvis uno modo consideret rationem entis praecisam & abstractam, non tamen in ea sistit, sed considerat omnes

can in a certain way be demonstrated.[75] But incomplex principles can be understood in two ways. In the first way, as true causes that are in some way really distinct from the effects or properties which are demonstrated by means of them. And principles or causes of this sort are not without qualification necessary to the nature_r of an object, since they are not necessary for constructing true demonstrations, as is clear from *Post. An.* I,[76] for God is a knowable object, and of him not only are attributes demonstrated *a posteriori* and from effects, but also *a priori*, by inferring one attribute from another, for example, immortality from immateriality, and being a free agent from being intelligent. In the second way, that is called a principle or cause which is the ground_r of another thing insofar as these are objectively conceived and distinguished. And this genus of principle is sufficient to serve as the middle term of a demonstration, since it suffices for the purposes of giving a formal ground_r, as it were, on account of which such a property agrees with the thing_r. Therefore, even if we grant that being as being does not have causes taken properly and rigorously in the first way, still, it has some ground_r of its properties. And in this way such grounds_r can also be found in God, for it is by appeal to God's infinite perfection that we give the cause of his being unique, and similarly regarding other attributes of his. For this reason, we can also turn this part of the argument to contrary effect, for being as being is of itself a knowable object having both a formal ground_r that suffices, and principles that suffice, for demonstrating properties of it. Therefore, some science can concern itself with it, this science being none other than metaphysics. But whether being as being in some way has true and real causes, we shall say below, in the disputation on causes.[77]

30. To the confirmation,[78] I reply, with St. Thomas, *ST* I, q. 4, art. 2, ad 3,[79] that although being, taken precisely and as distinguished by reason, is less perfect than inferior grades that include being itself and something else, nevertheless, without qualification being or existence_e

A demonstration can be made without causes that are really distinct from their effects.

St. Thomas.

<hr />

75. See *DM* 1.4.15–27.

76. See Cajetan, *In Posteriorum analeticorum libros* (Venetiis: Impensis nobilis viri Luceantonii de giunta florentini, die 9 Julii 1519), fols. 44vb–45rb.

77. See *DM* 12.

78. See the final sentence of *DM* 1.1.27.

79. Thomas Aquinas, *Sancti Thomae Aquinatis opera omnia* (Leonina), t. 4, p. 52b.

perfectiones essendi quas in re ipsa potest habere ens, saltem absque concretione ad materiam sensibilem, & ita includit perfectissima entia, a quibus maxima perfectio huius scientiae sumenda est, si in ordine ad res quas contemplatur, consideretur. Nam, si ad modum etiam speculandi, & scientiae subtilitatem, ac certitudinem inspiciamus, magna ex parte sumitur ex abstractione obiecti, a qua potest interdum habere maiorem perfectionem in ratione scibilis, quanvis fortasse in suo esse perfectius non sit.

itself, according as it is found in reality with as much perfection as it can have in respect of its being$_e$, is something most perfect. Therefore, although this science in one way considers the prescinded and abstracted nature$_r$ of being, nevertheless, it does not stop at that, but considers all the perfections of existence$_e$ that a being can have in reality, at least free of concretion in sensible matter, and thus it includes the most perfect beings, from which the greatest perfection of this science is derived, if it is considered in relation to the things$_r$ that it deals with. For, if we also consider the science's method of investigation, and its penetration and certitude, this is to a great degree derived from the abstraction of its object, from which abstraction it can sometimes have a greater perfection when viewed as a knowable [object], even if it is not, perhaps, more perfect in its being$_e$.

How the nature$_r$ of being is more perfect and less perfect than its inferiors.

SECTIO II.

UTRUM METAPHYSICA VERSETUR CIRCA RES OMNES SECUNDUM PROPRIAS RATIONES EARUM.

Ratio dubitandi pro utraque parte. 1. Ex dictis in praecedente Sectione, videtur inferri pertinere ad hanc scientiam de omni ente, & secundum omnem rationem entis disserere, quia scientia quae tractat de aliquo genere ut de obiecto adaequato, tractat etiam de omnibus speciebus sub illo contentis, ut de Philosophia constat. Et ratio est, quia alias non erit adaequatio inter tale obiectum & talem scientiam: plura enim sub uno extremo quam sub alio continebuntur: ergo pari ratione scientia, quae speculatur ens in quantum ens[11] ut adaequatum obiectum, omnia quae sub illo continentur, considerat. In contrarium vero est, quia, si hoc ita esset, supervacaneae essent omnes aliae scientiae, praesertim illae quae proprias rerum naturas inquirunt, quandoquidem totum hoc sola Metaphysica sufficienter praestaret.

Prima opinio. 2. Ad declarandam hanc difficultatem, & materiam in qua Metaphysica versatur, eiusque fines, ac terminos clarius & distinctius aperiendos, proposita nobis est praesens quaestio. In qua *Aegidius.* AEgid. 1. Metaph. q. 22. & in principio Poster. affirmat Metaphysicam de omnibus rebus & earum proprietatibus usque ad ultimas species seu differentias earum considerare. Quam sententiam defendit *Antonius* Antonius Mirandul. libr. 13. de *Mirand.* evers. singul. certam. Sect. 6. & ⟨13a⟩ 7. Qui consequenter affirmat caeteras scientias non esse a Metaphysica totaliter diversas, sed esse partes eius, seu potius omnes esse partes unius scientiae, communi autem usu distingui, & numerari ut plures propter commoditatem & usum earum in addiscendo, quia ita docentur, & addiscuntur ac si essent distinctae, idque propter rerum varietatem.

11. Reading "in quantum ens" here with C$_1$, C$_2$, G$_2$, M$_1$, M$_2$, M$_3$, P$_1$, P$_2$, S, V$_1$, V$_2$, V$_3$, and V$_4$. The following omit these words: M$_4$, V$_5$, and Vivès.

SECTION 2

WHETHER METAPHYSICS IS CONCERNED WITH ALL
THINGS$_R$ ACCORDING TO THEIR PROPER NATURES$_R$.

———

1. From what has been said in the preceding section, it seems to follow that it pertains to this science to treat of every being in accordance with every nature$_r$ of being, since a science that treats of some genus as its adequate object also treats of all the species contained under it, as is clear in the case of philosophy. And the reason is: because otherwise there will not be an adequation between such an object and such a science, for more things will be contained under the one extreme than under the other. Therefore, for the same reason, the science that investigates being as being as its adequate object considers all the things that are contained under it. But in favor of the contrary opinion is the fact that, if this were so, all the other sciences would be superfluous, especially those which inquire into the proper natures of things$_r$, since metaphysics on its own would sufficiently provide for all of this. *Reason for doubt on both sides.*

2. The present question is put forward to us for consideration in order to clear up this difficulty and in order to reveal more clearly and distinctly the matter with which metaphysics is concerned, as well as its limits and boundaries. Regarding this question, Giles of Rome, in *Metaph.* I, q. 22,[80] and at the beginning of *Post. An.,*[81] asserts that metaphysics considers all things$_r$ and their properties, as far as their ultimate species and their differences. Antonio Bernardi della Mirandola, *On the Abolition of the Duel,* book XIII, secs. 6 and 7,[82] defends this opinion. Consistently with this, he affirms that other sciences are not *The first opinion.* *Giles of Rome.* *Antonio Bernardi della Mirandola.*

---

80. Giles of Rome, *Metaphysicales Quaestiones Aureae Domini Aegidii Romani,* fols. 10vb–11va.

81. Perhaps: Giles of Rome, *Expositio super libros Posteriorum* (Venetiis: per Simonem de Luere, sumptibus domini Andree Torresani de Asula, 18 May 1500), fol. 4vb.

82. Antonio Bernardo Mirandulano, *Eversionis singularis certaminis libri XL* (Basileae: Henricum Pertri, 156–?), pp. 269–73.

73

Fundamen-
tum.[12] 3. Fundarique potest amplius haec sententia primo in autoritate Aristotel. 1. Metaphysic. cap. 2. dicente, Metaphysicam esse universalem scientiam, quia de omnibus rebus disputat. Et libr. 4. in principio ait hanc scientiam universaliter de ente disputare, & in fine text. 2. addit. *Aristotel.* *Sicut est unus sensus unius obiecti, & eorum quae sub ipso continentur, ita unam scientiam hanc speculari ens in quantum ens, & species eius, & species specierum,* & libr. 1. Posteriorum capit. 23. ait, eiusdem scientiae esse considerare totum & partes, id est genus & species, seu praedicata universalia & specialia, & lib. 6. Metaphy. capit. 1. dicit Metaphysicam quod quid est rerum omnium considerare.

4. Secundo argumentor in hunc modum, quia non repugnat dari unam scientiam, quae de rebus omnibus hoc modo consideret: ergo danda est huiusmodi scientia, tum quia non sunt distinguendae & multiplicandae scientiae sine causa, tum etiam quia intellectus acquirit scientias perfectiori modo quo potest: perfectius autem est rerum omnium scientiam unitam acquirere, quam divisam, ergo: sed huiusmodi scientia non potest esse alia nisi Metaphysica, quae dignissima & universalissima est omnium quae naturaliter [10b] esse possunt. Primum antecedens probatur, quia una est intelligendi facultas, quae circa ens in quantum ens hoc modo versatur, descendendo ad omnes proprias & specificas rationes entium: ergo potest acquirere unum scientiae habitum, quo facilis reddatur & prompta ad totum ens eodem modo cognoscendum: oportet enim ut iste habitus tam universalis sit, sicut est potentia ipsa, alioqui non potest perfecte illa potentia bene disponi ad omnes actus suos ad perfectam scientiam necessarios. Ut, verbi gratia, ad perfectam scientiam non satis est scire quid unumquodque sit, sed necesse est illud a caeteris distinguere, ut verbi gratia, hominem a le-

12. Reading "*Fundamentum*" here with C$_1$, C$_2$, G$_2$, M$_1$, M$_2$, M$_3$, M$_4$, P$_1$, P$_2$, S, V$_1$, V$_2$, V$_3$, and V$_4$. V$_5$ and Vivès place this word next to the following paragraph.

altogether diverse from metaphysics, but are parts of it—or rather, that all sciences are parts of a single science—and that by common usage they are distinguished and numbered as several for the sake of convenience and advantage in the learning of them, since in this way they are taught and learned as if they were distinct, and this on account of the variety of things_r.

3. This opinion can also be founded, first, on the authority of Aristotle, *Metaph.* I, ch. 2, when he says that metaphysics is the universal science because it treats of all things_r.[83] And in book IV, at the beginning, he says that this science treats universally of being,[84] and at the end of text 2 he adds: "just as there is one sense for one object and for those things which are contained under it, so also this single science investigates being as being, and its species, and the species of its species."[85] And in *Post. An.* I, ch. 23, he says that it belongs to the same science to consider a whole and its parts, that is, a genus and its species, or both universal and special predicates.[86] And in *Metaph.* VI, ch. 1, he says that metaphysics considers the what-it-is of all things_r.[87]

4. Second, I argue thus: because it is not absurd for there to be a single science that considers all things_r in this way. Therefore, there must be such a science, both because sciences ought not to be distinguished and multiplied without cause, and also because the intellect acquires sciences in the most perfect way it can, and it is more perfect to acquire a united science of all things_r than it is to acquire a divided science. Therefore. But a science of this sort cannot be any other than metaphysics, which is the most worthy and universal of all the sciences that can naturally exist_e. The first antecedent is proved because the faculty of understanding—which concerns itself with being as being in this way, by descending to all the proper and specific natures_r of beings—is one. Therefore, it can acquire a single habit of science by which it is made ready and quick to cognize the whole of being in the same way, for this habit must be as universal as the power itself, otherwise that power cannot be perfectly well-disposed to all those of its

Foundation.

Aristotle.

83. Aristotle, *Metaph.* I, ch. 2, 982a8–9 and 982a21–23.
84. Aristotle, *Metaph.* IV, ch. 1, 1003a21–26.
85. See Aristotle, *Metaph.* IV, ch. 2, 1003b19–22.
86. Aristotle, *Post. An.* I, ch. 28, 87a38–39.
87. Aristotle, *Metaph.* VI, ch. 1, 1025b7–16.

one & ab angelo, & sic de caeteris, quod tamen nulla scientia praestare
potest, nisi quae universaliter consideret omnia secundum proprias rationes eorum, per quas ⟨13b⟩ distinguuntur, quia non potest distinctio
inter extrema cognosci nisi cognitis ambobus secundum proprias rationes in quibus distinguuntur, ut per se notum est, & docet Aristotel. 3.
de anim. cap. 2.

5. Unde argumentor tertio, quia si quid obstaret huic universalitati
Metaphysicae, maxime, quod non omnes rationes entium abstrahant
a materia secundum esse: sed hoc non obstat, quia necessario dicendum est, Metaphysicam descendere ad considerandas plures rationes
seu quidditates entium quae sine materia esse non possunt. Distinguit
enim Metaphysica ens finitum in decem prima genera praedicamento-
rum: rursusque substantiam in materialem & immaterialem distinguit:
non posset enim ad immaterialem descendere nisi eam a materiali dis-
cerneret, neque etiam posset hoc praestare, nisi propriam rationem &
quidditatem substantiae materialis ut sic prius traderet: spectat ergo
hoc ad Metaphysicae munus: imo, cum nos immaterialia non nisi ad
modum privationum cognoscamus, prius oportet scire quid materialis
substantia seu materia sit, ut per carentiam eius immaterialem substantiam apprehendamus. Atque ita Aristotel. 7. & 8. Metaphysicae ex professo disputat de substantia materiali, & de principiis eius intrinsecis,
quae sunt materia, & forma.

acts which are necessary for perfect science—so that, for example, it is not enough for perfect science that one know what each thing is, but it is also necessary to distinguish each thing from the rest, as, for instance, the human being from the lion and from the angel, and likewise regarding the rest, which, however, no science can accomplish except for that which universally considers all things according to their proper natures$_r$, through which they are distinguished, since a distinction between extremes cannot be cognized unless both are cognized according to the proper natures$_r$ in respect of which they are distinguished, as is known$_n$ *per se*, and as Aristotle teaches in *De anima* III, ch. 2.[88]

5. For this reason, I argue, third: because if something stood in the way of this universality of metaphysics, it would be, above all, the fact that not all natures$_r$ of beings abstract from matter with respect to existence$_e$. But this is no obstacle, since it must necessarily be said that metaphysics descends in order to consider multiple natures$_r$ or quiddities of beings that cannot exist$_e$ without matter. For metaphysics distinguishes finite being into the ten primary genera of the categories, and in turn it distinguishes substance into material and immaterial, for it could not descend to immaterial substance unless it distinguished it from material substance, nor also could it accomplish this unless it first taught the proper nature$_r$ and quiddity of material substance as such. Therefore, this is part of the function of metaphysics. In fact, since we do not cognize immaterial things except by way of privations, one must first know what material substance or matter is, in order that we might apprehend immaterial substance through the absence of matter. And so

88. Aristotle opens this chapter of *De anima* by raising the question whether we perceive that we see (for example) by means of sight itself or by means of some other sense (425b12–13). He then offers two arguments against the latter option (425b13–17), the first of which (425b13–15) takes it to be a problematic consequence of this option that color (say) will be perceived both by sight and by that sense by which we perceive that we see. In his commentary on this chapter, Francisco de Toledo asserts that Simplicius, Themistius, and Philoponus take these two arguments to be conclusive, holding that Aristotle denies that the common sense perceives the external senses' proper sensibles. Toledo argues that this is a mistake, and that Aristotle later accepts the ostensibly problematic consequence because he attributes to the common sense the role of discriminating between (say) white and sweet: this, Toledo observes, is something that the common sense can do only if it perceives the external senses' proper sensibles. This consideration may be what Suárez has in mind here. See Francisco de Toledo, *Commentaria una cum quaestionibus in tres libros Aristotelis De Anima* (Compluti: Apud Ioannem Gratianum, 1577), fol. 176rb–vb.

6. Rursusque idem argumentum in accidentibus fieri potest, ut in qualitatibus, relationibus, & similibus. Sed peculiarem difficultatem inferunt quaedam prima genera, quae omnino materiam concernunt, ut sunt quantitas, habitus, & situs, quorum rationes proprias Metaphysica tradit, ut adaequatam divisionem entis, quae ad nullam aliam scientiam pertinere potest, conficiat. Quarto, vel supponimus Metaphysicam esse unum habitum simplicem, vel collectionem plurium quasi partialium. Si primum dicatur, necesse est consequenter dicere Metaphysicam praecise considerare rationem entis ut sic, & ad nullam particularem seu minus universalem rationem entis descendere, quod est plane falsum, ut constat ex dictis Sect. praeced. & patebit amplius ex dicendis. Sequela probatur, quia non potest idem habitus simplex attingere rationem communem secundum se ac praecisam, & ad particulares descendere, ut declarabimus Sect. sequenti. Si autem posterius dicamus, scilicet solum esse unum habitum collectione plurium partialium, nulla erit ma[11a]ior ratio conficiendi ⟨14a⟩ unam scientiam quae versetur circa ens ut sic, & circa quaedam entia, quam circa omnia in particulari: quia utrumque aeque commode fieri potest collectione plurium.

Praecedens opinio refutatur. Aristotelis in primis testimonio.

7. Haec vero sententia ab omnibus fere scriptoribus ut a mente Aristotelis, & a veritate aliena reiicitur: expresse enim ipse Aristoteles lib. 1. ca. 2. cum dixisset, *Sapientem scire omnia,* subdit, *ut possibile est scire non habentem singulariter eorum scientiam:* & infra hoc declarans dicit, *Eum qui habet universalem scientiam, quodammodo omnia scire, quae subiecta sunt universalibus.* Dicit autem, *quodammodo,* quia non scit illa simpliciter & secundum propria ex vi talis scientiae, sed quatenus sub universali continentur. Clarius libr. 4. in principio distinguit hanc scientiam a caeteris, *quia speculatur ens ut ens est,*[13] *& quae ei per se insunt: nullae autem caeterarum universaliter de ente prout ens est con-*

---

13. Reading *"est,"* here with all the early editions. Vivès omits this word.

it is that, in *Metaph*. VII and VIII, Aristotle *ex professo* treats of material substance and its intrinsic principles, which are matter and form.

6. And again, the same argument can be made regarding accidents, for instance, regarding qualities, relations, and the like. But a special difficulty presents itself regarding certain primary genera that are altogether conjoined with matter, such as quantity, habit, and situation, the proper natures$_r$ of which metaphysics teaches in order to produce an adequate division of being, which can pertain to no other science. Fourth, either we suppose that metaphysics is a single, simple habit, or we suppose that it is a collection of several partial habits, as it were. If the first is affirmed, then it must consequently be said that metaphysics precisely considers the nature$_r$ of being as such, and that it descends to no particular or less universal nature$_r$ of being, which is plainly false, as is clear from the things that have been said in the previous section, and as will be clearer from the things that are to be said later. The consequence is proved because the same simple habit cannot reach a nature$_r$ that is prescinded and common in itself while also descending to particular natures$_r$, as we shall make clear in the next section.[89] But if we affirm the second, namely, that it is only one habit through an assemblage of several partial habits, there is no greater reason to make it a single science concerned with being as such and *certain* beings than there is to make it a single science concerned with being as such and *all* beings in particular, for either can be made through an assemblage of several habits in an equally suitable way.

7. However, this opinion is rejected by almost all writers as foreign to both the truth and the thought of Aristotle, for in book I, ch. 2, after saying that "the wise human being knows all things," Aristotle himself expressly adds: "insofar as it is possible to know them without having science of them individually."[90] And later, while clarifying this, he says that "he who has universal science knows in a certain way all things that are subject to the universals."[91] And he says "in a certain way" because the person who has universal science does not, by virtue of such a science, know all things without qualification and in terms of what

89. See *DM* 1.3.3–5 and 1.3.13.
90. Aristotle, *Metaph*. I, ch. 2, 982a8–10.
91. Aristotle, *Metaph*. I, ch. 2, 982a21–23.

siderant, sed eius aliquam partem abscindentes quod ei accidit (id est convenit) *speculantur ut Mathematicae scientiae.* Distinguit ergo hanc scientiam a caeteris quae circa particularia entia versantur:[14] non ergo haec considerat partem illam entis quam aliae abscindunt. Idem repetit libr. 6. a principio, ubi tres speculativas scientias distinguit, Philosophiam, Mathematicam, & naturalem Theologiam, quas distinguit tum ex abstractione obiectorum, tum etiam consequenter ex rebus de quibus tractant, tum denique ex modo quo procedunt & demonstrant, ut infra declarabimus. Atque hanc divisionem scientiarum speculativarum secuti sunt omnes Aristotelis interpretes, & fere omnes Philosophi, ut latius traditur in primo Posteriorum.

Averroes.
D. Thomas.

8. Est ergo secunda sententia ab his omnibus recepta, Metaphysicam non considerare entia omnia secundum omnes gradus seu rationes speciales, prout a Philosopho, vel Mathematico considerantur. Unde Averr. 2. Physic. comment. 22. ait, Metaphysicam solum considerare materiam ut est quoddam ens: Physicam vero considerare illam ut est subiectum formae: & idem fere repetit 4. Metaphysi. comment. 9. & super alia loca Aristotelis citata. Et D. Thom. eisdem locis, & super Boetium de Trinitate in quaest. de divis. scient. art. 4. ad sextum. Ratio ⟨14b⟩ etiam contra priorem sententiam sic explicari potest, quia tribus modis intelligi potest hanc scientiam contemplari res omnes secundum proprias rationes earum. Primo ut non sola ipsa, sed aliae scientiae distinctae a Metaphysica de eis speculentur, ita tamen ut cognitio earum quae per alias scientias habetur, non sit vere ac proprie scientifica, sed alicuius ordinis inferioris: & solum appelletur scientia vulgari modo, quia habet aliquam certitudinem, vel ex sensu, vel ex aliqua fide humana: ad eum modum quo scientia subalternata, quando est sine subal-

Non sola
Metaphysica
est scientia.

14. Reading "versantur" here with C_1, C_2, G_2, M_1, M_2, M_3, P_1, P_2, S, V_1, V_2, V_3, and V_4. The following have "versatur": M_4, V_5, and Vivès.

is proper to them, but insofar as they are contained under a universal. More clearly, in *Metaph.* IV, at the beginning, he distinguishes this science from the others, "because it investigates being insofar as it is being and the things that are in it *per se*: and none of the other sciences considers being as being universally, but, separating off some part of being, they investigate what happens to belong to it"—that is, what agrees with it—"as the mathematical sciences do."[92] Aristotle, therefore, distinguishes this science from the others which concern themselves with particular beings. Therefore, this science does not consider that part of being which the others separate off. He says the same thing again in book VI, near the beginning, when he distinguishes the three speculative sciences, philosophy, mathematics, and natural theology, which he distinguishes both by appeal to the abstraction of their objects, and also, consequently, by appeal to the things_r of which they treat, and also, finally, by appeal to the way they proceed and demonstrate,[93] as we shall make clear below. And all of Aristotle's interpreters, as well as almost all philosophers, follow this division of the speculative sciences, as it is taught more fully in *Post. An.* I.[94]

8. It is, therefore, the second opinion that is accepted by all these thinkers, that is, that metaphysics does not consider all beings according to all special grades or natures_r, as they are considered by the philosopher or mathematician. For this reason, Averroes, in *Phys.* II, comment 22, says that metaphysics considers matter only insofar as it is a kind of being, but that physics considers it insofar as it is the subject of form.[95] And he says almost the same thing again in *Metaph.* IV, comment 9,[96] and in connection with the other passages in Aristotle

Averroes.
St. Thomas.

92. Aristotle, *Metaph.* IV, ch. 1, 1003a21–26.

93. Aristotle, *Metaph.* VI, ch. 1.

94. In Suárez's day *Post. An.* I, chs. 27–29, constituted a single chapter, which was commonly taken to be devoted to the distinction between, and a comparison of, the theoretical sciences. According to two common chapter divisions of the *Posterior Analytics* current in Suárez's day (one used by Francisco Toledo, the other by Giacomo Zabarella) this single chapter is labeled ch. 23. The division used by Cajetan, on the other hand, labels this chapter ch. 22. See Zabarella's commentary on this chapter, *Opera Logica* (Coloniae: Lazari Zetzneri, 1597), cols. 980–90.

95. In fact, Averroes makes these claims in *Phys.* II, comment 21. See Averroes, *Aristotelis opera cum Averrois Commentariis*, vol. 4, fol. 56C (mislabeled "56G").

96. In comment 9 on *Metaph.* IV, Averroes makes no such claim, so far as I can tell. But in *Metaph.* VI, comment 2, he does say that the physicist's consideration of matter is for the

ternante, scientia appellatur. Et hic modus declarandi hanc sententiam falsus est: primo enim supponit falsam sententiam de subalternatione aliarum scientiarum a Metaphysica, de qua paulo post dicemus. Secundo supponit, alias scientias seclusa Metaphysica non habere propriam evidentiam ex propriis principiis, quod est plane falsum. Sequela patet, quia si habent hanc evidentiam, nihil illis deest ad veram & propriam rationem scientiae: falso ergo negatur cognitionem earum esse vere & proprie scientificam. Minor ve[11b]ro patet, quia est contra experientiam, nam Mathematica habet propria principia evidentia, & per se nota, ex quibus per evidentes demonstrationes procedit, nec nititur aliquo testimonio, aut fide humana, ut per se notum est, sed evidentia cogente intellectum. Neque etiam nititur sensu, nam, per se loquendo, abstrahit a materia sensibili, & consequenter ab effectibus sensibilibus. Quod si aliquando utitur figuris visibilibus, solum est ut mens perfecte apprehendat terminos principiorum, ut possit intrinsecam eorum connexionem perspicere.

Aliae scientiae a Metaphysica ex propriis[15] *principiis habent omnimodam evidentiam.*

De Mathematica probatur.

15. Reading *"propriis"* here with C_1, C_2, G_2, M_1, M_2, M_3, M_4, P_1, P_2, S, V_1, V_2, V_3, and V_4. V_5 and Vivès have *"propris."*

that have been cited.[97] And St. Thomas says this in the same places,[98] and when treating of Boethius's *On the Trinity*, in the question on the division of the sciences, art. 4, ad 6.[99] An argument against the first opinion can also be set forth as follows, for the claim that this science considers all things$_r$ according to their proper natures$_r$ can be understood in three ways. First, as the claim that not only this science, but other sciences distinct from metaphysics, investigate them, but in such a way that the cognition of them that is had by means of the other sciences is not truly and properly scientific, but belongs to some inferior order, and is called science only in an everyday sense, since it has some certainty, either from sense-perception or from some sort of human faith, in the way a subalternate science is called a science in the absence of its subalternating science. And this way of explaining the opinion is false. For, first, it assumes a false view regarding the subalternation of the other sciences to metaphysics, of which we shall speak a little later.[100] Second, it assumes that in the absence of metaphysics other sciences do not have an evidence all their own derived from their proper principles, which is clearly false. The consequence is clear, since if they have this evidence, they are lacking in nothing required for the true and proper nature$_r$ of science. Therefore, it is falsely denied that their cognition is truly and properly scientific. And the minor is clear, since it is contrary to experience, for mathematics has evident proper principles that are known$_n$ *per se*, from which it proceeds by means of evident demonstrations, nor does it depend on some testimony or hu-

Metaphysics is not the only science.

Sciences other than metaphysics have every kind of evidence from their proper principles.

This is proved in the case of mathematics.

---

sake of form. See Averroes, *Aristotelis opera cum Averrois Commentariis*, vol. 8, fol. 146D. Costantino Esposito (Francisco Suárez, *Disputazioni metafisiche* I–III, 2nd ed., trans. Costantino Esposito [Firenze & Milano: Giunta Editore S.p.A. & Bompiani, 2017], 632n60) refers us here to *Metaph.* VII, comment 9, where Averroes claims that the physicist considers prime matter as a principle of change, while the metaphysician considers it insofar as it is a substance in potency. See Averroes, *Aristotelis opera cum Averrois Commentariis*, vol. 8, fols. 159M–160A.

97. Averroes, *Aristotelis opera cum Averrois Commentariis*, vol. 8, fol. 64E–G, fol. 146D, and vol. 1, part 2a, fols. 374B–381B.

98. Thomas Aquinas, *In duodecim libros metaphysicorum Aristotelis expositio*, pp. 12–13 (bk. I, lect. 2, n. 36), p. 151 (bk. IV, lect. 1, n. 532), p. 295 (bk. VI, lect. 1, n. 1147), and Thomas Aquinas, *In libros Posteriorum Analyticorum expositio*, bk. I, lect. 41, in: *Sancti Thomae de Aquino opera omnia* (Roma & Paris: Commissio Leonina & Vrin, 1989), t. 1*-2, pp. 15–56.

99. The reference is to q. 5, art. 4, ad 6 of Thomas Aquinas's commentary on the *De Trinitate* of Boethius. See Thomas Aquinas, *Sancti Thomae de Aquino opera omnia* (Leonina), t. 50, p. 156b.

100. See below, *DM* 1.5.46–52.

De Philosophia. 9. Philosophia vero quanvis non habeat tantam evidentiam sicut Mathematica, habet tamen sibi propriam & accommodatam: quia etiam non fundatur per se in humana autoritate: quod si in aliqua parte ita procedit, quoad illam non est scientia, sed mere fides & opinio, neque mutabit rationem suam, aut evidentior fiet propter connexionem cum Metaphysica: fundatur ergo per se in evidentia suorum principiorum, quam etiam non habet primario ex Metaphysica, sed ex habitu principiorum. Quod si quis dicat hanc evidentiam in Philosophia solum esse a posteriori & ab effectibus per sensum cognitis: respondetur fatendo in nobis magna quidem ex parte ita contingere propter imperfectionem nostram: ⟨15a⟩ tamen hoc nihil referre ad id de quo agimus: nam illae res physicae, quae tam imperfecte per Philosophiam cognoscuntur a nobis, non cognoscuntur perfectius aut evidentius per Metaphysicam. Quod si res aliquae naturales perfectiori modo cognosci possunt ab intellectu humano corpori coniuncto, ut re vera possunt, in his non[16] expectatur maior evidentia a Metaphysica, sed in ipsa Philosophia per se haberi potest: nam, licet incipiat per sensum, non tamen semper fundatur in illo, sed utitur illo ut ministro ad percipiendas per intellectum rerum naturas, quibus cognitis conficit demonstrationem a priori per principia per se & ex terminis evidentia intellectui, nec potest fingi alius modus quo per Metaphysicam habeatur perfectior scientia aut evidentior huiusmodi naturalium rerum: est ergo gratis confictus huiusmodi dicendi modus.

10. Aliter ergo intelligi potest quod Metaphysica tractet de omnibus entibus secundum omnes rationes eorum, scilicet, quia Metaphysica,

---

16. Reading "non" here with S, V$_1$, and V$_2$. The following omit "non": C$_1$, C$_2$, G$_2$, M$_1$, M$_2$, M$_3$, M$_4$, P$_1$, P$_2$, V$_3$, V$_4$, V$_5$, and Vivès.

man faith, as is known_n *per se*, but rather on an evidence that compels the intellect. Nor also does it depend on sense-perception, for, speaking *per se*, it abstracts from sensible matter and consequently from sensible effects. And if it sometimes makes use of visible figures, it is only in order that the mind might perfectly apprehend its principles' terms, so as to be able to perceive their intrinsic connection.

9. But philosophy, although it does not have as great an evidence as mathematics, nevertheless has an evidence that is proper and proportioned to it, since it too is not *per se* founded on human authority. But if in some part it proceeds in this way, with respect to that part it is not a science, but only faith and opinion, nor will it change its nature_r or become more evident on account of a connection with metaphysics. It is, therefore, *per se* founded on the evidence of its own principles, which evidence, moreover, it does not have primarily from metaphysics, but from the habit of principles. But if someone should say that this evidence in philosophy is only *a posteriori*, and from effects cognized by the senses, I reply by acknowledging that, in us, to a great extent indeed, it happens in this way, on account of our imperfection. However, this has nothing to do with the matter at hand, for those physical things_r which are so imperfectly cognized by us through philosophy are not cognized more perfectly or more evidently through metaphysics. And if some natural things_r can be cognized in a more perfect way by the human intellect when joined to the body, as they really can, then with respect to these, a greater evidence is not expected from metaphysics, but can be had *per se* in philosophy itself. For although it begins with the senses, nevertheless, it is not always founded on them, but it uses the senses as an instrument in order to perceive the natures of things_r through the intellect, and when these are cognized, it produces an *a priori* demonstration by means of principles that are *per se* evident to the intellect from their terms, nor can another way be imagined in which a more perfect or more evident science of such natural things_r is had through metaphysics. Therefore, such a way of speaking is fashioned pointlessly.

In the case of philosophy.

10. The claim that metaphysics deals with all beings according to all their natures_r can therefore be understood in another way, namely, because metaphysics, as the most universal science, embraces all these things by its power and efficacy, so to speak, even if each of the other,

tanquam scientia universalissima, omnia haec complectitur virtute &
efficacia sua (ut sic dicam) etiam si aliae scientiae particulares aliquam
partem huius obiecti possint attingere proprio & particulari modo,
quanvis scientifico & in suo genere perfecto. Itaque sicut causa particularis & universalis, sensus particularis, & universalis, distincti sunt,
& universalis attingit quidquid particularis, quanvis non e contrario, ita
existimari posset de hac scientia & de caeteris. Veruntamen hic etiam
modus nihil habet probabilitatis,[17] primo, quia, ut ex discursu proxime
facto sumi potest, nullus est possibilis naturalis modus demonstrandi
proprias res physicas, aut mathematicas, altior ac perfectior quam is
quem servant ipsae scientiae particulares: ergo superflue & sine causa
ponuntur scientiae particulares distinctae, si est una universalis quae
ad illa omnia descendat. Deinde, quia hae scientiae non sunt excog-
itandae ut facultates seu potentiae distinctae, sed ut habitus eiusdem
facultatis propriis illius actibus acquirendi, ut ad similes [12a] actus
eliciendos illam facilem reddant: ergo si Metaphysica specularetur res,
verbi gratia, naturales secundum proprias rationes earum ut sic, non
acquireretur per actus nobiliores quam sint ii quos Philosophia de eisdem rebus exercere posset, quia neque quoad eam partem haberent
maiorem evidentiam, neque altiora principia: ergo nulla esse posset
ratio multiplicandi hos ⟨15b⟩ habitus circa easdem res: neque potentia
indigeret habitu facilitante ad illos actus, circa quos iam haberet Phil-
osophicam scientiam.

11. Tertio itaque modo intelligi illa opinio potest confundendo
omnes scientias in unam Metaphysicam, ita ut intelligamus has denominationes vel conceptus Mathematicae, Philosophiae, ac Metaphysicae solum esse denominationes seu conceptus inadaequatos
eiusdem scientiae. Et hic sensus pertinet magis ad quaestionem de distinctione scientiarum, ut sunt quidam habitus, vel qualitates, quam ad
quaestionem de obiecto, quam modo tractamus. Certum est enim ex
dictis Metaphysicam secundum illum conceptum obiectivum qui huic
voci respondet, non versari circa res omnes in particulari, quia hoc ipso

---

17. Reading "probabilitatis" here with all of the early editions. Vivès reads "probabili-
taris."

particular sciences can reach some part of this object by a method that is particular and proper to it, though scientific and perfect in its own genus. Thus, just as a particular cause and a universal one, and a particular sense and a universal one, are distinct, and the universal reaches whatever the particular does, but not vice versa, so also could the same be thought regarding this science and the other ones. However, this way of understanding the claim has no plausibility, either—in the first place, because, as can be gathered from the argument just made, there is no possible natural way of demonstrating proper physical or mathematical things_r that is higher and more perfect than that which the same particular sciences employ. Therefore, distinct particular sciences are posited superfluously and without cause if there is a single universal science that descends to all those things. In the second place, because these sciences are not to be conceived as distinct faculties or powers, but rather as habits of the same faculty, to be acquired by its proper acts, in order that they might make it ready to elicit similar acts. Therefore if, for example, metaphysics investigated natural things_r according to their proper natures_r as such, it would not be acquired by acts that are nobler than those which philosophy could exercise regarding the same things_r, since they would have, with respect to that part, neither a greater evidence nor higher principles. Therefore, there could be no reason to multiply these habits that are about the same things_r, nor would a power need a habit that makes it ready for those acts for which it already has philosophical science.

11. This opinion, then, can be understood in a third way, namely, by combining all the sciences into a single metaphysics, in such a way that we understand these denominations or concepts of mathematics, philosophy, and metaphysics to be only denominations or inadequate concepts of the same science. And this interpretation bears on the question regarding the distinction of the sciences insofar as they are certain habits or qualities more than it does on the question we are now dealing with, regarding the object. For it is certain from what has been said that metaphysics, according to that objective concept which corresponds to this name, does not concern itself with all things_r in particular, since, by the very fact that the mind is understood to concern itself with natural

quod mens versari intelligitur circa res naturales, vel Mathematicas ut sic, iam intelligitur transilire terminos Metaphysicae, & Philosophia, vel Mathematica uti. Sicut quanvis memoria non distinguatur ab intellectu re ipsa, sed ratione formali obiectiva, non dicetur proprie & formaliter versari circa res ut praesentes, sed solum circa praeteritas ut sic. Addo deinde (quidquid sit de illis tribus scientiis, Philosophia, Mathematica, & Metaphysica quo modo unaquaeque earum per se una sit, quod paulo post breviter attingemus) per se se incredibile esse eas omnes vere ac proprie unicam scientiam humanam esse. Primo quidem quia hoc per se notum visum est omnibus fere Philosophis. Secundo, quia agunt de rebus omnino diversis, & fere nullam inter se habent connexionem quantum ad ea quae sunt propria uniuscuiusque. Tertio, quia multum differunt in modo procedendi: nam Philosophus vix recedit a sensu: Metaphysicus vero procedit per principia universalissima & maxime abstracta, Mathematicus vero medio quodam modo procedit: qui modi procedendi oriuntur ex illa vulgari triplici abstractione a materia. Quod si hae tres scientiae distinctae sunt, non minus distinguitur Metaphysica ab aliis duabus quam aliae duae inter se, quia res a materia separatae, de quibus tractat, non minus imo magis distant a caeteris quam reliqua omnia inter se, tum in perfectione entis, tum in abstractione, tum etiam in modo ratiocinandi, & difficultate ac subtilitate ipsiusmet scientiae: cum ergo Mathematica distincta a Philosophia sit omnium consensu ob diversam abstractionem, modumque procedendi omnino ⟨16a⟩ diversum, idem maiori ratione censendum est de Metaphysica respectu illarum: ergo non versatur circa res omnes quas aliae scientiae considerant secundum proprias rationes quibus ab eis considerantur.

things$_r$, or mathematical ones, it is, as such, already understood to go beyond the boundaries of metaphysics, and to employ philosophy or mathematics. In the same way, although memory is not distinguished from intellect in reality, but rather by its objective formal character$_r$, it will not properly and formally be said to concern itself with things$_r$ as present, but only with things past, as such. I add, in the next place, that (whatever might be the case regarding those three sciences, philosophy, mathematics, and metaphysics, when it comes to the question of how each of them is *per se* one, which issue we shall briefly touch on a little later[101]) it is *per se* unbelievable that they are all truly and properly a single human science. First, indeed, because the opposite has seemed to almost all philosophers to be known$_n$ *per se*. Second, because they deal with things$_r$ that are altogether diverse, and they have almost no connection with each other when it comes to those things which are proper to each. Third, because they differ greatly in their manner of proceeding, for the philosopher hardly withdraws from sense, but the metaphysician proceeds by means of the most universal and most abstract principles, while the mathematician proceeds in a kind of middle way—which ways of proceeding arise from that well-known threefold abstraction from matter. But if these three sciences are distinct, metaphysics is no less distinguished from the other two sciences than these two are from each other, because things$_r$ separate from matter, of which it treats, are no less—nay, are in fact more—distant from the rest than the rest are from each other, whether in respect of the perfection of being, in respect of abstraction, or in respect of the same science's mode of reasoning and difficulty and subtlety. Since, therefore, mathematics is distinct from philosophy by common consent, on account of their diverse abstractions and altogether diverse ways of proceeding, the same must, with greater reason, be thought about metaphysics in relation to them. Therefore, as regards all the things$_r$ that the other sciences consider, metaphysics does not consider them according to those proper natures$_r$ in accordance with which they are considered by the other sciences.

101. See below, *DM* 1.3.

Opinio tenenda, & pro ea
prima conclusio.

12. Haec posterior sententia vera est, & tenenda, quam ut distinctius proponamus & [12b] confirmemus, & ut clarius constet de quibus rebus nobis in discursu huius doctrinae tractandum sit, nonnullae propositiones subiiciendae sunt. Dico ergo primo, quanvis haec scientia consideret ens in quantum ens, & proprietates quae ipsi ut sic per se conveniunt, non tamen sistit in praecisa & quasi actuali ratione entis ut sic, sed ad aliqua inferiora consideranda descendit secundum proprias eorum rationes. Tota haec assertio constat ex dictis in praecedente sectione: & quoad priorem partem de ente in quantum ens confirmari potest ex adductis inter referendam secundam sententiam. Quoad alteram vero partem confirmari potest ex dictis circa primam sententiam: & statim amplius declarabitur. Solum est animadvertendum, quod Dialectici dicunt, genus considerari posse vel ut totum actuale, vel ut potentiale, seu (quod idem est) considerari posse ut abstractum abstractione praecisiva, id est, secundum id tantum quod in sua ratione formali actu includit in suo conceptu obiectivo sic praeciso, vel abstractione totali, ut abstrahitur tanquam totum potentiale includens inferiora in potentia: hoc (inquam) quod de genere dicitur, posse suo modo applicari ad ens in quantum ens: nam & habet suam rationem formalem quasi actualem, quae praecisa secundum rationem considerari potest, & inferiora habet, quae suo modo in potentia includit secundum rationem. Quando ergo ratio aliqua communis assignatur ut adaequatum obiectum alicuius potentiae, vel habitus, non semper assignatur ut est quid actuale, & omnino praecisum abstractione formali, sed ut includit aliquo modo inferiora: sicut ens naturale vel substantia materialis dicitur esse subiectum adaequatum Philosophiae, non tantum secundum praecisam rationem substantiae materialis ut sic, sed etiam secundum proprias rationes inferiorum substantiarum materialium, corruptibilium vel incorruptibilium, &c. Sic ergo, cum Metaphysica dicitur versari circa ens in quantum ens, non est ⟨16b⟩ existimandum sumi ens omnino ac formaliter praecisum, ita ut excludantur omnia inferiora secundum proprias rationes, quia haec scientia non sistit in

*The opinion to be held, and a first
conclusion in support of it.*

12. The second opinion is true and is to be affirmed, and in order to
set it forth more distinctly and confirm it, and more clearly establish
what things_r are to be dealt with by us in the course of this doctrine,
some propositions must be laid down. I say, therefore, first, that although this science considers being as being and the properties that *per
se* agree with it as such, nevertheless, it does not stop at the prescinded
and (as it were) actual nature_r of being as such, but rather it descends
in order to consider certain inferiors according to their proper natures_r.
This entire assertion is established by the things that have been said in
the preceding section. And with respect to its first part, concerning
being as being, it can be confirmed by appeal to the things that have
been adduced in reporting the second opinion. With respect to the
other part, it can be confirmed by appeal to the things that have been
said about the first opinion, and it will be further explained presently.
One must only note what the dialecticians say, that a genus can be
considered either as an actual whole or as a potential whole, or (and
this amounts to the same thing) that it can be considered either as
abstracted by a precisive abstraction—that is, according to that alone
which, in respect of its formal character_r, it actually includes in its objective concept thus prescinded—or as abstracted by a total abstraction,
insofar as it is abstracted as a potential whole that potentially includes
its inferiors.[102] I maintain that this, which is said of a genus, can in its
own way be applied to being as being, for it too has its own (as it were)
actual formal character_r, which can be considered prescinded according to reason, and it has inferiors which in its own way it potentially includes according to reason. When, therefore, some common nature_r is
assigned as the adequate object of some power or habit, it is not always
assigned insofar as it is something actual and altogether prescinded by
a formal abstraction, but insofar as it in some way includes inferiors,

*Being can
be conceived
both as an
actual whole
and as a
potential
whole.*

102. For an explanation of this distinction between two ways of considering a genus,
see *DM* 15.11.16. For an English translation of this text, see: Francis Suárez, *On the Formal
Cause of Substance: Metaphysical Disputation XV*, trans. J. Kronen and J. Reedy (Milwaukee:
Marquette University Press, 2000), 185–87.

sola consideratione illius rationis formalis actualis: sumenda ergo est illa ratio prout includit aliquo modo inferiora.

Quas rationes in particulari speculetur Metaphysica, quas non item. Aristotel.

13. Dico secundo. Haec scientia non considerat omnes proprias rationes seu quidditates entium in particulari, seu ut talia sunt, sed solum eas quae sub propria eius abstractione continentur, vel quatenus sunt cum illa necessario coniunctae. Haec est mens Aristotelis, & autorum quos citavi in secunda sententia, & aliorum qui de hac scientia scripserunt. Qui omnes distinguunt triplicem abstractionem in scientiis speculativis, & realibus, quales sunt tres supra numeratae, Physica, Mathematica, & Metaphysica: nam de aliis scientiis vel moralibus, vel rationalibus,[18] vel practicis alia est ratio, & modus considerandi unitatem obiecti, vel ex fine scientiae, vel ex modo procedendi, de quo

Scientiae speculativae reales qualiter in abstractione conveniant, differant qualiter.

alias. Illae ergo tres scientiae in aliqua abstractione conveniunt, nam omnes considerant de rebus in universali: differunt tamen in abstractione quasi formali & praecisiva a materia, nam Philosophia quanvis abstrahat a singularibus, non tamen a materia sensibili, id est, subiecta ac[13a]cidentibus sensibilibus, sed ea potius utitur in suo ratiocinandi modo. Mathematica vero abstrahit quidem secundum rationem a materia sensibili: non autem ab intelligibili, quia quantitas, quantumvis abstrahatur, non potest concipi nisi ut res corporea & materialis. Metaphysica vero dicitur abstrahere a materia sensibili & intelligibili, & non solum secundum rationem, sed etiam secundum esse, quia rationes entis quas considerat, in re ipsa inveniuntur sine materia: & ideo in proprio & obiectivo conceptu suo per se non includit materiam. De qua triplici abstractione, & partitione harum trium scientiarum per has abstractiones ex professo disseritur in libris Posteriorum. Nunc nobis

18. Reading "vel rationalibus" here with all the older editions that I've consulted. Vivès omits these words.

just as natural being or material substance is said to be the adequate subject of philosophy, not only according to the prescinded nature_r of material substance as such, but also according to the proper natures_r of inferior material substances, either corruptible or incorruptible, etc. In this way, therefore, when metaphysics is said to deal with being as being, it must not be thought that being is taken as prescinded completely and formally, in such a way that all inferiors according to their proper natures_r are excluded, since this science does not stop at just a consideration of that actual formal character_r. That nature_r, therefore, is to be taken insofar as it in some way includes inferiors.

What must be understood when metaphysics is said to consider being insofar as it is being.

13. I say, second: this science does not consider all the proper natures_r or quiddities of beings in particular, or insofar as they are such, but only those which are contained under its proper abstraction, or insofar as they are necessarily connected to that abstraction. This is the view of Aristotle, and of those authors whom I cited in connection with the second opinion, and it is also the view of others who have written about this science. All of these thinkers distinguish a threefold abstraction in real and speculative sciences, and of this sort are the three sciences mentioned above, that is, physics, mathematics, and metaphysics. For when it comes to the other sciences, whether moral, rational, or practical, there is another basis_r for, and way of, conceiving the unity of such a science's object, whether it is by appeal to the science's end or to its manner of proceeding, which issue is discussed elsewhere. The former three sciences, therefore, agree in some abstraction, for they all consider things_r in a universal way, but they differ with respect to their formal and precisive abstraction from matter, as it were. For philosophy, although it abstracts from singulars, still does not abstract from sensible matter, that is, from matter that is the subject of sensible accidents, but rather it makes use of it in its mode of reasoning. Mathematics, on the other hand, does indeed abstract from sensible matter according to reason, but not from intelligible matter, since quantity, however much it is abstracted, cannot be conceived except as a corporeal and material thing_r. Moreover, metaphysics is said to abstract from sensible and intelligible matter, and not only according to reason, but also with respect to existence_e, since the natures_r of being that it considers are in reality found without matter, and therefore it

Which natures_r metaphysics considers particularly, and which it does not. Aristotle.

How the real speculative sciences agree with respect to their abstractions, and how they differ with respect to them.

Modus distinguendi scientias per diversam abstractionem a materia quam aptus.

sufficiat hactenus non esse inventam aptiorem rationem distinguendi has scientias, & aliunde hanc videri satis convenientem: nam, cum hae scientiae sint de rebus ipsis, sintque maxime speculativae, ideoque abstractione utantur, ut constituant obiectum scibile, de quo possint demonstrationes fieri: recte ex diverso modo abstractionis intelligitur variari obiectum scibile ut sic: & ideo so⟨17a⟩let dici haec abstractio, quatenus in ipso obiecto fundamentum habet, ratio formalis sub qua talis obiecti in ratione scibilis. Item, quia res eo sunt perfectius intelligibiles, quo magis abstrahunt a materia: & similiter cognitio quo est de obiecto immaterialiori, & consequenter abstractiori, eo est certior: & ideo ex diverso gradu abstractionis seu immaterialitatis, recte consideratur varietas obiectorum scibilium, & scientiarum. Ex hac autem recepta doctrina facile intelligitur, & probatur assertio posita, quia scientia non transgreditur limites sui obiecti formalis seu rationis formalis sub qua sui obiecti[19]: considerat autem quidquid sub illa continetur: ergo haec scientia considerat omnia entia seu rationes entium quae sub praedicta abstractione continentur: & ultra non progreditur, nam caetera ad Physicam, vel Mathematicam spectant.

Rationem substantiae ut sic, & accidentis, ut sic considerat Metaphysica. D. Thomas. Quid sit abstrahere a materia secundum esse.

14. Ut hoc autem clarius intelligatur, dico tertio. Haec scientia sub ratione entis considerat rationem substantiae ut sic, & rationem etiam accidentis. De hac assertione nullus dubitat: & patet facile ex principio posito, quia illae duae rationes abstrahunt a materia secundum esse: ut enim supra diximus, & recte notavit D. Thom. in prolog. Metaphysicae, non solum dicuntur abstrahere a materia secundum esse illae rationes entium quae nunquam sunt in materia, sed etiam illae quae possunt esse in rebus sine materia, quia hoc satis est, ut in sua ratione formali materiam non includant, neque illam per se requirant. Accedit

19. Reading "obiecti" here with C_1, C_2, G_2, M_1, M_2, M_3, M_4, P_1, P_2, S, V_1, V_2, V_3, V_4, and V_5. Vivès reads "subiecti."

does not *per se* include matter in its proper and objective concept. This threefold abstraction, as well as the division of these three sciences by appeal to these abstractions, is *ex professo* discussed in the books of the *Post. An.*[103] For now, let it suffice for us that so far no more suitable basis_r for distinguishing these sciences has been found, and that, in any case, this one seems fitting enough. For, since these sciences are about things_r themselves, and are most of all speculative, and therefore employ abstraction in order to constitute a knowable object about which demonstrations can be made, the knowable object as such is rightly understood to be varied in accordance with diverse modes of abstraction. And therefore, this abstraction, insofar as it has a foundation in the object itself, is usually called the "formal aspect_r under which" of such an object in its character_r as a knowable [object]. Further, since things_r are more perfectly intelligible the more they abstract from matter, and similarly, cognition is more certain to the extent that it is of a more immaterial, and consequently more abstract, object, it follows that the variety of both knowable objects and sciences is rightly conceived in terms of diverse grades of abstraction or immateriality. But on the basis of this received doctrine the assertion set forth is easily understood and proved, since a science does not transgress the limits of its formal object, or the limits of its object's "formal aspect_r under which," but it considers whatever is contained under it. Therefore, this science considers all beings or natures_r of beings that are contained under the aforementioned abstraction, and it does not go any further, for the rest are the concern of physics or mathematics.

    14. In order that this might be understood more clearly, I say, third: this science considers, under the nature_r of being, the nature_r of substance as such and also the nature_r of accident. No one doubts this claim, and it is easily seen from the principle laid down, since these two natures_r abstract from matter with respect to existence_e. For as we said above, and as St. Thomas rightly notes in his prologue to the *Metaphysics*,[104] not only are those natures_r of beings which are nowhere in matter

The manner of distinguishing sciences by diverse abstractions from matter—how apt it is.

Metaphysics considers the nature_r of substance as such & the nature_r of accident as such.

St. Thomas

---

103. See Aristotle, *Post. An.* I, ch. 27. See also Toledo's commentary *ad loc.* in: Francisco de Toledo, *Commentaria una cum quaestionibus in universam Aristotelis logicam* (Venetiis: apud Juntas, 1580), fol. 212vb, and fols. 214rb–215ra.

104. Thomas Aquinas, *In duodecim libros metaphysicorum Aristotelis expositio*, p. 2.

etiam quod hae rationes sunt scibiles, & habere possunt attributa veluti adaequata & propria, & ad aliam scientiam non spectant: pertinent ergo ad hanc: non potest enim intellectus humanus, si perfecte sit dispositus, carere huiusmodi scientia. Unde, sicut Philosophia considerans de variis speciebus substantiarum materialium, considerat subinde communem rationem materialis substantiae, & adaequata principia, & proprietates eius: rursusque agens de variis speciebus viventium, considerat communem rationem viventis ut sic, & propria principia, & proprietates eius: ita scientia humana (ut sic dicam) considerans varios gradus & rationes entium, necesse est ut consideret communem rationem entis. Item, cum va[13b]rias substantias speculetur, & varia accidentia, necesse est ut consideret communes rationes substantiae & acci⟨17b⟩dentis: hoc autem non praestat nisi per hanc universalem, & principem scientiam.

Quae aliae rationes sub ente ad Metaphysicam considerationem pertineant.

Notatu dignum.

15. Atque hinc constat (ne eadem repetamus) idem dicendum esse de omnibus rationibus communibus, quae sub ente, substantia, & accidente ita abstrahi possunt, ut sint in rebus sine materia: huiusmodi sunt ratio entis creati vel increati, substantiae finitae, aut infinitae, & similiter accidentis absoluti vel respectivi, qualitatis, actionis, operationis aut dependentiae, & similium. De quibus observandum est plures posse abstrahi rationes communes rebus materialibus, & immaterialibus, quarum consideratio iuxta principium positum in rigore deberet ad hanc scientiam spectare, ut est communis ratio viventis, quae abstrahi potest a rebus materialibus & immaterialibus: item communis ratio cognoscentis & intelligentis, sicut etiam communis ratio entis necessarii seu incorruptibilis ab hac scientia considerantur: tamen quia plures ex praedictis rationibus ut a nobis cognoscuntur, non nisi ex diversis animarum gradibus cognosci possent, ideo nihil de illis potest hic convenienter dici, praeter ea quae in scientia de anima dicuntur: ideoque in eum locum ea praedicata reiicimus, quae ex operationibus vitae sumuntur, & communia sunt.

said to abstract from matter with respect to existence$_e$, but also those which *can* be in things$_r$ without matter, since this is sufficient for them not to include matter in their formal characters$_r$, and for them not to require it *per se*. It is also added that these natures$_r$ are knowable and can have attributes that are, as it were, adequate and proper, and that they are not the concern of another science. They pertain, therefore, to this one, for the human intellect cannot lack such science if it is perfectly disposed. For this reason, just as philosophy, in considering the various species of material substances, at the same time considers the common nature$_r$ of material substance, its adequate principles, and its properties—and again, in treating of the various species of living thing, it considers the common nature$_r$ of living thing as such, its proper principles, and its properties—so also is it necessary that human science (so to speak) consider the common nature$_r$ of being when it considers the various grades and natures$_r$ of beings. Further, when it investigates various substances, and various accidents, it is necessary that it consider the common natures$_r$ of substance and accident, and this it cannot manage except by means of this universal and most eminent science.

What abstracting from matter with respect to existence$_e$ is.

15. And hence it is established (so as not to repeat the same things) that the same must be said of all the common natures$_r$ which can be abstracted under being, substance, and accident in such a way that they are in things$_r$ without matter. Of this sort are the nature$_r$ of created or uncreated being, the nature$_r$ of finite or infinite substance, and likewise the nature$_r$ of absolute or relative accident, the nature$_r$ of quality, the nature$_r$ of action, the nature$_r$ of operation, the nature$_r$ of dependence, and the natures$_r$ of similar things. With regard to these, it must be noticed that several natures$_r$ common to material and immaterial things$_r$ can be abstracted, consideration of which, according to the principle laid down, ought strictly to be the concern of this science—for instance, the common nature$_r$ of living thing, which can be abstracted from material and immaterial things$_r$; further, the common nature$_r$ of cognizant and intelligent thing, and also the common nature$_r$ of necessary or incorruptible being, are considered by this science. However, since several of the mentioned natures$_r$, insofar as they are cognized by us, cannot be cognized except by appeal to the diverse grades of souls, nothing about

What other natures$_r$ contained under being are considered by metaphysics.

Something worthy of note.

Praedicata solis immaterialibus rebus communia, huius sunt considerationis.

16. Secundo ulterius a fortiori infertur pertinere ad hanc scientiam tractare in particulari de omnibus entibus seu rationibus entium, quae non nisi in rebus immaterialibus inveniri possunt, ut est communis ratio substantiae immaterialis, ratio primae seu increatae substantiae, & spiritus etiam creati, & omnium specierum, seu intelligentiarum quae sub ipso continentur. Solum est attendendum, has substantias praesertim creatas, valde imperfecte posse naturaliter cognosci, ad summum secundum quasdam communes rationes, & negativos conceptus: non tamen secundum proprias, & specificas differentias: eo tamen modo quo cognosci possunt, ad hanc scientiam potissimum pertinere earum contemplationem, ut supra dictum est. Non enim pertinet proprie, & per se ad Physicam nisi fortasse secundum quandam rationem communem extrinsecam, & non satis certam, scilicet quatenus angeli sunt motores caelestium orbium: per se autem & quoad cognitionem essentiae, & proprietatum intelligentiarum, ⟨18a⟩ quae naturaliter haberi potest, excedunt Physicam facultatem, quia sunt a sensibus remotissimae, & ideo earum cognitio difficilior est, & altior. Pertinet ergo ad hanc scientiam, quae hominem perficit secundum id quod in eo praestantissimum est, & in quo eius foelicitas naturalis magna ex parte consistit, id est, in contemplatione rerum altissimarum, ut Aristotel. dixit 10. Ethic. cap. 7.

Aristoteles.

Communis ratio causae, & quatuor generum causarum, & potissimae illarum causalitates ad Metaphysicam spectant.

17. Tertio colligitur ex dictis pertinere ad hanc scientiam tractare de communi ratione causae, & de singulis causarum generibus ut sic, & de primis ac potissimis causis seu rationibus causandi totius universi. Declaro singula, quia in primis ratio causae & effectus, ut sic, ex se communis est rebus materialibus & immaterialibus: nam in Deo, qui summe immaterialis est, ratio causae reperitur, & in angelis ratio effectus, & omnibus entibus creatis quatenus entia finita sunt, commune [14a] & essentiale est, ut ab aliqua causa emanent: & ad ipsa etiam creata entia, vel materialia, vel immaterialia secundum communem rationem aliquod genus operationis, vel causalitatis pertinet. Rursus haec ratio causae non tantum secundum communem rationem

them can suitably be said here aside from what is said in the science of the soul, and therefore we have left to that place those predicates which are taken from, and are common to, the operations of life.

16. Second, *a fortiori* it is further inferred that it pertains to this science to treat particularly of all beings or natures$_r$ of beings that cannot be found except in immaterial things$_r$—for instance, the common nature$_r$ of immaterial substances, the nature$_r$ of first or uncreated substance, and also the nature$_r$ of created spirit, as well as the natures$_r$ of all the species or intelligences that are contained under it. It is only to be observed that these substances, especially the created ones, can be naturally cognized [only] very imperfectly, at most in accordance with certain common natures$_r$ and negative concepts, but not in accordance with their proper and specific differences. Nevertheless, the contemplation of them in the way they can be cognized pertains most of all to this science, as was said above. For it does not pertain properly and *per se* to physics, except perhaps according to a certain common character$_r$ that is extrinsic and not sufficiently certain—namely, insofar as angels are movers of the heavenly spheres. But *per se* and with respect to the cognition that can naturally be had of the intelligences' essence and properties, they surpass the physical faculty, since they are most remote from the senses, and therefore the cognition of them is more difficult and loftier. It pertains, therefore, to this science, which perfects the human being with respect to what is foremost in her, and in which her natural happiness consists to a great degree, that is, in the contemplation of the highest things$_r$, as Aristotle says, *Ethics* X, ch. 7.[105]

17. Third, it is gathered from what has been said that it pertains to this science to deal with the common concept$_r$ of cause, with the individual genera of causes as such, and with the whole universe's primary and most important causes or causalities. I shall make this clear regarding each individually. For, in the first place, the concepts$_r$ of cause and effect, as such, are of themselves common to material and immaterial things$_r$, since in God, who is supremely immaterial, the concept$_r$ of cause is found, and in angels the concept$_r$ of effect, and it is common and essential to all created beings, insofar as they are finite beings, that they emanate from some cause. And also, some genus of operation, or of

Predicates common only to immaterial things$_r$ belong to this consideration.

Aristotle.

The common concept$_r$ of cause, the concepts$_r$ of the four genera of cause, and their principal causalities are the concern of metaphysics.

105. Aristotle, *Nic. Eth.* X, ch. 7.

causae, sed etiam secundum speciales & distinctos causandi modos, ex se abstrahit a materia secundum esse: nam ratio causae efficientis ut sic per se non requirit materiam, & multo minus ratio finis. Item haec ratio agentis liberi & a proposito. Item ratio causae exemplaris, seu ratio causae agentis per proprium exemplar vel ideam. Rursus causa materialis & formalis, quanvis prout in substantiis reperiuntur, non videantur a materia abstrahere: tamen quatenus secundum communes rationes suas a substantiis & accidentibus abstrahunt, a materia etiam separantur: pertinet ergo ad Metaphysicam haec genera causarum distinguere, & singulorum rationes explicare. Et quia ipsa sapientia est, & suprema naturalis scientia, ad eam pertinet primas rerum causas, vel potius primas rationes causandi in prima causa considerare: eiusmodi autem sunt ratio causae efficientis & finalis: hae namque secundum suam perfectionem supremam nec materiam requirunt, neque ipsam aut aliud genus causae supponunt, neque imperfectionem requirunt, sed per se ac primario in prima causa, quae est Deus, coniunguntur: secus vero est de ratione materiae ac ⟨18b⟩ formae: hae namque necessario supponunt aliam causam priorem a qua oriantur saltem efficienter, & finaliter: & ideo non computantur inter causas seu rationes causandi simpliciter primas: & ideo earum exacta cognitio non pertinet ad Metaphysicum nisi secundum rationes communes talium causarum: non tamen secundum eas res in quibus tales rationes causandi reperiuntur, quae sunt materia & forma substantialis: nam licet hae a Metaphysica attingantur, tamen integra earum scientia a Philosopho traditur.

18. Illud denique circa hoc considerandum est, variis, scilicet, titulis seu rationibus pertinere ad Metaphysicum hanc causarum considerationem: nam si virtus causandi, vel causalitas ipsa, vel relatio inde resultans, considerentur ut sunt entia quaedam, pertinent ad hanc scientiam ut obiectum eius, non quidem ut adaequatum (ut quidam falso

causality, pertains, in accordance with a common concept$_r$, to all these same created beings, whether material or immaterial. Again, of itself this concept$_r$ of cause abstracts from matter with respect to existence$_e$, not only according to the common concept$_r$ of cause, but also in accordance with special and distinct modes of causing, for the concept$_r$ of an efficient cause, as such, does not *per se* require matter, and much less so does the concept$_r$ of an end. Likewise, the concept$_r$ of a free and intentional agent. Likewise, the concept$_r$ of an exemplar cause, or the concept$_r$ of a cause acting through a proper exemplar or idea. In addition, although, insofar as they are found in substances, the material cause and the formal cause do not seem to abstract from matter, nevertheless, they too are separated from matter insofar as they abstract from substances and accidents according to their common concepts$_r$. Therefore, it pertains to metaphysics to distinguish these genera of causes and to explain the concepts$_r$ of each individually. And since metaphysics is wisdom itself, and the supreme natural science, it pertains to it to consider the first causes of things$_r$, or rather, to consider the primary causalities in the first cause. But such are the concept$_r$ of the efficient cause and the concept$_r$ of the final cause, for these, according to their supreme perfection, do not require matter, nor do they presuppose it or another genus of cause, nor do they require imperfection; rather, they are *per se* and primarily joined in the first cause, which is God. But it is otherwise with the concepts$_r$ of matter and form, for these necessarily presuppose another prior cause from which they originate at least efficiently and finally, and therefore they are not counted among causes or causalities that are primary without qualification, and therefore exact cognition of them does not pertain to the metaphysician, except according to the common concepts$_r$ of such causes, but not when it comes to the things$_r$ in which such causalities are found, which are matter and substantial form. For, although these are reached by metaphysics, nevertheless, complete knowledge of them is handed down by the philosopher.

18. Finally, in connection with this, it is to be observed that this consideration of causes pertains to metaphysics on a number of counts or for various reasons. For if the power of causing, or causality itself, or the relation resulting therefrom, are considered insofar as they are certain beings, they pertain to this science as its object, not indeed as its

dicebant, quod supra tetigimus), sed ut pars obiecti, quia haec tantum sunt quaedam entia, seu modi entium, non vero in se concludunt totam latitudinem entis. Si vero consideretur ratio vel virtus causae in ordine ad ipsam causam, scilicet quatenus est proprietas seu attributum eius rei quae causa dicitur, sic pertinet ad hanc scientiam considerare de causa, non ut de obiecto, vel parte obiecti, sed ut de attributo quodam obiecti, vel partis eius: atque hoc modo quia haec scientia considerat de Deo, consequenter in eo considerat rationem primae causae finalis, efficientis, & exemplaris: & considerans de angelis, inquirit quam virtutem causandi habeant in reliqua entia: & tractans de substantia ut sic, speculatur quam causalitatem habeat circa accidentia, & sic de aliis. Denique si consideretur ratio causae in ordine ad effectum, id est, quatenus eius cognitio necessaria est ad exactam effectus cognitionem, sic etiam pertinet ad hanc scientiam causarum cognitio, non ut obiectum, neque ut proprietas obiecti, sed ut principium seu causa obiecti seu partis eius. [14b]

Animae ne rationalis consideratio sit Metaphysici muneris.

19. Duae vero supersunt difficultates circa dicta. Una est de anima rationali, an eius consideratio ad Metaphysicum pertineat, sive in ratione entis, sive in ratione causae consideretur: est enim haec anima substantia quaedam immaterialis, & consequenter abstrahit a materia secundum esse, unde etiam abstrahit in propriis operationibus[20] suis. Hac ergo ratione videri potest ⟨19a⟩ propria & specifica consideratio huius animae ad hanc scientiam pertinere. Quod videtur confirmare Arist. 1.

Aristotel.

de partib. cap. 1. significans Physicum non considerare de omni anima. In contrarium vero est, quia anima rationalis, etiam ut rationalis est, est forma naturalis habens essentialem ordinem ad materiam, & ut sic est principium suarum operationum, etiam earum quas per corpus exercet, etiam secundum eum peculiarem modum quo ab homine exercentur. Sed haec controversia tractari solet ex professo in principio librorum de

Toletus.

Anima, ubi videri potest Cardin. Toletus quaest. 2. prooemiali.

---

20. Reading "in propriis operationibus" here with C₁, C₂, G₂, M₁, M₂, M₃, P₁, P₂, S, V₁, V₂, V₃, and V₄. The following have "in propriis rationibus": M₄, V₅, and Vivès.

adequate object (as some have falsely said, which is a point we touched on above), but as part of its object, since these are only certain beings, or modes of beings, but do not include in themselves the whole breadth of being. If, however, the causality or power of a cause is considered in relation to the cause itself, namely, insofar as it is a property or attribute of that thing_r which is called a cause, then in this way it pertains to this science to consider cause, not as its object, nor as a part of its object, but as a certain attribute of its object, or as a certain attribute of a part of its object. And in this way, since this science considers God, it consequently considers in him the character_r of primary final, efficient, and exemplar cause. And in considering angels, it inquires what power of causing they have with respect to the remaining beings. And in treating of substance as such, it investigates what causality it has with respect to accidents, and likewise regarding other things. Finally, if the concept_r of cause is considered in relation to an effect, that is, insofar as cognition of it is necessary for exact cognition of an effect, in this way also a cognition of causes pertains to this science, not as an object, nor as a property of an object, but as a principle or cause of its object, or as a principle or cause of a part of its object.

19. But there remain two difficulties regarding what has been said. *Whether consideration of the rational soul is a task of metaphysics.* One concerns the rational soul: does a consideration of it pertain to the metaphysician, whether it is viewed as a being or as a cause? For this soul is a certain immaterial substance, and consequently it abstracts from matter with respect to existence_e, and thus also it abstracts from matter in its proper operations. For this reason, then, a proper and specific consideration of this soul can seem to pertain to this science. And Aristotle seems to confirm this in *On the Parts of Animals* I, ch. 1, when *Aristotle.* he indicates that the physicist does not consider every kind of soul.[106] But opposed to this is the fact that the rational soul, even as rational, is a natural form having an essential relation to matter, and as such it is a principle of its own operations, including those operations which it exercises through the body, even in the special way they are performed by the human being. But this controversy is normally dealt with *ex pro-*

---

106. Aristotle, *On the Parts of Animals* I, ch. 1, 641a32–b10.

20. Nunc breviter dicitur huius animae considerationem remittendam esse in postremam & perfectissimam partem Philosophiae naturalis. Primo, quia scientia de homine ut homo est, physica est: eiusdem autem artificis est de toto, & de essentialibus eius partibus considerare. Deinde, quia licet anima habeat esse subsistens & separabile a materia quantum ad actualem coniunctionem: non tamen quantum ad aptitudinem, nec quantum ad ordinem ad materiam, & consequenter neque quantum ad perfectam cognitionem, tam essentiae, quam proprietatum & operationum eius: omnis autem cognitio per materiam Physica est. Non est ergo dubium, quin cognitio animae quantum ad substantiam eius, & proprietates per se illi convenientes, & modum seu statum existendi vel operandi quem habet in corpore, ad Physicum pertineat. De statu vero animae separatae, & modo operandi quem in eo habet, considerare, putant aliqui ad Metaphysicum per se pertinere: quod est probabile, quia secundum eam rationem videtur omnino fieri abstractio a materia, & nihil de anima prout in illo statu cognosci posse nisi per analogiam quandam & proportionem ad reliquas substantias immateriales. Nihilominus tamen, quia ad perfectionem scientiae spectat integre atque complete subiectum suum considerare, commodius haec omnia in Philosophia tractantur, maxime quia haec consideratio animae & statuum eius, quasi in partes divisa, & in diversis scientiis tradita, prolixitatem parit & confusionem: & ideo in discursu huius operis a consideratione animae rationalis tam coniunctae, quam separatae abstinebimus. Praesertim, quia etiam de angelis propter eandem causam perpauca dicturi sumus, quia integra eorum consideratio & contemplatio a Theologis merito iam usurpata est, ⟨19b⟩ quam totam huc traducere alienum esset a naturali scientia, & consequenter a nostro instituto: res autem obiter attingere, aut imperfecte tractare, aut nullius, aut parvae utilitatis esset. Atque eadem fere ratio est de cognitione Dei, quanvis quia de Deo plura possunt naturaliter cognosci, quam de intelligentiis, & quia eius cognitio naturalis, magis est ad perfectionem huius scientiae necessaria, nonnulla de ipso dicemus, quatenus vel a Philosophis tacta sunt, vel ratione naturali inveniri possunt. [15a]

fesso at the beginning of *De anima*, where Cardinal Francisco Toledo   *Toledo.*
can be seen to discuss it, q. 2 of the proem.[107]

20. For now, it is briefly said that the consideration of this soul is to
be left to the final and most perfect part of natural philosophy. First, because the science of the human being, insofar as she is a human being,
is physical, and it pertains to the same expert to consider a whole and
its essential parts. Second, because although the soul has existence$_e$ that
is subsistent and separable from matter as regards actual conjunction,
nevertheless, it is not such as regards aptitude, or as regards its relation
to matter, and consequently neither is it such with respect to the perfect
cognition of both its essence and its properties and operations. But every cognition through matter is physical. There is, therefore, no doubt
that cognition of the soul, as regards its substance, the properties that
per se agree with it, and the mode or state of existing or operating that
it has in the body, pertains to physics. But some think that it pertains
per se to the metaphysician to consider the state of the separated soul
and the mode of operating that it has in that state, and this is plausible,
since in accordance with that consideration$_r$ an abstraction seems to be
made from matter altogether, and nothing regarding the soul, insofar
as it is in that state, can be cognized except by a certain analogy with,
and proportion to, other immaterial substances. Nevertheless, since it
pertains to the perfection of a science to consider its subject wholly and completely, all these things are more appropriately dealt with
in philosophy, especially since this consideration of the soul and its
states, when divided into parts and handed down in diverse sciences,
generates prolixity and confusion. And therefore, in the course of this
work we shall abstain from a consideration of the rational soul, both
when joined to, and when separated from, matter—especially since,
for the same reason, we are going to say very few things about angels,
for the complete consideration and contemplation of them has now
rightly been taken over by the theologians, and to transfer that entire
consideration and contemplation to this place would be foreign to a
natural science, and consequently foreign to our purpose; and to touch
on things$_r$ in passing, or to treat of them imperfectly, would be of little

---

107. Francisco de Toledo, *Commentaria una cum quaestionibus in tres libros Aristotelis
De Anima*, fols. 3rb–7ra.

21. Altera difficultas erat de communibus rationibus substantiae materialis & aliis quae materiam includunt, vel sine materia esse non possunt: haec vero in argumentis tangitur, & in solutionibus eorum expedietur.

Rationibus oppositae sententiae satisfit.

22. Ad primam ergo rationem dubitandi in principio positam solutio patet ex dictis: non est enim necesse ut scientia quae considerat universalem rationem, in particulari descendat ad omnia quae sub tali ratione continentur, sed solum ad ea quae eandem rationem scibilis, seu eandem abstractionem participant. Quocirca quanvis, considerando convenientiam realem in communi ratione entis, non videatur esse maior ratio de quibusdam entibus particularibus quam de aliis, ut sub hanc scientiam cadant secundum proprias rationes, considerando tamen convenientiam in abstractione a materia secundum esse, quae est inter quasdam speciales rationes entium, cum ipsamet communi & abstractissima ratione entis, datur sufficiens ratio ob quam haec scientia ad particularia quaedam entia descendat, & non ad alia.

Quorundam entium in particulari consideratio cur ad Metaphysicam pertineat, non vero aliorum.

23. Ad primum vero fundamentum primae sententiae sumptum ex Aristotelis testimoniis patet responsio ex dictis, dicitur enim haec scientia universaliter considerare de ente, quia abstractissimam rationem entis in quantum ens considerat: & de omnibus quae in eadem abstractione & ratione scibilis[21] cum illa conveniunt. Et eodem modo dicitur tractare de omnibus rebus, scilicet quatenus entia sunt: & quia docet principia generalia, & communia omnibus rebus. Specialem vero difficultatem videntur habere verba illa libr. 4. text. 2. ubi dicitur huius scientiae esse considerare ens & eius species, ac species specierum. Quidam respondent eam distributionem esse accommodate intelligen-

Difficilis Aristotelis locus exponitur.

---

21. Reading "scibilis" with C_1, C_2, G_2, M_1, M_2, M_3, M_4, P_1, P_2, S, V_1, V_2, V_3, and V_5. The Vivès edition has "scibili." The relevant text is omitted from the scan of V_4.

or no use. And almost the same consideration_r applies to cognition of God, although, since more things can naturally be cognized about God than about the intelligences, and since natural cognition of him is more necessary to the perfection of this science, we shall say some things about him, insofar as they are either touched on by philosophers or can be discovered by natural reason.

21. The other difficulty concerned the common natures_r of material substance and other natures_r which include matter or cannot exist_e without matter. But this difficulty is touched on in the arguments and will be dispatched in the refutations of them.

22. The refutation of the first reason for doubt set forth at the beginning,[108] then, is clear from the things that have been said. For it is not necessary that a science which considers a universal nature_r descend in particular to all the things which are contained under that nature_r, but only that it descend in particular to those things which participate in the same concept_r of knowable [object], or in the same abstraction. Therefore, although, when considering their real agreement in the common nature_r of being, there seems not to be a greater reason why some particular beings, rather than others, should fall under this science according to their proper natures_r, nevertheless, when one considers the agreement that certain special natures_r of beings have in their abstraction from matter with respect to existence_e, together with this common and most abstract nature_r of being, there is a sufficient reason for this science to descend to some particular beings, and not to others.

The arguments for the opposite view are dealt with.

Why the particular consideration of some beings, but not others, belongs to metaphysics.

23. From what has been said, the reply to the first opinion's first foundation, taken from Aristotle's testimonies,[109] is clear. For this science is said to consider being universally because it considers the most abstract nature_r of being as being, as well as all those things which agree with it in the same abstraction and concept_r of knowable [object]. And in the same way it is said to treat of all things_r, namely, insofar as they are beings, and because it teaches principles that are general and common to all things_r. But those words from *Metaph.* IV, text 2, where it is said that it pertains to this science to consider being and its species, and the

A difficult passage in Aristotle is explained.

108. See *DM* 1.2.1 above.
109. See *DM* 1.2.3 above.

dam,[22] scilicet de speciebus entis proximis & remo⟨20a⟩tis sub eadem abstractione scibilis contentis. Sed melius D. Tho. & alii antiqui, quos Fonseca sequitur, ad hoc respondet, aliter construendo literam Aristotelis, quae sic habet secundum versionem antiquam, *Entis in quantum ens quascunque species speculari unius est scientiae genere, & species specierum.* In quibus verbis illa duo *& species specierum* aequivoca sunt: possunt enim coniungi ita ut unum determinet aliud: & referantur ad ens, & ad species specierum entis: & hunc sensum significat clare versio Argyropoli, & in eo procedit expositio data. Aliter vero possunt illa duo verba disiungi, & ad diversa referri, scilicet ad species rerum scibilium, & ad species scientiarum: & hoc recte significavit Fonseca vertens hoc modo. *Entis quotquot sunt species, unius scientiae genere est, & specierum species*[23] *contemplari*: atque ita sensus erit, unius scientiae genere esse contemplari species entis in communi, & in genere: variarum tamen specierum scientiarum esse contemplari varias species entis secundum proprias & specificas rationes scibilis. Atque ex hoc sensu confirmatur nostra sententia, nam si per scientiam unam in genere[24] intelligamus in rigore commune genus scientiae, ex hoc loco habetur non pertinere ad aliquam scientiam in specie contemplari omnia entia secundum omnes specificas rationes eorum, sed hoc pertinere ad genus scientiae speculativae in communi: ad scientias autem specificas spectare particularia obiecta scibilia se[15b]cundum proprias rationes eorum. Si autem per scientiam unam in genere intelligamus scientiam generalem ratione obiecti, qualis est Metaphysica, sic etiam ex hoc loco habetur huiusmodi scientiam solum considerare omnes species entis sub communi ratione entis, vel substantiae: scientias autem speciales considerare species entis sub propriis & specificis rationibus.

22. Reading "intelligendam" here with C_1, C_2, G_2, M_1, M_2, M_3, M_4, P_1, P_2, S, V_1, V_2, V_3, and V_5. Vivès has "intelligendum." The relevant text is omitted from the scan of V_4.

23. Reading "*specierum species*" here with V_1, V_2, and S. The following have "*species specierum*": C_1, C_2, G_2, M_1, M_2, M_3, M_4, P_1, P_2, V_3, V_4, V_5, and Vivès.

24. Reading "in genere" here with S, V_1, and V_2. The following omit these words: C_1, C_2, G_2, M_1, M_2, M_3, M_4, P_1, P_2, V_3, V_4, V_5, and Vivès.

species of its species,[110] seem to present a special difficulty. Some reply that this distribution is to be understood in a suitable way, namely, as having to do with the proximate and remote species of being contained under the same abstraction of knowable [object]. But St. Thomas[111] and other earlier thinkers, whom Fonseca follows, reply to this in a better way, by otherwise construing Aristotle's text, which reads thus in an old version: "*Entis in quantum ens quascumque species speculari unius est scientiae genere, & species specierum.*"[112] Among these words, these two, "*species specierum*," are equivocal, for they can be conjoined in such a way that one determines the other and the reference is to being and to the species of the species of being. John Argyropoulos's version clearly has this sense,[113] and the exposition given is in line with this sense.[114] But in another way those two words can be disjoined and referred to diverse things, namely, to the species of knowable things_r and to the species of the sciences, and this Fonseca has rightly signified by rendering the text thus: "It pertains to a science that is generically one to consider the species of being, however many there are, and it pertains to the species to consider the species."[115] And thus the sense will be that it pertains to a science that is generically one to consider the species of being universally and in general, but that it pertains to the various species of the sciences to consider the various species of being according to

110. Aristotle, *Metaph.* IV, ch. 2, 1003b21–22.

111. Thomas Aquinas, *In duodecim libros metaphysicorum Aristotelis expositio*, pp. 150 and 153 (bk. VI, lect. 1, n. 547).

112. The Latin here is ambiguous in a way that is difficult, indeed impossible, to replicate in English. I therefore leave it untranslated. Suárez will identify two ways in which the sentence might be understood. The *Translatio Anonyma sive Media* of the *Metaphysics* renders the relevant Greek text as "*entis in quantum ens quotcumque species speculari unius est scientie genere et species specierum.*" See Aristotle, *Aristoteles Latinus III.2, Metaphysica: Translatio anonyma sive "media,"* ed. G. Vuillemin-Diem (Leiden: Brill, 1976), p. 61. William of Moerbeke renders the same text as "*entis in quantum ens quascumque species speculari unius est scientie genere, species autem specierum.*" See *Aristoteles Latinus III.3.2, Metaphysica: Recensio & translatio Guillelmi de Moerbeka*, ed. G. Vuillemin-Diem (Leiden & Köln: Brill, 1995), p. 68. Both of these renderings are quite close to the version that Suárez quotes here.

113. Argyropoulos's translation renders the relevant Greek text as: "*eius quod est ut ens, quaecunque sunt species, unius est scientiae genere, & specierum species contemplari.*" See *Aristotelis Stagiritae de Prima Philosophia seu Metaphysicorum Libri XII, Ionanne Argyropylo Byzantino interprete*, fol. 23v.

114. By the "exposition given" Suárez means the interpretation of the text on which the first foundation relies. See *DM* 1.2.3 above.

115. Pedro da Fonseca, *Commentariorum in libros Metaphysicorum Aristotelis tomus primus*, col. 668.

24. Ad secundum respondetur non posse dari unam scientiam humanam, & propriis actibus humani ingenii acquisitam, quae universaliter illud perficiat quoad omnia scibilia secundum omnes rationes eorum: alioqui non solum illae tres scientiae speculativae, Philosophia, Mathematica, & Metaphysica, sed etiam morales & rationales, ac denique omnes in unam coalescerent, quae esset adaequata perfectio intellectus humani, quod est incredibile, quia cum actus & discursus humani ingenii, sint tam varii, & tam particu⟨20b⟩lares & distincti, atque independentes inter se, non est verisimile fieri posse ut omnes concurrant ad eandem scientiam generandam. Neque id est necessarium ad effectum de quo in argumento fit mentio, scilicet ad iudicandum de diversitate rerum distinctarum, quae ad diversas scientias pertinere dicuntur: quia unaquaeque scientia tradens cognitionem sui obiecti, sufficienter reddit facilem intellectum ad distinguendum illud a reliquis, si tamen reliqua cognoscantur, unde duae scientiae possunt se se iuvare & concurrere ad huiusmodi iudicia, maxime si una praebeat veluti formale[25] medium: alia vero quasi ministret materiam cui medium illud applicatur. Ita enim fere in proposito contingit: ut enim intellectus iudicet, & demonstret unum esse diversum ab alio, v. g. equum a leone, ex Metaphysica sumit formale medium, quod est ratio diversitatis, seu quid sit esse diversum, & illud applicat seu attribuit equo & leoni, quo-

---

25. Reading "formale" here with all of the early editions. Vivès has "formalem."

their proper and specific concepts$_r$ of knowable [object]. And according to this sense our opinion is confirmed, for if by a science that is generically one we understand, in strictness, the common genus of science, then the passage's meaning is that it does not pertain to some specific science to consider all beings according to all of their specific natures$_r$, but that this, rather, pertains to the genus of speculative science in general, whereas to consider particular knowable objects according to their proper natures$_r$ pertains to specific sciences. But if by a science that is generically one we understand a science that is general by reason of its object, as metaphysics is, then in this way also the passage's meaning is that a science of this sort only considers all the species of being under the common nature$_r$ of being or substance, but that the special sciences consider the species of being under their proper and specific natures$_r$.

24. To the second foundation,[116] I reply that there cannot be a single human science, acquired by proper acts of the human intellect, which universally perfects it with respect to all knowable [objects] in accordance with all of their natures$_r$. Otherwise, not only those three speculative sciences—philosophy, mathematics, and metaphysics—but also the moral and rational sciences, and finally all sciences, would coalesce into a single science that would be the adequate perfection of the human intellect. But this cannot be believed, for since the acts and reasonings of the human mind are so various and so particular and distinct, and independent of each other, it is implausible that it could happen that all of them should come together in order to generate one and the same science. Nor is it necessary for the effect that was mentioned in the argument, namely, judging about the diversity of distinct things$_r$ which are said to pertain to diverse sciences, since each science, in furnishing cognition of its object, sufficiently renders the intellect ready to distinguish it from other objects, provided that these other objects are cognized. And for this reason two sciences can help each other and concur in judgments of this sort, especially if one furnishes, as it were, a formal middle term, while the other supplies, as it were, the matter to which this middle term is applied. And this is precisely what happens in the present case, since, in order for the intellect to judge and demonstrate

A single acquired human science cannot embrace all knowable [objects] according to their proper natures$_r$.

---

116. See *DM* 1.2.4 above.

rum conceptus seu rationes ex philosophia sumit: tamen quia medium est quasi formale demonstrationis, ideo talis demonstratio, Metaphysica censetur, & hoc modo dicitur esse Metaphysicae munus diversitatem in rebus ostendere: & eodem modo dicitur demonstrare quidditates rerum: quia medium demonstrandi quidditatem in ratione quidditatis, Metaphysicum est, quia rationem quidditatis ut sic cognoscere, proprium est Metaphysicae.

25. Ad tertium respondent aliqui distinguendam esse in Metaphysica duplicem rationem. Una est scientiae particularis, sub qua ratione negant attingere materialia, ut sic. Alia est, quatenus est communis ars, aliisque scientiis vel artibus praeest: hoc enim munus tribuit illi Aristotel. in hoc prooemio, & primo Poster. cap. 7.[26] tex. 23. ubi per scientiam omnium dominam Metaphysicam intelligit, ut omnes exponunt, sub hac ergo ratione dicunt Metaphysicam cognoscere res materiales, ut materiales sunt, imo & materiam istam, quatenus pura potentia passiva est. Quod si obiicias, quia non potest scientia transgredi obiectum suum: sub eadem distinctione respondent, id verum esse de scientia ut particularis scientia est, non vero ut communis ars. Veruntamen distinctio, & responsio maiori indigent declaratione. Nam illae duae rationes non distinguuntur ex natura rei in habitu Metaphysicae, tanquam duae partes eius in re ipsa distinctae, sed solum consideratione, & prae[16a]cisiva abstractione nostra per ⟨21a⟩ inadaequatos conceptus: nam Metaphysica non nisi ratione sui obiecti abstractissimi, & universalissimi dicitur esse universalis scientia, & principia universalia tradere, ideoque posse alias scientias iuvare, ergo non potest illa duo munera divisim (ut sic dicam) seu per diversas sui partes praestare, sed simul dum suum obiectum proprium perfecte tractat, consequitur quidquid perfectionis habet super alias scientias, & confert omnem utilitatem quam ad illas praestare potest: illa ergo partitio est tantum secundum rationem nostram. Igitur fieri non potest, ut Metaphysica transcendat rationem

---

26. Reading "cap. 7" with S, C_1, C_2, G_2, M_1, M_2, M_3, M_4, P_1, P_2, S, V_1, V_2, V_3, and V_4. The following read "c. 17": V_5 and Vivès.

that one thing is diverse from another—for example, that the horse is diverse from the lion—it takes from metaphysics a formal middle term, which is the concept$_r$ of diversity, or what it is to be diverse, and it applies or attributes it to the horse and the lion, whose concepts or natures$_r$ it takes from philosophy. Nevertheless, since the middle term is, as it were, the formal element of a demonstration, such a demonstration is judged metaphysical, and in this way it is said to be a function of metaphysics to show the diversity of things$_r$. And in the same way it is said to demonstrate the quiddities of things$_r$, because the middle term for demonstrating a quiddity as a quiddity is metaphysical, since to cognize the concept$_r$ of quiddity as such is proper to metaphysics.

25. To the third foundation,[117] some reply that a twofold aspect$_r$ is to be distinguished in metaphysics. One is that of a particular science, in accordance with which aspect$_r$ they deny that metaphysics reaches material things as such. The other pertains to metaphysics insofar as it is a common art and presides over the other sciences or arts, for Aristotle attributes this function to it in the proem[118] and in *Post. An.* I, ch. 7, text 23, where by the science that rules them all he understands metaphysics, as all commentators explain.[119] In accordance with the latter aspect$_r$, then, metaphysics, they say, cognizes material things$_r$ insofar as they are material, and in fact also cognizes this matter insofar as it is pure passive potency. But if you object on the grounds that a science cannot go beyond its object, they reply, by appeal to the same distinction, that this is true of the science insofar as it is a particular science,

117. See *DM* 1.2.5 above.

118. Aristotle, *Metaph.* I, ch. 1, 982a14–19 and 982b4–10.

119. Aristotle, *Post. An.* I, ch. 9, 76a16–22. The words "*scientia que est illorum domina omnium*" ("the science that is ruler of them all"), rendering the Greek "ἐπιστήμη ἡ ἐκείνων κυρία πάντων" (76a18), appear at this point in the *Translatio Anonyma* of the *Posterior Analytics*. See *Aristoteles Latinus IV.1–4. Analytica Posteriora*, ed. L. Minio-Paluello and B. G. Dod (Bruges & Paris: Desclée de Brouwer, 1968), p. 124. William of Moerbeke's translation renders the same Greek text as "*scientia illorum domina omnium.*" See *Aristoteles Latinus IV.1–4. Analytica Posteriora*, p. 295. The translation used by Francisco de Toledo has "*scientia illorum domina omnium.*" See his *In universam Aristotelis logicam*, fol. 176va. The translation used by Zabarella has "*eorum scientia domina omnium.*" See his *Opera Logica*, col. 779. Note that the texts of the *Posterior Analytics* used by Toledo and Zabarella differ with respect to how they divide each of the work's two books into chapters. The text referenced by Suárez here is located in bk. I, ch. 7, of Toledo's text, but in bk. I, ch. 9, of Zabarella's text, which suggests that the chapter division used by Suárez is the one followed by Toledo, rather than the one followed by Zabarella.

formalem sui obiecti tam secundum unam rationem quam secundum aliam. Et confirmatur, nam si Metaphysica ut esse dicitur ars[27] universalis, transcendit abstractionem suam, & in rebus materialibus quatenus tales sunt, versatur, ergo in hoc nullum habet terminum, aut limitem, sed ad omnia obiecta aliarum scientiarum, secundum omnes rationes eorum descendet,[28] & sic inciditur in omnia incommoda, quae contra alias sententias intulimus. Sequela vero patet, tum quia si ex ratione formali obiecti, non assignatur talis terminus, non est unde assignetur: tum quia si Metaphysicus attingit proprium obiectum philosophiae v. g. ut constituat illud, etiam attingeret omnium scientiarum obiecta, & in ipsa philosophia oporteret omnes species naturalium entium contemplari, ut si forte plures sunt philosophiae, earum obiecta secernat, si vero est una, quomodo ex tot rebus unum eius obiectum confletur, declaret.

26. Existimo ergo, Metaphysicam sub nulla ratione consideratam transilire proprie rationem formalem sui obiecti, nec attingere mate-

27. Reading "ars" here with S, V_1, and V_2. The following omit this word: C_1, C_2, G_2, M_1, M_2, M_3, M_4, P_1, P_2, V_3, V_4, V_5, and Vivès.

28. Reading "descendet" here with C_1, C_2, G_2, M_1, M_2, M_3, M_4, P_1, P_2, S, V_3, V_4, V_5, and Vivès. The following read "descendat": V_1 and V_2.

but not insofar as it is a common art. Nevertheless, the distinction and the reply require greater clarification, for those two aspects_r are not distinguished *ex natura rei* in the habit of metaphysics as two parts of it that are in reality distinct, but are distinguished only by our consideration, and by our precisive abstraction through inadequate concepts. For metaphysics is said to be a universal science, and to teach universal principles, and thus to be capable of helping the other sciences, only by reason of its most abstract and universal object. Therefore, it cannot perform those two functions separately, so to speak—that is, through diverse parts of it—but while it treats perfectly of its proper object it obtains at the same time whatever perfection it has over the other sciences and confers all the benefit that it can render them. Therefore, that division is only according to our reason. Therefore, it is impossible for metaphysics to transcend the formal character_r of its object, either in accordance with the one aspect_r or in accordance with the other. And this is confirmed, for if metaphysics, insofar as it is said to be a universal art, transcends its abstraction and concerns itself with material things_r insofar as they are such, then it has no boundary or limit in this respect but will descend to all the objects of the other sciences according to all of their natures_r, and in this way one falls into all the difficulties that we adduced against the other opinions. The consequence is clear, both because if such a boundary is not assigned by appeal to the formal character_r of the object, there is no basis upon which it might be assigned, and also because, if the metaphysician reaches the proper object of philosophy—in order to constitute it, for example—she will also reach the objects of all the sciences, and in philosophy itself she will have to consider all the species of natural beings, so that, if by chance there are several philosophies, she might distinguish their objects, whereas if there is one philosophy, then so that she might show how its single object is forged from so many things_r.

26. I think, therefore, that metaphysics, considered under no aspect_r, properly goes beyond the formal character_r of its object, nor does it reach material things, unless it does so in some way that is in conformity with its abstraction. Nor, finally, do I think that it is universal, or that it serves the other sciences, except under that aspect_r in accordance with which it perfectly exhausts its object. But in order

rialia nisi concernendo aliquo modo abstractionem suam: nec denique esse universalem, aut deservire ad alias scientias nisi sub ea ratione, qua perfecte exhaurit obiectum suum. Ut autem hoc declarem, dico in primis, Metaphysicam non attingere rationem substantiae materialis, & alias similes quae sine materia non reperiuntur, nisi quatenus illarum cognitio propria necessaria est ad tradendas generales divisiones entis in decem summa genera, & alias similes, usque ad propria obiecta aliarum scientiarum praescribenda: hoc enim munus proprium est huius scientiae, ut sumitur ex 6. 7. & 8. Metaphysicae: & quia ad nullam aliam scientiam hoc pertinere potest ut per se facile constat. Item quia sine his divisionibus non posset ⟨21b⟩ Metaphysica suum obiectum exacte cognoscere, nec secundum communem rationem entis, quae cum analoga sit, non satis distincte cognoscitur non distinguendo modos quibus contrahi potest, neque secundum eas proprias & speciales rationes, quae a Metaphysica per se & exacte contemplandae sunt, quia non potest has rationes perfecte attingere nisi ab aliis eas separet ac distinguat.

27. Secundo dicitur, quoniam rationes universales quas Metaphysica considerat, transcendentales sunt, ita ut in propriis rationibus entium imbibantur, hinc fieri, ut dum Metaphysicus attingit nonnullos gradus entium, quae materiam includunt, ut ab illis separet caeteros gradus qui ad se directe & per se pertinent, de illis abstracte consideret rationes & proprietates quae communes sunt entibus abstrahentibus a materia, & ipsis etiam materialibus entibus, etiam ut [16b] talia sunt specificative, conveniunt. Ut verbi gratia, distinguit Metaphysica substantiam in materialem & immaterialem: vel ut substantiae immaterialis propriam rationem & considerationem assumat, vel quia ad scientiam pertinet proprias partes sui obiecti aliquo modo considerare: ut dicitur primo Poster. cap. 23. Tradita autem huiusmodi divisione, substantiam immaterialem per se & directe considerat, omnia in universum tractando quae de illa cognosci possunt: substantiam autem materialem non ita contemplatur, sed solum quatenus necesse est ad distinguendam illam a substantia immateriali, & ad cognoscendum de illa omnia Metaphysica praedicata, quae illi ut materialis est, conveniunt, ut v. g. esse compositam ex actu & potentia, & modum huius compositionis, & quod sit quoddam ens per se unum; & similia.

to make this clear, I say, in the first place, that metaphysics does not reach the nature_r of material substance, or other similar natures_r that are not found without matter, except insofar as the proper cognition of them is necessary for teaching the general divisions of being into the ten highest genera, and other similar ones, so as to prescribe the proper objects of the other sciences. For this function is proper to this science, as is gathered from *Metaph.* VI, VII, and VIII, and also because this function can pertain to no other science, as is easily seen *per se*. In addition, because without these divisions metaphysics could not accurately cognize its object, neither according to the common nature_r of being—which, since it is analogical, is not cognized in a sufficiently distinct way without distinguishing the modes by which it can be contracted—nor according to those proper and special natures_r which are to be considered *per se* and accurately by metaphysics, since it cannot perfectly reach these natures_r unless it separates and distinguishes them from others.

27. Second, I say that, since the universal concepts_r considered by metaphysics are transcendental in such a way that they are conceived in the proper natures_r of beings, it results that, when the metaphysician reaches some grades of beings that include matter, and this so as to separate from them other grades that pertain directly and *per se* to herself, in connection with these, she abstractly considers concepts_r and properties which both are common to beings that abstract from matter and also agree specificatively with material beings themselves, even insofar as they are such. For example, metaphysics distinguishes substance into material and immaterial, either in order to obtain the proper nature_r and consideration of immaterial substance, or because it pertains to a science to consider the proper parts of its object in some way, as is said in *Post. An.* I, ch. 23.[120] However, once such a division is handed down, it considers immaterial substance *per se* and directly, treating generally of all the things that can be cognized about it, but it does not consider material substance in this way, but only to the extent that is necessary for distinguishing it from immaterial substance, and for cognizing about it all the metaphysical predicates that agree with

---

120. Aristotle, *Post. An.* I, ch. 28, 87a38–39.

28. Tertio, in forma ad argumentum respondetur ideo Metaphysi-cam non considerare in particulari omnia entia, quia non transcendit propriam abstractionem sui obiecti: gradus autem quosdam genericos considerare, qui attingunt materiam, non omittendo suam abstractio-nem, tum quia illosmet abstrahit a materia quatenus est subiecta motui & sensui, solumque considerat illos secundum communes rationes ac-tus, seu formae, & potentiae, & similes: tum etiam, quia solum indirecte attingit proprias rationes eorum in ordine ad propriam abstractionem, scilicet, ut declaret quomodo in eis reperiantur communia & transcen-dentia praedicata, & quomodo ab eis distinguantur alii gradus ⟨22a⟩ vel genera quae vere ac secundum rem ab omni materia abstrahunt. Et hoc est²⁹ quod Arist. 4. Metaph. text. 5. significavit, cum dixit, *Philosophi est de omnibus posse speculari: si enim non Philosophi, quis erit, qui con-siderabit, si idem Socrates, & Socrates sedens, aut si unum uni contrari-um, &c?* Philosophiam enim per antonomasiam vocat Metaphysicam, ad quam dicit pertinere considerare diversitatem rerum in communi, quia idem & diversum sunt passiones entis: & hoc declarat praedicto exemplo, quod affectandae fortassis obscuritatis gratia in quodam in-dividuo posuit, cum constet scientiam non descendere ad individua, ex 1. Posterior. c. 7. & lib. 3. Metaph. cap. 13.

29. Quartum argumentum est revera difficile, attingit enim difficul-tatem de scientiae unitate, qualis sit, quae non potest hoc loco exacte tractari: attingemus tamen illam breviter sectione sequente.

---

29. Reading "est" here with C_1, C_2, G_2, S, V_1, and V_2. The following omit this word: M_1, M_2, M_3, M_4, P_1, P_2, V_3, V_4, V_5, and Vivès.

it insofar as it is material—for example, being composed from act and potency, and the mode of this composition, and the fact that it is a kind of being that is *per se* one, and the like.

28. Third, I reply in form to the argument that metaphysics, therefore, does not consider all beings particularly, since it does not transcend the proper abstraction of its object, and it considers certain generic grades that reach matter, but not by setting aside its abstraction, both because it abstracts these grades from matter insofar as matter is subject to motion and sense, and considers them only in terms of those common concepts$_r$ of act, or form, and potency, and the like, and also because it only indirectly reaches their proper natures$_r$ in relation to its proper abstraction—namely, so as to make clear how common and transcendental predicates are found in them, and how other grades or genera that truly and really abstract from all matter are distinguished from them. And this is what Aristotle, *Metaph.* IV, text 5, indicates when he says: "It pertains to the philosopher to be able to investigate all things, for if not to the philosopher, who will there be who considers whether Socrates and Socrates seated are the same, or whether one thing has a single contrary?"[121] etc. For he calls metaphysics philosophy by antonomasia, and he says that it pertains to metaphysics to consider the diversity of things$_r$ in general, since the same and the diverse are passions of being. And this he makes clear by means of the mentioned example, which, perhaps in order to feign some obscurity, he places in a certain individual, although it is clear, from *Post. An.* I, ch. 7,[122] and *Metaph.* III, ch. 13,[123] that a science does not descend to individuals.

29. The fourth argument[124] is really difficult, since it involves the difficulty regarding the unity of a science, namely, of what sort this unity is, which difficulty cannot be dealt with accurately in this place. Nevertheless, we shall touch on it briefly in the next section.

121. Aristotle, *Metaph.* IV, ch. 2, 1004a34–b4.

122. Aristotle, *Post. An.* I, ch. 8, 75b21–30.

123. According to the chapter divisions of Suárez's day, there is no *Metaph.* III, ch. 13. Perhaps he means *Metaph.* III, ch. 4, 999b1–3, located in *Metaph.* III, text 12.

124. See *DM* 1.2.6 above.

Sectio III.

Utrum Metaphysica sit una tantum scientia.

———

1. Explicato obiecto Metaphysicae, facile erit eius essentialem rationem exponere: quoniam vero essentia & unitas rei, vel sunt idem, vel intrinsece coniuncta, ideo simul explicanda est eius unitas, praesertim quia sermo est de unitate specifica, nam de numerica nulla est quaestio, cum constet in diversis hominibus[30] multiplicari hanc scientiam secundum numerum, sicut & reliqua accidentia. In eodem autem certum est non multiplicari in ordine ad easdem res, [17a] an vero respectu diversarum ipsa etiam distinguatur, & consequenter in eodem subiecto multiplicari possit, pendet ex priori quaestione de unitate eius specifica seu essentiali. Quoniam vero haec unitas per genus & differentiam declaratur recte, eo quod species ex genere & differentia constat, ideo supponimus id quod certum ac per se notum est, Metaphysicam esse vere ac proprie scientiam, ut Aristoteles, in principio Metaphysicae, & aliis innumeris locis docuit, & constat ex definitione scientiae, quae ex 1. Poster. & 6. Ethicor. cap. 3. sumitur, scilicet, quod sit cognitio seu habitus praebens certam ac evidentem cognitionem rerum necessariarum per propria earum principia & causas, si sit scientia perfecta & a priori. Haec autem omnia in hac doctrina inveniuntur, quantum est ex vi & ratione obiecti eius, & ⟨22b⟩ ideo non est dubium quin haec sit in se scientia, quanvis fortasse in nobis non semper, vel non quoad omnia, statum vel perfectionem scientiae assequatur. Constat ergo hanc scientiam contineri sub genere scientiae. Imo ex dictis facile constare potest contineri sub genere speculativae scientiae, ut Arist. dixit 1. Metaph. cap. 2. & lib. 2. cap. 1. quia circa res maxime speculativas, & quae ad opus non ordinantur, versatur, ut inferius commodius

Metaphysica vere ac proprie scientia.

Metaphysica scientia speculativa.

---

30. Reading "hominibus" here with S, V₁, and V₂. The following omit this word: C₁, C₂, G₂, M₁, M₂, M₃, M₄, P₁, P₂, V₃, V₄, V₅, and Vivès.

WHETHER METAPHYSICS IS ONLY ONE SCIENCE.

———

1. Since the object of metaphysics has been explained, it will be easy to expound its essential concept$_r$. However, since the essence and unity of a thing$_r$ are either the same or intrinsically conjoined, its unity must be explained at the same time, especially since the discussion concerns specific unity, for there is no question regarding its numeric unity, since it is clear that this science is numerically multiplied in diverse human beings, just as other accidents are. And it is certain that in the same human being it is not multiplied in relation to the same things$_r$, but whether it is distinguished in relation to diverse ones, and consequently can be multiplied in the same subject, depends on the prior question regarding its specific or essential unity. But since this unity is rightly explained through a genus and difference, because a species is constituted from a genus and difference, we assume what is certain and *per se* known$_n$, that metaphysics is truly and properly a science, as Aristotle teaches at the beginning of the *Metaphysics*[125] and in countless other places, and as is clear from the definition of science that is taken from *Post. An.* I[126] and *Ethics* VI, ch. 3[127]—namely: that it is a cognition or habit furnishing certain and evident cognition of necessary things$_r$ through their proper principles and causes, if it is a perfect and *a priori* science. But all these things are found in this doctrine, insofar as they depend on the capacity and nature$_r$ of its object, and therefore there is no doubt that this is in itself a science, even if, perhaps, in us it does not always, or in all respects, attain to the state or perfection of a science. It is, therefore, clear that this science is contained under the genus of

Metaphysics is truly and properly a science.

125. Aristotle, *Metaph.* I, chs. 1–2.
126. Aristotle, *Post. An.* I, ch. 2.
127. Aristotle, *Nic. Eth.* VI, ch. 3, 1139b18–36.

Metaphysica ab aliis scientiis distinguitur.

declarabimus, attributa huius scientiae explicando. Deinde constat ex dictis, hanc scientiam esse essentialiter distinctam a reliquis scientiis speculativis ac realibus, ut sunt Philosophia & Mathematica: unde fit etiam consequens habere illam ut sic unitatem aliquam ratione obiecti a nobis explicati. Sub qua ratione definiri potest, Metaphysicam esse scientiam quae ens in quantum ens, seu in quantum a materia abstrahit secundum esse, contemplatur.

Metaphysicae definitio.

Metaphysica ne una sit in specie subalterna, an vero in infima.

2. Difficultas ergo in praesenti tractanda superest an haec unitas sit generica vel specifica, & consequenter an illa differentia quae sumitur ex habitudine ad obiectum adaequatum a nobis expositum, sit subalterna ita ut sub ea possint plures specificae designari, vel potius sit una indivisibilis atque ultima. Multi enim priori modo de illa existimant: quorum sententia suaderi potest primo, quia in obiecto a nobis constituto abstractiones variae possunt assignari: in primis enim est illa duplex abstractio a materia secundum esse, aut necessario aut permissive tantum, quae videtur sufficiens ad variandum secundum speciem obiectum scibile ut sic, & consequenter scientiam. Rursus inter res quae necessario existunt sine materia, videtur ut minimum valde diversa abstractio Dei qui est omnino purus actus, & ab omni etiam Metaphysica compositione abstrahit, ab abstractione aliarum intelligentiarum, quae licet materia careant, compositae tamen sunt, eisque attributa longe diversa conveniunt. Possunt ergo sub generali Metaphysicae unitate tres saltem scientiae specie distinctae constitui. Una quae versetur circa ens in quantum ens, & ad summum descendat ad communes rationes substantiae, & accidentis, & ad novem genera, quae sub illo continentur: secunda, quae intelligentias creatas: tertia vero, quae solum Deum contempletur: nam sicut in eo solo naturalis beatitudo consistit, ita videtur danda scientia ⟨23a⟩ naturalis, quae secundum ultimam & specificam rationem suam Deum solum attingat. Neque for[17b]tasse deerit qui in plura membra hanc scientiam partiatur iuxta diversos gradus ab-

Prima opinio.

science. In fact, from what has been said, it can easily be seen that it is contained under the genus of speculative science, as Aristotle says in *Metaph.* I, ch. 2,[128] and book II, ch. 1,[129] since it is concerned with things_r that are most of all speculative, and not ordered to an operation, as we shall more conveniently make clear below, while explaining the attributes of this science.[130] Further, it is clear from what has been said that this science is essentially distinct from the other speculative and real sciences, such as philosophy and mathematics. And from this it also follows as a consequence that this science, as such, has some unity by virtue of the object that has been explained by us. In accordance with this account_r, metaphysics can be defined as the science that considers being as being, or being insofar as it abstracts from matter with respect to existence_e.

2. There remains, then, a difficulty that is to be dealt with here, namely, whether this unity is generic or specific, and consequently, whether that difference which is taken from the relation to the adequate object explained by us is subaltern in such a way that several specific ones can be designated under it, or is rather indivisibly one and ultimate. For many conceive it in the former way, and their view can be urged, first, because in the object constituted by us various abstractions can be identified. For, to begin with, there is that twofold abstraction from matter with respect to existence_e—either necessary or merely permissive—which seems sufficient to vary the knowable object as such specifically, and consequently sufficient to vary the science specifically as well. Again, among things_r that necessarily exist without matter, it seems, at least, that the abstraction of God—who is altogether pure act and abstracts even from every metaphysical composition—is very different from the abstraction of the other intelligences—which, although they lack matter, are nevertheless composite—and very different attributes agree with them. Therefore, under the general unity of metaphysics at least three specifically distinct sciences can be constituted: one that is concerned with being as being, and at most descends to the common natures_r of substance and accident, and to the nine genera

---

128. Aristotle, *Metaph.* I, ch. 2, 982a30–b28.
129. Aristotle, *Metaph.* II, ch. 1, 993b19–23.
130. See *DM* 1.5.

stractionis in ipsis communibus rationibus entis in quantum ens, vel substantiae in quantum substantia, & sic de aliis.

3. Secundo principaliter argumentor in hunc modum, quia si haec scientia est una, maxime quoad habitum iudicativum, qui in mente relinquitur ex actibus eius: nam species intelligibiles quibus haec scientia utitur, certum est esse quamplurimas, & non unam tantum: similiterque constat actus eius esse varios, & multiplices, non solum numero, sed etiam specie differentes: quis enim dubitaret diversum esse actum quo iudicamus omne ens esse unum, seu unitatem esse passionem entis: & quo iudicamus intelligentias esse immortales, vel aliquid simile? Si ergo unitas specifica in Metaphysica excogitari potest, solum est quoad habitum iudicativum: sed in eo etiam constitui non potest: ergo in nullo esse potest. Probatur minor, quia si ille habitus est unus specie, vel est omnino simplex in sua entitate secundum ordinem ad obiectum (omissa pro nunc compositione, si qua est, per solam intensionem, aut radicationem in subiecto) vel est qualitas composita: neutrum autem dici posse videtur. Primum probatur, quia cum habitus Metaphysicae ad varia iudicia, & de rebus distinctissimis inclinet, ut sit ipsis actibus quasi commensuratus, non videtur posse per unam & eandem simplicem qualitatem ad omnes illos inclinare, seu omnes efficere.

4. Quod secundo ita declaratur, quia habitus Metaphysicae primo acquiritur per unum actum circa unum obiectum, v. g. circa hanc conclusionem: *Omne ens est verum*, vel aliam[31] similem: deinde per alios actus augetur & extenditur ad alias conclusiones valde diversas, in quo augmento necesse est aliquid realitatis vel entitatis illi addi, quia

---

31. Reading "aliam" here with S, V_1, and V_2. The following have "etiam" instead: C_1, C_2, G_2, M_1, M_2, M_3, M_4, P_1, P_2, V_3, V_4, V_5, and Vivès.

which are contained under the latter; a second that considers created intelligences; and a third that considers only God. For, just as natural beatitude lies in him alone, so also it seems there must be a natural science which reaches God alone in accordance with an ultimate and specific concept_r. Nor, perhaps, will someone be lacking who divides this science into more members in accordance with diverse grades of abstraction belonging to the common natures_r of being as being, of substance as substance, and so on regarding the others.

3. Second, I argue chiefly in this way: because, if this science is one, it is one most of all with respect to the judicative habit which is left in the mind as a result of its acts. For it is certain that the intelligible species which this science employs are very numerous, and not only one. And similarly, it is clear that its acts are various and multiple, differing not only in number, but also in species. For who would doubt that the act by which we judge that every being is one, or that unity is a passion of being, is diverse from that by which we judge the intelligences to be immortal, or something similar? If, therefore, specific unity in metaphysics can be conceived, it is only with respect to the judicative habit. But specific unity cannot be founded on the judicative habit either. Therefore, it can be founded on nothing. The minor is proved, because if that habit is one in species, either it is altogether simple in its entity according to its relation to the object—setting aside, for now, composition (if there is any) through intension alone or through rooting in a subject—or it is a composite quality. But it seems that neither can be said. The first cannot be said because, since the habit of metaphysics inclines to various judgments, and concerns the most distinct things_r, if it is to be commensurate, as it were, with the acts themselves, then it cannot, it seems, incline to all these acts or produce them all by means of one and the same simple quality.

4. This can be made clear, in the second place, as follows: because the habit of metaphysics is first acquired through a single act regarding one object—for example, regarding this conclusion: "Every being is true," or another similar one. Then, by means of other acts, it is increased and extended to other, very different conclusions, and in the case of this habit, when it is increased, it is necessary that there be some reality or entity added to it, since it is impossible to understand a real

impossibile est intelligere augmentum reale sine additione reali. Haec autem additio non potest esse sufficiens per modum intensionis solius, quia hoc augmentum non tantum est ex diversa participatione subiecti secundum maiorem & maiorem radicationem ipsius formae in ipso, sed est ex parte ipsiusmet habitus per maiorem extensionem ad obiectum: ergo requiritur additio ex parte ipsiusmet habitus, quatenus ei aliquid additur, quo novum obiectum, seu novam conclu⟨23b⟩ sionem respiciat, ut aperte docuit Divus Thomas agens de habitibus *D. Thom.* in communi, 1. 2. quaest. 52 artic. 1. & 2. non potest ergo huiusmodi habitus esse omnino simplex, ut respicit totam latitudinem sui obiecti. Quod vero neque compositus esse possit, & tamen esse vere unus in specie, probatur primo, quia id quod primo acquiritur in habitu per actus unius speciei: & quod additur per actum specie distinctum, sunt etiam inter se specie distincta: ergo non componunt unum habitum secundum speciem. Antecedens patet, tum quia actus quibus illi generantur, sunt specie distincti, tum etiam quia inclinant ad similes actus specie distinctos: tum praeterea, quia non est maior ratio distinctionis inter actus ipsos secundos, quam inter inclinationes, quae per modum actus primi manent ad similes actus inclinantes, iis quibus genitae sunt, & consequenter commensuratae, & proportionatae ipsis: tum denique, quia si non esset [18a] distinctio specifica inter illa duo; nec numerica esset necessaria, sed sufficeret augmentum per modum intensionis. Consequentia autem prior probatur, quia ex duabus qualitatibus specie distinctis non potest una qualitas, & unius speciei componi.

5. Responderi potest, illa duo non distingui specie totali, sed partiali, ideoque posse qualitatem integram, simpliciter unam ex eis componi tanquam ex partibus heterogeneis. Sed contra, nam interrogo qualis sit hic compositionis modus, nam, aut est per veram & realem unionem illarum qualitatum (quae dicuntur partiales) non tantum in eodem subiecto, sed etiam inter se: vel est solum per adunationem in eodem subiecto. Neutrum dici potest, nam primum non videtur satis posse intelligi, aut explicari, nam interrogo qualis sit illa unio. Aut enim est per immediatam coniunctionem unius cum alio: & hoc non, quia talis

increase without a real addition. And this addition cannot be sufficient if it is by way of intension alone, since this increase is not merely due to the diverse participation of the subject which results from a greater rooting of the same form in itself, but rather concerns the habit itself, giving it a greater extension with respect to its object. Therefore, an addition is required on the side of the habit, insofar as something is added to it, by virtue of which it concerns a new object or new conclusion, as St. Thomas plainly teaches in treating of habits in general, *ST* I-II, q. 52, arts. 1 and 2.[131] A habit of this sort, therefore, cannot be altogether simple insofar as it is related to the whole extension of its object. But that it cannot be composite and yet truly one in species, either, is proved, in the first place, because what is first acquired in a habit by means of acts of one species, and what is added by means of an act that is distinct in species, are also distinct from each other in species. Therefore, they do not compose a habit that is specifically one. The antecedent is clear, because the acts by which they are generated are distinct in species; and also because they incline to similar acts that are distinct in species; and in addition, because the ground$_r$ of distinction between the same second acts is no greater than that between those inclinations which both remain as first acts and incline to acts which are similar to those by which they were generated, and to which they are consequently commensurate and proportioned; and finally, because if there were no specific distinction between those two things,[132] neither would a numerical distinction be necessary, but an increase by way of intension would suffice. And the earlier consequence is proved because one quality of a single species cannot be composed of two qualities distinct in species.

5. One can reply that those two things are not distinguished by a total species, but by a partial one, and therefore that a complete quality, one without qualification, can be composed from them as from heterogeneous parts. But to the contrary, I ask: of what sort is this mode of composition? For, either it is through a true and real union of those qualities (which are called partial), not only in the same subject,

St. Thomas.

---

131. Thomas Aquinas, *Sancti Thomae Aquinatis opera omnia* (Leonina), t. 6, pp. 330–34.

132. Sc. between "what is first acquired in a habit by means of acts of one species, and what is added by means of an act that is distinct in species."

unio non intervenit, nisi inter ea quae se habent ut potentia & actus, vel ut forma & materia, accidens & subiectum, terminus & res terminabilis: nullo autem ex his modis illa duo inter se comparantur, ut per se constat, quia utraque respicit per se suum obiectum, & non requirit aliam ut ab ea terminetur, vel actuetur. Vel uniuntur per modum cuiusdam continuationis in aliquo termino communi, ut creduntur uniri gradus intensionis: & hic modus unionis etiam est intellectu difficillimus. Primo quidem, quia nulla est sufficiens ratio ad fingendum illum. Secundo,[32] quia oportet assignari aliquem indivisibilem terminum, in quo illa duo uniantur. Quod ta⟨24a⟩men non videtur posse fieri, quia ille terminus etiam debet respicere aliquod obiectum: nullum est autem ad quod possit tendere, quia nec simul tendit in utrumque obiectum illorum partialium habituum seu actuum, per quos geniti sunt, neque est ulla ratio, ob quam magis tendat in unum, quam in aliud: nec fingi potest novum obiectum, in quod tendat, cum nullum aliud fuerit per actus cognitum, seu iudicatum. Tertio, quia in actibus non potest requiri talis unio, neque talis indivisibilis terminus in quo uniantur: alias omnes actus scientiae Metaphysicae possent in unum coalescere, & realiter uniri, quod est inintelligibile: ergo neque in habitu est talis unio, quia non potest aliquid esse in habitu, quod non fuerit in actibus: Si autem actus non habent inter se unionem, non habent unde, vel quo illam efficiant. Et hae rationes procedunt, etiam si illi duo partiales[33] habitus fingantur esse eiusdem rationis, & speciei. Si autem specie differunt, addi potest quarta ratio, scilicet, quia ea quae differunt specie, non possunt per se esse continua, neque habere proprium terminum communem.

---

32. C_1, C_2, G_2, M_1, M_2, M_3, M_4, P_1, P_2, V_3, V_4, V_5, and Vivès all omit the words "nulla est sufficiens ratio ad fingendum illum. Secundo, quia." These words are found in S, V_1, and V_2.

33. Reading "partiales" here with S, V_1, and V_2. The following read "particulares" instead: C_1, C_2, G_2, M_1, M_2, M_3, M_4, P_1, P_2, V_3, V_4, V_5, and Vivès.

but with each other as well, or it is only through a conjunction in the same subject. Neither can be said, for the first seems not to admit of being sufficiently understood or explained, for I ask: of what sort is that union? For either it is through an immediate conjunction of one thing with another, but this is not the case, since such a union does not take place except between things that are related as potency and act—whether as form and matter, as accident and subject, or as terminus and terminable thing$_r$—and in none of these ways are those two things related to each other, as is clear *per se*, since each is *per se* related to its own object and does not need the other so as to be terminated or actuated by it. Or they are united by means of a kind of continuation in some common terminus, as grades of intension are believed to be united, and this mode of union is also most difficult to understand. First, indeed, because there is no sufficient reason to suppose it. Second, because some indivisible terminus must be assigned in which those two things are united. It seems, however, that this cannot be done, since that terminus also must be related to some object; but there is no object to which it could be directed, since it is not directed simultaneously to both of the objects of those partial habits, or to both objects of the acts through which these partial habits were produced; nor is there any reason why it should be directed to one rather than the other; nor can one imagine a new object to which it is directed, since nothing else was cognized or judged through the acts. Third, because such a union cannot be required in acts, nor can such an indivisible terminus in which they are united. Otherwise all acts of the science of metaphysics could merge into a single act and really be united, which is unintelligible. Therefore, neither is there such a union in the habit, since there cannot be something in the habit that was not in the acts. But if the acts do not have a union with each other, then they do not have the resources or means to produce it. And these arguments succeed even if those two partial habits are imagined to be of the same nature$_r$ and species. But if they differ in species, a fourth argument can be added, namely: because those things which differ in species cannot be *per se* continuous, nor can they have a proper common terminus.

6. Tandem, si propter has rationes dicatur illas qualitates solum componere unum habitum per adunationem in eodem subiecto, sequitur primo non esse veram unitatem in hac scientia, sed tantum per accidens ratione subiecti, maxime si (ut videtur probabilius) qualitates illae specie distinguuntur. Sequitur secundo eadem ratione ex omnibus habitibus scientiarum componi unam scientiam per adunationem in eodem subiecto.

7. Duae difficultates seu quaestiones tanguntur in argumentis propositis. Prima est propria & [18b] specialis huius loci, an Metaphysica sit una scientia specie, nec ne. Secunda est generalis & eiusdem rationis in omnibus scientiis, & fere in omnibus habitibus acquisitis, an sint simplices qualitates, vel compositae secundum extensionem ad obiecta.

Variae hac super re opiniones.

8. Circa priorem partem, quae est propria huius loci, aliqui sentiunt, Metaphysicam non esse unam scientiam specie, sed genere: & ad minus continere sub se tres illas species praedictas, scilicet, de Deo, qui omnino abstrahit & a materia, & ab omni vestigio materiae, ut existimari potest omnis compositio: item ab omni mutatione & vicissitudine: & de intelligentiis creatis, quae neque abstrahunt ab omni compositione, neque[34] ab omni mutatione, tum locali, tum intellectus & voluntatis: abstrahunt tamen intrinsece & ⟨24b⟩ essentialiter a materia & motu physico: & de ente, quod solum permissive abstrahit a materia secundum esse. Neque est hoc contra divisionem scientiae speculativae datam ab Aristotele in Physicam, Mathematicam, & Metaphysicam, quia illa non est divisio in ultimas species, sed subalternas, ut constat de Mathematica, quae plures scientias sub se continet.

Metaphysica est una scientia specie. Aristoteles.

9. Nihilominus asserendum est cum communi sententia Metaphysicam simpliciter esse unam scientiam specie. Haec enim videtur clara mens Aristotelis in toto prooemio, seu capit. 1 & 2. lib. 1. Metaph. ubi semper de hac scientia tanquam de una specie loquitur, eique tanquam uni & eidem attribuit nomina & attributa, quae partim illi conveniunt, secundum quod versatur circa Deum & intelligentias: sic enim vocatur

34. Reading "ab omni compositione, neque" here with all of the early editions. Vivès omits these words.

6. Finally, if, on account of these arguments, it is said that those qualities only compose a single habit by means of a conjunction in the same subject, it follows, first, that there is no true unity in this science, but only an accidental unity by virtue of the subject, especially if (as seems more plausible) those qualities are specifically distinct. It follows, second, for the same reason, that, by means of this conjunction in the same subject, all the habits of the sciences compose a single science.

7. Two difficulties or questions are touched on in the arguments presented. The first is proper and particular to this place, namely, whether metaphysics is specifically one science, or not. The second is general and of the same nature, in the case of all sciences and almost all acquired habits, namely, whether they are simple qualities or are instead composite according to the extension they have relative to their objects.

8. With respect to the first difficulty, which is proper to this place, some think that metaphysics is not specifically one science, but one generically, and that it contains under itself at least the three species mentioned earlier, namely: a science of God, who abstracts altogether both from matter and from every image of matter (as every composition can be thought to involve), and likewise from every change and succession; a science of created intelligences, which abstract neither from every composition nor from every change, whether local or intellectual or volitive, although they abstract intrinsically and essentially from matter and physical motion; and a science of being, which only permissively abstracts from matter with respect to existence$_e$. Nor is this contrary to the division of speculative science given by Aristotle into physics, mathematics, and metaphysics, since this is not a division into ultimate species, but into subaltern ones, as is clear in the case of mathematics, which contains several sciences under it. *Various opinions on this issue.*

9. Nevertheless, it must be asserted, with the common opinion, that metaphysics is without qualification specifically one science. For this seems to be Aristotle's clear meaning in the entire proem, that is, in *Metaph.* I, chs. 1 and 2, where he always speaks of this science as specifically one and attributes to it, as to one and the same science, names and attributes that in part agree with it insofar as it is concerned with God and the intelligences (for thus is it called theology, or divine science, and first philosophy) and in part agree with it insofar as it is concerned *Metaphysics is specifically one science. Aristotle.*

Theologia, seu scientia divina, & prima Philosophia: partim ut versatur circa ens in quantum ens, & prima attributa, & principia eius, qua ratione dicitur scientia universalis, & Metaphysica: *sapientia* autem vocatur, quatenus haec omnia complectitur, & prima principia, primasque rerum causas contemplatur. Item in lib. 4. ubi ex professo tractare videtur de obiecto huius scientiae, dicit illam esse unam & considerare omnia quae a materia sunt separata.[35] Unde in discursu & modo tradendi hanc doctrinam, satis indicat eam esse scientiam unam in specie, & saepe indifferenter ait ens in quantum ens esse adaequatum obiectum huius scientiae, eiusque praecipuam partem esse substantiam, vel simpliciter, vel immaterialem, ac primam, ut patet ex lib. 4. cap. 2 & 3. & lib. 7. cap. 1. & lib. 12. in quo de Deo & de intelligentiis cognitionem tradit, eamque dicit esse praecipuam huius doctrinae partem, ad quam quodammodo caeterae ordinantur. Ac denique lib. 6. ca. 1, & lib. 11. cap. 6. abstractionem a materia secundum esse constituit ut adaequatam rationem formalem sub qua obiecti huius scientiae. Si autem distincta esset scientia quae ageret de ente ut ens est, ab ea quae tractat de ente immateriali, & re ipsa a materia separato, illa prior non participaret proprie ac perfecte huiusmodi abstractionem, neque ageret de primis rerum causis, neque alia haberet, quae Aristoteles Metaphysicae tribuit. Et hoc fere

D. Thom.   argumento concludit D. Thom. 1. 2. q. 57. arti. 2. sapientiam naturalem tantum esse unam, cum habitus aliarum scientiarum plures sint, ubi necesse est loqui de unitate specifica, nam se⟨25a⟩cundum genus, etiam aliae scientiae unitatem habent: haec autem sapientia non est nisi Metaphysica. Nec potest dici sa[19a]pientiam vocari solam eam partem seu scientiam ultimam Metaphysicae, quae de Deo agit, quia illa praecise sumpta non considerat prima principia communia omnibus scientiis, neque illa corroborat & confirmat, quod ad sapientiam spectat: sicut e contrario pars illa prior Metaphysicae, quae agit de ente ut sic, per se sola non considerat omnes altissimas causas: & ideo etiam illa praecise sumpta non habet propriam rationem sapientiae: oportet ergo ut una & eadem scientia haec omnia complectatur. Et hoc ipsum docuit idem Divus Thomas super citata loca Aristotelis, & praecipue in prologo Metaphysicae: idemque sentiunt reliqui expositores antiqui, & moderni.

---

35. Reading "'separata" here with S, V$_1$, and V$_2$. The following read "secreta" instead: C$_1$, C$_2$, G$_2$, M$_1$, M$_2$, M$_3$, M$_4$, P$_1$, P$_2$, V$_3$, V$_4$, V$_5$, and Vivès.

with being as being, its primary attributes, and its principles (for which reason it is called the universal science and metaphysics). And it is called "wisdom" insofar as it embraces all these things and considers first principles and the first causes of things_r. Further, in book IV, where he seems *ex professo* to treat of the object of this science, he says that it is one science and that it considers all things that are separate from matter.[133] Thus, in his discussion and in his way of handing down this doctrine, he sufficiently indicates that it is specifically one science, and he often indifferently says that being as being is the adequate object of this science, and that its principal part is substance, either substance without qualification, or immaterial and primary substance, as is clear from book IV, ch. 2 and ch. 3,[134] and from book VII, ch. 1, and from book XII,[135] in which he hands down cognition of God and the intelligences[136]; and he says that this cognition is the principal part of this doctrine, to which the other parts are in some way ordered.[137] And finally, in book VI, ch. 1,[138] and book XI, ch. 6,[139] he establishes abstraction from matter with respect to existence_e as the adequate "formal aspect_r under which" of this science's object. If, however, the science which treats of being as being were distinct from that which treats of being that is immaterial and really separate from matter, the former science would not participate properly and perfectly in such an abstraction, nor would it treat of the first causes of things_r, nor would it have the other features that Aristotle attributes to metaphysics. And with nearly this same argument St. Thomas concludes, *ST* I-II, q. 57, art. 2,[140] that natural wisdom is only one, while the habits of the other sciences are several—and here he must be speaking of specific unity, since the other sciences also have generic unity. But this wisdom is none other than metaphysics. Nor can it be said that only that final part or science of metaphysics which treats of God is called wisdom, for this

St. Thomas.

---

133. There is no mention of matter in *Metaph.* IV, ch. 1. Suárez likely has *Metaph.* VI, ch. 1, in mind.

134. Aristotle, *Metaph.* IV, ch. 2, 1003a33–b19, ch. 3, 1005a19–b11.

135. Aristotle, *Metaph.* XII, ch. 1, 1069a18–b2.

136. Aristotle, *Metaph.* XII, chs. 6–10.

137. Aristotle, *Metaph.* VII, ch. 11, 1037a10–17.

138. Aristotle, *Metaph.* VI, ch. 1, 1026a10–16.

139. Aristotle, *Metaph.* XI, ch. 7, 1064a28–b6.

140. Thomas Aquinas, *Sancti Thomae Aquinatis opera omnia* (Leonina), t. 6, p. 365b.

10. Ratio vero huius sententiae est, quia nullum est sufficiens fundamentum ad hanc scientiarum multiplicationem: & alioqui omnia ea, quae in hac scientia tractantur, adeo sunt inter se connexa, ut non possint commode diversis scientiis attribui. Eo vel maxime, quod ratione eiusdem abstractionis omnia conveniunt in eadem ratione scibilis: nam licet Deus, & intelligentiae secundum se consideratae, videantur altiori quodam gradu & ordine esse constitutae, tamen prout in nostram considerationem cadunt, non possunt a consideratione transcendentium attributorum seiungi. Unde etiam confirmatur, nam perfecta scientia de Deo & aliis substantiis separatis, tradit cognitionem omnium praedicatorum quae in eis insunt: ergo etiam praedicatorum communium, & transcendentium. Neque est eadem ratio de inferioribus scientiis, v. g. Philosophia, quae licet consideret de materiali substantia, non tamen propterea contemplatur praedicata communia, & transcendentia, quae illi etiam insunt: quia cum illa sit inferior scientia, non potest ascendere ad abstractiora, & difficiliora praedicata cognoscenda, sed per altiorem scientiam cognita supponit. At vero scientia de Deo, & intelligentiis est suprema omnium naturalium, & ideo nihil supponit cognitum per altiorem scientiam, sed in se includit quidquid necessarium est ad sui obiecti cognitionem perfectam, quantum per naturale lumen haberi potest: eadem ergo scientia quae de his specialibus obiectis tractat, simul considerat omnia praedicata, quae illis sunt cum aliis rebus communia: & haec est tota Metaphysica doctrina, est ergo una scientia. ⟨25b⟩

part, taken precisely, does not consider the first principles common to all the sciences, nor does it strengthen and confirm them, which is a task belonging to wisdom—just as, conversely, that prior part of metaphysics which treats of being as such does not, by itself alone, consider all the highest causes, and therefore it, too, taken precisely, does not have the proper nature_r of wisdom. It must, therefore, be the case that one and the same science embraces all these things. And this is the very thing that St. Thomas teaches in connection with the cited passages in Aristotle, and especially in the prologue to the *Metaphysics*.[141] And the remaining expositors, ancient and modern, believe the same.

10. The reason for this opinion is that there is no sufficient foundation for this multiplication of sciences. And in any case, all those things which are dealt with in this science are so interconnected that they cannot suitably be attributed to diverse sciences, especially in view of the fact that, by reason of the same abstraction, they all agree in the same concept_r of knowable [object], for although God and the intelligences, considered in themselves, seem to be constituted in some higher grade and order, nevertheless, insofar as they fall under our consideration, they cannot be separated from a consideration of transcendental attributes. For the following reason also is the opinion confirmed: because perfect science of God and the other separate substances affords cognition of all the predicates that are in them. Therefore, it also affords cognition of the common and transcendental predicates. The same is not true of the lower sciences—for example, philosophy, which, although it considers material substance, yet does not for this reason consider the common and transcendental predicates that are in it, since, being a lower science, it cannot ascend in order to cognize more abstract and difficult predicates, but supposes them cognized by a higher science. However, the science of God and the intelligences is the highest of all the natural sciences, and therefore supposes nothing cognized by a higher science, but includes in itself whatever is necessary for perfect cognition of its object, insofar as this can be had by the natural

---

141. Thomas Aquinas, *In duodecim libros metaphysicorum Aristotelis expositio*, pp. 1–2, pp. 151–53 (bk. IV, lec. 1, ns. 534–47), pp. 164–65 (bk. IV, lec. 5, ns. 588–95), pp. 297–98 (bk. VI, lec. 1, ns. 1162–63), pp. 315–18 (bk. VII, lec. 1, ns. 1245–62), p. 536 (bk. XI, lec. 7, ns. 2259–64), pp. 567–68 (bk. XII, lec. 1, ns. 2416–23).

Rationi
primae
dubitandi
respondetur.

11. Atque ex his satisfactum est primae rationi dubitandi in principio positae: declaratum est enim, quo modo illa abstractio a materia secundum esse, quae permissiva dicitur, vel necessaria, non variet specificam rationem obiecti scibilis, tum propter connexionem[36] talium rerum & praedicatorum inter se, praesertim in ordine ad nostram cognitionem[37]: tum etiam propter eundem ordinem doctrinae, & certitudinis. Denique, quia illa diversitas abstractionis solum est secundum diversos conceptus rationis, quae diversitas sola per se non sufficit ad diversam scientiam constituendam, nisi alia maior ratio distinctionis occurrat. Alioqui quot sunt communia praedicata abstrahibilia ab inferioribus, tot essent scientiae multiplicandae, & quot essent rerum species, tot etiam essent scientiae specie differentes, quod communiter non admittitur.

Metaphysica
unus ne
habitus.

12. Ad secundam dubitandi rationem non possumus [19b] in hoc loco ex professo satisfacere, quia, ut dixi, quaestio quae ibi tangitur, communis est omnibus scientiis, & fortasse inferius, tractando de qualitate, eam examinabimus. Nunc breviter dico difficillimum mihi videri velle defendere habitum Metaphysicae esse aut unam simplicem qualitatem, aut ita compositam, ut ex variis partialibus entitatibus, vera ac reali unione inter se unitis consurgat: quam difficultatem satis ostendunt quae in illo argumento proposita sunt. Quare facilius dici videtur huiusmodi scientiam includere partiales qualitates seu habitus, qui unam scientiam componere dicuntur non sola aggregatione per accidens in eodem subiecto, cui inhaerent, sed subordinatione aliqua ac dependentia quam inter se habent per ordinem ad idem subiectum, circa quod versantur: non enim necesse est in omnibus rebus eundem ordinem unitatis inveniri. Quod si quis inquirat, quisnam sit iste ordo

---

36. Reading "propter connexionem" with S, V_1, and V_2. Vivès has "propter necessariam connexionem." The following read "propter nostram connexionem": C_1, C_2, G_2, M_1, M_2, M_3, M_4, P_1, P_2, V_3, V_4, and V_5.

37. Reading "ad nostram cognitionem" here with S, V_1 and V_2. The following read "ad cognitionem": C_1, C_2, G_2, M_1, M_2, M_3, M_4, P_1, P_2, V_3, V_4, V_5, and Vivès.

light. Therefore, the same science that treats of these special objects at the same time considers all the predicates that are common to them and other things$_r$, and this is the whole of metaphysical doctrine. It is, therefore, a single science.

11. And in this way the first reason for doubt set forth at the be-ginning has been dealt with.[142] For it has been made clear how that abstraction from matter with respect to existence$_e$, which is called per-missive or necessary, does not vary the specific concept of the knowable object, both because of the connection between such things$_r$ and predi-cates, especially in relation to our cognition, and also because [they be-long to] the same order of doctrine and certainty. And finally, because that diversity of abstraction is only according to diverse concepts of reason, and this diversity alone does not suffice *per se* for constituting a diverse science, unless another, greater ground$_r$ of distinction presents itself. Otherwise, sciences would have to be multiplied as many times as there are common predicates abstractable from inferiors, and there would be as many specifically different sciences as there are species of things$_r$—which is generally not granted. *Reply to the first reason for doubt.*

12. We cannot in this place *ex professo* satisfy the second reason for doubt, since, as I have said, the question that is touched on there is common to all the sciences, and we shall perhaps examine it below when treating of quality.[143] For now, I say briefly that to me it seems most difficult to want to defend either the claim that the habit of meta-physics is one simple quality or the claim that it is composed in such a way that it arises from various partial entities united to each other by a true and real union. And the difficulty is sufficiently shown by the things set forth in that argument. For this reason it seems easier to say that a science of this sort includes partial qualities or habits that are said to compose a single science, not *per accidens* merely by aggregation in the same subject of inhesion, but through some subordination and dependence they have among themselves by virtue of being concerned with the same subject. For it is not necessary that the same order of uni-ty be found in all things$_r$. But if someone should inquire what this order of subordination and dependence is, it can be answered that it consists *Whether metaphysics is a single habit.*

142. See *DM* 1.3.2 above.
143. See *DM* 44.11.

subordinationis & dependentiae: responderi potest consistere in habitudine ad idem obiectum, quod licet res varias complectatur, & diversas proprietates habeat, quae de illo demonstrantur, ita tamen inter se sunt connexae, ut harum cognitio ab illis pendeat, & se se mutuo in cognitione iuvent sub eadem ratione & modo scientiae, ac doctrinae. Sed haec res, ut dixi, magis accuratam postulat inquisitionem ac disputationem suo loco tradendam. ⟨26a⟩

in a relation to the same object, and that, although this object embraces various things, and has diverse properties that are demonstrated of it, nevertheless, they are interconnected in such a way that cognition of the latter depends on the former, and they aid each other mutually in cognition under the same method, and mode of science and doctrine. But this matter, as I have said, requires a more careful investigation and treatment, which must be handed down in its proper place.

———

1. Explicato obiecto, & essentia huius scientiae, oportebat nonnihil dicere de causis eius: sed quoniam de materiali, formali, & efficiente nihil proprium ac peculiare dicendum occurrit, ideo solum dicemus de causa finali. Materialis enim causa huius scientiae non est alia, nisi subiectum eius, quod constat esse intellectum, nisi quis velit materiam circa quam ad materialem causam revocare: illa autem materia non est alia praeter obiectum scientiae de quo satis dictum est. Rursus cum ipsa scientia forma quaedam sit, non habet aliam causam formalem propriam, sed habet essentiam suam seu rationem formalem, habet etiam obiectum, quod quatenus speciem tribuit, rationem quandam formae habere dicitur, saltem extrinsecae. Denique, cum haec scientia acquisita sit, per proprios actus tanquam per proximam causam efficientem fit: in quo nihil speciale habet praeter ea quae communia sunt caeteris habitibus acquisitis. Igitur solus finis & munus huius scientiae explicanda supersunt: haec enim duo ita in praesenti coniuncta sunt, ut unum potius esse videantur: est autem haec scientia quoad habitum propter suam operationem, quam proxime elicit: hoc enim commune est omni habitui, neque aliquid in particulari habet habitus huius scientiae, quod nova declaratione indigeat. De ipsa vero operatione seu actu huius scientiae explicandum est qualis sit, & quem finem habeat, & inde constabit quaenam fuerit huius scientiae necessitas, vel utilitas.

Quae sit materialis causa Metaphysicae. Quae formalis.

Quae efficiens.

2. Dico ergo primo finem huius scientiae esse veritatis contemplationem propter se ipsam. Ita docet Aristoteles 12. Metaph. c. 2. & lib. 2.

Quis finis Metaph. Aristotel.

How Many Functions Does This Science Have, What Is Its End, and What Is Its Utility?

———

1. The object and essence of this science having been explained, something must be said about its causes. But since there is nothing peculiar and special that needs to be said about its material, formal, and efficient causes, we shall speak only of its final cause. For the material cause of this science is none other than its subject, which, clearly, is the intellect, unless someone should wish to reduce "the matter concerning which" to the material cause—but this matter is none other than the object of this science, about which enough has been said. Moreover, since a science itself is a kind of form, it does not have another proper formal cause, but has its own essence or formal character$_r$. It also has an object, which, insofar as it determines its species, is said to have a certain character$_r$ of form, at least of extrinsic form. Finally, since this science is acquired, it comes to be through proper acts as through a proximate efficient cause, in which respect it has nothing special in addition to those things which are common to other acquired habits as well. So only the end and function of this science remain to be explained, for these two are so conjoined in the present case that they seem rather to be one. But as far as the habit is concerned, this science exists$_e$ for the sake of its operation, which it proximately elicits, for this is common to every habit, nor does the habit of this science have something particular that requires a new clarification. But regarding the very operation or act of this science, it must be explained of what sort it is, and what end it has, and from this it will be clear what the necessity or utility of this science is.

What the material cause of metaphysics is.

What the formal cause is.

What the efficient cause is.

2. I say in the first place, then, that this science's end is the contemplation of truth for its own sake. This is what Aristotle teaches in

What the end of metaphysics is.

Aristotle.

c. 1. ubi id probat primo a priori, quia ea scientia maxime est pro[20a] pter veritatis cognitionem, & propter se ipsam, quae de primis rerum causis, & principiis, & de rebus dignissimis considerat: huiusmodi enim res aptissimae sunt ut sciantur, & earum cognitio maxime expetibilis est: sed haec scientia versatur in cognitione altissimarum rerum & causarum, ut constat ex his quae de obiecto illius diximus: ergo haec scientia maxime est propter se, & ⟨26b⟩ propter veritatis cognitionem. Secundo, quia haec scientia non inquirit veritatis cognitionem propter operationem: ergo propter se ipsam: non est enim inter haec invenire medium. Antecedens autem probatur ab Aristotele duplici signo: unum est quod homines propter admirationem & causarum ignorationem hanc scientiam invenire coeperunt: ergo propter cognitionem, & non alterius operis gratia, eam inquisierunt. Secundum signum est, quia homines, cum eis omnia ad hanc vitam necessaria suppeterent, hanc scientiam investigarunt: non ergo propter alium usum, sed ad expellendam ignorantiam, atque adeo propter ipsam veritatis cognitionem, eam inquisierunt. Tertio nos id probare possumus, quia scientia quae cognitionem ordinat ad operationem, proxime disputat de rebus operabilibus ab homine: haec autem scientia non tractat de huiusmodi rebus, sed de nobilissimis entibus, & de universalissimis rationibus entis, & maxime abstractis.

3. Sed si quis recte consideret, tam assertio posita, quam ea quae ex Aristotele in eius confirmationem adduximus, communia sunt omnibus speculativis scientiis, & maxime naturali Philosophiae, & ita ex dictis rationibus recte infert Aristoteles hanc scientiam, speculativam esse, & non practicam, quia proxime non ordinatur ad opus, sed sistit in veritatis cognitione, quod (ut dixi) commune est universae naturali philosophiae. Ut ergo in assertione posita proprius finis huius scientiae declaretur, subintelligere oportet eam esse propter cognitionem earum veritatum, quae de ipso ente ut tale est, & de rebus quae secundum esse abstrahunt a materia, demonstrari possunt. Atque ita proprius finis eius est declarare naturam, proprietates & causas entis in quantum ens, & partium eius, quatenus secundum esse a materia abstrahunt.

Metaph. XII, ch. 2,[144] and book II, ch. 1,[145] where he proves this, first, *a priori*, because the science which considers the first causes and principles of things$_r$, as well as the most worthy things$_r$, is most of all for the sake of cognizing truth, and for its own sake, for such things$_r$ are most suited to being known, and the cognition of them is most desirable. But this science is concerned with the cognition of the highest things$_r$ and causes, as is clear from the things that we have said about its object. Therefore, this science is most of all for its own sake, and for the sake of cognizing truth. Second, because this science does not seek cognition of truth for the sake of an operation. Therefore, it seeks cognition of truth for its own sake, for between these there is no middle ground. And the antecedent is proved by Aristotle by means of a twofold sign. One is that human beings began to discover this science on account of wonder and an ignorance of causes; therefore, they sought it for the sake of cognition, and not for the sake of some other operation. The second sign is that human beings sought out this science when they had got all the things necessary for this life; therefore, they did this not for the sake of some further utility, but in order to expel ignorance, and so they sought it for the sake of the very cognition of truth. Third, we can prove this because a science that orders cognition to an operation most immediately treats of things$_r$ that can be done by human beings; however, this science does not deal with such things$_r$, but with the most noble beings and the most universal and abstract natures$_r$ of being.

3. But if someone rightly reflects, he shall see that both the assertion laid down and the things we have adduced from Aristotle for its confirmation are common to all the speculative sciences, and especially to natural philosophy, and so from the mentioned arguments Aristotle rightly infers that this science is speculative, and not practical, since it is not proximately ordered to work, but stops at cognition of the truth, which (as I've said) is common to the whole of natural philosophy as well. Therefore, in order to make clear, in the assertion advanced, the proper end of this science, one must understand in addition that this

---

144. In Suárez's time, *Metaph.* XII, ch. 2 contained part of our bk. XII, ch. 1, and the whole of our bk. XII, ch. 2 (1069a30–b34). There is no mention of the end of metaphysics in this portion of the text, however. The Latin text's "12" would seem to be a misprint: see Aristotle, *Metaph.* I, ch. 2, 982a30–b28.

145. Aristotle, *Metaph.* II, ch. 1, 993b19–31.

4. Atque hinc colligitur prima necessitas seu utilitas huius doctrinae, nimirum ut perficiat intellectum secundum se (ut sic dicam) & propter perfectissimas res, rerumque rationes cognoscendas. Intellectus enim humanus licet in corpore sit, & ideo ministerio sensuum & phantasmatum indigeat, tamen secundum se spiritualis est, & vim habet res omnes, etiam spirituales & divinas, percipiendi: propter quod, *quodammodo divinus*, appellatus est ab Aristotele lib. 1. de anima, text. 82. Philosophia igitur naturalis videtur intellectum perficere, prout utitur sensibus, ⟨27a⟩ & circa sensibilia versatur. Mathematicae vero scientiae illum videntur perficere, prout aliquo modo abstrahit ab externorum sensuum experimento, cum dependentia tamen ab imaginatione, seu phantasia. Haec autem doctrina intellectum illustrat secundum se, abstrahens, quantum in corpore fieri potest, a sensibus, & phantasia: & res spirituales ac divinas contemplans, rationesque ac principia omnibus rebus communia, & generalia attributa entium, quae a nulla inferiori scientia considerantur.

5. Secundo vero addendum est, scientiam Metaphy[20b]sicae non solum propter se ipsam esse convenientem, sed etiam ad alias scientias perfecte acquirendas esse valde utilem. Haec assertio sumitur ex *Aristotel.* Aristotele, 1. Metaph. c. 2. & lib. 3. c. 2. ubi inter alias conditiones sapientiae ponit, quod reliquae scientiae illi ministrent, ipsa vero aliis praesit, eisque (ait Aristoteles) praecipiat, non imperio practico, quod ad prudentiam potius, vel morales scientias spectat, sed directione speculativa: & subdit huiusmodi esse Metaphysicam respectu aliarum scientiarum, quia de praestantissimis rebus, & de primis rerum causis, ac de ultimo fine & summo bono disputat. Addit etiam primo Poster. c. 7. Metaphysicam solam versari circa prima principia reliquarum scientiarum. Sunt enim duplicia principia scientiarum, ut in eodem lib. docet c. 8. quaedam propria, quae in unaquaque scientia declarantur:

science is for the sake of cognizing those truths which can be demonstrated of both being itself as such and things$_r$ that abstract from matter with respect to existence$_e$. And thus its proper end is to make clear the nature, properties, and causes of being as being, and the natures, properties, and causes of its parts, insofar as they abstract from matter with respect to existence$_e$.

4. And from this is inferred the primary necessity or utility of this doctrine: namely, to perfect the intellect in itself (so to speak) and to cognize the most perfect things$_r$ and natures$_r$ of things$_r$. For the human intellect, although it is in a body and therefore needs the help of both the senses and phantasms, is nevertheless spiritual in itself and has the power to perceive all things$_r$, including spiritual and divine things$_r$—for which reason it is called "in a certain way divine" by Aristotle in *De anima* I, text 82.[146] Natural philosophy, therefore, seems to perfect the intellect insofar as it uses the senses and concerns itself with sensible things. But the mathematical sciences seem to perfect it insofar as it abstracts in some way from the experience of the external senses, although with a dependence on imagination or phantasy. However, this doctrine illuminates the intellect in itself, abstracting, to the extent that this can be done in the body, from the senses and phantasy, and contemplating spiritual and divine things$_r$, and natures$_r$ and principles common to all things$_r$, and the general attributes of beings, which are considered by no inferior science.

5. But in the second place, it must be added that the science of metaphysics is not only fitting on its own account, but is also very useful for perfectly acquiring the other sciences. This claim is taken from Aristotle, *Metaph.* I, ch. 2, and book III, ch. 2,[147] where he mentions, among other features of wisdom, that other sciences serve it, while it is set over the others, and it commands them (Aristotle says), not with a practical dominion, which is rather the concern of prudence or the moral sciences, but with a speculative direction, and he adds that metaphysics is such in relation to the other sciences because it deals with the most excellent things$_r$, with the first causes of things$_r$, and with the ultimate

Aristotle.

---

146. This text is *De anima* I, ch. 5, 410b10–15, but Aristotle does not here call the human intellect divine. Suárez may have in mind *De anima* I, ch. 4, 408b29–30.

147. Aristotle, *Metaph.* I, ch. 2, 982a14–19, and *Metaph.* III, ch. 2, 996b10–14.

alia communia multis, vel potius omnibus scientiis, quia omnes illis utuntur, ut res subiecta postulat, & quatenus ab eis caetera particularia principia pendent, ut ibidem Philosophus ait, & libr. 4. Metaph. text. 7. Cum ergo omnes scientiae ab his principiis maxime pendeant, necesse est ut per hanc scientiam maxime perficiantur: quia, ut supra dictum est, horum principiorum cognitio & contemplatio ad nullam specialem scientiam pertinere potest, cum ex abstractissimis, & universalissimis terminis constet. Sic igitur est haec scientia ad aliarum

D. Thom.   consecutionem & perfectionem valde utilis. Unde D. Tho. in princip. Metaph. & in 2. d. 3. q. 2. art. 2. dicit, Metaphysicam esse ordinativam aliarum scientiarum, quia considerat rationem entis absolute: aliae vero secundum determinatam rationem entis, & in 2. d. 24. q. 2. art. 2. ad 4. ait Metaphysicam dirigere alias scientias. Denique ex his quae de obiecto & materia circa quam versatur, diximus, id facile probari potest, quia haec ⟨27b⟩ scientia considerat supremas entium rationes, & universalissimas proprietates, & propriam rationem essentiae & esse, & omnes modos distinctionis qui sunt in rebus: at sine horum omnium distincta cognitione non potest perfecta particularium rerum cognitio haberi. Quod experimento etiam cognosci potest: omnes enim aliae scientiae saepe utuntur principiis Metaphysicae, aut ea supponunt, ut in suis demonstrationibus vel ratiocinationibus progredi possint: unde saepe contingit ex ignoratione Metaphysicae in aliis scientiis errare.[38]

38. Reading "errare" here with M_1, P_1, P_2, S, V_1, and V_2. The following have "errari": C_1, C_2, G_2, M_2, M_3, M_4, V_3, V_4, V_5, and Vivès.

end and highest good. He also adds, in *Post. An.* I, ch. 7, that metaphysics alone concerns itself with the first principles of the other sciences.[148] For the principles of the sciences are twofold, as Aristotle teaches in the same book, ch. 8.[149] Some are proper, and these are made clear in each of the sciences. Others are common to many sciences, or rather to all of them, since all the sciences use them to the extent required by their subject matter, and insofar as other particular principles depend on them, as the Philosopher says in the same place and in *Metaph.* IV, text 7.[150] Since, therefore, all sciences depend to the greatest degree on the latter principles, it is necessary that they should be perfected to the greatest degree by this science, for, as was said above, the cognition and consideration of these principles can pertain to no special science, since such a principle is constituted from the most abstract and universal terms. In this way, therefore, this science is very useful for the attainment and perfection of the others. Accordingly, St. Thomas, at the beginning of the *Metaphysics*[151] and in *Sent.* II, d. 3, q. 2, art. 2,[152] says that metaphysics is ordinative with respect to the other sciences, since it considers the nature$_r$ of being absolutely, while the other sciences do so in relation to a determinate nature$_r$ of being. And in *Sent.* II, d. 24, q. 2, art. 2, ad 4,[153] he says that metaphysics directs the other sciences. Finally, this can easily be proved by appeal to the things we have said about the object and "matter concerning which" of this science, since this science considers the highest natures$_r$ of beings, and the most universal properties, and the proper concepts$_r$ of essence and existence$_e$, and all the modes of distinction that are in things$_r$, and without a distinct cognition of all these things a perfect cognition of particular things$_r$ cannot be had. And this can also be cognized by experience, for all the other sciences often use the principles of metaphysics, or assume them, in order to be able to advance in their demonstrations or reason-

St. Thomas.

148. Aristotle, *Post. An.* I, ch. 9, 76a16–22.
149. Aristotle, *Post. An.* I, ch. 10, 76a37ff.
150. Aristotle, *Metaph.* IV, ch. 3, 1005a19–b2.
151. Thomas Aquinas, *In duodecim libros metaphysicorum Aristotelis expositio*, p. 1a (prologue).
152. Suárez seems to be referring, rather, to *Sent.* II, d. 3, q. 3, art. 2. See Thomas Aquinas, *S. Thomae Aquinatis opera omnia*, ed. Robert Busa (Stuttgart-Bad Cannstatt: Frommann-Holzboog, 1980), 1:136c.
153. Thomas Aquinas, *S. Thomae Aquinatis opera omnia* (ed. Busa), 1:194b.

Solvitur obiectio.

6. Dices, cum haec scientia Metaphysicae maxime propter se ipsam inquiratur, quo modo potest esse utilis ad alias: nam quod est utile ad alia, est propter illa. Respondetur, Dupliciter contingit aliquid dici utile ad aliud: uno modo tanquam medium ordinatum ad aliud: alio modo utile ad aliud dicitur tanquam causa superior & eminentior, influens suo modo in aliud. Hoc igitur posteriori modo est Metaphysica utilis ad inferiores scientias, & ideo non repugnat, sed potius est valde consentaneum ac consequens, quod sit maxime propter se, & aliis valde utilis seu proficua. Priori autem modo caeterae scientiae ordinantur ad Metaphysicam, quatenus omnis alia cognitio, tam speculativa, quam practica, ordinatur ad supremam contemplationem, in qua naturalis hominis foelicitas consistit. Ita fere D. Tho. 3. contra Gent.[39] c. 25. ratione 6. ubi sic inquit. *Hoc autem modo se habet Philosophia prima ad alias scientias speculativas: nam ab ipsa omnes aliae dependent, utpote ab ipsa accipientes sua principia, [21a] & directionem contra negantes principia, ipsaque prima philosophia tota ordinatur ad Dei cognitionem, sicut ad ultimum finem.*

Ad aliud multipliciter aliquid utile.

D. Thom.

7. Sed ut haec Metaphysicae munera exactius intelligantur, oportet in specie declarare, quae sint officia, quae circa alias scientias exercet, & quomodo illa exequatur.

Quomodo Metaphysica circa obiecta aliarum scientiam versetur, eave[40] demonstret.

8. Primum itaque attribui solet Metaphysicae, quod unicuique scientiae obiectum praescribat, &, si necesse sit, illud esse demonstret, quod significavit Averroes 3. de coelo, comm. 4. dicens Metaphysicae

Averroes.

39. Reading "3 contra Gentes" here with M_1, P_1, P_2, S, V_1, and V_2. The following have "2 contra Gentes": C_1, C_2, G_2, M_2, M_3, M_4, V_3, V_4, V_5, and Vivès.

40. Reading "*eave*" here with S, V_1, and V_2. The following have "*ut ea*": C_1, C_2, and G_2. The following have "*ea ut*": M_1, M_2, M_3, M_4, P_1, P_2, V_3, V_4, V_5, and Vivès.

ings. Thus it often happens that, through an ignorance of metaphysics, one makes mistakes in the other sciences.

6. You will say: since this science of metaphysics is sought most of all for its own sake, in what way can it be useful for other sciences? For what is useful for other things is for their sake. I reply: it happens in two ways that something is called useful for another. In one way, as a means ordered to something else. In the other way, one thing is called useful for another as a higher and more eminent cause, flowing in its own way into the other thing.[154] It is, then, in this second way that metaphysics is useful for the lower sciences, and therefore it is not absurd, but rather altogether fitting and consistent, that it be most of all for its own sake and also very useful or advantageous for the other sciences. But the other sciences are ordered to metaphysics in the first way insofar as every other cognition, both speculative and practical, is ordered to the highest contemplation, in which the natural happiness of the human being consists. This is precisely the view of St. Thomas, in *Summa contra gentiles* III, ch. 25, argument 6,[155] where he speaks thus: "But it is in this way that first philosophy is related to the other speculative sciences: for all the others depend on it, inasmuch as they receive their principles from it, as well as guidance against those who deny their principles, and first philosophy itself is wholly ordered to the cognition of God as to an ultimate end."

7. But so that these functions of metaphysics might be understood more precisely, we must make clear specifically what services it performs in relation to the other sciences, and how it performs them.

An objection is refuted.

One thing is useful for another in several ways.

St. Thomas.

How metaphysics is concerned with the objects of the other sciences, or demonstrates them.

8. First, then, metaphysics is normally thought to prescribe to each science its object, and, if necessary, to demonstrate that it exists$_e$, which

---

154. Suárez sometimes uses the verb here translated "flow into" (*influere*) transitively, with "*esse*" ("existence$_e$" or "being$_e$") as its direct object. Thus he speaks of how causes "flow being$_e$" (so to speak) into their effects.

155. Thomas Aquinas, *Sancti Thomae Aquinatis opera omnia* (Romae: Typis Riccardi Garroni, 1926), t. 14, p. 66b.

esse defendere, ac verificare (sic enim loquitur) subiecta particularium scientiarum. Ratio vero esse potest, quia, ut Aristoteles docet 1. Poster. ⟨28a⟩ scientia non probat, sed supponit suum subiectum[41] esse, & quid sit: ergo oportet ut aliunde sumat: ergo cum non semper id sit per se notum, saepeque indigeat aliqua declaratione & probatione, oportet illud sumere ex aliqua superiori scientia, quae non potest esse nisi Metaphysica, ad quam spectat considerare essentiae, quidditatis, & ipsius esse rationem.

Obiectio.   9. Dices, Quomodo potest Metaphysica de obiectis aliarum scientiarum demonstrare quod sint: nam si sermo sit de actuali existentia, haec non requiritur ut res scientiae obiiciantur, sed quasi per accidens se habet: unde demonstrari non potest, praesertim de entibus creatis, cum illis non necessario conveniat: quod si aliquo modo ex effectibus probari potest, id magis videtur ad Philosophum naturalem pertinere, qui ex effectibus[42] sensibilibus philosophatur. Si vero sermo sit de esse in aptitudine seu in potentia, hoc non potest de uno subiecto demonstrari, quia nullum est medium quo demonstrari possit: sicut etiam non potest de subiecto scientiae demonstrari quid sit, quia nullum est medium quo unicuique rei propria essentia conveniat: sed immediate ac per se se illi convenit. Adde, quod haec scientia non potest descendere ad particularia obiecta singularium scientiarum, quia non potest suam propriam abstractionem transcendere: sicut ergo propter hanc causam non potest demonstrare proprietates eorum, ita neque ostendere, an sint, vel quid sint. Praeterea, si aliae scientiae huius ope indigerent, ut ab ea sumerent obiecta sua, non possent ante hanc scientiam addisci: quod est falsum, ut constat experientia: nam licet haec scientia dignitate prima sit, non tamen generatione. Denique, si necessarium est ut haec scientia aliarum obiecta demonstret, necessaria erit alia scientia, quae huic deserviat ad ostendendum proprium eius obiectum, quia ipsa non potest demonstrare subiectum suum esse, sed supponere debet: neque illud est ita per se notum, quin aliqua ostensione indigeat.

41. Reading "subiectum" here with C$_1$, C$_2$, G$_2$, M$_1$, M$_2$, M$_3$, M$_4$, S, V$_1$, V$_2$, V$_3$, V$_4$, and V$_5$. The following have "obiectum" instead: P$_1$, P$_2$, and Vivès.

42. Reading "effectibus" here with all of the early editions. Vivès has "effectibas."

is what Averroes indicates, *On the Heavens* III, comment 4,[156] saying *Averroes.*
that it pertains to metaphysics to defend and verify (for he speaks thus)
the subjects of the particular sciences. And the following can serve as
a reason for this view: because, as Aristotle teaches in *Post. An.* I,[157] a
science does not prove, but assumes, that its subject exists$_e$ and what
it is. Therefore, it must take this from elsewhere. Therefore, since this
is not always known$_n$ *per se*, and often requires some clarification and
proof, it must take it from some higher science, which can only be
metaphysics, to which it pertains to consider the concepts$_r$ of essence,
quiddity, and existence$_e$.

9. You will say: how can metaphysics demonstrate, regarding the *Objection.*
objects of the other sciences, that they exist$_e$? For if the discussion concerns actual existence, this is not required in order for things$_r$ to be
objects of a science, but is, as it were, *per accidens*. And this is why
it cannot be demonstrated, especially regarding created beings, since
actual existence does not necessarily belong to them. And if it can in
some way be proved from effects, this seems rather to pertain to the
natural philosopher, who philosophizes from sensible effects. But if the
discussion concerns existence$_e$ in aptitude or potency, this cannot be
demonstrated of a single subject, for there is no middle term through
which it might be demonstrated, just as it also cannot be demonstrated, of a science's subject, what it is, because there is no middle term
through which the essence of each thing$_r$ agrees with it; rather, the
essence agrees with it immediately and *per se*. In addition, this science
cannot descend to the particular objects of the individual sciences,
since it cannot transcend its own proper abstraction. Therefore, just as,
for this reason, it cannot demonstrate their properties, so neither can
it prove whether they exist$_e$, or what they are. Furthermore, if other
sciences needed the help of this science in order to get their objects
from it, they could not be learned before this science. But this is false,
as is clear from experience, for although this science is first in respect
of dignity, still, it is not first in respect of generation. Finally, if it is

---

156. Averroes, *Averrois Cordubensis commentum magnum super libro De celo & mundo Aristotelis*, ed. R. Arnzen, G. Endress, and F. Carmody (Leuven, Belgium: Peeters, 2003), 2:490.
157. Aristotle, *Post. An.* I, ch. 10, 76b3–6.

   10. Respondetur ad primam difficultatem, hanc scientiam ita iuvare alias ad ostendenda[43] earum obiecta esse vel quid sint, sicut ipsae de obiectis suis hoc supponunt. Scientiae autem, per se loquendo, non supponunt suum obiectum actu existere: hoc enim, ut argumentum factum probat, accidentarium est ad rationem scientiae: illam excipio quae est de Deo, cuius esse est de ⟨28b⟩ quidditate eius: in aliis vero rebus ad scientiam & demonstrationem non est necessaria existentia ea[21b]rum, nisi fortasse interdum ex parte nostra ad inquirendam & inveniendam scientiam, quia nos ex rebus ipsis scientiam accipimus. Igitur haec scientia non demonstrat aliarum obiecta actu existere, sed ea solum de causa dici potest alia obiecta esse, quia praebet principia ad ostendendum in quo gradu entium talia obiecta collocentur, & quam quidditatem habeant. Hoc autem praestat haec doctrina, declarando in primis ipsam rationem entis, & essentiae seu quidditatis, & in quo consistat, & deinde distinguendo varios gradus entium, sub quibus omnia obiecta scientiarum continentur. Quocirca quanvis a priori & in se non possit per proprium medium intrinsecum demonstrari obiectum scientiae esse, & quid sit, tamen quoad nos ostendi potest ex signis seu effectibus, declarando in primis, quid requiratur ad rationem entis, & in quo ratio essentiae consistat, & quam connexionem cum talibus signis vel effectibus habere possit: quae omnia non nisi per principia huius doctrinae exacte ostenduntur.

11. Accedit etiam, quod per causas extrinsecas, ut sunt finalis & efficiens, potest interdum ostendi aliquod obiectum esse, quod maxime

---

43. Reading "ostendenda" here with S, V₁ and V₂. The following have "ostendendum": C₁, C₂, G₂, M₂, M₃, M₄, P₂, V₃, V₄, V₅, and Vivès. The following have "ostendendam": M₁ and P₁.

necessary that this science demonstrate the objects of the other sciences, another science will be necessary which serves this one by proving its object, since it cannot demonstrate that its own subject exists$_e$, but must assume this; nor is this object so known$_n$ *per se* that it stands in no need of some proof.

10. To the first difficulty, I reply that this science helps the others *Reply.* prove that their objects exist$_e$, or what they are, just as these sciences assume this regarding their own objects. But speaking *per se*, sciences do not assume that their object actually exists, for this, as the argument that was made proves, is accidental to the nature$_r$ of science. I except the science of God, whose existence$_e$ belongs to his quiddity. But in the case of other things$_r$, their existence is not necessary for science and demonstration, except, perhaps, in relation to us sometimes, so that we might investigate and discover the science, since we receive science from things$_r$ themselves. Therefore, this science does not demonstrate that the objects of the other sciences actually exist; rather, it is only for the following reason that it can be said [to show] that other objects exist$_e$: because it supplies principles to show in what grade of beings such objects are located, and what quiddity they have. And this doctrine does this, first of all, by making clear the very nature$_r$ of being and the concept$_r$ of essence or quiddity, and in what they consist, and second, by distinguishing the various grades of beings under which all the objects of the sciences are contained. For this reason, although the object of a science cannot *a priori* and in itself be demonstrated to exist$_e$ through a proper intrinsic middle term, nor can what it is, nevertheless, with respect to us it can be shown from signs or effects, by making clear, first, what is required for the nature$_r$ of being, and in what the concept$_r$ of an essence consists, and what connection it can have with such signs or effects—all of which cannot accurately be shown except through this doctrine's principles.

11. In addition, through extrinsic causes, such as the final and efficient, it can sometimes be shown that some object exists$_e$, which is done especially through primary and universal causes, which this science considers. For instance, we can show that angels exist$_e$ because they are necessary to the perfection of the universe and are of such a nature that it is not impossible for them to be made by God.

fit per primas & universales causas, de quibus[44] haec scientia considerat, ut ostendere possumus angelos esse, quia & ad perfectionem universi sunt necessarii, & talis sunt naturae, ut non repugnaverit a Deo
fieri.

12. Atque ita etiam constat, quomodo possit haec scientia tale
munus exercere circa obiecta particularium scientiarum, etiam si infra
illius abstractionem esse videantur. Nam in primis, ut supra Sect. 2.
tetigimus, quanvis Metaphysica per se non versetur circa res omnes
secundum proprias rationes earum, tamen aliquo modo attingit illas,
quatenus scilicet necesse est ad proprias rationes explicandas, vel divisiones tradendas, & proprios gradus Metaphysicos secernendos ab
aliis, quae divisiones Metaphysicae multum aliis scientiis deserviunt
ad sua subiecta praescribenda, & ab aliis secernenda. Ac deinde non
semper necesse est ut Metaphysica per se ipsam immediate ostendat
singularium scientiarum obiecta, sed satis est quod tribuat principia,
& declaret terminos, quibus aliae scientiae uti possunt ad supponenda,
vel ostendenda, quantum necesse fuerit, obiecta sua. ⟨29a⟩

Metaphysica prior omnibus scientiis doctrinae ordine.

13. Unde consequenter fatendum est, si ordo doctrinae spectetur
secundum se, Metaphysicam esse caeteris priorem, quod non solum ex
hoc munere, sed etiam ex alio quod statim explicabimus, colligi potest:
nam confirmat aliquo modo omnium scientiarum principia. Deinde
transcendentales rationes entis declarat, sine quarum cognitione vix
potest in aliqua scientia quidpiam exacte tractari. Ac denique quandam
habet singularem connexionem cum dialectica, quam inferius declarabo, ratione cuius effectum fortasse est ut magna pars huius doctrinae
a modernis Dialecticis confuse tractetur. Nihilominus tamen ratione

Quare ultima addiscatur.

nostri modi cognoscendi haec scientia postremum locum sibi vendi-
cavit, ut constat ex usu omnium, & ex ipsamet Aristotelis inscriptione:
nam propterea hanc scientiam *Transphysicam seu Postphysicam* vocavit.

D. Thom.

Et ratio est, quam tetigit D. Tho. in 1. Metaph. c. 1. lect. 2. & Avicen. lib.

Avicenna.

1. suae Metaph. c. 3. quia res, quae a materia abstrahunt secundum esse,
licet secundum se sint maxime intelligibiles, a nobis tamen non inveni-

---

44. Reading "quibus" here with S, V_1, and V_2. The following have "quo": C_1, C_2, G_2, M_1,
M_2, M_3, M_4, P_1, P_2, V_3, V_4, V_5, and Vivès.

12. And so it is also clear how this science can perform such a function with respect to the objects of the particular sciences, even if they seem to be below its abstraction. For, in the first place, as we mentioned above in the second section, although metaphysics is not concerned *per se* with all things$_r$ according to their proper natures$_r$, nevertheless, it reaches them in some way, namely, insofar as this is necessary in order to explain its own natures$_r$, or in order to teach divisions and distinguish its own metaphysical grades from others, and these metaphysical divisions are of great service to the other sciences for fixing their subjects and distinguishing them from others. And second, it is not always necessary that metaphysics *per se* and immediately prove the objects of the individual sciences; rather, it is enough that it provides principles and makes clear terms which other sciences can use to assume or prove their objects, to whatever extent necessary.

13. For this reason, it must consequently be admitted that, if the order of doctrine is considered in itself, metaphysics is prior to the other sciences, and this can be gathered not only from this function, but also from another that we shall explain presently; for it in some way confirms the principles of all the sciences. Further, it makes clear the transcendental concepts$_r$ of being, absent cognition of which hardly anything can be dealt with accurately in some science. And finally, it has a certain special connection to dialectic—which connection I shall make clear below—as a result of which, perhaps, a great part of this doctrine is treated of confusedly by modern dialecticians. Nevertheless, because of our mode of cognition, this science claims for itself the last place, as is clear from the practice of all, and from Aristotle's title itself, since it is for this reason that he called this science "transphysics" or "postphysics." And the reason is—as St. Thomas touches on in *Metaph.* I, ch. 1, lec. 2,[158] as does Avicenna, in book I of his *Metaph.*, ch. 3[159]—

Metaphysics is prior to all the sciences in the order of doctrine.

Why it is learned last.

St. Thomas.

Avicenna.

---

158. See Thomas Aquinas, *In duodecim libros metaphysicorum Aristotelis expositio*, pp. 13–14 (bk. I, lect. 2, ns. 45–46), commenting on a passage from *Metaph.* I, ch. 2.
159. Avicenna, *Liber de philosophia prima, sive scientia divina I–IV*, pp. 20–21.

untur nisi per motum,[45] ut constat ex 12. Metaph. Et similiter rationes entis universalissimae [22a] & abstractissimae,[46] quanvis secundum se sint notiores, praesertim quoad quaestionem an sint, tamen, quid sint, & quas proprietates habeant, difficile a nobis cognoscitur, & saepe incipere oportet a particularibus & sensibilibus, ut ad illas pertingere possimus, & hoc modo dixit Arist. 1. Metaph. c. 2. universalissima esse cognitu difficillima. Unde loquendo de ordine quoad nos, non semper necesse est hanc scientiam aliis praemitti: semper tamen supponuntur aliqua principia huius scientiae, vel termini metaphysici, quatenus aliquo modo cognosci possunt virtute naturalis luminis intellectus, & prout satis est ad discurrendum, & progrediendum in aliis scientiis, quanvis non tam exacte & perfecte, sicut fit comparata hac scientia.

Universalissima, cognitu difficillima.

14. Ad ultimam confirmationem dicitur hanc scientiam in hoc superare reliquas, quod ipsa non solum supponit suum obiectum esse, sed etiam, si necesse sit, illud esse ostendit, propriis principiis utens, per se loquendo: nam per accidens interdum utitur alienis & extraneis propter excellentiam sui obiecti, & defectum nostri intellectus, qui non ⟨29b⟩ potest illud perfecte attingere ut in se est, sed ex inferioribus rebus. Cum autem dicitur scientiam supponere suum obiectum esse, intelligitur, per se loquendo, ut notavit Caiet. prima parte, q. 2. art. 3. per accidens vero non inconvenit scientiam aliquam demonstrare quoad nos obiectum suum. Quod si illa scientia suprema sit, non indiget ope alterius, sed vi sua id praestare potest: & huiusmodi est Metaphysica in ordine naturalium scientiarum, sicut etiam id Theologia habet in ordine supernaturali.

Scientia quomodo supponat suum obiectum.

45. Reading "motum," here with S, V₁, and V₂. The following have "modum,": C₁, C₂, G₁, M₁, M₂, M₃, M₄, P₁, P₂, V₃, V₅, and Vivès. The relevant text is missing from the scan of V₄.

46. Reading "universalissimae & abstractissimae" with V₁, V₂, and S. The following read "universalissime et abstractissime": C₁, C₂, G₂, M₁, M₂, M₃, M₄, P₁, P₂, V₃, and V₅, and Vivès. The relevant text is omitted from the scan of V₄.

because things$_r$ which abstract from matter with respect to existence$_e$, although they are in themselves most intelligible, are nevertheless not discovered by us except through motion, as is clear from *Metaph.* XII. And likewise, as regards the most universal and abstract natures$_r$ of being, even though they are in themselves more known$_n$, especially with respect to the question of whether they exist$_e$, still, when it comes to the question of what they are, and what properties they have, this is cognized by us with difficulty, and often we must begin with particular and sensible things in order to be able to reach them. And it is with this in mind that Aristotle says, *Metaph.* I, ch. 2, that the most universal things are the most difficult to cognize.[160] For this reason, regarding the order as it relates to us, it is not always necessary that this science precede the others. Nevertheless, some principles of this science, or metaphysical terms, are always assumed insofar as they can in some way be cognized by means of the intellect's natural light, and insofar as this suffices for reasoning and making progress in the other sciences, although not so exactly and perfectly as happens when this science has been acquired.

The most universal things are the most difficult to cognize.

14. To the final confirmation it is said that this science surpasses the rest in this respect: it not only supposes that its object exists$_e$, but also, if necessary, shows that it exists$_e$, using its own principles, speaking *per se*. For *per accidens* it sometimes uses foreign and extraneous principles on account of both the excellence of its object and the limitation of our intellect, which cannot perfectly reach this object as it is in itself, but does so from lower things$_r$. And when it is said that a science assumes that its object exists$_e$, this is understood to be the case speaking *per se*, as Cajetan notes, *ST* I, q. 2, art. 3[161]; *per accidens*, however, it is not impossible for some science to demonstrate its object in relation to us. But if that science is the highest science, it does not need the assistance of another science but can accomplish this by its own power, and of this sort is metaphysics in the order of the natural sciences, just as theology is in the supernatural order.

How a science assumes its object.

160. Aristotle, *Metaph.* I, ch. 2, 982a23–25.
161. Thomas Aquinas, *Sancti Thomae Aquinatis opera omnia* (Leonina), t. 4, p. 32a.

Quomodo Metaphysica prima principia
confirmet ac tueatur.

15. Secundum munus praecipuum, quod huic scientiae tribuitur, est prima principia confirmare ac defendere. Hoc munus tribuit huic *Aristotel.* scientiae Arist. 1. Poster. c. 7. & 1. Physic. c. 1. & illud ex professo tradit atque exercet 4. Metaph. ca. 3. ubi commentatores omnes idem tra- *Proclus.* dunt, & Proclus lib. 1. Comment. in Euclid. c. 4. ubi etiam Mathematicis scientiis ait Metaphysicam suppeditare principia. Quale autem sit hoc munus, & cur, vel quo modo ad hanc scientiam pertineat, non est facile *Prima* ad explicandum. Et ratio difficultatis est primo, quia prima principia *difficultatis* sunt per se, naturaliter, ac sine discursu nota: haec autem scientia, cum *ratio.* essentialiter scientia sit in omnibus partibus suis, in nulla earum potest nisi per discursum, & consequenter circa conclusiones, & propositiones mediatas versari: ergo nullum munus proprium circa prima principia *Secunda.* potest exercere. Secundo, quia alias confunderetur habitus Metaphys- icae cum habitu primorum principiorum, quia Metaphysica usurparet proprium munus illius habitus: unde non oporteret eos distinguere, contra Aristotelem 6. Ethic. ca. 3. ubi quinque virtutes intellectus dis- tinguit, & inter eas ponit intellectum, id est habitum principiorum, & sapientiam, quam esse Metaphysicam constat ex eodem in prooe- mio huius operis. Prima sequela patet, quia ad habitum principiorum pertinet assensum praebere primis principiis cum maiori evidentia & certitudine, quam omnis scientia: quandoquidem omnis scientiarum evidentia ab illo habitu pendet: ergo Metaphysica non potest confir- mare prima principia, aut robur aliquod adde[22b]re assensui illorum, *Tertia.* nisi munus habitus primorum principiorum usurpet. Tertio, quia vel haec scientia ⟨30a⟩ exercet hoc munus, explicando tantum terminos ex quibus prima principia constant: & hoc non est munus scientiae, neque ad illud est necessarius aliquis habitus iudicativus, sed solum conve- niens apprehensio, & terminorum explicatio. Vel exercet hoc munus, demonstrando aliquo modo ipsa principia: & rursus interrogo, an hoc intelligatur de demonstratione a priori, vel a posteriori. Et primum dici non potest, quia prima principia ut sic sunt immediata, unde a priori demonstrari non possunt. Si autem sumantur ut non sunt immediata quoad nos, quale est illud principium quo prima passio praedicatur de

In what way metaphysics confirms and defends first principles.

15. The second principal function assigned to this science is to confirm and defend first principles. Aristotle assigns this function to this
science in *Post. An.* I, ch. 7,[162] and in *Phys.* I, ch. 1,[163] and he *ex professo*
presents it and performs it in *Metaph.* IV, ch. 3, where all commentators
teach the same thing; and also Proclus, book I, his commentary on
Euclid, ch. 4, where he says that metaphysics furnishes principles to the
mathematical sciences.[164] But it is not easy to explain what sort of function this is, and why, or in what way, it pertains to this science. And the
reason for the difficulty is, first, because first principles are known$_n$ *per
se*, naturally, and without reasoning. But this science, since it is essentially a science in all of its parts, can in none of them be concerned with
anything except by reasoning, and consequently it can be concerned
with nothing but conclusions and mediate propositions. Therefore, it
can perform no function of its own concerning first principles. Second,
because otherwise the habit of metaphysics would be confounded with
the habit of first principles, since metaphysics would assume the proper
function of this habit, for which reason it would not be necessary to
distinguish them, contrary to what Aristotle says in *Ethics* VI, ch. 3,
where he distinguishes five virtues of the intellect and posits understanding among them, that is, the habit of principles, as well as wisdom,[165] which (as is clear from the same Aristotle in the proem of this
work[166]) is metaphysics. The first consequence is clear, because it pertains to the habit of principles to furnish assent to first principles with
greater evidence and certainty than every science does, since all the
evidence of the sciences depends on this habit. Therefore, metaphysics
cannot confirm first principles, or add some force to the assent to them,
unless it assumes the function of the habit of first principles. Third,

Aristotle.

Proclus.

The first reason for the difficulty.

The second.

The third.

---

162. Aristotle, *Post. An.* I, ch. 9, 76a16–22.
163. Aristotle, *Phys.* I, ch. 1, 184b25–185a5.
164. Proclus, *In Primum Euclidis Elementorum librum Commentariorum ad universam mathematicam disciplinam principium eruditionis tradentium Libri IIII* (Patavii: Excudebat Gratiosus Perchacinus, 1560), pp. 4–5.
165. Aristotle, *Nic. Eth.* VI, ch. 3, 1139b15–17.
166. See Aristotle, *Metaph.* I, chs. 1–2, 981b25–982a6.

definito, sic non est munus unius scientiae talia principia demonstrare, sed unaquaeque scientia in sua materia demonstrat ea quae ad ipsam pertinent, nec potest Metaphysica ad singula in specie descendere, ut ex dictis in sectionibus praecedentibus constat: ergo nihil proprium potest hac in parte Metaphysicae tribui. Secundum autem de demonstratione a posteriori non potest convenientius dici, quia hoc genus demonstrationis & scientiae non pertinet ad sapientiam, qualis est Metaphysica, sed pertinet vel ad experientiam, vel ad scientiam a posteriori, quam *scientiam quia* appellant, quae sine dubio est inferior, & distinctus habitus a scientia perfecta, qui[47] fortasse non est unus circa prima principia communia, & propria singularium scientiarum. Unde sicut perfectae sapientiae seu Metaphysicae adiungi potest in nobis aliquis imperfectus habitus demonstrans a posteriori prima principia communia, ad Metaphysicam spectantia, ita singulis scientiis particularibus adiungi potest similis habitus proportionatus, uniuscuiusque principia a posteriori demonstrans: quid est ergo quod in hoc munere proprium ac singulare habet metaphysica?

Propositae rationes dubitandi solvuntur singulatim. 16. Non possumus commodius ad hanc interrogationem respondere, & hoc munus declarare, quam per difficultates propositas breviter discurrendo. Et prima quidem facilis est: concedimus enim munus huius scientiae circa prima principia non esse elicere illum

47. Reading "qui" with S, V_1, and V_2. The following have "quia": C_1, C_2, G_2, M_1, M_2, M_3, M_4, P_1, P_2, V_3, V_4, V_5, and Vivès.

because either this science performs this function by explaining only the terms from which first principles are constituted, and this is not the function of a science, nor is some judicative habit necessary for this, but only a suitable apprehension and explanation of the terms; or this science performs this function by demonstrating these principles in some way, and then I further ask whether it is understood to do so by means of an *a priori* demonstration or an *a posteriori* one. The former cannot be said, because first principles, as such, are immediate and therefore cannot be demonstrated *a priori*. But if first principles are taken as not immediate in relation to us—of which sort is the principle by which a primary passion is predicated of the thing defined—then it is not the function of a single science to demonstrate such principles, but each science in its own subject matter demonstrates those which pertain to it; nor can metaphysics descend to individual principles specifically, as is clear from what has been said in the preceding sections. Therefore, in this regard nothing special can be assigned to metaphysics. But the second option, that is, that metaphysics demonstrates first principles by means of *a posteriori* demonstrations, cannot more rightly be said, since this genus of demonstration and science does not pertain to wisdom (and such is metaphysics), but pertains either to experience or to *a posteriori* science, which they call science "*quia*,"[167] which is without doubt inferior and a habit distinct from perfect science, and this habit is perhaps not a single habit in respect of common first principles and the proper principles of the individual sciences. For this reason, just as some imperfect habit which demonstrates *a posteriori* common first principles belonging to metaphysics can be joined in us to perfect wisdom or metaphysics, so can a similar, proportioned habit which demonstrates *a posteriori* the principles of each particular science be joined to individual particular sciences. With respect to this function, then, what is proper and special to metaphysics?

16. We cannot more appropriately reply to this question, and make this function clear, than by briefly running through the difficulties that were set forth. And the first, indeed, is easy: for we concede that the function of this science with respect to first principles is not to elicit

---

167. See below, *DM* 1.6.24, and p. 311, n. 303.

assensum evidentem & certum, quem intellectus lumine naturali ductus sine ullo discursu praebet primis principiis sufficienter propositis: hoc enim recte probat argumentum illud, & confirmat etiam secundum. Pertinebit ergo ad hanc scientiam aliquo discursu uti circa ipsa prima principia, ⟨30b⟩ quo illa confirmet aliquo modo ac defendat: quo modo autem id praestet, in secunda & tertia difficultate declarabitur.

17. Circa secundam aliqui tractare hoc loco solent, an habitus principiorum, quem Aristoteles intellectum appellavit, sit qualitas a potentia intellectiva in re ipsa distincta: & utrum sit qualitas a natura congenita, an potius acquisita. Qui enim negant hunc habitum esse qualitatem aliquam praeter ipsum naturale lumen intellectus, quod, quatenus natura sua est sufficienter propensum ad assensum primorum principiorum, illorum habitus appellatur, & non realiter neque ex natura rei, sed sola ratione a facultate intelligendi distinguitur: Qui (inquam) ita sentiunt, facile expedient difficultatem propositam, dicentes Metaphysicam distingui a naturali lumine intellectus, non vero distingui ab alio habitu, qui potest conferre intellectui facili[23a]tatem aliquam circa primorum principiorum assensum. Aliis vero (& quidem probabilius) videtur hanc quaestionem ab illa non pendere, nam sive habitus principiorum sit qualitas distincta, & per actus acquisita, sive non, necesse est Metaphysicam esse habitum ab illo distinctum: quia, ut in priori difficultate dicebam,[48] Metaphysicae munus non potest esse praebere assensum simplicem seu absque discursu primis principiis. Qui autem ponunt illum habitum qualitatem distinctam, eius munus & utilitatem esse dicunt elicere promptius & facilius cum intellectu ipsummet assensum simplicem & immediatum primorum principiorum: ergo, etiam si ponamus habitum principiorum esse propriis actibus acquisitum, non propterea confundere illum debemus cum habitu Metaphysicae.

18. Non ergo sunt hae quaestiones connexae, neque una ab altera pendet. Et (ut ego opinor) Aristoteles utrumque posuit, scilicet, & habitum principiorum esse virtutem distinctam a sapientia, ut constat ex

---

48. Reading "dicebam" here with M_1, P_1, P_2, S, V_1, and V_2. The following have "dicebant": C_1, C_2, G_2, M_2, M_3, M_4, V_3, V_4, V_5, and Vivès.

that evident and certain assent which the intellect, led by the natural light, bestows without any reasoning on first principles when they are sufficiently set forth, for that argument rightly proves this, and the second confirms it also. It will therefore pertain to this science to use some reasoning in connection with these first principles, in order to confirm them in some way and defend them. But how it accomplishes this will be made clear in discussing the second and third difficulties.

17. With regard to the second difficulty, some are wont in this place to treat of the question whether the habit of principles, which Aristotle calls understanding, is a quality distinct in reality from the intellective power, and whether it is a quality innate by nature or rather acquired. For those who deny that this habit is some quality over and above the natural light of the intellect—which light, insofar as it is by its nature sufficiently inclined to assent to first principles, is called the habit of them and is distinguished from the faculty of understanding not really, nor *ex natura rei*, but only by reason—these people, I say, will easily resolve the difficulty set forth by saying that metaphysics is distinguished from the natural light of the intellect but is not distinguished from another habit that can confer on the intellect a certain readiness in connection with the assent to first principles. To others, however, it seems (more probably indeed) that this question does not depend on that one, for whether the habit of principles is a distinct quality and is acquired through acts or not, it is necessary that metaphysics be a habit distinct from it, since, as I said in connection with the previous difficulty, the function of metaphysics cannot be to furnish an assent to first principles that is simple or without any reasoning. But those who posit that that habit is a distinct quality say that its function and usefulness is to more promptly and readily elicit, together with the intellect, the very same simple and immediate assent to first principles; therefore, even if we suppose that the habit of principles is acquired by proper acts, we ought not for that reason to confound it with the habit of metaphysics.

18. These questions, therefore, are not connected, nor does one depend on the other. And (as I think) Aristotle asserted both, namely, that the habit of principles is a virtue distinct from wisdom, as is clear from the cited passage in *Ethics* [VI, ch.] 3,[168] and that it is a habit we acquire

168. Aristotle, *Nic. Eth.* VI, ch. 3, 1139b15–17.

citato loco 3. Ethic. & esse habitum quem nostris actibus comparamus, ut ex eodem loco, & ex 2. Poster. c. ult. facile sumi potest. Nam in priori loco manifeste ponit illum inter habitus seu virtutes intellectus: si autem non esset res distincta ab ipsa facultate intelligendi, impropriissime, imo & falso diceretur esse habitum intellectus. In posteriori autem loco apertius sentit esse habitum non a natura inditum, sed acquisitum: non per discursum, sed per simplices actus ex sola ⟨31a⟩ terminorum propositione, & intelligentia comparatos. Et revera hoc posterius sequitur ex illo priori: nam si hic habitus non esset facilitas aliqua usu comparata ad similes actus promptius eliciendos, nulla esset[49] ratio, aut fundamentum, cur existimaretur esse qualitas aliqua distincta ex natura rei a lumine naturali intellectus, seu ab ipsa facultate intelligendi: tum quia, ut Arist. dixit 3. de anim. c. 4. intellectus natura sua est pura potentia in ordine intelligibilium, & tanquam tabula rasa: tum etiam quia si natura ipsa dedisset totam vim, quae ex parte potentiae necessaria est ad eliciendos hos actus, non tantum quoad substantiam, sed etiam quoad promptitudinem & facilitatem, supervacaneum fuisset multiplicare entitates in ipsa facultate intelligendi, sed ipsa posset & deberet in suamet intrinseca entitate fortior & efficacior constitui, neque esset ullum indicium ad illam distinctionem entitatum colligendam: sicut si voluntas natura sua ita est prompta & facilis ad amandum bonum in communi, ut non possit per actus promptior & facilior reddi, optimum argumentum est, non habere illam promptitudinem per habitum innatum, sed per suammet entitatem. Et similiter visus quia ex natura sua habet totam inclinationem & efficacitatem, quam ex parte sua habere potest ad eliciendum actum videndi, recte colligimus habere totam illam vim & inclinationem per intrinsecam facultatem & entitatem suam indivisibilem, & non per

D. Thom. aliquam aliam a natura inditam. Unde D. Tho. 1. 2. q. 51. art. 1. sensit hunc habitum non esse naturalem secundum se, sed quoad inchoationem quandam, quia scilicet actus per quos acquiritur, non sunt per discursum habiti, sed immediate ab ipso naturae lumine profluunt, quanvis in principio & ante habitum non emanent cum tanta promptitudine & facilitate, sicut post acquisitum habitum: de qua re late in 2. Posteriorum [23b] disputavimus, & fortasse in sequentibus nonnihil addemus.

---

49. Reading "esset" here with C_1, C_2, G_2, M_1, M_2, M_3, P_1, P_2, S, V_1, V_2, V_3, and V_4. The following have "esse": M_4, V_5, and Vivès.

through our acts, as can easily be gathered from the same place and from *Post. An.* II, final chapter.[169] For in the former passage, he clearly places it among the habits or virtues of the intellect, and if it were not a thing distinct from the very faculty of understanding, it would most improperly—and in fact falsely—be called a habit of the intellect. And in the latter passage, he more clearly takes it to be a habit, not implanted by nature, but acquired, and acquired not through reasoning, but through simple acts prepared for by the mere presentation and understanding of terms. And really this latter point follows from that earlier one, for if this habit were not a sort of readiness, obtained by practice, for more promptly eliciting similar acts, there would be no reason or foundation for judging it to be some quality distinct *ex natura rei* from the natural light of the intellect, or from the very faculty of understanding—both because, as Aristotle says in *De anima* III, ch. 4,[170] the intellect by its nature is a pure potency in the order of intelligibles, and like a blank slate, and also because, if nature itself had given the whole force which is necessary on the side of the potency for eliciting these acts, not only with respect to substance, but also with respect to promptness and readiness, it would have been superfluous to multiply entities in the same faculty of understanding, but the faculty of understanding itself could be, and would have to be, constituted more powerful and more efficacious in its own intrinsic entity, nor would there be any sign on the basis of which one might infer that distinction of entities. In the same way, if the will by its own nature is prompt and ready for loving the good in general in such a way that it cannot be made more prompt or readier by acts, this is the best proof that it does not have that promptness thanks to an inborn habit, but rather thanks to its very entity. And similarly regarding sight: since it, by virtue of its own nature, has the entire inclination and power that it can have, on its side, for eliciting an act of seeing, we rightly infer that it has that whole power and inclination thanks to its intrinsic faculty and indivisible entity, and not thanks to some other faculty and entity placed in it by nature.

169. According to the chapter divisions of the *Post. An.* in Suárez's day, the final chapter of the work—labeled ch. 18 in the version used by Toledo and Suárez and ch. 15 in the version used by Zabarella (see p. 113, n. 119 above)—begins a little later than our *Post. An.* II, ch. 19, does, at 99b17 (at "περὶ δὲ τῶν ἀρχῶν").

170. Aristotle, *De anima* III, ch. 4, 429a13–24 and 429b29–430a2.

Qualiter Metaphysica versetur circa prima principia, qualiter principiorum habitus.

19. Hac ergo sententia supposita, ad secundam difficultatem negatur sequela, nam Metaphysica aliter versatur circa principia prima, quam habitus principiorum. Nam in primis Metaphysica non versatur circa prima principia formaliter ut principia sunt, sed ut sunt aliquo modo conclusiones: at vero habitus versatur formaliter circa principia ut ⟨31b⟩ talia sunt, & veritates immediatae: & ideo hic habitus attingit sine discursu, Metaphysica vero, mediante aliquo discursu. Hinc rursus habitus principiorum non addit proprie aliquam evidentiam, vel certitudinem assensui principiorum qui ex sola natura haberi potest, sed addit facilitatem & promptitudinem in exercenda illa evidentia & certitudine: Metaphysica vero addit certitudinem & evidentiam, quia novo modo, & per novum medium facit assentiri eidem veritati. Est autem attente considerandum, hoc augmentum non esse intensivum, sed extensivum. Primo quidem, quia Metaphysica non auget evidentiam, vel certitudinem, imo neque intensionem ipsiusmet assensus quem elicit habitus principiorum: quia, ut dixi, Metaphysica nullo modo operatur circa illum assensum, sed circa obiectum seu materiam eius praebet novum assentiendi modum, per actum utique distinctum. Secundo, quia si hos actus inter se conferamus, revera non est certior aut evidentior assensus Metaphysicae, quam assensus habitus principiorum, ut argumentum factum probat, quia semper necesse est assensum Metaphysicae in aliquibus primis principiis ut per se notis niti. Et hac ratione dicimus Metaphysicam non augere intensive evidentiam, vel certitudinem circa prima principia, sed extensive tantum, novam eorum evidentiam, & certitudinem praebendo.

For this reason, St. Thomas, *ST* I-II, q. 51, art. 1,[171] judges that this habit   *St. Thomas.*
is not in itself natural, but natural with respect to a sort of beginning,
since, namely, the acts through which it is acquired are not had through
reasoning, but flow forth immediately from the very light of nature,
although in the beginning and before the habit they do not emanate
with such great readiness and facility as they do after the habit has been
acquired: which issue we have discussed at length in *Post. An.* II, and
perhaps we will add something about it in what follows.

19. This opinion having been supposed, then, in response to the
second difficulty, the consequence is denied, since metaphysics is concerned with first principles otherwise than the habit of principles is.
For, in the first place, metaphysics is not concerned with first principles   *In what way*
formally, insofar as they are principles, but rather insofar as they are in   *metaphysics*
is concerned
some way conclusions. However, the habit formally concerns principles   *with first*
insofar as they are such and immediate truths, and therefore this habit   *principles,*
and in what
reaches them without reasoning, whereas metaphysics reaches them   *way the habit*
through some sort of reasoning. Hence, again, the habit of principles   *of principles*
is.
does not properly add some evidence or certainty to that assent to principles which can be had by nature alone, but rather adds a facility and
readiness in the use of that evidence and certainty. Metaphysics, by
contrast, adds certainty and evidence, since it produces assent to the
same truth in a new way and by a new means.[172] It is carefully to be
noted, however, that this increase is not intensive, but extensive. First,
indeed, because metaphysics does not increase the evidence or certainty, nor in fact the intension, of the very assent which the habit of principles elicits, for, as I have said, metaphysics in no way operates on that
assent, but rather, regarding its object or matter, furnishes a new mode
of assent by means of an act that is assuredly distinct. Second, because
if we compare these acts to each other, the assent of metaphysics is really not more certain or evident than the assent of the habit of principles,
as the argument that was made proves, since it is always necessary that
the assent of metaphysics depend on some first principles as known$_n$
per se. And for this reason we say that metaphysics does not intensively

171. Thomas Aquinas, *Sancti Thomae Aquinatis opera omnia* (Leonina), t. 6, pp.
325b–26a.

172. The Latin word here translated "means" is also sometimes rendered "middle term."

20. Circa tertiam difficultatem attingitur alia quaestio, scilicet quibus modis versetur Metaphysica circa prima principia, iuvando & confirmando intellectum in assensu eorum. In qua breviter dicendum est doctrinam hanc praestare hoc munus duobus modis in tertia difficultate insinuatis. In primis enim tradit & declarat rationem ipsorum terminorum, ex quibus prima principia constant. Quod fere experientia ipsa patet in discursu huius doctrinae, tum apud Aristotelem, praesertim lib. 5. 7. 8. & 9. tum etiam apud alios autores, & ex his quae in disputationibus sequentibus dicemus, constabit: traditur enim in hac scientia, quid sit ens, quid substantia, quid accidens, quid totum, quid pars, quid actus, quid potentia, ex quibus terminis, & ex aliis similibus, prima principia constant. Cum enim haec principia in re non habeant intrinsecum, & quasi formale medium, quo illorum extrema connectantur, per se cognoscuntur ex cognitione terminorum: unde nihil magis potest ad eo-⟨32a⟩rum cognitionem iuvare, quam scientifica, & evidens notitia terminorum, seu rationum eorum, qualis est illa quae in hac scientia traditur. Neque enim verum est quod in praedicta difficultate tertia sumebatur, scilicet hoc munus non pertinere ad scientiam quae discurrendo & iudicando procedit, sed ad simplicem terminorum apprehensionem: nam licet, per se loquendo, ex parte simplicium rerum & termi[24a]norum non requiratur demonstratio, imo neque compositio ad intelligendum, quid unumquodque sit, aut significet, tamen quoad nos saepe potest hoc demonstrari, praesertim utendo divisione constante ex oppositis membris, & demonstrando quid res non sit (quod frequenter est nobis notius) & inde concludendo quid sit. Saepe etiam hoc fit, tradendo aliquas descriptiones rationum simplicium, quae sunt quoad nos notiores, & illis utendo ut mediis ad demonstrationes efficiendas, quae ad scientiam humanam acquirendam interdum sufficiunt. Atque hinc tandem intelligitur hunc modum illustrandi prima principia praecipue & immediate exerceri in hac scientia circa illa prima principia quae universalissima sunt, & constant terminis abstractioribus, id est, significantibus res aut rationes rerum quae sine materia possunt existere: nam, ut diximus, haec sunt quae, per se loquendo, sub obiecto Metaphysicae continentur: cumque illa sit suprema scientia, per se sufficiens est ad tradendum &

Terminorum cognitio ad complexa principia cognoscenda maxime confert.

increase the evidence or certainty regarding first principles, but only extensively, by furnishing them with a new evidence and certainty.

20. With respect to the third difficulty, another question is raised, namely, in what ways is metaphysics concerned with first principles when it helps and strengthens the intellect in its assent to them? Regarding this question, it must briefly be said that this doctrine performs this function in the two ways that were indicated in the third difficulty. For, in the first place, it teaches and makes clear the concepts$_r$ of the very terms from which first principles are constituted. This is plain by experience in the course of this doctrine, both in Aristotle, especially books V, VII, VIII and IX, and also in other authors, and it will be clear from the things that we shall say in the following disputations. For in this science one is taught what a being is, what a substance is, and what an accident is; what a whole is, what a part is; what an act is, what a potency is; and first principles are composed from these and similar terms. For since these principles do not in reality have an intrinsic and quasi-formal middle term by which their extremes might be connected, they are cognized *per se* from the cognition of their terms. For this reason nothing can help more in the cognition of them than the sort of scientific and evident knowledge$_n$ of their terms or concepts$_r$ that is handed down in this science. For what is assumed in the mentioned third difficulty is not true, namely, that this function does not pertain to science, which proceeds by reasoning and judging, but to the simple apprehension of terms. For although, speaking *per se*, as far as simple things$_r$ and terms themselves are concerned, neither a demonstration nor even a composition is required in order to understand what each is or signifies, nevertheless, in relation to us, this can often be demonstrated, especially by using a division constituted from opposed members, and by demonstrating what a thing$_r$ is not (which is frequently better known$_n$ by us) and thence concluding what it is. This is also often done by teaching some descriptions of simple concepts$_r$ that are, with respect to us, better known$_n$, and by using them as middle terms in constructing demonstrations, which sometimes suffice for the acquisition of human science. And hence, finally, it is understood that this way of making first principles clear is especially and immediately employed in this science in connection with those first principles which are the most universal

The cognition of terms most especially contributes to the cognition of complex principles.

explicandum rationes omnium rerum, & terminorum, quae sub obiecto eius clauduntur. At vero non ita proxime & immediate descendit ad proxima & particularia principia singularium scientiarum, & ad terminos ex quibus constant, sed solum illa attingit altero ex duobus modis superius explicatis, scilicet vel quatenus necesse est ad proprias definitiones tradendas, propriosque terminos explicandos, vel quatenus in eis generales rationes, & praesertim transcendentales, includuntur, sine quarum cognitione & adminiculo non potest aliqua ratio seu quidditas cuiuscunque rei in particulari explicari.

21. Alter modus quo haec scientia versatur circa prima principia, est, demonstrando illa seu veritatem & certitudinem illorum. Quod variis modis praestare potest. Primo dicunt aliqui Metaphysicam demonstrare principia a priori, non quidem per causam intrinsecam formalem, vel materialem, quia (ut recte probat argumen⟨32b⟩ tum factum) in his principiis immediatis non habet locum tale genus demonstrationis, sed per extrinsecam causam finalem,[50] efficientem, & exemplarem: nam, quia Metaphysica considerat primas causas, etiam Deum ipsum, qui sicut est prima veritas, ita est causa omnis veritatis, saltem extrinseca omnibus praedictis modis, potest saltem per hanc causam demonstrare veritatem, non tantum primorum principiorum, sed etiam conclusionum. Hic tamen modus demonstrandi rarissime aut nunquam exercetur in hac doctrina: &, si attentius consideretur, vix habere potest locum: nam in primis quod attinet ad causam efficientem, haec non habet locum in universalissimis principiis constantibus ex terminis communibus Deo & creaturis: nam sicut respectu Dei nulla potest dari causa efficiens, ita nec respectu illorum principiorum quae in Deo ipso veritatem habent, ut est illud: *Quodlibet est, vel non est*: &, *Impossibile est aliquid de eodem affirmare, & negare.* Atque hinc etiam constat haec principia non posse per causam finalem demon-

Universalissima principia non possunt per causas demonstrari.

50. Reading "finalem" here with S, V_1, and V_2. The following have "formalem": C_1, C_2, G_2, M_1, M_2, M_3, M_4, P_1, P_2, V_3, V_4, V_5, and Vivès.

and are constituted from very abstract terms, that is, from terms that signify things$_r$ or natures$_r$ of things$_r$ which can exist without matter. For, as we have said, these are those which, speaking *per se*, are contained under the object of metaphysics, and since it is the highest science, it suffices *per se* for teaching and explaining the natures$_r$ of all things$_r$ and terms which are included under its object. But it does not in this way descend proximately and immediately to the proximate and particular principles of the individual sciences, and to the terms from which they are composed, but rather it only reaches them in one of the two ways explained above, namely, either insofar as is necessary for teaching its own definitions, and for explaining its own terms, or insofar as general concepts$_r$, and especially transcendental ones, are included in them, without the cognition and assistance of which concepts$_r$ some nature$_r$ or quiddity of any thing$_r$ cannot be distinctly explained.

21. The other way this science concerns itself with first principles is by demonstrating them, or by demonstrating their truth and certainty. It can accomplish this in various ways. First, some say that metaphysics demonstrates principles *a priori*, not indeed through an intrinsic formal or material cause—since (as the argument made rightly proves) in the case of these immediate principles such a genus of demonstration has no place—but through an extrinsic cause, that is, through a final, efficient, or exemplar cause. For since metaphysics considers first causes, and also God himself (who, just as he is the first truth, is a cause of every truth, at least an extrinsic cause in all the ways mentioned), it can at least demonstrate the truth, not only of first principles, but also of conclusions, through this cause. However, this way of demonstrating is most rarely, or never, employed in this doctrine, and if it is more attentively considered, it can hardly play a role. For, first, with respect to the efficient cause, this cause has no place in the most universal principles constituted from terms common to God and creatures, since, just as, with respect to God, there can be no efficient cause, so neither can there be an efficient cause with respect to those principles which hold true of God himself, such as this one: "Any given thing either is or is not," and this one: "It is impossible to affirm and deny something of the same thing." And hence it is also clear that these principles cannot be demonstrated through a final cause, since the final cause is related to produc-

strari, quia causa finalis est in ordine ad effectionem, & operationem: & ideo quae abstrahunt ab efficiente, abstrahunt etiam a fine. Rursùs hinc fieri videtur, etiam illa principia, quae solis creaturis communia sunt, [24b] quatenus sub scientiam cadunt, non posse per causam efficientem, vel finalem demonstrari: quia ut sic abstrahunt ab actuali existentia, & consequenter ab efficientia, nam omnis efficientia est circa rem existentem, seu quae ad exitum perducitur, ut, verbi gratia, *omne totum esse maius sua parte*, verum est, omni efficientia seclusa, & sic de caeteris. Et hinc ulterius non videtur hic possibilis probatio per causam exemplarem, tum quia quod abstrahit ab efficiente causa, abstrahit etiam ab exemplari: nam exemplar est id, ad cuius similitudinem efficiens operatur, & comparatur tanquam ars, vel ratio operandi respectu efficientis intellectualis: si ergo veritas horum principiorum abstrahit ab efficiente, etiam abstrahit ab exemplari causa: tum etiam, quia essentiae rerum ut sic non pendent[51] a causa exemplari: ergo nec veritas primorum principiorum. Antecedens patet, quia homo, verbi gratia, non ideo est animal rationale, quia Deus talem illum cognoscit, seu quia in exemplari divino talis repraesentatur, sed potius ideo talis cognoscitur, quia ex se postulat talem essentiam.

22. Sed ad haec dici ⟨33a⟩ potest haec principia abstrahere quidem ab efficientia actuali, non tamen ab efficientia possibili, & consequenter non omnino abstrahere a causa efficiente, exemplari, & finali: ut enim infra dicemus, quanvis essentiae creaturarum abstrahi possint ab esse, non tamen ab ordine ad esse, sine quo intelligi non potest vera & realis essentia: eadem ergo ratione prima principia communia entibus creatis veris & realibus, etiam si secundum necessariam connexionem abstrahant a tempore & actuali existentia, non tamen ab ordine ad esse, scilicet, quia cum tali connexione possent existere, & non aliter: & hoc modo possunt etiam habere respectum ad praedictas causas, & per eas demonstrari. Ut si quis probet omne totum esse maius sua parte, quia ita potest a Deo fieri, & non aliter: vel hominis essentiam esse animal

---

51. Reading "essentiae rerum ut sic non pendent" with C₁, C₂, G₂, M₁, M₂, M₃, M₄, P₁, P₂, S, V₁, V₂, V₃, and V₄. The following have "essentia rerum ut sic non pendet": V₅ and Vivès.

tion and operation, and therefore those things which abstract from the efficient cause also abstract from an end. And from this, furthermore, it seems to result that those principles also which are common only to creatures, insofar as they fall under a science, cannot be demonstrated through an efficient or final cause, since, as such, they abstract from actual existence and consequently from efficiency, for every efficiency has to do with an existing thing$_r$ or with that which is being effected. For example, that "every whole is greater than its part" is true setting aside all efficiency, and similarly in other cases. And hence, furthermore, it does not seem that a proof through an exemplar cause is possible here. First, because what abstracts from an efficient cause also abstracts from an exemplar cause, for an exemplar is that the likeness of which an efficient cause directs its operation toward, and it is related as an art or ground$_r$ of operation to an intellectual efficient cause; if, therefore, the truth of these principles abstracts from the efficient cause, it also abstracts from the exemplar cause. And also because the essences of things$_r$ as such do not depend on an exemplar cause, and therefore neither does the truth of first principles. The antecedent is clear, since the human being, for example, is not a rational animal because God cognizes her to be such, or because she is so represented in the divine exemplar; rather, the human being is cognized to be such because of herself she requires such an essence.

22. But to these things it can be said that these principles do indeed abstract from actual efficiency, but not from possible efficiency, and that consequently they do not abstract altogether from the efficient, exemplar, and final cause. For, as we shall say below,[173] although the essences of creatures can be abstracted from existence$_e$, nevertheless, they cannot be abstracted from a relation to existence$_e$, without which relation a true and real essence cannot be understood. For the same reason, therefore, even if first principles common to true and real created beings abstract, with respect to necessary connection, from time and actual existence, nevertheless, they do not abstract from a relation to existence$_e$, since they could exist with such a connection, but not otherwise; and in this way they can also have a relation to the men-

The objection is met.

---

173. See *DM* 2.4.14.

rationale, quia in ea[52] potest a Deo condi, & non in alia. Et similiter ex causa finali potest ostendi hominem esse animal rationale, quia potest ad Deum cognoscendum & amandum institui. Vel ex causa exemplari, quia in divina idea talis repraesentatur: non enim haberet homo talem essentiam realem, nisi in Deo haberet tale exemplar: nec repugnat sub diversis rationibus utrumque verum esse, scilicet & Deum cognoscere hominem esse talis essentiae, quia revera talis est: & hominem habere talem essentiam, quia in Deo talem habet ideam.

23. Quae responsio declarat quidem hunc modum demonstrandi non semper esse impossibilem, nec inutilem. Quanquam enim hi modi demonstrandi in singulis primis principiis non omnes locum habeant: nam quod tria & quatuor sint septem, non est necesse ut habeat causam finalem, & sic de aliis principiis, in quibus est veritas ex connexione extremorum, non quidem ordinata ad aliquem finem, quia praedicatum non declarat proprietatem aliquam vel essentiam subiecti, sed identitatem potius, seu repugnantiam oppositorum,[53] ut patet in hoc: *quodlibet est, vel non est,* & similibus, in quibus dicti modi demonstrandi per causas extrinsecas locum non habent. Nihilominus tamen ad multa principia applicari possunt, praesertim illa demonstratio quae est per causam finalem, nam essentiae rerum, & proprie[25a]tates causam finalem habent, per quam possint demonstrari, si talis causa aliunde per se nota sit, vel per aliud notius principium ostendi possit, hoc enim in omni demonstratione necessarium est. ⟨33b⟩

Per efficiens, finem, & exemplar primum demonstrare non potest naturale lumen.

24. Addo vero ulterius, saepe hoc probationis genus excedere vim naturalis luminis intellectus humani, & pertinere potius ad Metaphysicam divinam (ut sic dicam) vel supernaturalem, quam naturalem. Nam exemplaria divina, nisi in se ipsis videantur, esse non possunt ratio aut

52. Reading "ea" here with S, V_1, and V_2. The following have "eo" instead: C_1, C_2, G_2, M_1, M_2, M_3, M_4, P_1, P_2, V_3, V_4, V_5, and Vivès.

53. Reading "oppositorum" with all of the early editions. Vivès has "popositorum."

tioned causes, and can be demonstrated through them. For instance, if someone should prove that every whole is greater than its part because it can in this way be made by God, but not otherwise; or that rational animal is the essence of the human being because she can be established by God in that essence, but not in another. And similarly, from a final cause it can be shown that the human being is a rational animal because she can be made in order to cognize and love God. Or from the exemplar cause, because she is so represented in the divine idea, for the human being would not have such a real essence unless she had such an exemplar in God. Nor is it absurd for both to be true in different senses, namely, that God cognizes the human being to be of such an essence because she really is such, and that the human being has such an essence because she has such an idea in God.

23. This reply makes it clear indeed that this way of demonstrating is not always impossible or useless. For although these ways of demonstrating are not all applicable to every first principle—for it is not necessary that the proposition that three and four are seven have a final cause, and likewise in the case of other principles in which the truth is due to the connection of the extremes but is not ordained to some end, since the predicate does not make clear some property or the essence of the subject, but rather an identity or an incompatibility of opposites, as is clear in the case of this principle, "Any given thing is or is not," and the like, to which the mentioned ways of demonstrating through extrinsic causes do not apply—nevertheless, they can be applied to many principles, especially that demonstration which is through the final cause, for the essences and properties of things$_r$ have a final cause through which they can be demonstrated, if such a cause is otherwise known$_n$ *per se*, or can be shown through another, better known$_n$ principle, for this is necessary in every demonstration.

24. But I add, furthermore, that often this genus of proof exceeds the power of the human intellect's natural light and pertains to divine (so to speak) or supernatural metaphysics, rather than to natural metaphysics. For the divine exemplars, unless they are seen in their very selves, cannot be the ground$_r$ or means[174] of cognizing some truth, and

The natural light cannot demonstrate through the first efficient, final, and exemplar cause.

174. Again, the Latin word here translated "means" is in some contexts rightly translated as "middle term."

medium cognoscendi aliquam veritatem: non possunt autem in se ipsis videri per Metaphysicam naturalem, imo non potest haec scientia ostendere Deum habere haec vel illa exemplaria rerum, nisi a posteriori ex rebus ipsis, sicut ex artificio in re effecto[54] cognoscimus qualem ideam in artifice habuerit. Atque eadem ratio est de causa efficiente prima: quandiu enim non agnoscimus virtutem Dei in se, non possumus ex illa cognoscere quales possint ab ea res fieri, sed potius ex rebus factis virtutem Dei investigamus, quanvis, cognita virtute Dei ex quibusdam effectibus, possit per illam demonstrari quid in aliis facere possit. Et similiter ex perfectione & efficientia eius possumus investigare finem & perfectionem operum eius, ut quod ad eum spectet omnia propter se condere, vel perfectum facere universum. Ex quo possumus ulterius colligere, quas naturas rebus cognitis tribuerit, quem philosophandi *Aristoteles.* modum attigit Aristoteles libr. 12. Metaphysicae in fine.

Demon-
stratio per
deductionem
ad impossibile
Metaphysici
muneris est.
25. Praeter hos demonstrandi modos, qui parum sunt usitati, est alius per deductionem ad impossibile, & hoc modo ostenduntur omnia principia per deductionem ad illud, *Impossibile est de eodem simul idem affirmare & negare*: Et quia hoc est generalissimum principium huius doctrinae proprium, ideo huiusmodi demonstrandi genus ad hanc sapientiam spectat: de illo autem principio & usu eius dicturi sumus plura inferius disputatione 3. Denique ad augendam hanc certitudinem circa prima principia, plurimum conferre potest consideratio ipsius luminis intellectualis, quo ipsa principia prima manifestantur, & reflexio circa illud, & reductio ad fontem unde dimanat, scilicet ipsum divinum lumen. Sic enim recte colligimus prima principia, vera esse, quia ipso naturali lumine immediate, & per se vera ostenduntur, quia in huiusmodi modo assentiendi non potest hoc lumen decipi, aut ad falsum inclinare, quia est participatio divini luminis in suo gene-
Psalmus 4. re & ordine perfecta. ⟨34a⟩ Unde est illud Psal. 4. *Quis ostendit nobis bona? Signatum est super nos lumen vultus tui Domine.* Unde Aristoteles in principio scientiae de anima, illam scientiam iudicavit esse valde certam, quia lumen ipsum intellectuale contemplatur, in quo haec

---

54. Reading "effecto" with C_1, C_2, G_2, M_1, M_2, M_3, P_1, P_2, S, V_1, V_2, and V_3. The following have "effecta": M_4, V_5, and Vivès. The following has "effectu": V_4.

they cannot be seen in their very selves through natural metaphysics. In fact, this science cannot show that God has these or those exemplars of things_r except *a posteriori* from the things_r themselves, just as we cognize from a piece of art produced in reality what sort of idea it had in the artisan. And the same argument holds regarding the first efficient cause, for as long as we do not cognize the power of God in itself, we cannot cognize, by appeal to it, what sorts of things_r can be made by it, but rather we investigate the power of God by appeal to the things_r that have been made, even though, once the power of God is cognized from certain effects, one can demonstrate through it what it can do in other cases. And similarly, from his perfection and efficiency we can investigate the end and perfection of his works, for instance, that it pertains to him to establish all things for his own sake, or to make the universe perfect. From this we can in addition gather what natures he has assigned to the things_r cognized, which manner of philosophizing Aristotle touches on in *Metaph.* XII, at the end.[175]

Aristotle.

25. In addition to these ways of demonstrating, which are rarely used, there is another, through deduction to the impossible, and in this way all principles are proved through deduction to this one: "It is impossible to affirm and deny the same thing of the same thing at the same time." And since this is the most general principle proper to this doctrine, such a genus of demonstration pertains to this wisdom. But regarding that principle and its use we shall say more below, in the third disputation.[176] Finally, for the purpose of increasing this certainty regarding first principles, a consideration of the intellectual light itself, by which first principles themselves are made manifest, can be of great use, as can reflection on this light and the tracing of it back to the source from which it emanates, namely, the divine light itself. For in this way we rightly gather that first principles are true, since they are immediately and *per se* shown to be true by means of the natural light itself, because in such a mode of assenting this light cannot be deceived or incline to the false, since it is a participation of the divine light that is perfect in its own genus and order. For this reason, we find in Psalm 4: "Who shows good things to us? The light of your counte-

Demonstration through deduction to the impossible is a task of the meta-physician.

Psalm 4.

175. Aristotle, *Metaph.* XII, ch. 10.
176. See *DM* 3.3.

sapientia illam scientiam superat: nam altiori modo considerat vim, & perfectionem huius luminis secundum se, quatenus secundum esse abstrahit a materia, & quatenus certitudinem & infallibilitatem divini luminis participat.

Deductio ad impossibile quomodo sit demonstratio a priori, quomodo a posteriori.

26. Dices huiusmodi ostensionem primorum principiorum non esse a priori, sed a posteriori tantum: non enim haec principia vera sunt, quia per infallibile lumen cognoscuntur, sed potius quia vera sunt[55] & immediata, ideo per tale lumen manifestantur. Respondeo, concedendo hanc probationem non esse a priori, si veritas principiorum in esse rei (ut ita dicam) consideretur, potest tamen aliquo modo dici a priori in ratione cognoscibilis seu [25b] evidentis & certi: recte enim a priori ostenditur aliquam propositionem esse certam, quia a Deo revelatur, vel esse evidentem, quia demonstratione probatur: Sic ergo ostendi potest haec principia esse evidentissima, quia ipso lumine naturali immediate manifestantur. Atque haec probatio & reflexio maxime confert ad confirmandum intellectum, eiusque certitudinem augendam, saltem ex parte subiecti, in assensu principiorum.

Illatio.

Soncinas.
Iavellus.

Aristoteles.

27. Ex his ergo satis declaratum est, quomodo prima principia contineantur sub obiecto seu materia, circa quam haec scientia versatur, quodque munus circa illa exerceat. Atque obiter colligi etiam potest, hoc quidem esse verum de primis & universalissimis principiis, non tamen[56] de illis solis, ut Soncinas, & Iavellus, & nonnulli alii voluerunt: quia, licet circa priora principia, per se loquendo, immediatius versetur haec doctrina, & pluribus modis illa demonstret, ut ex dictis patet, tamen etiam ad alia se extendit, quia nonnulli ex praedictis modis generales & communes omnibus sunt. Et ideo Aristoteles absolute de omnibus locutus est, dicens Metaphysicam demonstrare principia

55. Reading "sunt" here with S, V$_1$, and V$_2$. The following omit this word: C$_1$, C$_2$, G$_2$, M$_1$, M$_2$, M$_3$, M$_4$, P$_1$, P$_2$, V$_3$, V$_4$, V$_5$, and Vivès.

56. Reading "tamen" here with S, V$_1$, and V$_2$. The following omit this word: C$_1$, C$_2$, G$_2$, M$_1$, M$_2$, M$_3$, M$_4$, P$_1$, P$_2$, V$_3$, V$_4$, V$_5$, and Vivès.

nance is stamped upon us, Lord."[177] For this reason, at the beginning of the science of the soul, Aristotle judges that science to be very certain because it considers the intellectual light itself,[178] in which respect this wisdom surpasses that science, for it considers in a higher way the power and perfection of this light in itself, insofar as it abstracts from matter with respect to existence$_e$, and insofar as it participates in the certainty and infallibility of the divine light.

26. You will say that such a proof of first principles is not *a priori*, but only *a posteriori*, for these principles are not true because they are cognized by means of an infallible light, but rather it is because they are true and immediate that they are made evident through such a light. I reply by granting that this proof is not *a priori* if the truth of the principles in real being$_e$ (so to speak) is considered, but it can in some way be called *a priori* [when the truth of the principles is considered] in its character$_r$ as a cognizable [object], that is, as an evident or certain thing, for it is rightly proved *a priori* that some proposition is certain because it is revealed by God, or that it is evident because it is proved by a demonstration. In this way, therefore, it can be shown that these principles are most evident because they are immediately made manifest by the natural light itself. And this proof and reflection especially contributes to strengthening the intellect and increasing its certainty in its assent to principles, at least on the side of the subject.

27. On the basis of these things, then, it has been sufficiently explained how first principles are contained under the object or subject matter with which this science is concerned, and what function it performs with respect to them. And it can also be gathered in passing that this is indeed true of the first and most universal principles, but not of them alone, as Soncinas, Javelli, and some others would have it, since although this doctrine, speaking *per se*, more immediately concerns itself with prior principles, and demonstrates them in several ways, as is clear from the things that have been said, nevertheless, it also extends itself to others, since some of the aforementioned ways of demonstrating are general and common to all. And for this reason Aristotle

How a deduction to the impossible is an a priori *demonstration and how it is an* a posteriori *one.*

Inference.

Soncinas.
Javelli.

Aristotle.

177. Psalm 4:6.
178. Aristotle, *De anima* I, ch. 1, 402b1–4. See Francisco de Toledo, *Commentaria una cum quaestionibus in tres libros Aristotelis De Anima*, fols. 12ra–14ra.

omnium scientiarum, ut patet ex Prooemio, cap. 1. & 2. & ex lib. 4. Metaph. tex. 7. & ex 1. Poster. cap. 7. & ex 1. Topic. cap. 2. & 1. Physicor. cap. 2. ubi ait, si quis neget prima principia Geometriae, non pertinere ad Geometriam illa ⟨34b⟩ probare, sed ad primum Philosophum. Es- *D. Thomas* tque[57] aperta sententia D. Thomae, 1. 2. quaest. 57. art. 2. praesertim ad 1. & secundum. Et ratione potest facile ex dictis ostendi,[58] nam modi ostendendi prima principia, etiam in particularibus & propriis principiis aliarum scientiarum locum habent. Imo addit Divus Thom. citato loco ad hanc scientiam non solum pertinere confirmare intellectum in assensu principiorum, sed etiam conclusionum, quod intelligi potest remote & mediate, quia confirmando principia, virtute etiam confirmat conclusiones: vel materialiter tantum (ut sic dicam) quia interdum per altiores causas potest sapientia ostendere conclusiones, quae per alia media inferiora in aliis scientiis demonstrantur.

Non esse munus Metaphysicae
tradere instrumenta sciendi.

Aliquorum   28. Sunt qui existiment munus hoc etiam ad Metaphysicam per-
sententia.   tinere: nam licet Dialecticus definire doceat, dividere, &c. non tamen potest ex propriis principiis huiusmodi instrumenta declarare, eorumque rationem reddere, sed solum quoad quaestionem an sint, huiusmodi instrumenta tradere, & exponere: ad Metaphysicum autem spectare de illis disserere, eorum primas radices & causas declarando. Quod de singulis ita exponi potest, nam definitio declarat essentiam rei, sed rationem essentiae declarare ad Metaphysicam pertinet: ergo & perfectam rationem definitionis tradere, munus est Metaphysicae. Rursus, divisio declarat rerum distinctionem: sed de rerum distinctionibus agere munus est Metaphysicae: ergo & rationem divisionis explicare

---

57. Reading "Estque" with all of the early editions. Vivès has "Estqua."

58. Reading "Et ratione potest facile ex dictis ostendi," with S, V_1, and V_2: The following have "Et ratione facile ex dictis ostendi,": C_1, C_2, M_1, M_2, P_1, and P_2. The following have "Et rationem facile ex dictis ostendi,": G_2, M_3, M_4, V_3, V_4, and V_5. The following has "Et ratione facile ex dictis ostendi potest,": Vivès.

speaks without qualification about all of them, saying that metaphysics demonstrates the principles of all the sciences, as is clear from the proem, chs. 1 and 2,[179] and from *Metaph.* IV, text 7,[180] and from *Post. An.* I, ch. 7,[181] and from *Topics* I, ch. 2,[182] and *Phys.* I, ch. 2,[183] where he says that if someone denies the first principles of geometry, it does not pertain to geometry to prove them, but to the first philosopher. And it is the clear opinion of St. Thomas, *ST* I-II, q. 57, art. 2, especially ad 1 and ad 2.[184] And it can easily be shown by argument from the things that have been said, for the ways of proving first principles are applicable also to the particular and proper principles of the other sciences. In fact, St. Thomas adds in the place cited that it pertains to this science to strengthen the intellect not only in its assent to principles, but also in its assent to conclusions, which can be understood either remotely and mediately, since by strengthening principles it virtually strengthens conclusions as well, or only materially (so to speak), since wisdom can sometimes prove through higher causes conclusions that are demonstrated in other sciences through other, inferior middle terms.

It is not the function of metaphysics to
teach the instruments of knowledge.

28. There are some who hold that this task belongs to metaphysics as well, for although the dialectician teaches how to define, divide, etc., nevertheless, he cannot explain instruments of this sort from proper principles and give their reason, but he only, with respect to the question of "whether they are," teaches and expounds such instruments, whereas it pertains to the metaphysician to treat of them by making clear their first roots and causes. And this can be explained in detail as follows, for a definition makes clear the essence of a thing$_r$, but to make clear the concept$_r$ of essence pertains to metaphysics. Therefore, it is the

179. Aristotle, *Metaph.* I, chs. 1 and 2.
180. Aristotle, *Metaph.* IV, ch. 3, 1005a19–b1.
181. Aristotle, *Post. An.* I, ch. 9, 76a16–22.
182. Aristotle, *Top.* I, ch. 2, 101a36–b4.
183. Aristotle, *Phys.* I, ch. 2, 184b25–185a5.
184. Thomas Aquinas, *Sancti Thomae Aquinatis opera omnia* (Leonina), t. 6, pp. 365b–366a.

ad eam pertinet. Ad haec, omnis vis argumentationis, si formam eius spectemus, consistit in altero ex his principiis, *Quae sunt eadem uni tertio, sunt eadem inter se*: *Non potest idem simul de eodem affirmari, &* [26a] *negari*: Sed haec principia sunt propria Metaphysicae scientiae, ad quam pertinet tractare de eodem, & diverso: & de ente, & non ente, quae per affirmationem & negationem explicantur: ergo ex hoc etiam capite pertinet ad Metaphysicum, instrumentum sciendi tradere. Tandem scientia est spiritualis qualitas: ergo ut sic comprehenditur sub Metaphysicae obiecto: ergo eadem ratione pertinet ad Metaphysicam tradere rationem acquirendi scientiam, & declarare quibus modis aut instrumentis acquiratur: nam agere de fine & mediis, eiusdem est doctrinae; ⟨35a⟩ omnia autem haec ad scientiam tanquam ad finem ordinantur.

Reprobatur.   29. Sed haec sententia, nisi amplius declaretur, confundit Metaphysicam cum Dialectica, nam Dialecticae proprium munus est, sciendi modum tradere, quod non aliter facit, nisi docendo instrumenta sciendi, & eorum vim & proprietates demonstrando. Quocirca, ut, quid veritas rei habeat, exponamus, & unicuique scientiae suum proprium munus tribuamus, advertendum est, haec instrumenta sciendi proprie & formaliter inveniri in cogitationibus mentis, seu internis actibus intellectus, fundari vero in rebus, vocibus autem explicari. Scientia enim in actu quodam intellectus consistit, vel in habitu, iuxta diversas acceptiones scientiae, actualis scilicet & habitualis: & ideo necesse est ut propria sciendi instrumenta in ipso intellectu, & in actibus ipsius posita sint: nam, quia homo per discursum scientiam acquirit, & ad discursum perficiendum aliis prioribus operationibus, seu conceptionibus rerum indiget, ideo huiusmodi conceptiones mentis ita dispositae & ordinatae, ut ad scientiam acquirendam per se ac directe conferant, dicuntur instrumenta sciendi: sunt ergo huiusmodi instrumenta formaliter in operationibus mentis. Quia ergo mentis operationes ut rectae sint & verae, esse debent rebus ipsis proportionatae, & commensu-

function of metaphysics to teach the perfect account_r of definition as well. Further, division makes the distinction between things_r clear. But it is the task of metaphysics to treat of the distinctions between things_r. Therefore, it pertains to metaphysics to explain the concept_r of division as well. In addition, the entire force of argumentation, if we consider its form, depends on one of these principles: "Things that are the same as a third thing are the same as each other," and "The same thing cannot be affirmed and denied of the same thing at the same time." But these principles are proper to the science of metaphysics, to which it pertains to deal with the same and the diverse, and with being and non-being, which are explained through affirmation and negation. Therefore, for this reason too it pertains to the metaphysician to teach the instruments of knowledge. Finally, a science is a spiritual quality. Therefore, it is, as such, comprehended under the object of metaphysics. Therefore, for the same reason, it pertains to metaphysics to teach the method_r of acquiring science, and to make clear by which means or instruments it is acquired, for it belongs to the same doctrine to treat of the end and the means, and all these things are ordained to science as to an end.

29. But this opinion, unless it is more fully clarified, confounds metaphysics with dialectic, for it is a proper function of dialectic to teach the method of knowing, which it does not otherwise do than by teaching the instruments of knowledge, and by demonstrating their power and properties. For this reason, in order to explain the truth of the matter, and assign to each science its proper function, it must be noted that these instruments of knowledge are properly and formally found in the thoughts of the mind, or in the internal acts of the intellect, but are founded on things_r and are explained by means of words. For science consists in a certain act of the intellect, or in a habit, according to different acceptations of "science," namely, actual and habitual, and therefore it is necessary that the proper instruments of knowledge be situated in the intellect itself and in its acts. For, since the human being acquires science by reasoning, and needs other prior operations or conceptions of things_r in order to perfect her reasoning, such conceptions of the mind, so disposed and ordered that they assist *per se* and directly in the acquisition of science, are called instruments of knowledge. Therefore, instruments of this sort are formally in the operations of the mind.

ratae, ideo necesse est ut huiusmodi instrumenta aliquo modo in rebus ipsis fundentur: explicantur autem vocibus, quae a natura datae sunt ad exprimenda animi sensa, iuxta illud Aristotelis 1. Periherm. *Sunt autem ea quae in voce, earum, quae sunt in anima, passionum notae:* & illud Cicer. 1. de Oratore, *Hoc uno praestamus feris, quod loquimur inter nos, & quod exprimere dicendo sensa possumus.*

Vera in hoc sententia.

30. Sic ergo dicendum est non pertinere ad Metaphysicum directe tradere instrumenta sciendi, & modum ac dispositionem eorum docere, quam in conceptibus mentis habere debent, ut apta sint ad scientiam generandam. Probatur argumento supra insinuato, quia hoc spectat ad munus Dialecticae: qua ratione dixit Aristoteles 2. lib. Metaphys. cap. 3. *Absurdum esse scientiam simul & modum scientiae quaerere.* Quibus verbis docere voluit (ut omnes expositores tradunt) Dialecticam ante alias scientias, praesertim ante Metaphysicam, esse acquirendam, eo quod ad il⟨35b⟩lam spectat modum sciendi tradere: quod nihil aliud est, quam instrumenta sciendi docere, modumque aperire tractandi & probandi res scientiae accommodatum. Neque est verum Dialec-

Dialecticae[59] est an, & quid sint sciendi instrumenta, tractare.

ticam solum perfunctorie, & quoad an est (ut vocant) haec explicare, tum quia experimento constat non solum tradere Dialecticam leges recte definiendi, argumentandi aut demonstrandi, sed etiam rationes harum rerum: nam etiam [26b] a priori demonstrat, cur recta definitio & argumentatio tales conditiones & proprietates requirant, & similia: tum etiam quia alias non satis esset Dialectica ad scientiam acquiren-dam, sed oporteret etiam Metaphysicam praemittere, quod est plane falsum, & contra omnium sensum & usum. Sequela patet, quia nun-quam acquiritur vera scientia, nisi quis sciat se scire: nam scientia esse debet perfectum intellectuale lumen, quod se ipsum manifestat, alioqui non erit omnino evidens: non potest autem scire, quod sua cognitio est vera scientia, nisi sciat suam ratiocinationem esse veram demonstratio-nem, quod scire non potest, nisi sciat quid sit vera demonstratio, & cur

59. Reading "*Dialecticae*" with C_1, C_2, G_2, M_1, M_2, M_3, M_4, P_1, P_2, S, V_1, V_2, V_3, and V_4. The following have "*Dialectica*": V_5 and Vivès.

Since, therefore, the operations of the mind, if they are to be right and true, must be proportioned to, and commensurate with, things$_r$ themselves, it is necessary that such instruments be founded in some way on things$_r$ themselves. And they are explained by means of words, which have been given by nature in order to express the thoughts of the soul, according to the following text from Aristotle, *On Interpretation* I: "The things that are in speech are signs of passions that are in the soul,"[185] and according to this one, from Cicero, *On the Orator* I: "We excel the beasts in this single respect, the fact that we talk to each other, and the fact that we can express our thoughts by speaking."[186]

30. It must, therefore, be said that it does not pertain to the meta- *The true view.*
physician to directly teach the instruments of knowledge, or to teach the mode and disposition they should have in the concepts of the mind in order that they might be suited to generating science. This is proved by the argument introduced above, since this pertains to the task of the dialectician. For this reason, Aristotle says in *Metaph.* II, ch. 3, that "it is absurd to seek at the same time a science and that science's method."[187] With these words he wishes to teach (as all expositors tell us) that dialectic must be acquired before the other sciences, and especially before metaphysics, because it pertains to dialectic to teach the method of knowing, which is nothing other than to teach the instruments of knowledge, and to reveal the method of treating and proving things$_r$ that is suited to science. Nor is it true that dialectic explains these things *Dialectic* only in a superficial way, and with respect to the "whether it is" (as they *treats of the* call it), both because it is clear by experience that dialectic teaches not *instruments* only the rules for rightly defining, arguing or demonstrating, but also *of knowledge,* the reasons of these things$_r$—for it also demonstrates *a priori* why a *both with* correct definition and argumentation require such characteristics and *respect to the* properties, and the like—and also because otherwise dialectic would *"whether it* not be sufficient for acquiring science, but it would also be necessary *is" and with* to learn metaphysics beforehand, which is plainly false and against the *respect to the* thought and practice of all. The consequence is clear, since true science *"what it is."*

185. Aristotle, *De Int.*, ch. 1, 16a3–4.

186. Cicero, *De oratore*, 1.32, in: M. Tullius Cicero, *Rhetorica, Vol. 1: Libros de oratore tres continens*, ed. A. S. Wilkins (Oxford: Oxford University Press, 2016), 9.

187. Aristotle, *Metaph.* II, ch. 3, 995a13–14.

talibus principiis, talique forma ratiocinandi constare debeat. Si ergo Dialectica horum omnium rationem non redderet, sed potius fidem quandam illorum postularet, non posset ad veram scientiam acquirendam deservire, aut esse sufficiens. Et confirmatur quia demonstratio non est aptum instrumentum sciendi, nisi cognita ut demonstratio, id est, ut ratiocinatio necessario concludens ex principiis certis & evidentibus. Nam si quis conficiat rationem quae in se sit demonstratio, ab ipso autem non cognoscatur, sed existimetur ratio probabilis, vel procedens solum ex certis, non vero evidentibus, in illo non generabit veram scientiam, quia talis demonstratio sic proposita, vel est ineptum instrumentum, vel non satis applicatum ad talem effectum. Unde Dialectica ita tradit modum sciendi ut scientifice illum doceat: propter quod, qui recte de illa sentiunt, non tantum sciendi modum, sed etiam veram scientiam illam esse existimant: hoc igitur munus ad Dialecticam proprie & per se spectat, & non ad Metaphysicam.

Consectarium.   31. Atque hinc etiam fit eiusdem Dialecticae, & non Metaphysicae esse huiusmodi instrumenta tradere seu dirigere, prout vocibus exprimi, aut confici possunt (sub vocibus autem scripta complectimur, quia quoad hoc solum materialiter differunt) ⟨36a⟩ imo nec Dialectica ipsa directe & ex instituto circa haec versatur ut circa proprium obiectum & materiam suam, sed ex consequenti, & quasi ex quadam concomitantia hoc praestat. Cum enim voces a conceptibus oriantur, dum Dialectica conceptus dirigit & ordinat, consequenter docet quibus verbis, seu qua verborum forma exprimendi sint, ut vim habeant suadendi ac demonstrandi, quod totum & per se clarum est, & ex ipso Dialecticae usu perspicuum.

is never acquired unless someone knows that he knows, for science must be a perfected intellectual light that reveals itself, otherwise it will not be altogether evident. But one cannot know that one's cognition is true science unless one knows that one's reasoning is a true demonstration, and this one cannot know unless one knows what a true demonstration is, and why it must be composed from such principles and such a form of reasoning. If, therefore, dialectic did not give the reason of all these things, but rather demanded a sort of faith in them, it could not serve or be sufficient for acquiring true science. And this is confirmed, because a demonstration is not a suitable instrument of knowledge unless it is cognized as a demonstration, that is, as a piece of reasoning that draws its conclusion necessarily from certain and evident principles. For if someone produces an argument that is in itself a demonstration, but he does not cognize it as a demonstration, judging instead that it is a probable argument, or an argument proceeding only from certain, but not evident, premises, then it will not generate true science in him, for such a demonstration, thus set forth, is either an unsuitable instrument for, or not adequately directed to, such an effect. For this reason, dialectic teaches the method of knowing in such a way that it teaches it scientifically, and for this reason those who think correctly about it judge it to be, not only a method of knowing, but also a true science. This function, therefore, properly and *per se* pertains to dialectic, and not to metaphysics.

31. And thus it also follows that it pertains to the same dialectic, *Consequence.* and not to metaphysics, to teach or direct such instruments, insofar as they can be expressed by, or composed from, words (we include written words under words, since for present purposes they differ only materially). In fact, dialectic itself does not even directly and deliberately concern itself with these as with its proper object and subject matter, but it accomplishes this as a consequence and, as it were, by virtue of a certain concomitance. For since words arise from concepts, when dialectic directs and orders concepts, it consequently teaches by what words, or by what form of words, they must be expressed in order that they might have the power to persuade and demonstrate, and this is wholly and *per se* clear and, from the very practice of dialectic, evident.

32. Addendum vero est, quatenus haec instrumenta sciendi in rebus ipsis fundantur, eorum scientiam & cognitionem plurimum perfici per scientiam Metaphysicae,[60] ita ut quod circa omnes scientias & principia earum Metaphysicam praestare diximus, peculiari quadam ratione circa Dialecticam eiusque munera locum habeat. Hoc probat ratio dubitandi in principio posita, & declaratur in hunc modum. Nam peculiariter pertinet ad Metaphysicam cognitio essentiae, & quidditatis ut sic: definitio autem, cuius rationem ac formam Dialectica tradit, si sit perfecta, explicat rei essentiam & quidditatem, & ideo dum Metaphysica tradit quid[61] sit uniuscuiusque rei essentia & quidditas, plurimum confert ad perfectum definiendi modum. Praesertim quia non solum tradit Metaphysica rationem essentiae in communi, sed etiam intra suam abstractionem va[27a]rios essentiarum gradus ac modos declarat: ex quibus maxime pendet cognoscere, quibus partibus definitiones rerum constare debeant, aut quem modum definiendi in distinctis rebus (verbi gratia, in substantia, vel accidenti, & in re simplici, aut composita) tenere oporteat. Sic igitur Metaphysica plurimum perficit definiendi artem, quanvis directe & ex instituto illam non tradat. Simili modo contingit circa aliud instrumentum sciendi, quod est divisio, cuius leges & conditiones tradit dialectica: illae vero omnes fundantur in rerum distinctione seu oppositione: agere vero de variis distinctionibus rerum ad Metaphysicam pertinet: nam idem & diversum ad proprietates entis reducuntur, sicut unum & multa: & ideo, dum Metaphysica distinctiones varias rerum exacte declarat, artem etiam dividendi illustrat. De argumentatione autem seu demonstratione non videtur similis ratio, quia non fundatur proxime in essentia, vel aliqua proprietate entis, sicut definitio, & divisio: nihilominus alia via, etiam ⟨36b⟩ in hoc munere, Metaphysica Dialecticam iuvat, tam ex parte materiae, quam ex parte formae. Ex parte quidem materiae, quia dum Metaphysica fere omnium entium rationes distinguit ac separat, & generatim declarat quid sit res in essentia, quid etiam proprietates: quid res, quid vero modus: materiam subministrat demonstrandi, &

---

60. Reading "per scientiam Metaphysicae" here with C₁, C₂, G₂, M₁, M₂, M₃, M₄, P₁, P₂, S, V₁, V₂, V₃, and V₄. The following has "per scientiam Metaphys.": V₅. The following has "per scientiam metaphysicam": Vivès.

61. Reading "quid" here with C₁, C₂, G₂, M₁, M₂, M₃, M₄, P₁, P₂, S, V₁, V₂, V₃, and V4. The following have "quod": V₅ and Vivès.

32. However, it must be added that, insofar as these instruments of knowledge are founded on things$_r$ themselves, the science and cognition of them is greatly perfected by the science of metaphysics, and this in such a way that, what we have said metaphysics does, in relation to all the sciences and their principles, holds true for a certain special reason in relation to dialectic and its functions. The reason for doubt set forth at the beginning proves this, and it is made clear in this way. For the cognition of essence and quiddity as such pertains in a special way to metaphysics. And a definition, the nature$_r$ and form of which dialectic teaches, explains, if it is perfect, the essence and quiddity of a thing$_r$. And therefore, while metaphysics teaches what the essence and quiddity of each thing$_r$ is, it greatly contributes to the perfect method of defining—especially since metaphysics not only teaches the concept$_r$ of an essence in general, but it also makes clear within its own abstraction the various grades and modes of essences, on which especially depends the cognition of which parts the definitions of things$_r$ must be constituted from, or which method of definition must be adhered to in the case of diverse things$_r$ (for example, in the case of a substance or an accident, and in the case of a simple thing$_r$ or a composite one). In this way, therefore, metaphysics greatly perfects the art of defining, although it does not teach it directly and by design. Similarly for the other instrument of knowledge, which is division, the rules and characteristics of which dialectic teaches: these are all founded on the distinction or opposition of things$_r$, and it pertains to metaphysics to treat of the various distinctions of things$_r$,[188] for the same and the diverse are reduced to properties of being, such as the one and the many. And therefore, while metaphysics accurately explains the various distinctions of things$_r$, it also elucidates the art of dividing. But there seems not to be a like consideration$_r$ as regards argumentation or demonstration, since it is not founded proximately on the essence or some property of being, as definition and division are. Nevertheless, by another path, metaphysics helps dialectic in connection with this function as well, both with respect to matter and with respect to form. With respect to matter, to be sure, because while metaphysics distinguishes and di-

Metaphysics greatly elucidates the instruments of knowledge.

---

188. See *DM* 7, "On the Various Genera of Distinctions."

argumentandi, seu potius exacte declarat qualia esse debeant tam extrema, quam media demonstrationis. Ex parte vero formae, quia haec doctrina exacte declarat & ostendit omnia principia, in quibus omnis recta forma argumentandi nititur, ut sunt illa, *Quae sunt eadem uni tertio, sunt eadem inter se. Non potest idem de eodem simul affirmari & negari,* & similia.

Rationes pro opposita sententia solvuntur.

33. Ad rationes dubitandi in principio positas facilis est responsio ex dictis. Ad primam de definitione respondetur Metaphysicum quidem declarare in communi, quid sit essentia, & qualis etiam sit, simplex ne an composita, intra sui obiecti latitudinem, suamque abstractionem: Dialecticum autem tractare de modo quo a nobis concipienda est & declaranda distincte per definitionem, rei essentia & natura, seu ex quibus conceptibus aut vocibus componenda sit definitio, quas ve proprietates habere debeat ut apta sit: haec autem munera distincta sunt, quanvis se se mutuo iuvent: nam Dialectica iuvat Metaphysicam, sicut modus sciendi scientiam: Metaphysica autem iuvat dialecticam tamquam generalis scientia, quae proxime & exacte de rebus disserit, quas Dialectica, vel supponit, vel solum remote attingit. Atque eadem fere responsio applicanda est ad alteram partem de[62] divisione, nam Metaphysica tractat de distinctionibus rerum, prout in rebus ipsis sunt: dialectica vero de modo concipiendi & explicandi partitiones rerum. Similiter ad tertium membrum de argumentatione dicendum est, quod licet Metaphysica aliquo modo demonstret illa principia, eaque reducat ad illud universalissimum, *Quodlibet est vel non est,* seu *Impossibile est idem simul esse, & non esse,* tamen etiam Dialectica supponit simile principium ut per se notum, id est, non posse idem de eodem affirmari & negari: ad quod fere omnem vim & formam rectae argumentationis reducit, ut illius proprietates, & conditiones demonstret. [27b]

---

62. Reading "de" here with S, V_1, and V_2. The following read "ex" instead: C_1, C_2, G_2, M_1, M_2, M_3, M_4, P_1, P_2, V_3, V_4, V_5, and Vivès.

vides the natures$_r$ of almost all beings, and in a general way makes clear what a thing$_r$ is in its essence, and also what properties are, and what a thing$_r$ is, and what a mode is, it supplies the matter of demonstration and argumentation, or rather it accurately explains what the extremes and the middle terms of a demonstration must be like. And with respect to form, because this doctrine accurately explains and proves all the principles on which every correct form of argumentation depends, such as these: "Things that are the same as a third are the same as each other," and "The same thing cannot at the same time be affirmed and denied of the same thing," and the like.

33. As for the reasons for doubt that were set forth at the beginning, the answer is easy, given the things that have been said. To the first, having to do with definition, I reply that the metaphysician, within the scope of her object and her abstraction, does indeed make clear in a general way what an essence is, and also what it is like, whether simple or composite, and the dialectician discusses the way in which the essence and nature of a thing$_r$ should be conceived by us and distinctly explained by means of a definition, or from which concepts or words a definition is to be composed, or what properties it must have in order to be suitable. But these functions are distinct, although they aid each other, for dialectic assists metaphysics as the method of knowing assists science, whereas metaphysics assists dialectic as a general science which proximately and accurately treats of things$_r$ that dialectic either assumes or touches on only from a distance. And almost the same reply is to be given to the other part, regarding division, for metaphysics deals with the distinctions of things$_r$ insofar as they are in things$_r$ themselves, whereas dialectic deals with the manner of conceiving and explaining the divisions of things$_r$. Likewise, with respect to the third part, regarding argumentation, it must be said that, although metaphysics in some way demonstrates those principles, and reduces them to this most universal one: "Any given thing either is or is not," or "It is impossible for the same thing at the same time to be and not to be," nevertheless, dialectic also assumes a similar principle as *per se* known$_n$—namely, the principle that the same thing cannot be affirmed and denied of the same thing—to which nearly all the force and form of a correct argumentation reduces, in order to demonstrate its properties and characteristics.

34. Ad ultimum membrum de scientia respondetur, considerationem scientiae, ⟨37a⟩ prout est quaedam spiritualis qualitas mentis, & habitus, vel operatio eius talis conditionis & naturae, multiplicem esse posse. Una est mere speculativa, qua contemplamur quid sit talis res, & quas proprietates habeat: & haec consideratio, vel pertinet ad eam partem Philosophiae naturalis, quae de anima rationali tractat, si de humana tantum scientia, quae non est sine phantasia, sit sermo: vel, si abstracte & absolute loquamur de scientia, pertinebit ad Metaphysicam, nam est res vel proprietas abstrahens a materia secundum esse. Alia consideratio scientiae est quasi practica, & artificiosa, quae non est de habitibus, sed de actibus scientiae: nam ars circa operationes versatur: & solum habet locum haec consideratio in humana scientia, quae per compositionem & discursum perficitur: ars enim non versatur circa simplicia, sed circa composita: nam scopus artis est dirigere compositionem aliquam, vel concentum: unde forma artificiosa ex debita proportione & compositione partium seu rerum simplicium consurgit: haec ergo scientiae directio & consideratio ad dialecticam spectat, quae est ars sciendi, non ad Metaphysicam. Ut autem dialectica hoc munus exercere possit, non oportet quod exacte speculetur totam naturam & essentiam illius qualitatis quae est scientia, sed satis est, quod supponat esse operationem mentis, & aliquas eius proprietates tradat, quas ad veritatem exacte & sine errore manifestandam requirit, ut quod sit evidens, certa, & similes. Atque haec cognitio scientiae traditur a Dialectico, ut constat ex libris Posteriorum, eaque sufficit dialectico, ut ad eam tanquam ad finem suam artem & sciendi methodum dirigat. Alia denique consideratio scientiae potest dici moralis, quatenus usus, vel exercitium scientiae potest esse laude, vel reprehensione dignum: quod munus ad moralem Philosophiam, vel prudentiam spectat.

34. To the final part, regarding science, I reply that the consideration of science, insofar as it is a certain spiritual quality and habit of the mind, or an operation of it having a particular character and nature, can be manifold. One is purely speculative, by which we consider what such a thing$_r$ is, and what properties it has, and this consideration either pertains to that part of natural philosophy which treats of the rational soul, if the discussion concerns only human science, which is not without imagination, or, if we are speaking abstractly and absolutely about science, it pertains to metaphysics, for it is a thing$_r$ or property that abstracts from matter with respect to existence$_e$. Another consideration of science is, as it were, practical and has to do with art, which is not about the habits, but the acts, of a science, since art is concerned with operations. And this consideration has place only in the case of human science, which is perfected through composition and reasoning, for art does not concern itself with simples, but with composites, since the goal of art is to direct some composition or union, for which reason an artificial form arises from a due proportion and composition of parts or simple things$_r$. Therefore, this direction and consideration of science belongs to dialectic, which is the art of knowing, and not to metaphysics. But in order that dialectic might perform this task, it is not necessary that it carefully investigate the whole nature and essence of that quality which is science, but it is enough that dialectic assume that it is an operation of the mind, and that it teach some of its properties which it requires for the accurate manifestation of the truth without error—for instance, that it is evident, certain, and the like. And this cognition of science is handed down by the dialectician, as is clear from the books of the *Posterior Analytics*, and it suffices for the dialectician's task of directing his art and the method of knowing to science as to his end. Finally, another consideration of science can be called moral, insofar as the use or exercise of science can be worthy of praise or censure, and this function belongs to moral philosophy or prudence.

Sectio V.

Utrum Metaphysica sit perfectissima scientia speculativa, veraque sapientia.

—

1. Explicando causam finalem & utilitatem huius scientiae, simul effectum eius declaravimus: nam tota eius utilitas in operatione & effectu eius posita est: reliquum ergo est ut de illius attributis pauca dicamus, quae ex materia subiecta, & ex fine illius facile colligi poterunt.

Prima conclusio

2. Dico primo Meta⟨37b⟩phys. scientiam esse speculativam omnium perfectissimam. Ita docet Arist. li. 1. c. 2. & li. 2. c. 1. & li. 3. c. 2. & omnes interpretes. Estque satis probata haec assertio ex dictis. Nam sect. praeced. ostendimus finem huius scientiae esse veritatis cognitionem, & ex se in ea sistere: scientia autem ex hoc fine vocatur speculativa, ut Arist. li. 6. docet, & inferius suo loco tractabitur. In sect. autem prima ostensum est obiectum huius scientiae esse nobilissimum, tam in esse obiecti, propter summam abstractionem, quam in esse rei propter nobilissima entia, quae comprehendit. Omnis autem scientia habet nobilitatem suam ex obiecto suo: est ergo haec scientia speculativa, omnium praestantissima. [28a]

Quaestiuncula.

3. Interrogabit autem fortasse aliquis an haec scientia pure speculativa sit, vel etiam practica: ut enim nunc suppono, non repugnat eandem scientiam, vel cognitionem simul eminenti ratione speculativam esse & practicam: id enim Theologi attribuunt scientiae divinae, non tantum ut in ipso Deo est, sed etiam ut participatur a nobis, vel per visionem claram, vel per obscuram Theologiam & fidem: ergo etiam in scientiis acquisitis & naturalibus esse poterit aliqua, quae hanc eminentiam participet, simulque sit speculativa & practica. Quod si alicui, maxime huic doctrinae, convenire debet. Primo, quia est suprema omnium sci-

SECTION 5

WHETHER METAPHYSICS IS THE MOST PERFECT
SCIENCE AND TRUE WISDOM.

---

1. In explaining the final cause and usefulness of this science, we have at the same time made clear its effect, for its entire usefulness is located in its operation and effect. It remains, then, to say a few things about its attributes, which can easily be gathered from its subject matter and end.

2. I say, first, that metaphysics is the most perfect speculative science of them all. This is what Aristotle teaches in *Metaph.* I, ch. 2, book II, ch. 1, and book III, ch. 2, as do all of his interpreters.[189] And this claim is sufficiently proved by appeal to what has been said. For in the preceding section we showed that this science's end is the cognition of truth, and that of itself it stops at the truth; but a science is called speculative because it has this as its end, as Aristotle teaches in *Metaph.* VI,[190] and this will be discussed below in its place. And in the first section it was shown that the object of this science is the noblest, both in the being$_e$ of an object, on account of its supreme abstraction, and in real being$_e$, on account of the noblest beings that it embraces. But every science has its nobility from its object. Therefore, this speculative science is the most excellent of them all. *First conclusion.*

3. Someone will perhaps ask whether this science is purely speculative, or also practical, since, as I now suppose, it is not impossible for the same science or cognition to be eminently speculative and practical at the same time, for theologians attribute this to divine science, not only as it is in God himself, but also as it is participated in by us, either by a clear vision, or by an obscure theology and faith. Therefore, among the acquired and natural sciences as well, there can be one that participates *A minor issue.*

---

189. Aristotle, *Metaph.* I, ch. 2, 982a14–19, 982a30–982b10, *Metaph.* II, ch. 1, 993b19–31, *Metaph.* III, ch. 2, 996b8–13.
190. Aristotle, *Metaph.* VI, ch. 1, 1025b18–1026a32.

195

entiarum, omnibusque imperat, prout in prooemio Aristoteles dixit. Deinde quod naturalem Dei cognitionem, quantum naturae lumine fieri potest, perficiat: ex Dei autem cognitione pendet iudicium rectum de agendis: ergo hoc etiam iudicium per hanc scientiam dirigitur atque adeo ex ea parte practica est. Et declaratur in hunc modum, nam haec scientia demonstrat attributa divina quae naturae lumine demonstrari possunt, inter quae sunt esse summe bonum, esse ultimum finem omnium, esse primam veritatem: ergo haec omnia demonstrat haec scientia: ergo etiam demonstrabit Deum esse super omnia diligendum, quia hoc debetur ei quatenus summe bonus, & ultimus finis est. Rursus demonstrat haec scientia Deum habere omnium providentiam: esseque sapientissimum & iustissimum: ergo consequenter etiam docebit eum esse timendum, & illi esse fidendum, & similia: quae omnia ad mores & praxim spectant. Denique non alia ratione Theo⟨38a⟩logia infusa merito existimatur eminenter practica, & speculativa, nisi quia sub altiori lumine considerat in Deo illam rationem finis ultimi, consequendi per media moralia & practica: ergo idem erit de naturali Metaphys. ut sub inferiori lumine procedit, servata proportione.

Responsio. 4. Nihilominus dicendum est, doctrinam hanc nihil habere practicae scientiae, sed tantum esse contemplatricem. Ita sumitur ex Aristotele, & aliis expositoribus, nam licet expresse non attingant hanc quaestionem, tamen dum simpliciter docent, hanc scientiam esse speculativam, & aut tacent de practica, aut certe id negant, plane sentiunt esse pure speculativam. Accedit quod Aristoteles in libris Ethicorum ex professo disputavit de beatitudine hominis tanquam de prima regula moralium actionum: Beatitudo autem hominis consistit in Deo ut est finis ultimus omnium, & singulari modo creaturae rationalis: illa ergo consideratio non spectat ad Metaphysicam: ergo nulla alia consideratio superest, sub qua possit haec doctrina esse practica. Quia si est practica, maxime moralis: nam per se notum est non esse factivam seu directivam operationum artis, imo nec actionum intellectualium,

Aristoteles.

in this eminence and is at the same time speculative and practical. But if this pertains to some acquired and natural science, it should pertain especially to this doctrine. First, because it is the highest of all the sciences and rules them all, as Aristotle says in the proem.[191] Second, because it perfects the natural cognition of God insofar as this can be done by the light of nature, and right judgment about action depends on cognition of God. Therefore, this kind of judgment also is directed by this science, and so this science is in this respect practical. And this is made clear in the following way, for this science demonstrates the divine attributes that can be demonstrated by the light of nature, among which are: to be supremely good, to be the ultimate end of all things, to be the first truth. Therefore, this science demonstrates all these things. Therefore, it will also demonstrate that God is to be loved above all things, since this is due to him insofar as he is supremely good and the ultimate end. Again, this science demonstrates that God has providence over all things and is the wisest and most just. Therefore, it will consequently also teach that he is to be feared, and that faith is to be placed in him, and the like, all of which concern morals and practice. Finally, infused theology is deservedly judged eminently practical and speculative for no other reason than because under a higher light it considers in God that character, of highest end which is to be achieved by moral and practical means. Therefore, the same will be true of natural metaphysics, proportionately, insofar as it proceeds under an inferior light.

4. Nevertheless, it must be said that this doctrine is in no way a *Reply.* practical science, but is only contemplative. This is how it is understood in accordance with Aristotle and other expositors, for, even if they do not explicitly touch on this question, nevertheless, since they teach without qualification that this science is speculative, and either keep silent about its being practical or definitely deny this, they clearly think that it is purely speculative. In addition, in the books of the *Ethics,* Aristotle *ex professo* treats of the human being's beatitude as the primary *Aristotle.* rule of moral actions.[192] But the human being's beatitude lies in God insofar as he is the ultimate end of all things and in a special way the end of the rational creature. Therefore, that consideration does not per-

191. See Aristotle, *Metaph.* I, ch. 2, 982a14–19 and 982b4–7.
192. See Aristotle, *Nic. Eth.* I, chs. 1–4.

ut praecedente sectione dictum est: moralis autem non est, quia consideratio ultimi finis in ordine ad mores non est munus eius, sed moralis Philosophiae, ut dictum est.

Cur Theologia speculativa & practica, Metaphysica tantum speculativa.

    5. Ratio autem a priori reddi potest ex differentia inter supernaturalem Theologiam, & hanc naturalem: quae ex differentia luminis sub quo utraque procedit, sumenda est. Illa enim procedit sub lumine divinae revelationis fidei, quatenus mediate ac per discursum applicatur ad [28b] conclusiones in principiis fidei contentas: fides autem non solum revelat Deum ut finem ultimum omnium, sed etiam specialiter docet in eo consistere hominis Beatitudinem: ac proinde non solum revelat fides veritates speculativas circa Deum, sed etiam practicas: imo etiam fere omnia prima principia morum revelat: & eadem certitudine, atque ex se eodem modo circa haec omnia versatur: ex quibus discurrit Theologia, considerans non tantum speculative in Deo rationem ultimi finis, sed etiam moraliter in ordine ad media quibus est consequendus. At vero Metaphysica procedit tantum sub naturali lumine, quod non eodem modo, nec eadem certitudine ⟨38b⟩ omnia obiecta sua complectitur: & ideo Metaphysica non est habitus illi adaequatus, sed sub speciali quadam ratione, & abstractione perficit naturale lumen circa ea obiecta quae abstrahunt a materia secundum esse, ut diximus. Et ideo de Deo solum speculative considerat rationem ultimi finis & supremi boni, scilicet quatenus in se talis est, talisque cognosci potest lumine naturae, potius quantum ad *an est,* quam quantum ad *quid est.* Non vero considerat practice, quomodo hic finis sit ab homine consequendus, imo nec in particulari attingit, vel inquirit modum quo Deus est finis ultimus hominis, vel quo homo ipse potest attingere Deum, prout est suus finis ultimus: quia hoc iam est infra Metaphysicam abstractionem & contemplationem, & ad Philosophiam spectat, imo supponit considerationem physicam hominis, seu naturalem philosophiam, quae mere speculativa est: & spectat ad philosophiam moralem, quae quodammodo, & (ut ita dicam) inchoative, practica scientia est: de quarum scien-

tain to metaphysics. Therefore, there remains no other consideration under which this doctrine could be practical. For if it is practical, it is most of all moral, since it is known$_n$ *per se* that it is not productive or directive of the operations of art. In fact, neither is it productive or directive of intellectual actions, as was said in the previous section.[193] And it is not moral, since the consideration of the ultimate end in relation to morals is not its function, but the function of moral philosophy, as has been said.

5. An *a priori* reason can be given by appeal to the difference between supernatural theology and this natural theology, which is to be taken from the difference between the lights under which each proceeds. For the former proceeds under the light of faith in divine revelation, insofar as it is applied mediately and through reasoning to the conclusions contained in the principles of faith. But faith not only reveals God as the ultimate end of all things, but also particularly teaches that the human being's beatitude lies in him, and therefore, faith reveals not only speculative truths about God, but also practical ones. In fact, it also reveals almost all the first principles of morals, and of itself it deals with all these things in the same way and with the same certainty. And theology reasons from these things, considering the character$_r$ of ultimate end in God, not only speculatively, but also morally in relation to the means by which this end must be achieved. By contrast, metaphysics proceeds only under the natural light, which does not embrace all of its objects in the same way or with the same certainty, and therefore metaphysics is not a habit adequate to it, but under a certain special aspect$_r$ and abstraction it perfects the natural light as regards those objects which abstract from matter with respect to existence$_e$, as we have said. And therefore, regarding God, it considers the character$_r$ of ultimate end and highest good only speculatively, namely, insofar as God is in himself such and can be cognized to be such by the natural light, and this with respect to the "whether it is" rather than with respect to the "what it is." But it does not consider in a practical way how this end is to be achieved by the human being. In fact, neither does it particularly touch on or inquire after the way in which God is the ultimate end of the human

Why theology is speculative and practical, but metaphysics only speculative.

---

193. This sort of direction pertains to logic or dialectic.

tiarum distinctione non est hic dicendi locus. Fateor tamen, quod si de angelis prout in se sunt, haberi posset naturalis scientia Metaphysicae, ad illam pertineret non solum naturam eorum contemplari, sed etiam quomodo essent capaces ultimi finis sui, & in quo eorum beatitudo consisteret, quibusque mediis ad illam possent pervenire: quae scientia ex parte moralis esset, simulque praxim aliquam cum speculatione coniungeret: essetque tota Metaphysica, quia tota abstraheret a materia secundum esse. Veruntamen huiusmodi scientia, angelica potius esset, quam humana: nos enim de angelorum Beatitudine vix aliquid possumus nisi per analogiam ad nostram investigare: & ideo Metaphysica prout in nobis est, mere est speculativa omni ex parte, & ad moralia seu practica non descendit.

Secunda conclusio.

6. Dico 2. Metaphys. non solum scientia est, sed etiam naturalis sapientia. Hanc assertionem ponit, & ex professo probat Arist. li. 1. c. 1. & 2. & lib. 3. c. 2. Qui primum supponit esse in nobis aliquam virtutem intellectualem quae sit sapientia: quod etiam docuit idem Arist. 6. Ethi.

Aristoteles.

c. 2. & sequent. Estque communis omnium sapientium consensus: nam si nullus habitus hominis esset sapientia, nullus hominum sapiens dici posset, nam sapiens a sapientia est & dicitur, non enim est homo sapiens a natura, nec ex sola potentia seu facultate, ut est per se notum, alias omnes homines essent ⟨39a⟩ sapientes: sed sapiens fit homo aliquo usu, & habitu aut virtute: est ergo sapientia habitus. Rursus [29a] ex ipsa voce & omnium sensu constat significare habitum ad intellectum pertinentem, non quemcunque, sed perfectum, quique virtus intellectualis sit, & valde perfecta. Quod optimo discursu probat Aristoteles in prooemio cap. 1. distinguens experientiam ab arte, & artem a scientia, quae propter se quaeritur, & in causarum ac principiorum cognitione versatur: & concludens sapientiam esse debere aliquam huiusmodi scientiam.

being, or how the human being herself can reach God insofar as God is her ultimate end, for this is already below metaphysical abstraction and contemplation, and concerns philosophy. In fact, it presupposes a physical consideration of the human being, or natural philosophy, which is merely speculative, and it pertains to moral philosophy, which is, in a certain way and inchoatively (so to speak), a practical science. But this is not the place to speak of the distinction of these sciences. Nevertheless, I grant that if one could have a natural science of metaphysics regarding the angels as they are in themselves, it would pertain to it to consider not only their nature, but also how they are capable of their ultimate end, and in what their beatitude lies, and by what means they can arrive at it, and this science would in part be moral, and at the same time would conjoin some practice with speculation, and it would be entirely metaphysical, since it would abstract altogether from matter with respect to existence$_e$. Nevertheless, such a science would be angelic, rather than human, for we can hardly investigate anything regarding the beatitude of angels except by analogy with our own, and therefore, metaphysics, insofar as it is in us, is merely speculative in every respect and does not descend to moral or practical matters.

6. I say, second, metaphysics is not only a science, but also natural wisdom. Aristotle makes this claim and *ex professo* proves it in *Metaph.* I, chs. 1 and 2, and in book III, ch. 2.[194] He first assumes that there is in us some intellectual virtue that is wisdom. Aristotle also teaches this in *Ethics* VI, ch. 2 and following,[195] and it is the common view of all the wise, for if no habit of the human being were wisdom, no human being could be called wise, for the human being is wise, and is so called, from wisdom, since the human being is not wise by nature, nor by virtue of a power or faculty alone, as is known$_n$ *per se*, otherwise all human beings would be wise; rather, a human being becomes wise through the exercise [of some power] and through a habit or virtue. Wisdom, therefore, is a habit. Moreover, it is clear from the word itself and from the understanding of all that it signifies a habit belonging to the intellect, and not any habit, but a perfect one, and it is an intellectual virtue and a very perfect one. Aristotle proves this by an excellent line of reasoning in the proem,

Second conclusion.

Aristotle.

---

194. Aristotle, *Metaph.* I, chs. 1–2, 981b25–983a23, and *Metaph.* III, ch. 2, 996b8ff.
195. See especially *Nic. Eth.* VI, chs. 2, 3, and 7.

Multiplex sapientiae acceptio.

7. Est autem hoc loco advertendum, si attendamus vulgarem sermonem, interdum videri hoc sapientiae nomine significari, non unum determinatum habitum intellectus, sed rectitudinem quandam intellectualem ad bene iudicandum de rebus omnibus, consurgentem ex perfecta consecutione scientiarum omnium, ad eum modum quo iustitia in una acceptione non significat unum singularem habitum, sed concentum & rectitudinem omnium virtutum voluntatis. Atque ad hanc sapientiae acceptionem videntur optime accommodari descriptiones

4 Tusc. & 2. Officior.

illae Ciceronis, *Sapientia est rerum divinarum atque humanarum, causarumque quibus hae res continentur, scientia.* Atque eodem sensu videntur de sapientia locuti antiqui Philosophi, qui de ratione sapientiae aiebant esse, ut omnium rerum sit cognitio, etiam usque ad infimas species, & omnes proprietates earum: hoc enim non fit una scientia, sed omnium collectione. Imo, si de homine sit sermo, neque per omnes scientias simul sumptas tam exactam rerum omnium cognitionem assequitur: & ideo ipsi aiebant non esse in homine veram sapientiam, sed fucatam: nos autem verius dicimus esse in homine veram sapientiam, etiam naturalem, sed humanam, ac proinde valde limitatam. Alio vero modo, magisque apud sapientes usitato, sumitur sapientia pro aliquo peculiari habitu, idque dupliciter: est enim quaedam quae dicitur sapientia simpliciter: alia, quae tantum secundum quid: illa est quodammodo universalis, non praedicatione, aut omnium collectione, sed eminentia & virtute, ut statim declarabimus: haec est particularis, non tantum habitu, sed etiam materia, & virtute. De hac posteriori sapientia

Plato.

est longus sermo Socratis apud Platonem, dialog. 3. seu de ⟨39b⟩ sapien. ubi distinguit sapientiam artificum, & gubernatorum, & similes. Et hoc eodem modo videtur dixisse Paulus 1. Corinth. 3. *Ut sapiens architectus, fundamentum posui.* Dicitur enim sapiens in aliquo genere, vel materia, qui scientiam, vel artem quae circa eam versatur, perfecte novit, & per

D. Thomas.

supremas causas illius generis, ut notavit D. Tho. 2. 2. q. 45. art. 1. Alio denique modo (ut ibidem ait D. Thom.) quaedam particularis scientia, seu intellectualis virtus dicitur sapientia simpliciter, & hoc modo usus

ch. 1,[196] distinguishing experience from art, and art from science, which is sought for its own sake and has to do with the cognition of causes and principles, and concluding that wisdom must be some such science.

7. But it is to be noted in this place that, if we consider common speech, it sometimes seems that this name "wisdom" signifies not a single determinate habit of the intellect, but a certain intellectual correctness that serves for judging well about all things$_r$, arising from the complete acquisition of all the sciences, in the way that "justice," in one sense of the term, does not signify one particular habit, but the harmony and correctness of all the will's virtues. And the following account from Cicero seems to be most in conformity with this sense of "wisdom": "Wisdom is the knowledge of things$_r$ divine and human, and of the causes by which these things$_r$ are held together."[197] And the ancient philosophers who used to say that it pertains to the nature$_r$ of wisdom to be a cognition of all things$_r$, even as far as the lowest species, and all their properties, seem to have spoken of wisdom in the same sense, for this does not result from a single science, but from the acquisition of them all. In fact, if the discussion concerns the human being, she does not obtain so exact a cognition of all things$_r$ by means of all the sciences taken at the same time, and therefore the same people used to say that in the human being there is no true wisdom, but a counterfeit one. We, on the other hand, more truly say that in the human being there is a true wisdom, one that is also natural, but human and therefore very limited. However, in another way, a way more usual among the wise, wisdom is taken to be a special habit, and this in two ways, for there is a wisdom that is called wisdom without qualification, and another that is so called only in a qualified way. The former is in a certain way universal, not by predication, or by the acquisition of all the sciences, but eminently and virtually, as we shall immediately make clear. The latter is particular, not only with respect to the habit, but also with respect to its matter and virtually. There is a long discussion of this latter wisdom by Socrates in Plato, third dialogue, or *On Wisdom*, where he distinguishes the wisdom

---

196. Aristotle, *Metaph.* I, ch. 1.

197. Cicero, *De officiis*, 2.5, in: M. Tullius Cicero, *De officiis*, ed. M. Winterbottom (Oxford: Oxford University Press, 2016), pp. 69–70.

Aristoteles. est Aristoteles hac voce, lib. 6. Ethic. loco citato, & in praesenti: & hoc sensu tribuit Metaphysicae hanc dignitatem sapientiae.

Aliquot sapientiae proprietates.   8. Secundo, ad hoc probandum subiicit Aristoteles c. 2. conditiones sapientiae, quarum aliquae communes illi sunt cum aliis scientiis speculativis: aliae vero sunt illi propriae: & illae quae communes esse videntur, ita accipiendae sunt ut secundum quandam eminentiam, & *Prima.* singularem perfectionem, sapientiae conveniant. Prima ergo conditio est, sapientiam versari circa omnia, esseque omnium scientiam, ut possibile est. Haec conditio sa[29b]tis est a nobis exposita in sect. 2. ratio vero eius constabit ex dicendis.

Secunda.   9. Secunda conditio sapientiae ab Aristotele posita est, ut in rebus difficilioribus & a sensibus remotioribus versetur: nam ea cognoscere quae omnibus sunt obvia, quaeve sensibus percipiantur,[63] non ad sapientes, sed ad quoscunque vulgares homines spectat. Haec autem conditio intelligenda videtur de cognitione rerum difficiliorum, quanta homini possibilis est: non enim spectat ad hominis sapientiam altiora se quaerere, & quae lumine naturali cognosci non possint, quales sunt futurorum contingentium eventus, & similia, quae per humanam scientiam velle cognoscere, non sapientia est, sed temeritas. Sapientia igitur humana in rebus altioribus ac difficilioribus iuxta ingenii humani capacitatem versatur.

63. Reading "percipiantur" with M_1, P_1, S, V_1, and V_2. The following have "percipiuntur": C_1, C_2, G_2, M_2, M_3, M_4, P_2, V_3, V_4, V_5, and Vivès.

of the artisan from the wisdom of the one who governs, and the like.[198] And Paul seems to have spoken in this same way, 1 Cor. 3: "As a wise architect I have laid the foundation."[199] For a person is called wise in some genus or subject matter when she perfectly knows_n the science or art which concerns itself with that subject matter and knows_n it through the highest causes of that genus, as St. Thomas notes, *ST* II-II, q. 45, art. 1.[200] *St. Thomas.* Finally, in another way (as St. Thomas says in the same place[201]) a certain particular science or intellectual virtue is called wisdom without qualification, and in this way does Aristotle use this name in *Ethics* VI, *Aristotle.* in the passage cited,[202] and in the present passage,[203] and in this sense he assigns this dignity of wisdom to metaphysics.

8. Second, in order to prove this, in ch. 2 Aristotle adduces characteristics of wisdom,[204] some of which are common to it and the other speculative sciences, while some are proper to it. And those which *Some properties of wisdom.* seem to be common are to be taken in such a way that they agree with wisdom according to a certain eminence and singular perfection. The first characteristic, then, is that wisdom is concerned with all things, *The first.* and is the science of all things, insofar as this is possible. This characteristic was sufficiently explained by us in section 2, but its ground_r will be clear from the things that are to be said.

9. The second characteristic of wisdom set forth by Aristotle is that *The second.* it is concerned with things_r that are more difficult and more remote from the senses, for to cognize things that are obvious to all, or things of the sort that are perceived by the senses, does not pertain to the wise, but to the common run of human beings. And it seems that this characteristic is to be understood as having to do with the cognition of more difficult things_r insofar as this is possible for the human being, for it does not pertain to the human being's wisdom to seek out things that are higher than itself, and that cannot be cognized by the natural light, of which sort are the outcomes of future contingents, and the like.

---

198. See Plato, *Theages*, 123a–126a.
199. 1 Cor. 3:10.
200. Thomas Aquinas, *Sancti Thomae Aquinatis opera omnia* (Leonina), t. 8, p. 339a–b.
201. Thomas Aquinas, *Sancti Thomae Aquinatis opera omnia* (Leonina), t. 8, p. 339b.
202. Aristotle, *Nic. Eth.* VI, ch. 7.
203. Aristotle, *Metaph.* I, ch. 1.
204. Aristotle, *Metaph.* I, ch. 2, 982a4–19.

Tertia.   10. Tertia conditio est ut sit certissima cognitio: sub qua conditione etiam evidentia, & claritas[64] comprehenditur: quia naturalis certitudo, de qua sermo est, ex evidentia nascitur, eique commensuratur. Ratio autem perspicua huius conditionis est, quia sapientia significat perfectam scientiam, & eximiam cognitionem: maxima autem perfectio cognitionis humanae in certitudine, & evidentia posita est. ⟨40a⟩

Quarta.   11. Quarta conditio est ut sit aptior ad docendum, causasque rerum tradendas. Hoc ipsum significaverat Aristoteles c. 1. dicens, signum sapientis esse posse docere, & ad sapientem pertinere causas rerum cognoscere, ac tradere. Item in unaquaque arte vel scientia illum sapientiorem existimamus, qui rerum causas intimius & universalius comprehendit. Denique humana cognitio tunc perfectior est, cum causam assequitur, alioqui semper est imperfecta: cuius signum est, quia inquirentis animus non quiescit, donec causam inveniat. Igitur sapientia simpliciter illa erit, quae rerum causas altiores & universaliores assequitur; unde etiam fiet ut aptior sit ad docendum.

Quinta.   12. Quinta est, talem sapientiam maxime dignam esse quae propter se, sciendique causa appetatur: hoc enim ad dignitatem pertinet, ut per se constat: cum ergo sapientia dignitatem quandam, & excellentiam inter scientias obtineat, non est dubium, quin in eo genere scientiarum collocanda sit quae propter ipsum scire quaeruntur: & quod in eo habeat supremum quendam & excellentem gradum, atque adeo quod propter se sit maxime expetibilis.

Sexta.   13. Sexta proprietas sapientiae est praeesse aliis, potius quam eis ministrare: quod etiam est consonum dignitati eius: quo autem sensu accipiendum sit, statim declarabo. Solum circa has proprietates adverto

---

64. Reading "claritas" with C_1, C_2, G_2, M_1, P_1, P_2, S, V_1, and V_2. The following have "charitas": M_2, M_3, M_4, V_3, V_4, V_5, and Vivès.

To want to cognize these things through human science is not wisdom, but presumptuousness. Human wisdom, therefore, is concerned with higher and more difficult things_r in a manner consistent with the capacity of the human intellect.

10. The third characteristic is that it is the most certain cognition, *The third.* under which characteristic evidence and clarity are also included, since natural certainty, which is what the discussion is about, arises from evidence and is commensurate with it. And the manifest ground_r of this characteristic is: because wisdom signifies perfect science and uncommon cognition, and the greatest perfection of human cognition is found in certainty and evidence.

11. The fourth characteristic is that it is more suited to teaching and *The fourth.* to passing down the causes of things_r. Aristotle indicates this very thing in ch. 1, saying that a sign of the wise person is the ability to teach,[205] and that it pertains to the wise person to cognize and teach the causes of things_r.[206] Moreover, in each art or science we judge that person to be wiser who grasps the causes of things_r more deeply and universally. Finally, human cognition is more perfect when it reaches the cause, and is otherwise always imperfect. A sign of this is that the mind of the inquirer does not rest until it discovers the cause. Therefore, wisdom without qualification will be that cognition which reaches the higher and more universal causes of things_r, for which reason it results that it is more suited to teaching.

12. The fifth characteristic is that such wisdom is most worthy of *The fifth.* being sought for its own sake and for the sake of knowing, for this pertains to its worth, as is clear *per se*. Since, therefore, wisdom possesses a kind of dignity and superiority among the sciences, there is no doubt that it is to be placed in the genus of sciences that are sought for the sake of knowing itself, and that in this genus it holds a certain supreme and superior rank, and that it is, therefore, the most desirable on its own account.

13. The sixth property of wisdom is that it rules over the other sci- *The sixth.* ences, rather than serving them, and this also accords with its dignity. But in what sense this must be understood I shall immediately make

---

205. Aristotle, *Metaph.* I, ch. 1, 981b7–9.
206. Aristotle, *Metaph.* I, ch. 1, 981a24–b6.

Aristotelem in eis assignandis fere non loqui de sapientia, sed de sapiente: subintelligit tamen eam scientiam esse sapientiam, ratione cuius sapienti hae conditiones conveniunt. Quod si quis dicat non convenire has proprietates sapienti, ratione unius scientiae, sed ratione omnium, vel plurium simul: respondendum est id nunc superesse ostendendum, probando has conditiones reperiri in scientia Metaphysicae, simulque ostendetur esse unam quandam scientiam quae omnibus illis attributis aliis praeemineat, ideoque sit sapientia, illamque esse Metaphysicam.

Dictae proprietates sapientiae in Metaphysica reperiri, demonstrantur.[65]

14. Tertio igitur loco probat Aristo. dicto c. 2. has omnes conditiones in Metaphys. reperiri. Primam quidem, quia ille quodammodo novit subiecta omnia qui praeditus est scientia[66] universali: sed Metaph. est [30a] universalissima scientia: ergo est scientia rerum omnium eo modo quem sapientia requirit, scilicet quantum possibile est. De hac conditione satis dictum ⟨40b⟩ est supra, sectio. 2. & ex ibi dictis colligere licet, duobus vel tribus modis agere Metaphysicam de omnibus rebus. Primo confuse & in communi, quatenus agit de rationibus entis communibus omnibus rebus, aut omnibus substantiis, vel accidentibus, & consequenter de primis & universalissimis principiis, in quibus omnia principia reliquarum scientiarum aliquo modo fundantur. Secundo in particulari de rebus omnibus usque ad proprias differentias, & species; quod aliqualiter verum est, non tamen aeque, nec eodem modo in omnibus: nam in rebus vel rationibus rerum, quae abstrahunt a materia secundum esse, id est simpliciter verum ex parte ipsarum rerum: limitatur tamen ex imperfectione intellectus nostri. Itaque Metaphysica humana (de qua tractamus) de his demonstrat & disserit, quantum humanum ingenium naturali lumine potest. In rebus autem quae sensibilem, aut intelligibilem materiam seu quantitatem concer-

---

65. Reading "*Dictae proprietates sapientiae in metaphysica reperiri demonstrantur*" with M₁, P₁, P₂, S, V₁, and V₂. The following have "*Dictas proprietates sapientiae in metaphysica reperiri demonstratur*": C₁, C₂, and G₂. The following have "*Dictae proprietates sapientiae in Metaphysica reperiri demonstratur*": M₂, V₃, V₄, and Vivès. The following has "*Dicta proprietatis sapientia in Metaphysica reperiri demonstratur*": V₅. The individual words in M₃ and M₄ can't reliably be made out.

66. Reading "scientia" here with C₁, C₂, G₂, M₁, M₂, M₃, M₄, P₁, P₂, S, V₁, V₂, V₃, and V₄. The following have "scientiam": V₅ and Vivès.

clear. I only note regarding these properties that Aristotle, in assigning them, scarcely speaks of wisdom, but of the wise person; yet he also understands that wisdom is the science by virtue of which these characteristics agree with the wise person. But if someone should say that these properties do not agree with the wise person by virtue of a single science, but by virtue of all or several of them together, one must reply that for the moment the view remains to be confirmed, by proving that these characteristics are found in the science of metaphysics, and at the same time it will be shown that there is a certain single science that excels the others with respect to all these attributes and is therefore wisdom, and that this science is metaphysics.

14. In the third place, then, Aristotle proves, in the mentioned ch. 2, that all these characteristics are found in metaphysics.[207] The first, indeed, because he who is endowed with universal science in a certain way knows$_n$ all subjects. But metaphysics is the most universal science. It is, therefore, the science of all things$_r$ in the way wisdom requires—namely, insofar as this is possible. Of this characteristic enough has been said above in section 2, and from the things that were said there one can infer that metaphysics treats of all things$_r$ in two or three ways. First, confusedly and in a general way, insofar as it treats of the natures$_r$ of being that are common to all things$_r$, or common to all substances or accidents, and consequently treats of the first and most universal principles, on which all the principles of the other sciences are in some way founded. Second, it treats particularly of all things$_r$ as far as their proper differences and species, which is in some way true, though not equally or in the same way regarding all of them, for regarding the things$_r$ or natures$_r$ of things$_r$ that abstract from matter with respect to existence$_e$, this is without qualification true as far as the things$_r$ themselves are concerned, although it is limited as a result of our intellect's imperfection. And so human metaphysics (of which we are treating) demonstrates and deals with these things insofar as the human mind can do so by the natural light. But with respect to those things$_r$ which incorporate either sensible matter or intelligible matter, or quantity, this is not true without qualification, even on the part of

It is demonstrated that the mentioned properties are found in metaphysics.

207. Aristotle, *Metaph.* I, ch. 2, 982a19–b10.

nunt, non est id simpliciter verum, etiam ex parte ipsius scientiae, sed quatenus in eis reperiuntur transcendentalia praedicata, vel eis aliquo modo applicantur metaphysicae rationes & media abstrahentia a materia, ut per ea aliquid de eis demonstretur. Tertio addere possumus hanc scientiam agere de omnibus, non in se, sed in causis suis, quia disputat de universalissimis causis rerum omnium, & praesertim de Deo.

15. Posset ergo inquiri, quinam ex his modis ad rationem sapientiae sufficiat, & consequenter qua ex parte Metaphysica, sapientia sit, vel an solum sit sapientia, prout omnes hos modos comprehendit. Ad quod breviter dicendum videtur Metaphysicam requirere totam illam amplitudinem & cognitionem, ut sit absolute & simpliciter sapientia. Etenim si quis ex Metaphysica sciat communem rationem entis in quantum ens, & eius attributa ac principia, habet quidem inchoatam sapientiam, quandoquidem principia tenet universalia, quibus potest alia principia confirmare & diiudicare. Item, quia habet quandam scientiam, vel scientiae partem per se se valde appetibilem, & scitu dignissimam, & ad alias omnes scientias utilissimam; & quodammodo necessariam: esset ergo illa, aliqualis sapientia. Non tamen posset dici sapientia simpliciter: quae enim est simpliciter sapientia sine Dei cognitione? Item, quia ens inquantum ens, in eo praecise sistendo, licet in ratione obiecti scibilis sit satis perfectum propter eius abstrac⟨41a⟩tionem, subtilitatem & transcendentiam, tamen in esse rei habet minimam perfectionem, nam maior est in determinatis entibus: ad rationem autem sapientiae non satis est obiectum scibile sine dignitate rerum quae sciuntur. Tamen si in nomine vim faciamus, certe Metaphysica, si in ea entis abstractissima ratione sistat, non erit satis sapida scientia ut sapientia simpliciter possit appellari. E contrario vero si fingeretur Metaphysica quae de Deo, & non de ente tractaret, illa quidem plus aliquid haberet de ratione sapientiae, tum propter nobilitatem obiecti, quod re ipsa non minus abstractum est quam ens, [30b] licet non praedicatione aut universalitate, tum ob iucunditatem, quam maxime habet adiunctam talis contemplatio, tum denique ob virtualem continentiam & causalitatem, ex qua fit ut talis Dei cognitio facile pariat aliarum rerum cognitionem. Veruntamen huiusmodi cognitio Dei exacta ac demonstrativa non potest per naturalem Theologiam obtineri, non cognitis prius commu-

the science itself, but insofar as transcendental predicates are found in them, or insofar as metaphysical concepts_r and middle terms that abstract from matter are in some way applied to them, so that through these something might be demonstrated of them. We can add, in the third place, that this science treats of all things, not in themselves, but in their causes, since it treats of the most universal causes of things_r, and especially God.

15. It could, therefore, be inquired which, exactly, of these ways of dealing with all things suffices for the nature_r of wisdom, and consequently by virtue of which part metaphysics is wisdom, or whether metaphysics is wisdom only insofar as it involves all of these ways. To this one must, it seems, briefly reply that metaphysics requires all of that breadth and cognition to be wisdom absolutely and without qualification. For if someone knows, thanks to metaphysics, the common nature_r of being as being, and its attributes and principles, he does indeed have an inchoate wisdom, since he grasps universal principles by means of which he can confirm and judge other principles. Further, since he has a certain science, or part of a science, that is *per se* very worthy of desire, and most worthy of being known, and most useful and in a way necessary for all the other sciences, it would therefore be some sort of wisdom. But it could not be called wisdom without qualification, for what wisdom without qualification is there absent cognition of God? Further, although being as being, precisely considered, is sufficiently perfect as a knowable object on account of its abstraction, subtlety, and transcendence, nonetheless, in its being_e as a thing it has the least perfection, for it is greater in determinate beings, and a knowable object without the dignity of the things_r that are known is not enough for the nature_r of wisdom. Still, if we focus on the name,[208] certainly metaphysics, if it stops at that most abstract nature_r of being, will not be a science appetizing[209] enough to admit of being called wisdom without qualification.

---

208. The Latin words "*sapientia*" ("wisdom") and "*sapiens*" ("wise") are connected to the Latin verb "*sapire*," which can mean either "to be wise," "to be prudent," on the one hand, or "to taste of," "to savor of," on the other. Suárez will soon engage in a little wordplay that takes advantage of this ambiguity. The wordplay cannot be replicated in English, unfortunately.

209. The word here translated "appetizing" is "*sapida*," which can mean either *wise* or *savory*. "Savory" can of course be used to convey the idea of being desirable. The claim here seems to be, then, that metaphysics, in dealing only with being *qua* being taken precisely,

nibus rationibus entis, substantiae, causae, & similibus, quia nos non cognoscimus Deum nisi ex effectibus, & sub communibus rationibus, adiunctis negationibus quibus imperfectiones excludimus. Et ideo fieri non potest ut Metaphysica sit sapientia sub postrema ratione, nisi etiam primam includat. Si autem fingatur Metaphysica quae ex primo & secundo modo cognoscendi omnia, habeat quaecunque necessaria sunt ad cognoscendum Deum, eumque primario attingat & contempletur, illa quidem dici posset sapientia absolute, etiam si de aliis rebus parum aut nihil in specie cognosceret: esset tamen valde imperfecta, & mutila sapientia, quam necesse esset multa etiam de Deo ignorare, aut imperfecte attingere: quia cum Deus ex effectibus cognoscatur, ignoratis praecipuis effectibus, necessarium esset etiam ipsius Dei cognitionem esse diminutam. Et propter hanc causam merito Aristoteles, non partem Metaphysicae, sed totam illam appellavit sapientiam simpliciter, quam dixit esse unam tantum 6. Ethicor. capi. 7. & Divus Thomas 1. 2. quaestio. 57. articulo secundo.

16. Secundam conditionem sapientiae in Metaphysica reperiri probat Aristoteles, quia tractat de rebus maxime universalibus, & a sensu remotissimis: haec autem sunt nobis cognitu difficillima: nam cum nostra cognitio a sensu oriatur, quod a sensu longissime abest, difficile in nostram intelligentiam ca⟨41b⟩dit. Hinc vero occasione sumpta solent hoc loco[67] disputare interpretes, an intellectus noster in hoc statu directe cognoscat singularia, vel universalia tantum: & an inter ipsa

67. Reading "loco" here with S, V_1, and V_2. The following omit this word: C_1, C_2, G_2, M_1, M_2, M_3, M_4, P_1, P_2, V_3, V_4, V_5, and Vivès.

On the other hand, if one were to imagine a metaphysics that dealt with God, and not being, it would, to be sure, have more of the nature$_r$ of wisdom: first, on account of the nobility of its object, which is in reality not less abstract than being (although not by predication or universality), and second, on account of the agreeableness which contemplation of this sort most especially has joined to it, and third, on account of the virtual containment and causality thanks to which it happens that such cognition of God easily begets cognition of other things$_r$. Nevertheless, such exact and demonstrative cognition of God cannot be acquired by means of natural theology if the common natures$_r$ of being, substance, cause, and the like are not cognized beforehand, since we do not cognize God except from his effects, and in accordance with common concepts$_r$, with negations adjoined, negations by which we exclude imperfections. And therefore, it is not possible for metaphysics to be wisdom in accordance with this last concept$_r$ of it unless it also satisfies the first. But if one imagined a metaphysics that has, thanks to the first and second ways of cognizing all things, whatever is necessary for cognizing God, and it primarily reached him and contemplated him, then it could indeed be called wisdom absolutely, even if it cognized little or nothing in particular about other things$_r$. But it would be a very imperfect and truncated wisdom, and it would also necessarily be ignorant of, or imperfectly grasp, many things about God, for, since God is cognized from his effects, given an ignorance of his greatest effects, there would necessarily also be a diminished cognition of God himself. And for this reason Aristotle rightly called, not a part of metaphysics, but the whole of it, wisdom without qualification, which he said is only one, *Ethics* VI, ch. 7,[210] and St. Thomas, *ST* I-II, q. 57, art. 2.[211]

16. Aristotle proves that the second characteristic of wisdom belongs to metaphysics on the grounds that it treats of things$_r$ that are maximally universal and most remote from sense. And these things are the most difficult for us to cognize, for since our cognition arises from sense, what is furthest removed from sense falls with difficulty under

and not with God, would not be sufficiently desirable/wise to be called wisdom without qualification. Note the occurrence of "agreeableness" ("*iucunditas*") in the next sentence.

210. Aristotle, *Nic. Eth.* VI, ch. 7, 1141a22–25.

211. Thomas Aquinas, *Sancti Thomae Aquinatis opera omnia* (Leonina), t. 6, p. 365b.

universalia facilius cognoscat ea quae minus communia sunt, ut species ultima, & ideo verum sit quod hoc loco ait Aristoteles, *Universalissima esse cognitu difficillima.* Veruntamen prior ex his quaestionibus omnino aliena est a praesenti instituto: quid enim refert ad dignitatem Metaphysicae scientiae declarandam, aut ad praedictum Aristotelis textum intelligendum, quod singulare directe cognoscatur ab intellectu, nec ne? haec ergo quaestio omnino est a nobis in proprium locum, hoc est in scientiam de anima, remittenda. Speramus enim fore ut, adiuvante Deo, illius etiam scientiae disputationes pro viribus elaboratas aliquando tradamus. Quod si id assequi non potuerimus, sufficient quae a gravissimis autoribus de praedicta quaestione hactenus tradita sunt: statui enim de nulla re extra proprium locum, aut omnino extra methodum disserere, etiam si omittenda prorsus talis disputatio sit: minoris enim incommodi esse censeo aliquid tacere, quam importune peregrinis quaestionibus aliunde vocatis, lucidam ac distinctam methodum obscurare & confundere. [31a]

Universalia ne an singularia facilius cognoscat noster intellectus.

17. Atque eadem fere ratio est de posteriori quaestione, quam idcirco etiam omittam, attingendo tantum id quod necesse est ut sensus Aristotelis in citato loco intelligatur, ne sibi ipsi repugnare videatur. Etenim lib. 1 Physicorum statim in initio ait in scientia progrediendum esse ab universalioribus ad particularia, quia incipiendum est a notioribus nobis, & universaliora, notiora nobis sunt: hic vero ait hanc scientiam esse de rebus difficillimis, eo quod sit de universalissimis, quae sunt hominibus cognitu difficillima. Quam apparentem contra-

D. Tho. qualiter conciliet duo Aristotelis loca difficilia.

dictionem ita D. Thom. 1. Metaphys. ca. 2. lect. 2. conciliat ut intelligamus Aristotelem 1. Phys. locutum fuisse de simplici tantum apprehensione, & imperfecta cognitione rerum universalium, hic vero de scientifica cognitione, & complexa, qua proprias rationes universalium distincte cognoscimus, eorumque proprietates de illis demonstramus. Non enim semper ea quae facilius in mentem veniunt per simplicem apprehensionem, facilius etiam intime penetrantur & cognoscuntur:

our intelligence. For this reason, interpreters are wont in this place to take the opportunity to discuss the question of whether our intellect in its present state directly cognizes singulars, or only universals, and also the question of whether, among universals themselves, it more easily cognizes those which are less common, such as ultimate species, so that it is true what Aristotle says here, that is, that "the most universal things are the most difficult to cognize."[212] Nevertheless, the former question is altogether foreign to our present purpose, for what difference does it make to the task of showing the dignity of metaphysics, or to the task of understanding the mentioned text of Aristotle, that a singular is cognized directly by the intellect, or not? This question, then, is wholly to be referred by us back to its proper place, that is, to the science of the soul. For we hope that, with God's help, we will at some time produce disputations concerning this science, worked out to the best of our ability.[213] But if we are unable to accomplish this, the things that have thus far been taught on this question by the most serious authors will suffice. For I have resolved to treat of nothing outside its proper place, or altogether outside our method, even if such a disputation is wholly to be omitted, since I think it less unsuitable to remain silent about something than to obscure and confound the clear and distinct method with foreign questions inopportunely summoned from elsewhere.

17. And almost the same consideration$_r$ applies to the second question, which I shall therefore also pass over, touching only on what is necessary in order to understand Aristotle's meaning in the passage cited, lest he seem to contradict himself. For in *Phys.* I, immediately at the beginning,[214] he says that in a science one should proceed from more universal things to particular ones, since a beginning must be made from things more known$_n$ to us, and more universal things are more known$_n$ to us. Here, however, he says that this science is about the most difficult things$_r$ because it is about the most universal things, which are the most difficult things for human beings to cognize. St. Thomas, *Metaph.* I, ch. 2, in lecture 2,[215] resolves this apparent contradiction in

Whether our intellect cognizes universals or singulars more easily.

How St. Thomas reconciles two difficult passages in Aristotle.

---

212. Aristotle, *Metaph.* I, ch. 2, 982a23–25.

213. For Suárez's discussion of the question whether the intellect cognizes singulars, see Francisco Suárez, *Opera Omnia*, 3:722ff.

214. Aristotle, *Phys.* I, ch. 1, 184a16–26.

215. Thomas Aquinas, *In duodecim libros metaphysicorum Aristotelis expositio*, pp. 13–14 (n. 46).

quid enim facilius apprehendimus quam tempus, mo⟨42a⟩tum, & similia? Quid vero difficilius inquiritur quoad exactam cognitionem, tam rationis formalis, seu entitatis, quam proprietatum talium rerum? Sic ergo universaliora dicuntur notiora nobis quoad simplicem & imperfectam apprehensionem, quoad an est (ut sic dicam) quis enim non facilius concipiat hanc esse arborem, quam sit ne pyrus, aut ficus? Ad hos enim universaliores conceptus confusos, & imperfectos paucioribus indigemus, & ideo facilius illos formamus. Dum tamen illorum exactam cognitionem inquirimus, difficilius eam assequimur, eo quod sint a sensibus remotiores, ut hic dixit Aristoteles.

 18. Huic autem expositioni solum obstare video quod Aristoteles 1. Physic. non videtur tantum loqui de rudi illa & imperfecta universalium apprehensione, sed de scientifica cognitione: nam ex ea facilitate cognoscendi universaliora colligit ordinem in scientia servandum: scientia autem non debet procedere a notioribus quoad apprehensionem, sed quoad eam cognitionem quae per scientiam haberi potest: nam si scientifica cognitio difficilior est, nihil fere conferet quod simplex apprehensio facilior sit, ut iuxta convenientem methodum ab huiusmodi rebus sit incipiendum. Adde ipsa experientia constare etiam in cognitione scientifica facilius cognosci rationes communes, quam proprias, ut ens mobile aut naturale, quam coelum, vel hominem: & rationem entis, quam rationem substantiae, vel accidentis. Et ratio etiam id suadet, nam in scientia per se & directe intenditur distincta cognitio tam essentiae, quam proprietatum uniuscuiusque rei, vel rationis formalis: & universalia ipsa non tractantur aut sciuntur, per se loquendo, ut tota universalia seu potentialia sunt, sub qua ratione ipsorum distincta cognitio pendet ex cognitione rerum inferiorum: haec enim est veluti reflexiva cognitio & dialectica, quia illa proprietas seu ratio totius po-

such a way that we ought to understand Aristotle, in *Phys.* I, to have been speaking only of simple apprehension and the imperfect cognition of universal things$_r$, but here to be speaking of the complex and scientific cognition by which we distinctly cognize the proper natures$_r$ of universal things and demonstrate their properties of them. For the things that more easily come into the mind through simple apprehension are not always more easily inwardly penetrated and cognized as well. For what do we more easily apprehend than time, motion, and the like? But what is sought with greater difficulty than exact cognition of the formal character$_r$ or entity of such things$_r$ and exact cognition of their properties? In this way, then, more universal things are called more known$_n$ to us as far as simple and imperfect apprehension is concerned, with respect to the "whether it is" (so to speak), since who does not more easily conceive this to be a tree than a pear tree or a fig tree? For we need fewer things for those more universal, confused, and imperfect concepts, and therefore we form them more easily. But when we seek after exact cognition of them, we obtain this with greater difficulty, since they are more remote from the senses, as Aristotle says here.

18. The only thing I see standing in the way of this exposition is the fact that in *Phys.* I Aristotle does not seem to be speaking merely of that unwrought and imperfect apprehension of universals, but of scientific cognition. For from this facility for cognizing things that are more universal he infers that an order is to be observed in a science. But a science ought to proceed from things that are more known$_n$, not with respect to apprehension, but with respect to the cognition that can be had through science, for if scientific cognition is more difficult, the fact that simple apprehension is easier will scarcely be of help granted that, according to the appropriate method, a start is to be made from such things$_r$. In addition, it is clear by experience that in scientific cognition common natures$_r$ are more easily cognized than proper ones. For instance, mobile or natural being is more easily cognized than the heavens or the human being, and the nature$_r$ of being is more easily cognized than the nature$_r$ of substance or accident. And reason also urges this, for in a science what is *per se* and directly intended is distinct cognition of both the essence and the properties of each thing or formal character$_r$, and universals themselves are not dealt with or known, speaking *per se*, inso-

tentialis per intellectum potius convenit, quam re ipsa: sciuntur enim huiusmodi universalia in scientiis propriis ac realibus secundum proprias actuales essentias, & proprietates illis consentaneas, & adaequatas: sic autem facilius sciuntur uni[31b]versaliora, quia ab eis omnino pendet cognitio minus universalium: non vero e contrario, quia universaliora sunt de ratione inferioris, & non e converso. Atque haec obiectio non solum videtur concludere Aristotelem in 1. Physicor. de scientifica cognitione universaliorum fuisse locutum, sed ⟨42b⟩ etiam falsum esse haec universaliora esse difficiliora cognitu.

Aliorum conciliatio. 19. Quapropter nonnulli volunt Aristotelem hoc loco non de universalibus rationibus, sed de universalibus causis fuisse locutum, id est, non de universalibus quae in praedicando vocant, de quibus in primo Physicorum fuerat locutus, & de quibus procedit discursus factus, sed de universalibus in causando, ut sunt Deus, & intelligentiae. De quibus videtur etiam recte intelligi ratio Aristotelis, scilicet quia universalia sunt a sensibus remotissima: hoc enim est verum de his[68] universalibus in causando, de caeteris vero minime: nam cum haec sint etiam in singularibus materialibus, non videntur a sensu remota: nam hoc ens, vel haec substantia obiicitur sensui, sicut hoc animal vel hic homo, unde universaliora praedicata facilius obiiciuntur sensibus ratione suorum propriorum singularium, quam minus universalia, & ideo facilius cadit in intellectum nostrum saltem ex parte nostra animal quam homo, & substantia quam animal, & sic de aliis: quia, regulariter loquendo, & iuxta ordinarium modum quo nobis applicantur obiecta sensibilia, facilius imprimunt sensibus species seu phantasmata horum singularium.

68. Reading "his" here with M_1, P_1, P_2, S, V_1, and V_2. The following omit this word: C_1, C_2, G_2, M_2, M_3, M_4, V_3, V_4, V_5, and Vivès.

far as they are universal or potential wholes (in accordance with which conception_r of them distinct cognition of them depends on cognition of inferior things_r), for this sort of cognition is, as it were, reflexive and dialectical, since that property or character_r of [being a] potential whole agrees with them through an operation of the intellect rather than in reality. For such universals are known in proper and real sciences according to their proper actual essences, and according to the properties that agree with, and are adequate to, them. But in this way more universal things are more easily known, since cognition of less universal things altogether depends on them, but not vice versa, since the more universal belongs to the nature_r of the inferior, but not vice versa. And this objection seems to show not only that Aristotle was speaking of the scientific cognition of more universal things in *Phys.* I, but also that it is false that these more universal things are more difficult to cognize.

19. For this reason, some would have it that in this place Aristotle is speaking, not of universal natures_r, but of universal causes, that is, not of universals which are called universal with respect to predication (about which he spoke in *Phys.* I, and concerning which the presented line of reasoning succeeds), but of universals with respect to causation, such as God and the intelligences. The reason Aristotle gives seems also to be correctly understood as concerning these—namely, because universals are most remote from the senses. For this is true of these universals with respect to causation, but not at all of the others, for since the latter are also in individual material things, they seem not to be remote from the senses, for this being, or this substance, is an object of sense just as this animal or this man is, for which reason a more universal predicate is more easily presented to the senses by reason of its proper singulars than a less universal one is. And therefore animal falls more easily under our intellect than human being does, at least in relation to us, and substance more easily than animal, and so on regarding the rest, since—generally speaking, and according to the way sensible objects normally reach us—they more easily impress on the senses species or phantasms of these singulars.

Refutatur.

20. Nihilominus haec expositio reiicitur communiter ab interpretibus Aristotelis, licet enim fateantur dictum Philosophi esse verum etiam de universalibus causis: docent tamen eum proprie locutum fuisse de universalioribus praedicatis: tum quia haec proprie & simpliciter dicuntur universalia: tum etiam quia re vera etiam ex ea parte qua Metaphysica tractat de ente & substantia ut sic, est difficilior caeteris scientiis. Et in haec etiam praedicata cadit ratio Aristotelis, quod scilicet longius absunt a sensibus secundum suam abstractionem & praecisam rationem: hae namque communes rationes non habent propria singularia, sed mediis rationibus minus universalibus ad singularia descendunt.

Explicatur & approbatur conciliandi modus ex D. Thoma adductus.

21. Alias responsiones afferunt expositores tam in hunc Metaphysicae locum, quam in illum Physicor. & super 1. libr. Poster. cap. 2. & libr. 2. capit. 15. & 18. ubi etiam Aristoteles ait universalia esse naturae notiora, singularia nobis. Quibus omissis in priori responsione persistendum censeo, si paululum tamen explicetur. Dicendum ergo existimo Aristotelem in libr. 1. Physicorum locutum fuisse de ordine doctrinae, ⟨43a⟩ in qua dicit esse incipiendum ab universalioribus, quia nobis sunt notiora quoad simplicem & confusam cognitionem eorum, quatenus sunt quaedam tota potentialia & universalia. Nec refert quod in scientiis non intendatur cognitio confusa, sed distincta, quia Aristoteles non dicit universaliora esse notiora ea cognitione quae per scientiam intenditur, sed ea potius quae imperfecta supponitur, ut per scientiam per[32a]ficiatur. In hoc vero loco Metaphysicae non agit Aristoteles de ordine doctrinae a nobis observando, sed de perfecta scientia ipsorum obiectorum obtinenda, & hoc modo ait universaliora esse cognitu difficiliora. Quod tamen non asseruit simpliciter, sed cum hac limitatione *fere*: quia contingit interdum universaliora esse etiam quoad perfectam cognitionem nobis notiora: quia difficultas quae ex parte abstractionis in eis est, potest aliunde compensari: quo modo ens naturale ut sic, est nobis notius quam coelum, & ens quam angelus. Non obstante autem ea limitatione, concludit Aristoteles hanc scientiam esse de rebus difficillimis, quia in ea tanta est abstractio ut omnino praescindat a materia, & ab actionibus & proprietatibus sensibilibus ut tales sunt, & ideo nihil

20. Nevertheless, this exposition is commonly rejected by Aristotle's interpreters, for although they grant that what the Philosopher says is true of universal causes as well, nonetheless, they teach that he was speaking properly of more universal predicates, both because these are properly and without qualification called universals, and also because metaphysics is really more difficult than the other sciences also by virtue of that part of it which treats of being and substance as such. And the reason Aristotle gives applies to these predicates as well—namely, that they are further away from the senses according to their abstraction and prescinded nature$_r$, for these common natures$_r$ do not have proper singulars, but descend to singulars through the mediation of less universal natures$_r$.

21. Expositors bring forth other replies, both in connection with this passage in the *Metaphysics* and in connection with that one in the *Physics*, and also regarding *Post. An.* I, ch. 2,[216] and book II, chs. 15[217] and 18,[218] where Aristotle also says that universals are more known$_n$ by nature and singulars more known to us. But setting these aside, I find that one must stick to the earlier reply, provided that it is explained somewhat. I think, therefore, that it must be said that Aristotle, in *Phys.* I, is speaking about the order of doctrine, in which, he says, a beginning must be made from things that are more universal, since they are more known$_n$ to us when it comes to simple and confused cognition of them, insofar as they are certain potential and universal wholes. Nor does it matter that confused cognition is not aimed at in the sciences, but rather distinct cognition, since Aristotle does not say that more universal things are more known$_n$ by that cognition which a science aims at, but rather that they are more known$_n$ by that cognition which is assumed imperfect in order that it might be perfected through science. But in this passage of the *Metaphysics* Aristotle is not dealing with the order of doctrine that is to be observed by us, but with the perfect science of these objects that is to be obtained, and it is in this sense that he says that more universal things are more difficult to cognize. However, he does not assert this without qualification, but with this limitation:

216. Aristotle, *Post. An.* I, ch. 2, 71b33–72a5.
217. Aristotle, *Post. An.* II. ch. 13, 97b28–37.
218. Aristotle, *Post. An.* II, ch. 19, 99b32–end.

in eius obiecto esse potest unde difficultas ex tanta abstractione proveniens tollatur: atque haec satis sint de illa secunda conditione.

Dubium.　22. Circa tertiam conditionem sapientiae merito dubitari potest quo modo huic doctrinae conveniat, scilicet, esse certissimam. Et ratio difficultatis potissima oritur ex scientiis Mathematicis, quae videntur multo certiores, cum ex principiis evidentissimis, imo & sensu notissi- *Aristoteles.* mis procedant. Unde idem Aristoteles lib. 2. Metaphys. cap. 3. tex. 16. significat modum procedendi Mathematicae esse accuratissimum, & certissimum, eo quod a materia & mutatione abstrahat, a qua non abstrahit Philosophia, & licet Metaphysica videatur abstrahere, si res de quibus tractat, considerentur, prout tamen in nobis est, non videtur abstrahere, quia non considerat de rebus illis nisi ex effectibus sensibilibus qui in materia versantur. Unde idem Aristotel. lib. 2. tex. 1. ait res notissimas natura sua esse nobis ignotas, quia intellectus noster ita ad eas comparatur sicut verspertilionis visus ad lucem Solis. Et confirmatur, nam humana cognitio a sensu incipit, unde per sensum accipit claritatem & certitudinem: quo ergo fuerit cognitio de rebus a sensu remotioribus,[69] eo erit minus certa: sicut ergo ex hoc principio ⟨43b⟩ colligit Aristoteles supra hanc scientiam esse difficillimam, ita colligere potuit esse incertissimam. Imo haec duo videntur semper esse coniuncta, difficultas videlicet & incertitudo, aut minor certitudo: si ergo haec scientia est maxime difficilis, erit consequenter minus certa.

69. Reading "remotioribus" with M_1, P_1, P_2, S, V_1, and V_2. The following have "remotior" instead: C_1, C_2, G_2, M_2, M_3, M_4, V_3, V_4, V_5, and Vivès.

"usually."[219] For it sometimes happens that more universal things are more known_n to us even as far as perfect cognition is concerned, since the difficulty that attaches to them by virtue of their abstraction can be otherwise compensated for. It is in this way that natural being as such is more known_n to us than the heavens are, and being is more known_n to us than the angel is. Notwithstanding that limitation, however, Aristotle concludes that this science is about the most difficult things_r, since the abstraction in it is so great that it prescinds altogether from matter, and from sensible actions and properties insofar as they are such, and therefore, there can be nothing in the object of this science by means of which the difficulty resulting from so great an abstraction might be removed. And let these points suffice regarding the second characteristic.

22. Regarding the third characteristic of wisdom, it can justly be doubted how it is that being most certain agrees with this doctrine. *A doubt.* And the most powerful reason for this difficulty arises from the mathematical sciences, which seem much more certain, since they proceed from the most evident principles, and in fact from those most known_n to sense. For this reason Aristotle himself, in *Metaph.* II, ch. 3, text *Aristotle.* 16, indicates that mathematics' mode of proceeding is the most exact and certain, since it abstracts from matter and change, from which philosophy does not abstract,[220] and although metaphysics seems to abstract from matter and change, if the things_r of which it treats are considered, nevertheless, insofar as it is in us, it seems not to abstract from them, since it does not consider those things_r except on the basis of sensible effects that are found in matter. For this reason, Aristotle himself, in *Metaph.* II, text 1, says that the things_r which are by their nature most known_n are unknown to us, since our intellect is related to them as the bat's vision is related to the light of the sun.[221] And this is confirmed, for human cognition takes its start from sense, for which reason it receives clarity and certainty through sense. Therefore, the more cognition is of things_r remote from sense, the less certain it will be. Therefore, just as Aristotle above infers from this principle that this

---

219. "Usually" here translates "*fere.*" Aristotle's words here are: "σχεδὸν δὲ καὶ χαλεπώτατα ταῦτα γνωρίζειν τοῖς ἀνθρώποις, τὰ μάλιστα καθόλου (πορρωτάτω γὰρ τῶν αἰσθήσεών ἐστιν)" (*Metaph.* I, ch. 2, 982a23–25).
220. Aristotle, *Metaph.* II, ch. 3, 995a14–17.
221. Aristotle, *Metaph.* II, ch. 1, 993b9–11.

     23. Distinguendae videntur duae partes huius doctrinae: una est quae de ente ut ens est, eiusque principiis & proprietatibus disserit. Altera est quae tractat de aliquibus peculiaribus rationibus entium, praesertim de immaterialibus. Quoad priorem partem non dubium est quin haec doctrina sit omnium certissima, quod satis est ut haec proprietas ipsi absolute & simpliciter tribuatur: nam quoties comparatio fit inter habitus, secundum id quod in eis est optimum & maximum fieri debet, ut sumitur ex 3. Topic. ca. 2. sic ergo Aristoteles in dicto prooemio absolute ait hanc doctrinam esse certissimam, & videtur loqui de illa prout in nobis est. Et ratio eius est optima, & procedit de hac scientia quoad hanc partem, scilicet, quia ea scientia est certissima quae circa prima principia maxime versatur, & quae ex paucioribus rem conficit: ita vero se habet haec scientia: quia talis scientia magis est independens, habetque princi[32b]pia notiora, ex quibus alia principia robur & certitudinem accipiunt, ut declaratum est: sic enim res illae de quibus Mathematicae tractant, includunt communia & transcendentia praedicata, de quibus Metaphysica disserit: principia etiam Mathematica includunt Metaphysica, & ab illis pendent.

24. De altera vero parte huius scientiae quae in determinatis rationibus entis versatur, distinguendum est: potest enim esse scientia certior, aut secundum se, aut quoad nos. Scientia igitur harum rerum ex se se non est dubium quin sit certissima, & quod Mathematicas scientias antecellat. Nam certitudo scientiae hoc modo pensanda est ex obiecto: huiusmodi autem res, & substantiae immateriales sunt ex se aptae ad gignendam certissimam sui cognitionem: tum quia sicut sunt perfectiora entia, magisque necessaria, simpliciaque, & abstracta, ita in eis maior est veritas, maiorque certitudo principiorum. At vero ex parte intellectus nostri est haec scientia in nobis quoad hanc partem minus certa, ut experientia docet, & probant rationes dubii in principio

science is the most difficult, so likewise could he have inferred that it is the least certain. In fact, these two seem always to be conjoined, namely, difficulty and uncertainty, or less certainty. If, therefore, this science is the most difficult, it will consequently be less certain.

23. It seems that one must distinguish two parts of this doctrine. *Reply.* There is one that treats of being insofar as it is being, its principles, and its properties. There is another that deals with certain special natures$_r$ of beings, especially immaterial ones. With respect to the first part, there is no doubt that this doctrine is the most certain of all, and this suffices for this property to be assigned to it absolutely and without qualification, for whenever a comparison is made between habits, this should be done according to what is best and greatest in them, as is gathered from *Topics* III, ch. 2.[222] And therefore Aristotle says absolutely in the mentioned proem that this doctrine is the most certain, and he seems to be speaking of it insofar as it is in us. And his reason is the best and succeeds in the case of this science with respect to this part, namely: because that science which is most of all concerned with first principles, and accomplishes its task on the basis of fewer principles, is the most certain.[223] And that is how things stand with this science, since this science is more independent and has principles that are more known$_n$, from which other principles receive force and certainty, as has been explained. For in this way those things$_r$ of which mathematics treats include common and transcendental predicates, of which metaphysics treats, and mathematical principles also include metaphysical ones and depend on them.

24. Regarding the other part of this science, which is concerned with determinate natures$_r$ of being, one must make a distinction, for a science can be more certain either in itself or in relation to us. There is no doubt, then, that the science of these things$_r$ is of itself the most certain, and that it surpasses the mathematical sciences. For the certainty of a science must be measured in this way, by appeal to its object. But things$_r$ of this sort and immaterial substances are of themselves suited to producing the most certain cognition of themselves, since, just as they are more perfect beings and more necessary, simple, and abstract,

---

222. Aristotle, *Top.* III, ch. 2, 117b36–39.
223. Aristotle, *Metaph.* I, ch. 2, 982a25–28.

positae. Praesertim illa quod cum nostra cognitio a sensu oriatur, ob-scu⟨44a⟩rius & ex natura rei minus certo attingimus ea quae ab omni materia sensibili abstrahunt.

25. Dices primo, Ergo haec scientia prout in nobis est, semper est minus certa in hac parte, quam Mathematica: ergo simpliciter est minus certa, quia Metaphysica de qua agimus, non est alia nisi humana: haec autem tantum in nobis est, quid ergo refert ad nobilitatem Metaphysicae quod secundum se sit certior? illud enim erit verum de Metaphysica Angelica, non de nostra. Unde tractando de nostra, videtur involvi repugnantia in illa distinctione, secundum se, & prout in nobis: haec enim distinctio accommodata obiectis seu rebus cognitis optime quadrat, & ita est illa usus saepe Aristoteles in primo Posteriorum, & in principio Physi. & Metaph. at vero accommodata actibus, vel habitibus nostris nullo modo videtur posse habere locum, propter rationem factam: hic autem non de obiectis, sed de re ipsa loquimur. Respondent aliqui satis esse quod Metaphysica in angelis sit certior, quia eiusdem rationis est cum nostra, quia sub eadem ratione seu abstractione de his entibus disserit. Sed hoc non recte dicitur, quia illa scientia angelica est altioris rationis, primum quia illa vel est a priori & perfecta, scilicet, ut versatur circa res creatas, vel si est a posteriori ut de Deo, est per cognitionem perfectam nobiliorum effectuum. Deinde quia scientiae differunt genere ex modo procedendi: modus autem intelligendi angelorum est altior, simplicior, & essentialiter perfectior.

26. Respondetur ergo primo fortasse in aliquo statu posse Metaphysicam humanam esse perfectiorem & certiorem quam sint Mathematicae: nam licet, acquirendo hanc scientiam solis naturalibus viribus & ordinario modo humano, non possit tam perfecta[70] obtineri, si tamen noster intellectus iuvetur ab aliqua superiori causa in ipsomet discursu naturali, vel si ipsa scientia modo supernaturali fiat, licet res

---

70. Reading "perfecta" with C_1, C_2, G_2, M_1, M_2, M_3, P_1, P_2, S, V_1, V_2, V_3, and V_4. The following have "perfecte": V_5 and Vivès.

so is there greater truth in them, and greater certainty of principles. But in relation to our intellect, this science in us is, with respect to this part, less certain, as experience teaches and the reasons for doubt set forth at the beginning prove. Especially this one: that since our cognition arises from sense, we grasp those things which abstract from all sensible matter more obscurely and, by virtue of their nature, with less certainty.

25. You will say, first: therefore, insofar as it is in us, this science is always, with respect to this part, less certain than mathematics. Therefore, it is without qualification less certain, since the metaphysics we are discussing is none other than human metaphysics, and this alone is in us. What difference does it make to the nobility of metaphysics, therefore, that it is in itself more certain? For that will be true of angelic metaphysics, not of ours. For this reason, in treating of our metaphysics, an absurdity in that distinction—between "in itself" and "insofar as it is in us"—seems to be involved, for this distinction, when applied to the objects or things_r cognized, is perfectly appropriate, and it is often used in this way by Aristotle in *Post. An.* I, and at the beginning of the *Physics* and *Metaphysics*. But applied to our acts or habits, it seems out of place, for the reason given; and here we are speaking not of the objects, but of the thing_r itself. Some reply that it is enough that in angels metaphysics is more certain, because it is of the same nature_r with ours, since it treats of these beings under the same aspect_r or abstraction. But this is not rightly said, for that angelic science is of a higher nature_r, first because either it is *a priori* and perfect, namely, insofar as it concerns itself with created things_r, or, if it is *a posteriori*, as when it treats of God, it is through a perfect cognition of his nobler effects. And second, because sciences differ in genus according to their manner of proceeding, and angels' mode of understanding is higher, simpler, and essentially more perfect.

26. I reply first, therefore, that perhaps in some state human metaphysics can be more perfect and certain than mathematics is, for, although when acquiring this science only by means of our natural powers, and in the ordinary human way, it cannot be obtained so perfect, nevertheless, if our intellect is helped by some superior cause in its natural reasoning, or if this science comes about in a supernatural way, although the thing_r itself is natural, it can perhaps be so clear and evident that it surpasses mathematics. But since this reply is more theological

ipsa sit naturalis, potest forte esse tam clara & evidens ut Mathematicas superet. Quia vero haec responsio magis est Theologica quam Philosophica, addo ulterius, quanvis [33a] Metaphysica in nobis semper sit quoad hanc partem inferior Mathematica in certitudine, nihilominus simpliciter & essentialiter esse nobiliorem: ad quod multum refert, quod sit secundum se, & ⟨44b⟩ ex parte obiecti certior: nam dignitas obiecti maxime spectat ad dignitatem scientiae, & illa est quae per se redundat in scientiam: imperfectiones autem quae ex parte nostra miscentur, sunt magis per accidens: & ad hoc tendit distinctio data, in quo sensu nullam involvit repugnantiam.

2. Dubium.   27. Dubitabit secundo aliquis, nam hinc sequitur, hanc scientiam Metaphysicae quatenus de Deo agit, minus certam esse quoad nos, quam ut tractat de intelligentiis, quod tamen non videtur verum. Sequela sic deducitur ex ratione facta, nam si haec scientia est minus certa quoad nos, ut versatur circa res abstractas a materia, quia nostra cognitio a materialibus incipit: ergo, quo res de qua tractat Metaphysica, magis elongata & remota fuerit ab hac materia, eo Metaphysica, prout in illa versatur, erit minus certa: sed Deus summe distat a rebus materialibus & sensibilibus: ergo. Respondetur, negando sequelam, absolute loquendo. Duobus enim modis intelligi potest unam rem magis distare ab alia, scilicet perfectione seu entitate, & causalitate seu connexione effectus & causae. Priori modo magis distat Deus a materialibus rebus, quam spiritus creati: posteriori autem modo magis distant spiritus creati ab omnibus rebus creatis, quam Deus. Pendent enim omnia essentialiter a Deo, non a caeteris spiritibus, &, per se loquendo, omnia Deum imitantur, & aliquam eius similitudinem aut vestigium gerunt: quod vero inde resultet aliqua similitudo, vel convenientia cum angelis, est secundarium & accidentarium. Quia ergo nos ex rebus sensibilibus non utcunque consideratis, sed ut effectibus, ascendimus ad substantias separatas contemplandas, inde fit ut naturaliter certius assequamur Dei cognitionem, quam angelorum, quod ipso usu & experientia constabit amplius ex dicendis.

than philosophical, I add, furthermore, that even if, as regards this part of it, metaphysics in us is always inferior in certainty to mathematics, nevertheless, without qualification and essentially it is nobler. For as regards its nobility it matters much that it is more certain in itself and on the side of its object, since the worth of its object is most of all relevant to the worth of a science, and is that which redounds *per se* to the science, whereas the imperfections which are, on our side, introduced are more *per accidens*, and the given distinction aims at this, in which sense it involves no absurdity.

27. Second, someone will experience doubts because from this it follows that the science of metaphysics, insofar as it treats of God, is less certain in relation to us than it is insofar as it treats of the intelligences, which, however, seems not to be true. The consequence is inferred in the following way from the argument that was made. For if this science is less certain in relation to us insofar as it is concerned with things$_r$ abstracted from matter, because our cognition takes its start from material things, then the more the things$_r$ that metaphysics deals with are far away and remote from matter, the less certain will metaphysics be insofar as it is concerned with them. But God is most distant from material and sensible things$_r$. Therefore. I reply by denying the consequence, absolutely speaking. For one thing$_r$ can be understood to be distant from another in two ways, namely, with respect to perfection or entity, and with respect to causality or the connection of effect and cause. In the first way, God is more distant from material things$_r$ than created spirits are, but in the second way created spirits are more distant from all created things$_r$ than God is. For all things depend essentially on God, not on other spirits, and, speaking *per se*, all things imitate God and bear some resemblance to him or trace of him; and that from this there results some resemblance to, or agreement with, the angels, is secondary and accidental. Since, therefore, we ascend to the contemplation of separate substances not from sensible things$_r$ considered in any way whatsoever, but from sensible things considered as effects, it follows that naturally we achieve more certainly a cognition of God than we do a cognition of the angels, and from the things to be said this will become clearer by practice and experience.

3. Dubium.   28. Tertio potest dubitari, praesertim circa priorem partem positam, an haec scientia superet alias solum quoad principiorum certitudinem, vel etiam conclusionum. Nam ratio facta solum videtur procedere de principiis: at si hoc dicatur, sequitur non hanc scientiam, sed habitum principiorum, qui distinctus est, esse certiorem aliis scientiis. Unde obiter etiam dubitari potest, an sit haec scientia certior habitu principiorum. Nam si hoc dicatur, facile expeditur posita difficultas, ut per se constat: at hoc ipsum videtur difficillimum: nam haec scien⟨45a⟩tia nititur in ipsis primis principiis: quo modo ergo potest esse certior, quam illorum habitus, cum hic etiam verum sit axioma illud, *Propter quod unumquodque tale, & illud magis?*

D. Thom.   29. Ab hac posteriori parte incipiendo, D. Thom. 1. 2. quaestio. 2, artic. 2. ad secundum[71] significat sapientiam esse nobiliorem & certiorem etiam ipso habitu principiorum, sic enim ait: *Scientia pendet ab intellectu, sicut a principaliori, & utrumque pendet a sapientia, sicut a principalissimo, quae sub se continet & intellectum & scientiam:* sentit ergo Divus Thomas sapientiam esse intellectu seu habitu principiorum principaliorem & perfectiorem. [33b] Et rationem indicat, quia sapientia habet quidquid est perfectionis in habitu principiorum, & illud ipsum nobiliori modo, & praeterea aliquid amplius: est ergo perfectior. Antecedens declaratur, quia intellectus versatur circa prima principia, iudicium de illis ferendo: sed hoc ipsum habet sapientia, ut supra ostensum est, & ultra hoc versatur circa plura alia, quae ex principiis inferuntur, & circa res nobilissimas, & primas rerum causas, ut supra ostensum est. Rursus circa ipsamet prima principia versatur nobiliori modo sapientia, quia intellectus simplici tantum modo versatur, ferendo iudicium ex naturali & immediata efficacitate naturalis luminis intellectus: sapientia vero, reflexionem faciens supra ipsummet lumen, & originem illius contemplans, a qua ipsum habet totam certitudinem suam, illud assumit ut medium ad veritatem & certitudinem principiorum demonstrandam: hic autem modus iudicandi videtur altior,

---

71. Reading "1. 2. q. 2, a. 2, ad 2" here with C₁, C₂, G₂, M₁, M₂, M₃, M₄, P₁, P₂, S, V₁, V₃, V₅, and Vivès. Suárez, however, seems actually to have in mind *ST* I-II, q. 57, art. 2, ad 2. V₂ reads "1. q. 2, a. 2, ad 2." V₄ reads "2. q. 2, a. 2, ad 2."

28. Third, it can be doubted, particularly as regards the first part, *Third doubt.* whether this science surpasses others only with respect to the certainty of its principles, or also with respect to the certainty of its conclusions. For the argument made seems to succeed only regarding principles. But if this is said, it follows not that this science, but that the habit of principles, which is distinct, is more certain than the other sciences. For this reason, incidentally, it can also be doubted whether this science is more certain than the habit of principles. For if this is said, the difficulty set forth is easily resolved, as is clear *per se.* But this view seems most difficult, for this science depends on the same first principles: how, then, can it be more certain than the habit of them? For here also that axiom is true: "That on account of which each thing is such is such to a higher degree."[224]

29. Taking his start with this second issue, St. Thomas, *ST* I-II, q. 2, *St. Thomas.* art. 2, ad 2, indicates that wisdom is nobler and more certain than even the very habit of principles, for he speaks thus: "Science depends on understanding as on what is superior, and both depend on wisdom, which contains under itself both understanding and science, as on what is supreme."[225] St. Thomas, therefore, believes that wisdom is superior to, and more perfect than, understanding or the habit of principles. And he gives as a reason: because wisdom has whatever perfection there is in the habit of principles, and that in a nobler way, and besides this, something more; it is, therefore, more perfect. The antecedent is made clear because understanding is concerned with first principles, by passing judgment on them. But wisdom does the same, as was shown above, and beyond this is concerned with quite a few other things that are inferred from principles, regarding both the noblest things$_r$ and the first causes of things$_r$, as was shown above. Furthermore, wisdom is concerned with the very same first principles in a nobler way, because understanding is concerned with them only in a simple way, in that it passes judgment by means of the natural and immediate efficacy of the intellect's natural light, whereas wisdom, reflecting upon the very same light, and contemplating its origin, from which that light has all

---

224. See Aristotle, *Metaph.* II, ch. 1, 993b24–25.
225. Suárez seems actually to have in mind *ST* I-II, q. 57, art. 2, ad 2. See Thomas Aquinas, *Sancti Thomae Aquinatis opera omnia* (Leonina), t. 6, p. 366a.

magisque comprehensivus: ergo habet sapientia plus perfectionis quam intellectus, & quidquid nobilitatis est in intellectu, id habet perfectiori modo. Unde etiam videtur satisfieri difficultati in contrarium insinuatae: nam licet sapientia in principio & quasi via generationis pendeat ab intellectu, quia necesse est ut supponat aliqua principia, tamen secundum se, si perfecta sit, non pendet ab eo essentialiter, sed per se sufficit ad assentiendum principiis per propria media, & reflexionem supra ipsum lumen intellectuale, & fortasse ad eam perfectionem pervenire potest, ut iam sine ullo discursu formali principiis suis praebeat assensum. Atque eandem sententiam tenet Albertus lib. de apprehens. p. 6.[72] *Albertus.* habetque magnum fundamentum in Aristotele, libr. 1. Poster. capit. 7. tex. 23. ubi significat Metaphysicam esse ⟨45b⟩ omnium principem, eo quod sua principia demonstret: & lib. 6. Ethic. capit. 7. ubi sic ait, *Sapientem non solum ea scire, quae ex principiis cognoscuntur, sed etiam circa principia dicere vera oportet. Quare sapientia, & intellectus est & scientia, & (ut caput est) scientia rerum earum quae summis afficiuntur honoribus.* Non potuit autem intelligere sapientiam esse aggregatum ex intellectu & scientia aliqua, cum haec sigillatim distinxerit, ut virtutes diversas: intelligit ergo esse intellectum & scientiam secundum quandam eminentem perfectionem, ut ibi etiam expositores intelligunt: & disputat Buridan. quaest. 12. qui hanc sententiam insinuat in quaest. *Buridanus.* ult. eiusdem lib. 6. Ethicorum.

Metaphysica ne habitu principiorum certior. 30. Nihilominus aliqui probabiliter existimant limitandam esse hanc sententiam, ut nimirum sapientia praeferatur intellectui principiorum, ut versatur circa principia aliarum scientiarum, non vero ut versatur circa principia eiusdem Metaphysicae. Quae limitatio videtur *D. Thom.* sumi ex verbis quae Divus Thomas supra subiungit, dicens, sapientiam esse principalissimam, continereque sub se intellectum & scientiam,

---

72. Reading "p. 6" here with M_1, P_1, P_2, S, V_1, and V_2. The following editions have "p. 5": C_1, C_2, G_2, M_2, M_3, M_4, V_3, V_4, V_5, and Vivès.

of its certainty, assumes it as a middle term for demonstrating the truth and certainty of principles; and this way of judging seems higher and more comprehensive. Therefore, wisdom has more perfection than understanding, and whatever nobility there is in understanding wisdom has in a more perfect way. For this reason the difficulty that was introduced in support of the contrary position seems also to be resolved, for although wisdom in the beginning and in the course of generation (as it were) depends on understanding, since it is necessary that it assume some principles, nevertheless, in itself, wisdom, if it is perfect, does not depend on understanding essentially, but rather suffices *per se* for assenting to principles by means of its own middle terms and by means of reflection on the intellectual light itself, and it can perhaps arrive at such a perfection that it now furnishes assent to its principles without any formal reasoning. And Albert holds the same view, in the *Albert.* book *On Apprehension*, part 6,[226] and it has an important foundation in Aristotle, *Post. An.* I, ch. 7, text 23, where Aristotle indicates that metaphysics is the foremost of all the sciences because it demonstrates its own principles,[227] and also *Ethics* VI, ch. 7, where he says: "The wise person must not only know those things which are from principles, but must also say what is true regarding the principles. For this reason, wisdom is both understanding and science, and (insofar as it is highest) a science of those things, which are most of all honored."[228] But he could not have understood wisdom to be an aggregate of understanding and some science, since these he had severally distinguished as diverse virtues. He therefore understands it to be understanding and science according to a certain eminent perfection, as expositors of the passage also understand. And Buridan, q. 12, discusses this, and he teaches this *Buridan.* opinion in the final question of the same *Ethics* VI.[229]

30. Nevertheless, some judge with probability that this opinion must be limited so that, certainly, wisdom is preferred to the under-

Is metaphysics
more certain
than the habit
of principles?

226. See Albert the Great, *Opera omnia*, ed. Borgnet (Parisiis: Vivès, 1890), 5:603–7. Note that Albert is no longer considered to be the author of *De apprehensione*.

227. Aristotle, *Post. An.* I, ch. 9, 76a16–22.

228. Aristotle, *Nic. Eth.* VI, ch. 7, 1141a17–20.

229. The final question on *Ethics* VI is q. 22. See John Buridan, *Questiones Joannis buridani super decem libros ethicorum aristotelis ad nicomachum* (Paris: Ponset le Preux, 1513), fols. 127vb–128va and 138va–140ra.

Ut de conclusionibus (ait) *scientiarum diiudicans, & de principiis earundem*: ubi notandum est illud relativum, *earundem,* refert enim alias scientias a sapientia distinctas: ergo solum comparatur sapientia ad intellectum ut versatur circa principia aliarum scientiarum, & quia de illis
diiudicat, ideo[73] nobilior esse dicitur. At vero secus videtur accidere in
[34a] eadem sapientia comparata ad intellectum ut versatur circa principia ipsiusmet sapientiae: nam ab illo ut a proximo fonte habet suam
totam certitudinem. Item, ille habitus circa easdem res nobiliori modo
versatur, quia ille habitus non sistit in primis principiis abstractissimis,
pertinentibus ad ens ut sic, & ad alios terminos abstractos, ut est illud,
Quodlibet est, vel non est, & similia, sed etiam versatur circa prima principia substantiae ut sic, & Dei, & intelligentiarum ut sic: unde ad illum
proprie pertinet earum quidditates contemplari: nam quidditas rei per
simplicem cognitionem intelligitur, vel ex ea immediatum principium
constituitur, si a nobis per compositionem cognoscatur: ad sapientiam
vero pertinebit, proprietates harum rerum ex quidditate demonstrare.
Et quidem non videtur posse negari, quin cognitio illorum principiorum quibus haec scientia nititur, certior simplici⟨46a⟩ter sit, quam sit
ipsa scientia, quandoquidem ab illa pendet ut a propria causa, alterius
& superioris rationis in modo assentiendi. Nec refert, quod Metaphysica in sua principia reflectatur ut ea demonstret: semper enim necesse
est ut secundum propriam rationem suam per discursum procedat,
& prioribus principiis nitatur, quae ut notiora & certiora sumat: non
enim dicendum est eundem habitum acquisitum, per discursum & sine
discursu assentiri. Igitur absolute & universim comparando principia
Metaphysicae ad ipsam scientiam, certior est illorum cognitio. Et hoc
ipsum confirmat experientia, nihil enim demonstratur in Metaphysica,
quod sub ea ratione tam certum sit, sicut hoc principium, *Quodlibet est,
vel non est,* quatenus est per se notum.

---

73. Reading "diiudicat, ideo" here with C_1, C_2, G_2, M_1, M_2, M_3, P_1, P_2, S, V_1, V_2, V_3, and
V_4. The following editions read "diiudicat, & ideo": M_4, V_5, and Vivès.

standing of principles insofar as it is concerned with the principles of the other sciences, but not insofar as it is concerned with the principles of metaphysics itself. This limitation seems to be taken from the words that St. Thomas, above, adds when he says that wisdom is supreme and contains under itself understanding and science: "insofar as it judges," he says, "the conclusions of the sciences and their principles,"[230] in which the relative "their" is to be noted, for it refers to other sciences distinct from wisdom. Therefore, wisdom is only being compared to understanding insofar as it is concerned with the principles of the other sciences, and it is said to be nobler because it passes judgment on them. But things appear to turn out otherwise when wisdom is compared to understanding insofar as it is concerned with the principles of wisdom itself, for wisdom has its entire certainty from this as from its nearest source. Likewise, this habit is concerned with the same things$_r$ in a nobler way, since this habit does not stop at the first, most abstract principles that pertain to being as such and to other abstract terms (such as this principle: "Any given thing either is or is not," and the like), but is also concerned with the first principles of substance as such, of God, and of intelligences as such. For this reason it properly pertains to this habit to consider their quiddities, for the quiddity of a thing$_r$ is understood through simple cognition, or, if it is cognized by us through composition, it is constituted an immediate principle on account of simple cognition. But it will pertain to wisdom to demonstrate the properties of these things$_r$ from their quiddity. And indeed, it seems that it cannot be denied that the cognition of those principles on which this science depends is more certain without qualification than this science itself is, since this science depends on that cognition as on a proper cause that has a different and superior nature$_r$ when it comes to mode of assent. Nor does it matter that metaphysics reflects on its own principles in order to demonstrate them, for it is always necessary that, in accordance with its proper nature$_r$, it proceed by reasoning and depend on prior principles which it takes as more known$_n$ and more certain, for it must not be said that the same acquired habit assents both by reasoning and without reasoning. Therefore, comparing the princi-

St. Thomas.

---

230. Thomas Aquinas, *ST* I-II, q. 57, art. 2, ad 2. See Thomas Aquinas, *Sancti Thomae Aquinatis opera omnia* (Leonina), t. 6, p. 366a.

Sapientia omnibus aliis intellectualibus habitibus quomodo excellentior.
Aristoteles.
Fonseca.

31. Cum ergo sapientia praefertur omnibus aliis virtutibus intellectualibus, etiam intellectui principiorum, intelligi potest primo de sapientia ut includit sua principia, & comparatur ad alias scientias ut sua etiam principia, & conclusiones includunt: ita enim solere scientias considerari sumitur ex Aristotele 3. Metaphysic. capit. 2. tex. 5. ubi Fonseca id advertit. Dicitur autem Metaphysica excedere alias scientias quoad certitudinem tam conclusionum, quam etiam principiorum, non solum comparando principia ad principia, & conclusiones ad conclusiones: sic enim non esset propria comparatio scientiae ad intellectum, sed scientiae ad scientiam, & intellectus ad intellectum: in quo sensu etiam una scientia particularis dici potest certior quam intellectus principiorum, quia potest habere certiora principia. Igitur intelligi debet, etiam comparando conclusiones Metaphysicae ad principia propria aliarum scientiarum, dici Metaphysicam excedere in certitudine, quia discursus eius nititur principiis adeo notis & certis, ut possit generare assensum certiorem, quam sit simplex assensus aliquorum principiorum in aliis materiis: & propter alias rationes supra factas.

Habitus inevidentior evidentiori potest esse nobilior, & incertior certiori.

32. Vel secundo, & fortasse clarius, dici potest sapientia praeferri intellectui principiorum nobilitate, & excellentia simpliciter, non vero semper certitudine aut evidentia, praesertim respectu nostri, seu prout in nobis est: non enim semper nobilitas habitus, seu ipsius di⟨46b⟩gnitas, [34b] aut scientiae, cum certitudine aut evidentia convertitur: fides enim Christiana simpliciter in substantia aut specie sua est nobilior, quam naturalis Metaphysica, licet non sit ita clara & evidens: & naturalis Philosophia est nobilior, quam Mathematica, licet sit minus certa, propter obiecti nobilitatem, quae ad dignitatem simpliciter intellectualis virtutis magis confert, ut significavit Divus Thomas libr. 1.

Aristoteles. de anima capit. 1. & 1. part. q. 1. art. 5. ad 1. ubi adducit illud Aristotelis

ples of metaphysics absolutely and universally to this science itself, the cognition of the former is more certain. And experience confirms this very thing, for there is nothing demonstrated in metaphysics which, as such, is as certain as this principle, "Any given thing either is or is not," insofar as this principle is known$_n$ *per se*.

31. Since, therefore, wisdom is preferred to all other intellectual virtues, and even to the understanding of principles, this can, in the first place, be understood of wisdom insofar as it includes its principles and is compared to other sciences insofar as they too include their principles and conclusions. For that sciences are usually considered in this way is inferred from Aristotle, *Metaph.* III, ch. 2, text 5,[231] where Fonseca takes note of it.[232] But metaphysics is said to surpass the other sciences with respect to the certainty of both conclusions and principles, not only comparing principles to principles and conclusions to conclusions, for in this way there would not be a proper comparison of science to understanding, but rather a comparison of science to science and of understanding to understanding, and in this sense also one particular science can be called more certain than an understanding of principles, since it can have principles that are more certain. Therefore, it should be understood that, even when comparing the conclusions of metaphysics to the proper principles of other sciences, metaphysics is said to exceed them in certainty, because its reasoning depends on principles that are so known$_n$ and certain that it can generate an assent which is more certain than the simple assent to some principles in other matters, and because of other reasons given above.

In what way wisdom is more excellent than all other intellectual habits.

Aristotle.

Fonseca.

32. Or, in the second place, and perhaps more clearly, it can be said that wisdom is preferred without qualification to the understanding of principles in respect of nobility and excellence, but not always in respect of certainty or evidence, especially in relation to us, or insofar as it is in us. For the nobility of a habit, or its worth, or the nobility or worth of a science, is not always convertible with its certainty or evidence. For in its substance or species Christian faith is without qualification nobler than natural metaphysics, although it is not so clear and evident, and natural

A less evident habit can be nobler than a more evident one, and a less certain habit nobler than a more certain one.

231. Aristotle, *Metaph.* III, ch. 2, 997a15–25.
232. Pedro da Fonseca, *Commentariorum in libros Metaphysicorum Aristotelis tomus primus*, cols. 573–74.

lib. 1. de partibus animal. capit. 5: *Res superiores tametsi leviter attingere possimus, tamen ob eius cognoscendi generis excellentiam amplius oblectamur, quam cum haec nobis iuncta, omnia tenemus.* Et similem fere sententiam habet lib. 1. de coelo, capit. 12. Sapientia ergo sive Metaphysica etsi non sit certior in nobis, quam intellectus, saltem quoad sua principia, est tamen simpliciter nobilior & altior, quia attingit nobiliora entia, & supremas causas entium, nempe Deum & intelligentias, quas intellectus principiorum secundum proprias rationes earum non attingit, sed solum secundum communem rationem entis, & substantiae: nam licet de Deo & intelligentiis multa sint principia per se nota secundum se: tamen respectu nostri nihil est per se notum: nam, si Deum esse non est nobis per se notum, ut infra ostendemus, multo minus reliqua quae de his rebus in Metaphysica demonstrantur. Atque ita fit, ut de his rebus nihil per intellectum principiorum immediate cognoscamus, sed solum per sapientiam, & ideo sapientia nobilior sit, esto non sit certior suis principiis, prout in nobis existit: quia ad maiorem nobilitatem satis est, quod sit de rebus simplicioribus & secundum se certioribus, cum ea certitudine & evidentia quae per naturale lumen ingenii humani haberi potest. Unde beatitudo naturalis hominis (quod hoc maxime confirmat) non in aliquo actu intellectus principiorum, sed in actu & contemplatione sapientiae consistit, dicente Aristotele. 6. Ethicor. cap. 12. quod sicut sanitas est quaedam foelicitas corporis, ita sapientia est foelicitas animae: & ideo ibidem praefert illam prudentiae: nam prudentia ad sapientiam ut ad finem refertur: est namque (ut optime ait) sapientiae procuratrix prudentia: ita enim animum regit, ut eum pacatum reddat, & a perturbatione liberum, quod ad contemplationem sapientiae maxime necessarium est: idemque docet libr. 10. Ethicor. capit. 7. & 8.

philosophy, although it is less certain than mathematics, is nobler than it on account of the nobility of its object, which contributes more to the unqualified worth of an intellectual virtue, as St. Thomas indicates in *De anima* I, ch. 1,[233] and in *ST* I, q. 1, art. 5, ad 1,[234] where he adduces the following text of Aristotle from *On the Parts of Animals* I, ch. 5: "Even though we can reach superior things_r only slightly, still, on account of the excellence of this kind of cognition, we are more delighted than we are when we grasp all the things around us."[235] And he holds almost the same view in *On the Heavens* I, ch. 12.[236] Therefore, even if wisdom or metaphysics is not more certain in us than understanding, at least with respect to its own principles, it is nevertheless without qualification nobler and loftier, since it reaches nobler beings and the highest causes of beings, namely, God and the intelligences, which the understanding of principles does not reach according to their proper natures_r, but only according to the common natures_r of being and substance. For although there are many principles regarding God and the intelligences that are in themselves known_n *per se*, still, in relation to us nothing about them is known_n *per se*, for if the fact that God exists_e is not known_n to us *per se*, as we will show below,[237] much less are the other points that are demonstrated in metaphysics about these things_r. And so it happens that we cognize nothing about these things_r immediately through the understanding of principles, but only through wisdom, and therefore wisdom is nobler, even if, insofar as it exists in us, it is not more certain than its principles, since for its greater nobility it is enough that it be about things_r that are simpler and more certain in themselves, with that certainty and evidence which can be had through the natural light of the human intellect. For this reason, the natural beatitude of the human being (and this fact especially confirms our claim) consists not in some act of the understanding of principles, but in the act and contemplation of wisdom, with Aristotle saying in *Ethics* VI, ch. 12, that, just as health

Aristotle.

233. Thomas Aquinas, *Sancti Thomae de Aquino opera omnia* (Roma & Paris: Commissio Leonina & Vrin, 1984), t. 45, pt. 1, p. 5a.

234. Thomas Aquinas, *Sancti Thomae Aquinatis opera omnia* (Leonina), t. 4, p. 16b.

235. Aristotle, *On the Parts of Animals* I, ch. 5, 644b31–35.

236. Suárez would seem to have in mind a passage from bk. II, ch. 12, of Aristotle's *On the Heavens*. See, in particular, 291b25–28. See Averroes, *Averrois Cordubensis commentum magnum super libro De celo & mundo Aristotelis*, 2:388–89.

237. See *DM* 29.3.33.

33. Atque ex his constat etiam resolutio ⟨47a⟩ tertiae dubitationis quoad priorem partem eius: dicendum est enim hanc doctrinam esse certiorem aliis scientiis, non solum quoad principia, sed etiam quoad conclusiones. Quod quidem si intelligatur proportionate, indubitatum est, ut dixi, scilicet quod principia huius scientiae sunt certiora principiis aliarum scientiarum, & conclusiones huius, conclusionibus aliarum: hoc enim posterius ex priori sequitur: nam illae conclusiones certiores sunt, quae sequuntur ex certioribus principiis eodem genere illationis. Quod autem principia sint certiora, constat, quia sunt abstractiora & universaliora, & omnium prima, ut infra videbimus: unde deservi[35a]re possunt ad demonstrandum aliquo modo principia aliarum scientiarum, ut declaratum est. At vero si intelligatur illa comparatio absolute, & sine dicta proportione, id est, quod haec scientia secundum se totam, etiam secundum conclusiones suas, superet certitudine alias scientias, secundum totum quod in eis est, etiam quoad principia earum, sic comparatio est minus certa, & non necessaria ad nobilitatem & perfectionem sapientiae. Nihilominus tamen probabilis est, si loquamur de principiis propriis & particularibus aliarum scientiarum prout a nobis cognoscuntur: vix enim unum reperies quod ex sola terminorum cognitione tanta certitudine nobis innotescat, quanta potest ex principiis Metaphysicae manifestari.

is a certain happiness of the body, so is wisdom the happiness of the soul.[238] And therefore, in the same place, he prefers it to prudence, for prudence is related to wisdom as to an end, since prudence (as he well says) is wisdom's deputy, for prudence rules the mind in such a way that it renders it peaceful and free from disturbance, which is most of all necessary for the contemplation of wisdom; and he teaches the same in *Ethics* X, chs. 7 and 8.

33. And from these things the resolution of the third doubt is also clear as regards its first part, for it must be said that this doctrine is more certain than the other sciences, not only with respect to principles, but also with respect to conclusions. And indeed, if this is understood proportionately, it is undoubtedly true, as I said—that is, undoubtedly true that the principles of this science are more certain than the principles of the other sciences, and the conclusions of this science more certain than the conclusions of the other sciences. For the latter claim follows from the former, since conclusions are more certain when they follow, by the same kind of consequence, from principles that are more certain. And it is clear that the principles are more certain, since they are more abstract and universal, and the first of all, as we shall see below. For this reason they can serve to demonstrate in some way the principles of the other sciences, as has been made clear. But if that comparison is understood absolutely, and without the mentioned proportion—that is, if it is understood to mean that this science, taken as a whole, even in its conclusions, surpasses the other sciences in certainty, with respect to all that is in them, including their principles—in this way the comparison is less certain and not necessary for the nobility and perfection of wisdom. Nevertheless, it is still plausible, if we are speaking of the proper and particular principles of the other sciences insofar as they are cognized by us, for you will hardly find one that is of the sort to become known$_n$ to us, solely on the basis of a cognition of its terms, with as much certainty as it can be when it is made manifest from the principles of metaphysics.

---

238. Aristotle, *Nic. Eth.* VI, ch. 12, 1144a3–6.

Quomodo Metaphysica aptior ad docendum sit.

34. Quartam sapientiae conditionem, quae est esse aptiorem ad docendum, Aristoteles ita demonstrat, quia *illa scientia aptior est ad docendum, quae magis in causarum cognitione versatur: ii enim docent qui causam cuiusque rei afferunt.* Tacite autem subsumit hanc doctrinam maxime versari in causarum cognitione: & ita concludit esse aptissimam ad docendum, ideoque sapientiam esse. Hanc eandem conditionem declaravit Aristoteles fere toto capite primo huius prooemii seu primi libri. Ut enim concludat ad sapientiam pertinere, rerum supremas causas investigare, longe petito principio ait homines naturaliter appetere scientiam: nam hac maxime ratione sensus diligunt: & in caeteris quidem animalibus esse tantum cognitionem sensuum, & quaedam eorum habere etiam memoriam, & innatam quandam prudentiam, vel potius naturalem instinctum & sagacitatem, & aliqua etiam participare quendam disciplinae modum, nunquam tamen assequi perfectam ex⟨47b⟩perientiam: hominem autem per sensus cognoscere singularia, quae non solum memoria tenet, sed etiam inter se confert, & ita paulatim acquirit experientiam, quae solum circa singularia versatur. Per experientiam vero ultra progreditur, & artem inquirit, qua iam universalia cognoscat, eorumque rationes & causas inquirat, & ideo qui artem assecutus est, sapientior censetur, quam solum expertus, quia non solum an res sit, sicut expertus, sed etiam propter quid, & causam rei cognoscit. Et ideo (inquit) in quacunque arte architectos nobiliores & sapientiores putamus eos, qui non tantum activi sunt (quod suo modo commune est inanimatis) sed etiam causas rerum, rationesque cognoscunt. Et statim subiungit proprietatem in qua nos versamur, dicens, *Et prorsus signum sapientis est posse docere:* quod praestare potest qui causas rerum novit, non vero qui solos effectus expertus est.

In what way metaphysics is more suited to teaching.

34. Aristotle demonstrates the fourth characteristic of wisdom, which is that it is more suited to teaching, in the following way: because "that science is more suited to teaching which is more concerned with the cognition of causes, for they who make known the cause of each thing$_r$ teach."[239] And he tacitly assumes that this doctrine is most of all concerned with the cognition of causes, and so he concludes that it is the most suited to teaching, and that it is therefore wisdom. Aristotle explains this same characteristic in almost the whole of ch. 1 of this proem or first book. For in order to conclude that it pertains to wisdom to investigate the highest causes of things$_r$, he says, beginning from further back, that human beings naturally desire knowledge, since it is especially for this reason that they prize the senses, and that in other animals indeed there is only cognition of the senses, and that some of them also have memory, and a kind of inborn prudence, or rather a natural instinct and sagacity, and that some of them also participate in a certain sort of learning, although they never achieve perfect experience; but that through the senses the human being cognizes singulars, which she not only retains by means of memory, but also compares to one another, and in this way she gradually acquires experience, which only has to do with singulars. But through experience she advances further and seeks after art, by which she now cognizes universals, and inquires into their natures$_r$ and causes, and therefore, she who attains art is judged wiser than the person who has only experience, since she cognizes not only whether a thing$_r$ is, as the experienced person does, but also the thing$_r$'s reason why and cause. And therefore (he says) we think that, in any given art, those masters of the craft are nobler and wiser who are not only active (which is in its own way common also to inanimate things), but also cognize the causes and natures$_r$ of things$_r$. And he immediately adds the property with which we are concerned, saying: "And truly, it is a mark of the wise person to be able to teach,"[240] which can be done by the one who knows$_n$ the causes of things$_r$, but not by the one who has experience only of effects.

239. Aristotle, *Metaph.* I, ch. 2, 982a28–30.
240. Aristotle, *Metaph.* I, ch. 1, 981b7.

Dubium.   35. Circa hanc vero conditionem in primis dubitari potest, cur haec scientia aptior ad docendum existimetur quam reliquae: nam omnis scientia propria & a priori (inter has enim facienda est comparatio) demonstrat rem per suas causas: ergo tam apta est ad docendum unaquaeque [35b] scientia in sua materia, quam haec in sua. Neque ad hoc refert quod haec scientia de nobilioribus rebus tractet: nam hoc conferet quidem ut ipsa sit nobilior, non vero ut ad docendum sit aptior: nam ad hoc magis confert proportio effectus ad causam, quam nobilitas utriusque: tam accommodate enim docetur effectus inferior per suam propriam causam, quam superior per suam: haec ergo conditio vel nulla est specialis in Metaphysica, vel non est distincta a nobilitate obiecti. Quod si alicui scientiae haec proprietas attribui potest, certe potius Dialecticae esset tribuenda: nam illa docet discere, & docet docere: ergo aptior illa est ad docendum quam omnis alia. Atque ita Plato hoc munus Dialecticae accommodat in Dialogo de Ente, seu Sophista, & ideo ibidem, & 7. lib. de Repub. eam praefert omnibus scientiis.

Dubii solutio.   36. Ad priorem difficultatem respondetur, licet aliae scientiae demonstrent suas proprietates, vel effectus per proprias causas eis accommodatas, quia tamen illae causae non sunt primae, nec independentes, sed superioribus subordinatae, ideo non sunt ita aptae ad docendum aliae disciplinae, ac Metaphysica, quae primas rerum causas, & ⟨48a⟩ principia considerat. Itaque non solum excedit Metaphysica in obiecti nobilitate, sed etiam in causarum & principiorum independentia ac superioritate. Ex qua fit, ut haec scientia per se sola & sine alterius adminiculo plene & exacte doceat omnia quae sub obiectum illius cadunt: aliae vero scientiae in multis pendeant ab hac, ut exactam causarum cognitionem possint tradere, & ideo dicitur haec scientia aptior ad docendum.

37. Ad confirmationem respondetur duo esse quae ad docendum iuvant, scilicet methodum & modum docendi, & rerum ac causarum

35. But concerning this characteristic, it can, in the first place, be *A doubt.* doubted why this science is judged to be better suited to teaching than the others, for every science that is proper and *a priori* (for it is among these that a comparison is to be made) demonstrates a thing$_r$ through its causes. Therefore, each science is as suited to teaching in its own subject matter as this one is in its subject matter. Nor does it make a difference here that this science treats of nobler things$_r$, for this would indeed contribute to its being nobler, but not to its being better suited to teaching, for the proportion of effect to cause contributes more to this than the nobility of either does, since an inferior effect is taught through its proper cause as fittingly as a superior effect is taught through its cause. This characteristic, therefore, is either not at all peculiar to metaphysics, or not distinct from the nobility of its object. But if this can be attributed to some science as a property, it certainly ought rather to be attributed to dialectic, for dialectic teaches one how to learn, and it teaches one how to teach. Therefore, it is more suited to teaching than any other science. And thus Plato gives this task to dialectic in his dialogue on being, or the *Sophist*,[241] and for this reason he prefers it to all other sciences there and in book VII of the *Republic*.[242]

36. To the first difficulty, I reply that, although other sciences *Resolution of* demonstrate their properties or effects through proper causes appro- *the doubt.* priate to them, nevertheless, since those causes are not first, nor independent, but subordinated to superior ones, the other disciplines are not as suited to teaching as metaphysics, which considers the first causes and principles of things$_r$. And so metaphysics surpasses them not only with respect to nobility of object, but also with respect to independence and superiority of causes and principles. From this it follows that this science teaches fully and exactly, by itself alone and without the assistance of another science, all the things that fall under its object, whereas other sciences depend in many respects on it in order to be able to hand down an exact cognition of causes. And therefore this science is said to be more suited to teaching.

37. To the confirmation I reply that there are two things that aid teaching, namely, the method and manner of teaching, and the com-

241. Plato, *Sophist*, 253b–e.
242. Plato, *Republic* VII, 534b–535a.

comprehensionem. Quoad illud prius, ad Dialecticam pertinet docendi munus, & in eo sensu potest dici aptissima ad docendum, vel potius ad discendum, quoniam formam & methodum docendi tradit. Quantum vero ad posterius attinet, Metaphysica est ad docendum aptissima, quoniam docet demonstrandi media altiora, & efficaciora, & maxime a priori. Quia ergo hoc est potissimum & difficillimum in scientia: & quia ipsamet Dialectica quatenus scientia est, & per causas demonstrat, in hoc pendet aliquo modo a Metaphysica, ideo simpliciter haec est ad docendum aptissima. Nec aliud sensit Plato, qui Dialecticae nomine Metaphysicam saepe intelligit.

Quomodo Metaphysica a priori demonstret.   38. Secundo circa eandem conditionem, seu probationem eius, dubitari potest, quomodo haec scientia per causas possit demonstrare, cum habeat simplicissimum obiectum quod proprias causas habere non potest. Ens enim in quantum ens, nec secundum se, nec secundum nobilissimum obiectum sub eo communi contentum, proprias causas habere potest: ergo Metaphysica non potest per causas demonstrare, saltem in suprema sui parte, neque in ea quae universalissimas rationes entis considerat. Antecedens constat, quia Deus non habet causas, & consequenter neque ens ut ens, quod Deum comprehendit. Respondetur duplices esse causas, alias proprias, & quae re ipsa influunt in effectum, & alias [36a] latius dictas, quae sunt potius causae cognoscendi rem a priori, quam existendi, & proprie dicuntur rationes attributorum seu proprietatum quae de subiecto demonstrantur. Loquendo igitur de subiecto huius scientiae secundum abstractissimam rationem eius, abstractissimam (inquam) vel secundum rationem nostram, ut est ens in quantum ens: vel secun⟨48b⟩dum rem ipsam, ut est ens primum seu ipsum esse per essentiam, sic verum est non habere hanc scientiam proprias rei causas, per quas aliquid de suo obiecto demonstret, habet tamen rationes & media secundum modum concipiendi nostrum distincta ab extremis, quibus conficit demonstrationes a priori: nam ad huiusmodi demonstrationes, cum modo humano conficiantur, sufficit distinctio conceptuum cum aliquo fundamento in re, & quod proprietas per unum conceptum cognita, sit ratio alterius attributi demonstrati: & hoc modo demonstramus Deum esse ens perfectum, quia est ens

prehension of things_r and causes. With respect to the first, the task of teaching belongs to dialectic, and in that sense it can be called the most suited to teaching, or rather the most suited to learning, since it hands down the form and method of teaching. But with respect to the second, metaphysics is most suited to teaching, since it teaches middle terms of demonstration that are higher, more efficacious, and most of all *a priori*. Since, therefore, this is the most important and difficult thing in a science, and since dialectic itself, insofar as it is a science, also demonstrates through causes, and in this respect depends in some way on metaphysics, it follows that the latter science is without qualification most suited to teaching. Nor did Plato think otherwise, since by the name "dialectic" he often understands metaphysics.

38. Second, with respect to the same characteristic or its proof, it can be doubted how this science can demonstrate through causes, since it has the simplest object, which cannot have proper causes. For being as being can have proper causes neither in itself nor as regards the noblest object that is contained under that general one. Therefore, metaphysics cannot demonstrate through causes, at least not in its loftiest part, nor in that part which considers the most universal natures_r of being. The antecedent is clear, because God does not have causes, and consequently neither does being as being, which includes God. I reply that causes are twofold: some are proper, and these in reality flow into their effect, while others are more broadly so-called, and these are causes of cognizing a thing_r *a priori*, rather than causes of existing, and they are properly called grounds_r of the attributes or properties that are demonstrated of a subject. Therefore, speaking of the subject of this science in accordance with its most abstract nature_r—most abstract, I say, either according to our reason, as being *qua* being is, or in reality, as the first being or existence_e through essence is—in this way it is true that this science does not have proper real causes through which it demonstrates something of its object. However, it has grounds_r and middle terms that are, according to our mode of conceiving, distinct from the extreme terms, and by means of these middle terms it constructs *a priori* demonstrations. For it suffices for such demonstrations, when they are made in the human way, that there be a distinction of concepts with some foundation in reality, and that the property cognized through one concept be the ground_r

ab intrinseco necessarium, & unam proprietatem entis, vel substantiae eodem modo demonstramus per aliam. Et hunc demonstrationis modum comprehendit Aristoteles, cum dicit hanc scientiam docere rerum causas, id est, principia & radices ac rationes rerum, sive sint propriae causae Physicae, sive Metaphysicae rationes, quae solent etiam *D. Thom.* formales causae late appellari. Et hoc modo exponit Divus Thomas 6. lib. Metaphys. tex. 1. quod ibi Aristoteles ait, nempe inquiri in hac scientia principia & causas entium in quantum sunt entia. At vero quoad alias partes seu entia quae Metaphysica comprehendit sub obiecto suo, ut sunt entia creata, intelligentiae, &c. sic proprias habet causas reales seu in re ipsa vere influentes, per quas possit demonstrationes conficere, ut per se notum est.

Per quot causarum genera
demonstret Metaphysica.

39. Occurrit autem statim tertia interrogatio, an haec scientia ut versatur circa haec entia, demonstret per omnia causarum genera, an per aliqua tantum. Et in primis certum est saepissime & maxime *Per finalem* demonstrare per causam finalem, ut ex ipso usu constat, & quia haec *demonstrat.* est causarum prima & nobilissima, & quae maxime conferre solet ad rerum naturas, & proprietates, imo ad caeteras rei causas investigandas. *Per* Rursus etiam est certum demonstrare hanc scientiam per causam effi- *efficientem.* cientem, nam considerat de primo ente, quod est caeterorum omnium potissima causa efficiens, a qua caetera omnia essentialiter pendent. Et sub ea causa considerat etiam de intelligentiis, quae aliquam habent causalitatem in haec inferiora, & denique de aliis rerum causis, quatenus sub obiecto suo comprehendi possunt. ⟨49a⟩

of the other, demonstrated attribute. And in this way we demonstrate that God is a perfect being, since he is an intrinsically necessary being, and in the same way we demonstrate one property of being or substance through another. And Aristotle has this mode of demonstration in mind when he says that this science teaches the causes of things_r, that is, the principles and roots and grounds_r of things_r, whether they are proper physical causes or rather metaphysical grounds_r, which are also commonly called formal causes, in a broad sense. And it is in this way that St. Thomas explains, in *Metaph.* VI, text 1, what Aristotle says *St. Thomas.* there, namely, that the principles and causes of beings insofar as they are beings are sought in this science.[243] But with respect to the other parts or beings that metaphysics includes under its object, such as created beings, intelligences, etc., to this extent it does have proper causes that are real, or that in reality truly influence, by means of which causes it can produce demonstrations, as is known_n *per se.*

Through how many genera of cause
metaphysics demonstrates.

39. But a third question immediately presents itself: whether this *It* science, insofar as it is concerned with these beings, demonstrates *demonstrates* through all the genera of cause, or through some only. And, in the *through the* first place, it is certain that it very often and especially demonstrates *final cause.* through the final cause, as is clear from experience, and because the final cause is the first and noblest of the causes, and is especially wont to contribute to the investigation of the natures and properties of things_r, and even to the investigation of a thing_r's other causes. Furthermore, *Through the* it is also certain that this science demonstrates through the efficient *efficient cause.* cause, for it considers the first being, which is the most important efficient cause of all other things, on which all other things essentially depend. And under this cause it considers the intelligences as well, which have some causality with respect to lower things, and also, finally, oth-

---

243. Text 1 of *Metaph.* VI is 1025b3–28. So far as I can see, Thomas makes no attempt in the relevant *lectio* (bk. VI, lect. 1) to explain how the first philosopher can be said to deal with the causes and principles of being *qua* being even if God, who has no cause, is included under the subject of metaphysics. See Thomas Aquinas, *In duodecim libros metaphysicorum Aristotelis expositio*, pp. 295–96 (bk. VI, lect. 1, ns. 1144–55).

Obiectioni fit satis.

40. Dices, Causalitas causae efficientis tota[74] versatur circa rerum existentiam, scientia vero abstrahit ab existentia: non ergo potest per efficientem causam quidquam demonstrare. Respondetur primo, licet actualis dependentia a causa efficiente quatenus in actu exercito (ut sic dicam) non cadat per se sub scientiam, quia non est simpliciter necessaria, sed contingens & libera: habitu[36b]do tamen intrinseca ad causam efficientem, praesertim primam, est necessaria, & consideratur in scientia, multaeque proprietates rerum ex illa colliguntur. Nam ex eo quod creatura habet essentialem dependentiam a causa efficiente, colligitur non esse ens per essentiam, sed per participationem, & esse non esse de essentia eius, esseque ens finitum, & similia. Deinde dicitur, esto scientia non consideret existentiam rei in actu exercito, considerare tamen illam in actu signato, id est quid sit ipsa existentia, & quomodo unicuique rei conveniat aut convenire possit, atque ad hoc maxime confert causae efficientis consideratio. Unde etiam fit, ut de his rebus quae aliquo modo sunt entia necessaria, scientia contempletur ipsam existentiam actualem, & exercitam, quod maxime habet verum circa Deum, qui est simpliciter ens necessarium, & actu existens, cuius existendi necessitas non per efficientem causam, sed per negationem efficientis causae consideratur. De aliis vero rebus etiam inquiritur in scientia an aeternae sint, & quomodo dimanent a sua efficiente causa. Multa ergo in Metaphysica per hanc causam demonstrantur.

Per exemplarem.

41. Atque hinc etiam constat, posse hanc scientiam uti causa exemplari in demonstrationibus suis, si tamen veritatem ac proprietatem ipsius exemplaris possit attingere in se se, quod tamen rarum est, & in exemplaribus divinis, quae ideas vocant, impossibile naturaliter, quia non possunt illa divina exemplaria in se conspici, nisi Deus in se ipso videatur. Quacunque tamen ratione exemplaris causa cognoscatur, optimum medium est demonstrandi, & Metaphysicae maxime proprium,

---

74. Reading "tota" here with C₁, C₂, G₂, M₁, M₂, M₃, M₄, P₁, P₂, S, V₁, V₂, V₃, V₄, and V₅. Vivès omits this word.

er causes of things_r, insofar as they can be comprehended under its object.

40. You will say: the entire causality of the efficient cause has to do with the existence of things_r. But a science abstracts from existence. Therefore, it cannot demonstrate anything through the efficient cause. I reply, first, that although actual dependence on an efficient cause insofar as it is in exercised act (so to speak) does not fall *per se* under science, since it is not without qualification necessary, but rather contingent and free, nevertheless, the intrinsic relation to an efficient cause, especially to the first efficient cause, is necessary and is considered in a science, and from it one infers many properties of things_r. For, from the fact that a creature has an essential dependence on an efficient cause, it is inferred that it is not a being by its essence, but by participation, and that existence_e does not pertain to its essence, and that it is a finite being, and the like. Second, I say that, even if a science does not consider the existence of a thing_r in exercised act, nevertheless, it considers it in signified act, that is, what existence itself is, and how it agrees or can agree with each thing_r, and consideration of the efficient cause especially contributes to this. For this reason it also results that, regarding those things_r which are in some way necessary beings, a science considers existence itself that is actual and exercised, which is especially true with respect to God, who is without qualification a necessary being and actually existing, whose necessity of existing is considered not through an efficient cause, but through the negation of an efficient cause. Regarding other things_r, however, one also inquires in a science whether they are eternal, and how they emanate from their efficient cause. Many things in metaphysics, therefore, are demonstrated through this cause.

41. And from this it is also clear that this science can make use of the exemplar cause in its demonstrations, provided that it can reach the truth and property of the very exemplar in itself, which, however, is rare and, in the case of the divine exemplars (which they call ideas), naturally impossible, since those divine exemplars cannot in themselves be seen unless God is seen in himself. Still, in whatever way the exemplar cause is cognized, it is the best middle term for demonstrating, and the one most proper to metaphysics, for of itself it abstracts from matter and is more properly found in spiritual and intellectual things_r, and it is

nam ex se abstrahit a materia, & in rebus spiritualibus & intellectualibus proprius reperitur, & est quodammodo ratio aut forma per quam
agens operatur, & ita eadem est de illa ratio, quae de efficiente causa.

Quomodo per materialem.   42. De causa tandem materiali Soncinas 4. Metaphysic. ⟨49b⟩
quaestio. 15. absolute negat Metaphysicam demonstrare quicquam
per hanc causam. Ratio eius est, quia Metaphysica abstrahit ex parte
obiecti a materia: ergo & principia Metaphysicae abstrahunt a materia: ergo & demonstrationes. Sed haec sententia limitatione indiget,
nam causa materialis ut sic, & in tota sua latitudine sumpta, latius patet
quam materia sensibilis, aut intelligibilis seu quantitativa, a quibus abstrahit Metaphysicae obiectum. Assumptum declaratur, nam in rebus
spiritualibus vere datur causatio (ut sic dicam) materialis: substantia
enim spiritualis creata, vere est causa materialis suorum accidentium,
& multi arbitrantur essentiam esse causam materialem existentiae, &
naturam personalitatis, & terminum actionis quae ad illum tendit.
Quanquam ergo demus, Metaphysicam non uti materia propriissime
dicta in demonstrationibus suis, negari tamen non potest, quin saepe
utatur causa materiali, vel ad affirmandum, vel ad negandum aliquid.
Priori modo demonstrat, verbi gratia, accidentia angelica esse immaterialia, indivisibilia, & tota in toto, & tota in qualibet parte, quia sunt
in subiecto spirituali, &c. Posteriori autem modo demonstrat, illa accidentia non creari, quia pendent a suo subiecto in fieri & conservari,
& simi[37a]liter ex propria definitione causae materialis demonstrat,
essentiam non posse comparari ad existentiam ut subiectum. Denique
causalitas potentiae passivae ut sic materialis est, pertinet autem ad
Metaphysicum considerare potentiam passivam, & per eam demonstrare: ergo & per materialem causam. Addo ulterius ex supra dictis de
obiecto huius doctrinae, quod licet per se & ex primario instituto non
tractet de materia physica, tractat tamen aliquo modo de illa, scilicet,
quatenus necessarium est ad complendam sui obiecti tractationem, &
considerationem, & ad distinguendum actum a potentia, & formam
completam ab incompleta, & utramque a materia, ac denique ad col-
locandam materiam in eo gradu entis, in quo vere constituenda est: in
hac vero tractatione multa potest ex ratione communi causae materialis colligere ac demonstrare, ut per se notum videtur, & ex ipso usu
constabit. Non est ergo omnino aliena ab hac scientia demonstratio

in a certain way the ground$_r$ or form through which an agent operates, and so the same consideration$_r$ applies to both it and the efficient cause.

42. Finally, regarding the material cause, Soncinas, *Metaph.* IV, q. 15, absolutely denies that metaphysics demonstrates anything through this cause.[244] And his argument is: because, with respect to its object, metaphysics abstracts from matter; therefore, the principles of metaphysics also abstract from matter, and so too, therefore, do its demonstrations. But this opinion is in need of limitation, for the material cause, as such, and taken in its entire breadth, extends more widely than sensible matter and intelligible, or quantitative, matter, from which the object of metaphysics abstracts. And this assumption is made clear because in spiritual things$_r$ there truly is material causation (so to speak),[245] for a created spiritual substance is truly the material cause of its accidents, and many hold that essence is the material cause of existence, that a nature is the material cause of personality, and that a terminus is the material cause of an action that tends toward it. Therefore, although we grant that metaphysics does not make use of matter, most properly so-called, in its demonstrations, nevertheless, it cannot be denied that it often makes use of the material cause, either for affirming something or for denying something. In the first way, for example, it demonstrates that angelic accidents are immaterial, indivisible, and whole in the whole and whole in any part, since they are in a spiritual subject, etc. And in the second way metaphysics demonstrates that those accidents are not created, since they depend on their subject in their coming-to-be and being-conserved, and in a similar way, on the basis of the proper definition of material cause, it demonstrates that essence cannot be related to existence as a subject. Finally, the causality of a passive potency as such is material, and it pertains to the metaphysician to consider passive potency, and to demonstrate through it, and therefore through a material cause. On the basis of the things said above regarding the object of this doctrine, I add, furthermore, that although

In what way through the material cause.

---

244. Paul Soncinas, *Quaestiones Metaphysicales acutissimae*, pp. 23b–24b.

245. The Latin word here rendered "causation" is "*causatio*," the more common meaning of which is *plea* or *excuse*. As suggested by his parenthetical comment, "so to speak," Suárez would seem to have some scruples about using the term to mean *causation* or *causal action*. I count only eighteen occurrences of the word in the whole of the *Metaphysical Disputations*.

per materialem causam, quanvis aliae frequentius occurrant, magisque propriae huius doctrinae esse videantur.

43. De quinta proprietate nihil occurrit addendum his quae in priori conclusione, & in ⟨50a⟩ praecedente sectione dicta sunt. Ostensum est enim scientiam hanc esse maxime speculativam, & versari circa res propter se maxime expetendas ac cognoscendas: unde evidentissimum est hanc scientiam appetendam & quaerendam esse propter se ipsam. Item dictum est naturalem foelicitatem in aliquo actu huius scientiae positam esse: at foelicitas maxime expetitur propter se ipsam.

Metaphysica aliarum scientiarum
facile princeps.

44. Atque ex hac conditione facile intelligitur, sextam etiam sapientiae conditionem in Metaphysicam perfectissime convenire: unde Aristoteles in hunc modum eam demonstrat. Ea scientia maxime princeps est, ministrantique praeponitur, quae primas rerum causas considerat, praesertim finalem & ultimam, cuius gratia res fiunt: hoc autem est Metaphysicae munus: illa ergo est quae dominatur[75] reliquis disciplinis: ergo hoc etiam titulo ipsa est sapientia. At vero dicunt aliqui non hanc, sed moralem scientiam, praesertim politicam, habere hunc principatum, & quasi imperium in caeteras scientias, ut docte *Fonseca* ad hunc Aristotelis locum annotavit. Etenim praecipere ac dominari inter in-

Fonseca.

75. Reading "dominatur" here with M_1, P_1, P_2, S, V_1, and V_2. The following editions have "dominabitur": C_1, C_2, G_2, M_2, M_3, M_4, V_3, V_4, V_5, and Vivès.

it does not treat of physical matter *per se* and in accordance with its primary aim, nevertheless, it treats of it in some way, namely, insofar as this is necessary to complete the treatment and consideration of its object, to distinguish act from potency, to distinguish complete form from incomplete form, to distinguish each of these from matter, and finally, to locate matter in that grade of being in which it is truly to be established. But in this treatment one can infer and demonstrate many things from the common concept$_r$ of the material cause, as seems to be known$_n$ *per se*, and as will be clear from experience. Demonstration through the material cause is not, therefore, altogether foreign to this science, although other demonstrations occur more often in it and seem to be more proper to this doctrine.

43. Regarding the fifth property, nothing presents itself to be added to the things that were said in connection with the earlier conclusion[246] and in the preceding section. For it has been shown that this science is most of all speculative and concerned with things$_r$ that are most of all to be sought and cognized for their own sake. For this reason, it is most evident that this science is to be desired and pursued for its own sake. Further, it has been said that natural happiness is found in some act of this science, and happiness is most of all desired for its own sake.

Metaphysics is indisputably the
queen of the other sciences.

44. And from this characteristic it is easily understood that the sixth characteristic of wisdom also agrees most perfectly with metaphysics, for which reason Aristotle demonstrates it in the following way.[247] That science is especially preeminent, and is set over an auxiliary science, which considers the first causes of things$_r$, especially the final and ultimate cause for the sake of which things$_r$ are done. But this is the function of metaphysics. It is, therefore, the science that rules over the other sciences. Therefore, it is wisdom for this reason also. But some say that not this science, but moral science, and especially political science, has dominion and sovereignty, as it were, over the other sciences, as Fonseca   *Fonseca.*

246. See *DM* 1.5.2–5.
247. See Aristotle, *Metaph.* I, ch. 2, 982b4–7.

tellectuales virtutes practicis potius quam speculativis tribuendum est: praecipere enim practicus actus est, & Philosophia moralis, practica est, & in ea praecipua est politica, quae in ordine ad commune Reipublicae bonum cuncta praecipit: ergo. Et confirmatur, nam iuxta debitum rationis ordinem non boni mores ad scientiam, sed scientia ad bonos mores referenda est: scientia ergo illa quae bonos mores procurat, ei imperare debet quae in sola rerum speculatione sistit. Sed hae rationes si quid probant, potius de prudentia, quam de morali Philosophia procedunt, nam praecipere ad prudentiam pertinet, non ad Philosophiam: intendere autem bonos mores nec Philosophiae, [37b] nec prudentiae proprie convenit, sed voluntati, & virtutibus eius. Deinde probant quidem illae rationes prudentiam esse perfectiorem in ratione virtutis moralis, & sub ea ratione practice imperare, & consequenter dare etiam gratis possumus in ordine ad bonos mores aliquo modo praeire caeteris scientiis speculativis moralem philosophiam: non autem probant rationes illae vel absolute & simpliciter esse perfectiorem prudentiam Metaphysica, vel in genere virtutis intellectualis philosophiam moralem habere primatum. ⟨50b⟩

45. Oportet ergo in scientiis duo distinguere, scilicet veritatis contemplationem seu iudicium & infallibilem vim seu rectitudinem attingendi illam, & bonum usum talis scientiae & actuum eius, quatenus liberi sunt, & bene vel male, & propter honestum finem, & cum debitis circunstantiis possunt fieri, aut non fieri. Prior ratio est essentialis scientiae ut sic, imo in universum omni virtuti intellectuali hoc per se primo convenit, quanvis practica virtus ulterius ipsam veritatis cognitionem & iudicium ordinet ad opus: quod non pertinet ad maiorem perfectionem scientiae ut sic, sed potius est indicium minoris perfectionis, ut hic Aristoteles docuit in prooemio Metaphysicae, & fortasse inferius id attingemus, tractando de qualitatibus & habitibus mentis. Posterior ratio, scilicet usus scientiae, quod nimirum sit honestus, vel Reipublicae utilis, vel ad alios fines, est accidentalis scientiae ut sic, licet sit maxime necessaria homini. Imperare igitur scientiae usum hoc posteriori modo proxime spectat ad virtutes aliquas & ad prudentiam, & ad idem imperium magis conferunt scientiae morales, quam Meta-

learnedly notes on this passage of Aristotle.[248] For to direct and to rule ought to be attributed to the practical, rather than speculative, among the intellectual virtues, for to direct is a practical activity, and moral philosophy is practical, and in moral philosophy especially politics, which directs all things to the common good of the republic. Therefore. And this is confirmed, for according to the right order of reason, good morals are not to be referred to science, but science to good morals. Therefore, that science which attends to good morals ought to command that which stops at the mere contemplation of things$_r$. However, these arguments, if they prove something, succeed with respect to prudence, rather than moral philosophy, for to direct pertains to prudence, not to philosophy, and to aim at good morals properly agrees not with philosophy, or with prudence, but with the will and its virtues. Moreover, those arguments do indeed prove that prudence is more perfect as a moral virtue, and that, as such, it commands practically, and consequently we can also freely grant that in relation to good morals moral philosophy in some way directs the other, speculative sciences. But those arguments do not prove either that prudence is, absolutely and without qualification, more perfect than metaphysics, or that moral philosophy holds the highest rank in the genus of intellectual virtue.

45. In the sciences, therefore, one must distinguish two things: first, the contemplation or judgment of truth and the inerrant power or skill to reach it, and second, the good use of such a science and its acts, insofar as they are free and can be done, or not done, well or badly, for the sake of an honorable end, and with the appropriate circumstances. The first aspect$_r$ is essential to a science as such; in fact, in general this agrees *per se* and primarily with every intellectual virtue, although a practical virtue further orders the same cognition and judgment of truth to work, which is something that does not pertain to the greater perfection of a science as such, but is rather a mark of lesser perfection, as Aristotle teaches here in the proem of the *Metaphysics*,[249] and perhaps below we shall touch on this in treating of the qualities and habits of the mind.[250] The second

---

248. Pedro da Fonseca, *Commentariorum in libros Metaphysicorum Aristotelis tomus primus*, cols. 123–24.

249. See Aristotle, *Metaph.* I, ch. 1, 981b13–25, and ch. 2, 982b11–28.

250. See *DM* 44.13.19–54.

physica, & hoc proprie vocatur imperium practicum, quia respicit opus scientiae, magis ut est opus voluntatis, quam intellectus: usus enim est active in voluntate, quanvis interdum executio sit in intellectu. At vero dirigere scientias sub priori ratione, scilicet ad veri cognitionem, per se primo ac maxime pertinet ad Metaphysicam, a qua quodammodo accipiunt principia, & terminorum cognitionem, & obiecta, seu quidditates suorum obiectorum, iuxta ea quae in superioribus declarata sunt. Et ratione huius directionis & independentiae dici potest Metaphysica imperare aliis, imperio potius speculativo, quam practico: ratione cuius ipsa simpliciter eminet in ratione scientiae, & sapientiae. Addo denique, si Metaphysica consideretur quatenus in perfectissimo actu eius naturalis beatitudo hominis consistit, sic ad illam ut ad finem ordinari non solum alias scientias, sed etiam morales virtutes & prudentiam, nam haec omnia ad foelicitatem hominis ordinantur, & actiones omnes ad hunc finem optime referuntur, ut scilicet hominem disponant, aptumque reddant ad divinam contemplationem, quae formaliter seu elicitive ad hanc scientiam pertinet, licet habere debeat coniunctum amorem, qui ex tali contemplatione solet nasci. Atque hac etiam ratione concludit Aristoteles scientiam hanc omnibus impe⟨51a⟩rare, quia contemplatur summum bonum & ultimum finem simpliciter: sicut enim in artibus quae ad aliquem finem subordinantur, illa architectonica est, aliisque imperat, quae supremum finem in illo ordi[38a]ne considerat: ita Metaphysica, quae absolute contemplatur ultimum finem scientiarum, artiumque omnium, totiusque humanae vitae, dicitur imperare omnibus, esseque omnium princeps, non quia proprie & practice imperet, sed quasi virtute & eminenter. Non enim procedit Metaphysica, practice ostendendo quomodo ille finis obtinendus sit, aut alia in eum dirigenda, & ideo non proprie & formaliter imperat: ostendit tamen finem, in quem omnia dirigenda sunt,[76] eumque finem ultimum rerum omnium esse ostendit: & ideo ex parte rei cognitae, virtute & eminenter, quantum est ex se, omnibus imperat, omniaque in eum finem ac summum bonum dirigit.

---

76. Reading "dirigenda sunt" here with S, V_1, and V_2. The following editions omit "sunt": C_1, C_2, G_2, M_1, M_2, M_3, M_4, P_1, P_2, V_3, V_4, V_5, and Vivès.

aspect₁, namely, the use of a science—that, of course, it be honorable, or useful to the republic or for other ends—is accidental to science as such, although it is most especially necessary for the human being. Therefore, to command the use of a science in this latter way pertains immediately to some virtues and to prudence, and the moral sciences contribute more to this dominion than metaphysics does. And this is properly called a practical dominion, since it concerns the work of a science insofar as it is a work of the will rather than a work of the intellect, for use is actively in the will, although sometimes execution is in the intellect. But to direct the sciences in accordance with the first aspect₁, namely, to the cognition of truth, pertains *per se* and primarily and most of all to metaphysics, from which, in a certain way, [other sciences] receive their principles, the cognition of terms, and their objects, or the quiddities of their objects, in keeping with the things made clear above. And by reason of this direction and independence, metaphysics can be said to command the others by means of a speculative, rather than practical, dominion, for which reason it is, as a science and wisdom, preeminent without qualification. I add, finally, that if metaphysics is considered insofar as the natural beatitude of the human being consists in her most perfect act, then in this way not only the other sciences, but also the moral virtues and prudence, are ordered to it as to an end, for all of these things are ordained to the happiness of the human being, and all actions are best referred to this end, in order, namely, that they might dispose the human being and make her fit for divine contemplation, which formally or elicitively pertains to this science, although it should have a conjoined love, which usually arises from such contemplation. And for this reason, too, Aristotle concludes that this science commands all the others, because it contemplates the highest good and the ultimate end without qualification. For just as, among arts which are subordinated to some end, the one which considers the highest end in that order is architectonic and commands the others, so is metaphysics—which absolutely contemplates the ultimate end of the sciences, of all the arts, and of human life as a whole—said to command all of them and to be the foremost among them, not because it commands properly and practically, but because it commands, as it were, virtually and eminently. For metaphysics does not proceed by showing, practically, how that end is to be achieved, or how

Expeditur dubium de subalternatione aliarum
scientiarum ad Metaphysicam.

Aliquorum opinio.   46. Hic vero dubium occurrit circa conditionem hanc, an hoc imperium, vel directio Metaphysicae in alias scientias, tale sit, ut dicendae sint omnes scientiae ratione illius subalternari Metaphysicae. Non enim defuere, qui ita de hoc imperio Metaphysicae existimaverint, ut ratione illius omnes scientias subalternatas, solam vero Metaphysicam simpliciter, aut tantum subalternantem esse dixerint. Quam sententiam aliqui tribuunt Aristoteli, 1. Physicor. capit. 2. & lib. 1. Posteriorum capit. 7. & Platoni, lib. 7. de Repub. ubi de Metaphysica nomine Dialecticae disputat. Eamque insinuat D. Thom. opusculo de natura generis cap. 14. Alii vero simpliciter negant hanc subalternationem: & haec est communis & recepta sententia, ut videre licet in Iavello, 1. Metaphysic. quaest. 2. Soncinate, lib. 4. quaest. 9. Soto, 1. Physic. quaest. 11. Alii denique distinctione utuntur, & sub una ratione seu usu vocis *subalternationis*, docent posse Metaphysicam dici subalternantem, saltem aliquo modo, simpliciter vero negant. Lege Fonsecam, lib. 4. cap. 1. quaest. 2.[77]

Aristoteles.
Plato.
D. Thomas.
Aliorum placitum.
Iavellus.
Soncinas.
Soto.
Fonseca.

77. Reading "quaest. 2" here with S, V_1, and V_2. The following read "q. 1": C_1, C_2, G_2, M_1, M_2, M_3, M_4, P_1, P_2, V_3, V_4, V_5, and Vivès.

other things are to be directed to it, and therefore it does not properly and formally command. Nevertheless, it makes known the end to which all things should be directed, and it shows that it is the ultimate end of all things$_r$, and therefore, with respect to the thing$_r$ cognized, metaphysics, considered in itself, commands all the sciences virtually and eminently, and it directs all things to that end and highest good.

A doubt regarding the subalternation of the other sciences to metaphysics is resolved.

46. Here, however, a doubt presents itself regarding this characteristic, namely, whether this dominion or direction of metaphysics vis-à-vis the other sciences is such that all sciences must be said to be subalternated to metaphysics because of it. For there have been some who have thought this regarding this dominion of metaphysics, so that they have claimed that because of it all other sciences are subalternate, and that metaphysics alone is without qualification or only subalternating. Some attribute this view to Aristotle, *Phys.* I, ch. 2,[251] and *Post. An.* I, ch. 7,[252] and to Plato, *Rep.* VII,[253] where he discusses metaphysics under the name "dialectic." St. Thomas suggests the same in his short work, *On the Nature of the Genus*, ch. 14.[254] Others, however, unqualifiedly deny this subalternation, and this is the common and received view, as one can see in Javelli, *Metaph.* I, q. 2,[255] Soncinas, book IV, q. 9,[256] and Soto, *Phys.* I, q. 11.[257] Finally, others make use of

The opinion of some.

Aristotle.
Plato.
St. Thomas.
The view of others.
Javelli.
Soncinas.
Soto.

251. See Aristotle, *Phys.* I, ch. 2, 184b25–185a17.

252. According to the chapter divisions of the *Post. An.* used by Suárez, *Post. An.* I, ch. 7, begins at our *Post. An.* I, ch. 6, 75a28, and continues till the end of our *Post. An.* I, ch. 9. See Francisco de Toledo, *Commentaria una cum quaestionibus in universam Aristotelis logicam*, fols. 179va–180rb.

253. Plato, *Republic* VII, 531c–535a.

254. [Ps.-] Thomas Aquinas [Thomas Sutton], *De natura generis*, ch. 14, in: *Sancti Thomae Aquinatis opera omnia* (Parmae: Typis Petri Fiaccadori, 1864), 17:18b–20a.

255. Giovanni Crisostomo Javelli, *Opera* (Lugduni: Apud Antonium de Harsy, 1580), t. 1, pp. 711b–12b.

256. Paul Soncinas, *Quaestiones Metaphysicales acutissimae*, pp. 13a–14b.

257. To judge by the 1582 Salamanca edition of his *Super octo libros Physicorum Aristotelis Quaestiones*, Domingo de Soto devotes only eight questions to book I of Aristotle's *Physics*. However, at *Phys.* I, q. 1, ad 5 (fol. 6va), Soto does deny that physics is subalternate to metaphysics. See Soto, *Super octo libros physicorum Aristotelis quaestiones* (Salmanticae: ex Officina Ildefonsi à Terranova & Neyla, 1582).

Quae sit
subalternata
scientia.

47. Ne vero in nominum ambiguitate versemur, supponamus, proprie scientiam illam dici subalternatam alteri, quae essentialiter seu necessario ex natura rei ab illa pendet in esse scientiae, ita ut esse scientia non possit, nisi scientiae subalternanti coniungatur, & ab illa sumat evidentiam principiorum. Ratio autem huius ⟨51b⟩ est, quia scientia subalternata non habet principia per se nota & immediata, sed conclusiones demonstrabiles in superiori scientia, & ideo sicut omnis scientia ab habitu principiorum essentialiter pendet, ita subalternata a subalternante proprie dicta: quia utraque sumit a superiori virtute evidentiam principiorum. Dices, Unde constat subalternatam scientiam non posse habere principia per se nota, sed conclusiones alibi demonstrabiles, illi esse principia? Respondetur, hoc non posse nisi ad significationem vocis pertinere: nam in re constat esse aliquas scientias quae huiusmodi utuntur principiis, ut Medicina, Musica, &c. has ergo dicimus subalternatarum nomine significari. Nam illae quae principia habent immediata, proxime ac per se subordinantur habitui principiorum, & ideo non est cur respectu alterius scientiae subordinationem habe[38b]re dicantur, cum ab illa per se non pendeant: haec ergo dependentia unius scientiae ab alia, nomine subalternationis significatur.

Quae
conditiones
ad subalter-
nationem
requisitae.

48. Ex quo fit, ut subalternatio vera non sit, nisi inter scientias diversas: nam etsi in eadem scientia sit dependentia unius conclusionis ab altera usque ad principia prima,[78] non tamen ideo scientia dici potest, vel in totum, vel in partem subalternata, cum absolute tota scientia non alteri scientiae priori, sed immediate habitui principiorum subordinetur, sed ad summum dici potest una conclusio subordinata, vel subalternata demonstrationi alterius. Oportet ergo ut scientiae

---

78. Reading "principia prima" here with C₁, C₂, G₂, M₁, M₂, M₃, M₄, P₁, P₂, S, V₁, V₂, V₃, and V₄. The following editions omit "prima": V₅ and Vivès.

a distinction, and they teach that according to one account, or use of the term "subalternation" metaphysics can be called subalternating, at least in some way, but they deny that it is subalternating without qualification. See Fonseca, book IV, ch. 1, q. 2.[258]

Fonseca.

47. In order to avoid ambiguity, let us suppose that that science is properly called subalternate to another which essentially, or by virtue of its nature necessarily, depends on that other one for its being a science, in such a way that it cannot be a science unless it is joined with the subalternating science and acquires the evidence of its principles from it. The reason for this is that a subalternate science does not have principles that are immediate and known$_n$ *per se*, but principles that are conclusions demonstrable in a higher science, and therefore, just as every science essentially depends on the habit of principles, so does a subalternate science essentially depend on a subalternating science properly so-called, since both acquire the evidence of their principles from a superior virtue. You will say: how is it established that a subalternate science cannot have principles that are known$_n$ *per se*, but that conclusions, demonstrable elsewhere, are principles for it? I reply that the question can concern only the signification of the word, for in reality it is clear that there are some sciences which employ such principles, for instance, medicine, music, etc.; we say, therefore, that these are signified by the name "subalternate." For those sciences which have immediate principles are proximately and *per se* subordinated to the habit of principles, and therefore, there is no reason why they should be said to be subordinate to another science, since they do not depend *per se* on another one. Therefore, this dependence of one science on another is signified by the name "subalternation."

What a subalternate science is.

48. From this it results that there is true subordination only between diverse sciences. For even if, in one and the same science, there is a dependence of one conclusion on another all the way up to the first principles, nevertheless, a science cannot for this reason be called subalternate, either as a whole or in part, since the whole science is not absolutely subordinate to another prior science, but is rather immediately subordinate to the habit of principles. At most, one conclusion can be

What conditions are required for subalternation.

258. Pedro da Fonseca, *Commentariorum in libros Metaphysicorum Aristotelis tomus primus*, cols. 656–62.

distinctae sint, & quod inter se habeant praedictam dependentiam, & subordinationem. Contingit vero interdum scientiam aliquam non in omnibus suis principiis, neque in omnium conclusionum demonstrationibus, sed in quibusdam habere dictam dependentiam a scientia superiori: & tunc dicitur illi subalternata, non in totum, sed ex parte, seu partiali subordinatione, non totali: quo modo Geometria dicitur subalternari naturali Philosophiae, quia, licet utatur multis principiis indemonstrabilibus, aliqua tamen habet quae in Philosophia demonstrantur, ut illud, *A quolibet puncto in quodlibet punctum lineam duci*: quod in Physica demonstratur, quia nulla indivisibilia sunt immediata, eo quod ex indivisibilibus componi non possit continua quantitas.

Unde enascatur scientiae unius ad alteram subalternatio.

49. Oriri autem solet haec dependentia unius scientiae ab alia ex subor⟨52a⟩dinatione obiectorum: nam, sicut esse scientiae consistit in ordine ad obiectum, ita & principia sunt proportionata illi. Quapropter si obiecta duarum scientiarum non sunt inter se subordinata, utpote si sint genera vel species omnino condivisae, inter illas scientias non potest esse subalternatio. Oportet ergo ut haec subalternatio in obiectis fundetur, nimirum in eo, quod obiectum unius est idem cum obiecto alterius, adiuncta aliqua differentia accidentali, quae in esse entis sit per accidens, in esse autem scibilis sit aliquo modo per se, & constituat speciale obiectum scibile. Quando enim duo obiecta scientiae per se subordinantur, etiam in esse rei, scilicet ut genus & species: vel ut superius & inferius essentialiter, scientiae de illis obiectis non possunt esse subalternatae, saltem totaliter, quia, vel pertinent ad eandem scientiam, si in eadem omnino sint abstractione, vel certe, si scientiae diversae sint, erit utraque subalternans, quia utraque habere potest propria principia sumpta ex propria differentia obiecti quod considerat, vel ex prima passione, & per illa poterit demonstrare reliquas conclusiones, quae de posterioribus passionibus conficiuntur. Nam scientia de homine non considerat quae conveniunt homini ut animal est, sed tantum ut rationalis est, & in illis non subalternatur scientiae de animali, quia esse rationale immediate convenit homini, & ex hoc principio oriuntur aliae passiones hominis ut homo est. Quod si aliqua est quae pendeat ex

called subordinate or subalternate to the demonstration of another. The sciences must, therefore, be distinct, and the mentioned dependence and subordination must obtain between them. It occasionally happens, however, that some science has the mentioned dependence on a higher science, not as regards all of its principles, nor as regards the demonstrations of all of its conclusions, but as regards some of them, and then it is called subalternate to the higher science, not as a whole, but in part, or by a partial subordination, not a total one. In this way geometry is called subalternate to natural philosophy, since, although it makes use of many indemonstrable principles, it nevertheless has some principles that are demonstrated in philosophy, such as this one: "a line can be traced from any point to any point," which is something demonstrated in physics, on the grounds that no indivisibles are immediate, since a continuous quantity cannot be composed from indivisibles.[259]

49. This dependence of one science on another normally arises from the subordination of their objects, for, just as the being$_e$ of a science consists in a relation to an object, so also are principles proportioned to that. For this reason, if the objects of two sciences are not subordinate one to another—for example, if they are completely condivided species or genera[260]—then there can be no subalternation between those sciences. Therefore, this subalternation must be founded on the objects—without doubt, on the fact that the object of the one is the same as the object of the other, but with the addition of some accidental difference, which in respect of the being$_e$ of the being is *per accidens*, although in respect of its being$_e$ as a knowable [object] it is in some way *per se* and constitutes a special knowable object. For when two objects of knowledge are subordinate *per se* in real being$_e$ as well, namely, as genus and species, or as essentially superior and inferior, then the sciences of those objects cannot be subalternate, at least not totally, since, either they pertain to the same science, if they are in altogether the same abstraction, or at any rate, if the sciences are diverse, each will be subalternating, since each can have proper principles taken from the proper difference of the object that it considers, or from its primary passion, and by means of these it will be able to demonstrate the remaining conclusions that are

Whence arises the subalternation of one science to another.

259. See Aristotle, *Phys.* VI, ch. 1, 231a21–b18.
260. I.e., if they have the same proximate genus.

gradu sensitivo ut sic aliquo modo, aut ex speciali coniunctione sensibilis cum rationali, quantum ad id subalternabitur partialiter scientia
de homine scientiae de animali, non tamen omnino & totaliter.

50. Ad subalternationem ergo absolutam & tota[39a]lem, necesse
est ut subiectum subalternatae scientiae addat accidentalem differentiam subiecto scientiae subalternantis, ut linea visualis addit lineae,
numerus sonorus numero, humanum corpus sanabile humano corpori: nam ex hac coniunctione provenit, tum ut scientia quae specialiter
considerat proprietates ex illo coniuncto ut sic manantes, sit diversa a
scientia quae abstrahit ab illa compositione, & subiectum secundum se
considerat: tum etiam ut principia talis scientiae sint conclusiones superioris scientiae, quia nimirum proprietates talis compositi oriuntur
ex ipsis componentibus, & ex proprietatibus quas secundum se habent,
& in superiori scientia demonstrantur. De quibus omnibus ⟨52b⟩ in lib.
1. Posterior. capit. 11. latius disseritur: hic vero solum insinuata, & quasi
delibata sunt, ut breviter explicemus, quomodo Metaphysica sit affecta
ad alias scientias, etiam quoad hanc proprietatem.

drawn regarding the subsequent passions. For the science of the human being does not consider things that agree with the human being insofar as she is an animal, but only things that agree with her insofar as she is rational, and when it comes to the latter things, the science of the human being is not subalternate to the science of the animal, since to be rational agrees immediately with the human being, and from this principle arise other passions that belong to the human being insofar as she is a human being. But if there is some passion of the human being that depends in some way on the sensitive grade as such, or on a special conjunction of the sensitive with the rational, with respect to it the science of the human being will be partially subalternate to the science of the animal, but not completely and totally.

50. For absolute and total subalternation, therefore, it is necessary that the subject of the subalternate science add an accidental difference to the subject of the subalternating science, as visual line adds to line, sounding number adds to number, and curable human body adds to human body. For from such a composition it results, first, that the science which specifically considers the properties emanating from this composite as such is diverse from the science which abstracts from that composition and considers the subject in itself, and second, that the principles of such a science are conclusions of the superior science, since the properties of such a composite undoubtedly arise from the components themselves and from the properties that these components have in themselves, which are demonstrated in the superior science. All these things are discussed at some length in *Post. An.* I, ch. 11,[261] but here they have only been introduced and sampled, as it were,

261. In his references thus far to the *Post. An.*, Suárez seems to be using the division into chapters that is found in the text employed by Toledo in his commentary, rather than the division found in the text used by Zabarella in his commentary. (See p. 113, n. 119.) In Toledo's text, however, *Post. An.* I, ch. 11, coincides with our *Post. An.* I, chs. 14 and 15, and it is difficult to see how these chapters could be interpreted as offering a discussion of the subalternation of the sciences. Moreover, in Zabarella's text, *Post. An.* I, ch. 11, coincides with our *Post. An.* I, ch. 12, and although mention is made in this chapter of the subalternation of optics to geometry (77b1–2), it is difficult to see how this chapter could be characterized as discussing the subalternation of the sciences "at some length" (*latius*). Suárez seems actually to have had (what he and Toledo label) ch. 10 in mind, which is our *Post. An.* I, ch. 13. Rubio discusses the subalternation of the sciences during the course of commenting on this chapter. See Antonio Rubio, *Commentarii in Universam Aristotelis Dialecticam* (Compluti: Ex Officina Iusti Sanchez Crespo, 1603), vol. 2, cols. 560–87.

51. Ex dictis igitur non obscure colligitur nullam proprietatem scientiae proprie subalternantis convenire Metaphysicae respectu aliarum scientiarum. Primum enim non pendent omnino aliae scientiae in esse scientiae a Metaphysica, quia non pendent in omni evidentia & certitudine suorum principiorum. Habent enim sua principia immediata, & indemonstrabilia ostensive & directe: quod satis est ut possint habere evidentiam eorum immediate ab habitu principiorum, quae sufficit ad generandam scientiam. Etenim, licet Metaphysica demonstrare possit aliquo modo illa principia, illa tamen demonstratio non est simpliciter necessaria ad iudicium evidens talium principiorum, cum ex terminis possint evidenter cognosci, & illa demonstratio non sit proprie a priori, sed per deductionem ad impossibile, vel ad summum per aliquam extrinsecam causam. Metaphysica ergo non est simpliciter necessaria ad evidentiam horum principiorum: ergo neque ut habitus ex eis genitus sit vera scientia: ergo talis habitus non est scientia subalternata Metaphysicae. Rursus obiecta inferiorum scientiarum non sunt per accidens subordinata enti, aut substantiae, sed per se & essentialiter, ut patet in ente naturali, quod est obiectum Philosophiae, & de quantitate quae est obiectum Mathematicae. Et ratio est, quia sub ente nihil continetur per accidens, sed per se: quod si sit aliqua scientia quae agit de aliquo ente rationis, illa nullo modo subordinatur Metaphysicae quatenus agit de ente reali, quia ens rationis ut sic non continetur sub ente reali, sed est primo diversum: quatenus vero Metaphysica agit de ente rationis, sic quodlibet ens rationis, non per accidens, sed per se continetur sub ente rationis ut sic, quod Metaphysicus considerat: non ergo intercedit propria & totalis subalternatio. Quod ipse etiam usus docet, alias esset Metaphysica ante omnes scientias acquirenda, quoniam sine illa nulla scientia esse posset: oppositum autem habet usus propter causas supra tactas, & nihilominus verae demonstrationes fiunt ex principiis per se notis sine Metaphysica, & praesertim in Mathematicis: non intercedit ergo vera subalternatio. Quod ⟨53a⟩ autem in una vel altera conclusione intercedat interdum, id non repugnat, ut ex principiis positis facile intelligi potest.

in order that we might briefly explain how metaphysics is related to the other sciences as regards this property as well.

51. From what has been said, then, it is clearly inferred that no property of a properly subalternating science agrees with metaphysics in its relation to the other sciences. For, in the first place, the other sciences do not depend altogether for their being sciences on metaphysics, since they do not depend on it for the entire evidence and certainty of their principles. For they have their own immediate and indemonstrable principles ostensively and directly, which is enough for them to be able to have the evidence of them immediately from the habit of principles, and this evidence suffices for generating science. For, although metaphysics can in some way demonstrate these principles, nevertheless, that demonstration is not without qualification necessary for an evident judgment of such principles, since they can be cognized in an evident way from their terms, and that demonstration is not properly *a priori*, but through deduction to the impossible, or at most through some extrinsic cause. Metaphysics, therefore, is not without qualification necessary for the evidence of these principles. Therefore, neither is it necessary in order for the habit produced from these principles to be a true science. Therefore, such a habit is not a science subalternate to metaphysics. Moreover, the objects of inferior sciences are not subordinate *per accidens* to being or substance, but *per se* and essentially, as is clear in the case of natural being, which is the object of philosophy, and in the case of quantity, which is the object of mathematics. And the reason is: because nothing is contained *per accidens* under being, but only *per se*. But if there is some science which treats of some being of reason, it is in no way subordinate to metaphysics insofar as metaphysics treats of real being, since being of reason as such is not contained under real being, but is primarily diverse from it. And insofar as metaphysics treats of the being of reason, in this way any being of reason is contained not *per accidens*, but *per se*, under being of reason as such, which the metaphysician considers. A proper and total subalternation, therefore, does not obtain. And experience itself teaches this, otherwise metaphysics would have to be acquired before all the sciences, since without it there could be no science. But this is contrary to experience, for the reasons

52. Quod si extenso vocabulo quis velit subalter[39b]nationem vocare illam excellentiam, & quasi imperium quod Metaphysica habet in alias scientias, quatenus earum principia potest aliquo modo stabilire, & confirmare, & quatenus magnam lucem omnibus affert, vel quatenus attingit ultimum finem, vel foelicitatem hominis, non est cum eo contendendum, cum de nomine disceptatio sit, praesertim cum graves *Simplicius.* autores interdum eo genere locutionis utantur, ut videre licet in Simplicio libr. 1. Physicor. tex. 8. & Themist. in Paraphr. ad 1. lib. Poster. capit. 2. Aristoteles vero nunquam est usus illo loquendi modo, neque illam proprietatem ad rationem sapientiae requisivit, sed solum ut aliis scientiis quodammodo dominetur, quod longe diversum est, ut ex dictis constat.

Interrogationi respondetur.   53. Hactenus ergo satis probata est secunda assertio, Metaphysicam scilicet esse veram sapientiam. Interrogabit vero aliquis quo modo prior & posterior assertio cohaereant: nam Aristoteles in Ethicis scientiam & sapientiam ponit species condistinctas sub genere virtutis intellectualis: nos vero doctrinam hanc simul facimus &[79] scientiam & sapientiam. *D. Thom.* Hoc autem facili negotio expeditur, si dicamus cum D. Th. 1. 2. q. 57. ar. 2. ad 1. Sapientiam condistingui a scientia, non quia scientia non sit, sed quia in latitudine scientiae habeat specialem gradum & dignitatem. Unde fit scientiam dupliciter sumi, uno modo generice ut dicit habitum per demonstrationem acquisitum, ut in primo Poster. capit. 2. definitur, ubi hac ratione nulla mentio fit sapientiae in particulari, quia solum agitur de scientia sub illa generali ratione sub qua sapientiam complectitur, & sic procedit prior assertio a nobis posita. Alio modo accipitur scientia magis stricte, prout dicit habitum qui solum versatur circa conclusiones demonstrabiles, & non circa ipsa principia, id est

---

79. This "&" appears here in M$_1$, P$_1$, P$_2$, S, V$_1$, and V$_2$. It is omitted in the following editions: C$_1$, C$_2$, G$_2$, M$_2$, M$_3$, M$_4$, V$_3$, V$_4$, V$_5$, and Vivès.

touched on above, and moreover, true demonstrations are made from principles that are known_n *per se* without metaphysics, and especially in mathematics. Therefore, a true subalternation does not obtain. And that it does sometimes obtain in the case of one conclusion or another is not an obstacle, as can easily be seen from the principles laid down.

52. But if, using the term in an extended sense, someone should want to call "subalternation" that excellence and (as it were) domin-ion which metaphysics has over the other sciences, insofar as it can in some way fix and confirm their principles, and insofar as it sheds great light on all of them, or insofar as it attains the ultimate end or happi-ness of the human being, then one ought not to dispute this, since the controversy will in that case be about a name, especially since serious authors sometimes make use of that kind of talk, as one can see in Sim- *Simplicius.* plicius, *Phys.* I, text 8,[262] and Themistius, in his Paraphrase of *Post. An.* I, ch. 2.[263] But Aristotle never employed that manner of speaking, nor did he require that property for the nature_r of wisdom: he required only that it rule over the other sciences in some way, which is very different, as is clear from what has been said.

53. So far, then, the second assertion has been sufficiently proved, *A question is* namely, that metaphysics is true wisdom. But someone will ask how *answered.* the earlier and later assertions harmonize,[264] for in the *Ethics* Aristotle states that science and wisdom are condistinct species under the genus of intellectual virtue,[265] whereas we make this doctrine both a science and wisdom at the same time. But this problem is easily solved if we say with St. Thomas, *ST* I-II, q. 57, art. 2, ad 1,[266] that wisdom is condis- *St. Thomas.* tinguished from science, not because it is not a science, but because within the compass of science it has a peculiar rank and worth. From

262. Simplicius, *Commentarii in octo Aristotelis Physicae Auscultationis libros* (Venetiis: Apud Iuntas, 1551), fol. 8ra–8va (commenting on 184b25–185a5).

263. I suspect that "2" is a misprint for "20," or, at any rate, that Suárez means to refer to book I, ch. 20, of Themistius's paraphrase, which is devoted to *Post. An.* I, ch. 9. See The-mistius, *Paraphrasis in Aristotelis Posteriora, & Physica. In libro[s] item de Anima, Memoria & Reminiscentia, Somno & Vigilia, Insomniis, & Divinatione per Somnum* (Venetiis: Apud Hieronymum Scotum, 1554), fol. 5va.

264. The "earlier" assertion, introduced at *DM* 1.5.2, was that metaphysics is the most perfect of all the speculative sciences.

265. Aristotle, *Nic. Eth.* VI, ch. 3, 1139b14–17.

266. Thomas Aquinas, *Sancti Thomae Aquinatis opera omnia* (Leonina), t. 6, p. 365b.

pro habitu qui solum scientia est, & nullo modo intellectus, ad eum utique sensum quo Aristoteles dixit sapientiam esse intellectum & scientiam: & in hoc sensu scientia distinguitur a sapientia, & sic dicimus Metaphysicam non esse scientiam huiusmodi, sed sapientiam. ⟨53b⟩

this it follows that science is taken in two ways: in one way, generically, insofar as it means a habit acquired through demonstration, as it is defined in *Post. An.* I, ch. 2,[267] where for this reason no mention is made of wisdom in particular, since science is dealt with there in accordance with that general account, according to which it includes wisdom, and in this way the first assertion laid down by us is correct. In another way, science is taken more strictly insofar as it means a habit which has to do only with demonstrable conclusions, and not with principles themselves, that is, a habit which is only a science and in no way understanding, and it is certainly in this sense that Aristotle said that wisdom is understanding and science. And in this sense science is distinguished from wisdom, and so we say that metaphysics is not such a science, but wisdom.

267. Aristotle, *Post. An.* I, ch. 2, 71b9–19.

Sᴇᴄᴛɪᴏ VI.

Uᴛʀᴜᴍ ɪɴᴛᴇʀ ᴏᴍɴᴇs sᴄɪᴇɴᴛɪᴀs Mᴇᴛᴀᴘʜʏsɪᴄᴀ ᴍᴀxɪᴍᴇ ᴀʙ ʜᴏᴍɪɴᴇ ᴀᴘᴘᴇᴛᴀᴛᴜʀ ᴀᴘᴘᴇᴛɪᴛᴜ ɴᴀᴛᴜʀᴀʟɪ.

Ratio proponendi quaestionem. 1. Hanc quaestionem praecipue propono propter Aristotelem in prooemio Metaphysicae, ut occasione illius nonnulla declaremus, quae ex illo prooemio declaranda supersunt, ne aut ea omnino praetereamus, aut necessarium nobis sit ad ea iterum redire. Confert etiam huius dubitationis expositio ad dignitatem huius doctrinae amplius commendandam, ex eo quod naturae hominis ut rationalis est, maxime est conformis, vel potius summa naturalis eius perfectio.

Aristoteles. 2. Aristoteles ergo lib. 1. Metaphysicae capit. 1. & 2. videtur directe intendere partem affirmantem huius dubii, nimirum naturalem hominis [40a] appetitum maxime ad Metaphysicam attrahi. Quod ut persuadeat, praemittit axioma illud, *Omnis homo naturaliter scire desiderat.*

Quis sit sensus illius pronunciati,
Omnis homo naturaliter scire desiderat.

3. Circa quod in primis sensum Aristotelis exponere oportet, deinde propositionis veritatem. Tres ergo termini in illa propositione declarandi sunt: prior est appetere vel desiderare. Circa quem supponenda est primo vulgaris distinctio duplicis appetitus, innati, & elicitivi. Prior im-*Quis sit appetitus innatus.* proprie ac metaphorice dictus est appetitus: proprie vero nihil aliud est quam naturalis propensio, quam unaquaeque res habet in aliquod bonum, quae inclinatio in potentiis passivis nihil aliud est quam naturalis capacitas, & proportio cum sua perfectione: in activis vero est ipsa naturalis facultas agendi. Itaque in his omnibus appetitus non addit aliq-

SECTION 6

WHETHER, AMONG ALL THE SCIENCES, METAPHYSICS
IS MOST OF ALL DESIRED BY THE HUMAN BEING BY
MEANS OF A NATURAL APPETITE.

—

1. I propose this question especially on account of what Aristotle *Reason for* says in the proem of the *Metaphysics*, in order that we might, on the *proposing the* occasion of it, explain some things from that proem which remain to *question.* be explained, lest we either pass them by altogether or find it necessary to return to them again. An exposition of this doubt also contributes to underlining the worth of this doctrine, because it is most of all in agreement with the nature of the human being insofar as she is rational, or rather, it is her highest natural perfection.

2. Aristotle, then, in *Metaph.* I, chs. 1 and 2, seems immediately to *Aristotle.* aim at an affirmative reply to this question, namely, at the claim that the natural appetite of the human being is most of all drawn to metaphysics. In order to persuade us of this, he takes the following axiom as a premise: "Every human being naturally desires to know."[268]

> *What the meaning of this proposition is: "Every human*
> *being naturally desires to know."*

3. Regarding this, we must begin by making Aristotle's meaning clear, and then show the truth of the proposition. Therefore, three terms in that proposition must be explained: the first is "to seek" or "to desire." With respect to this term, the common distinction between two appetites—innate and elicitive—must first be assumed. The former *What an* is improperly and metaphorically called an appetite and is properly *innate* nothing other than a natural propensity which each thing_r has to some *appetite is.*

268. Aristotle, *Metaph.* I, ch. 1, 980a21.

275

uid ultra ipsam rei naturam, vel proximam facultatem, ratione cuius convenit rei talis appetitus. Neque in hoc appetitu distingui potest actus primus & secundus, quia hoc modo appetere non est agere aliquid, sed solum habere innatam talem propensionem, qualem habet gravitas ad centrum, etiam si nihil agat. Appetitus elicitivus est proprie appetitus, quia fertur in bonum ut bonum, illudque per proprium actum potest appetere. Unde duo sunt in hoc appetitu (loquimur in creaturis) unum est facultas appetendi, aliud appetitio ipsa. Primum reti⟨54a⟩nuit iam nomen appetitus, qui in sensitivum & rationalem dividitur: & hic appetitus ut sic etiam est innatus, si generatim de innato loquamur, quia cum ipsa natura datus est, & habet naturalem propensionem ad suum obiectum, & ad suum actum. Quia vero ita est innatus ut sit etiam elicitivus actualis appetitionis qua tendit in bonum formaliter, & quatenus bonum est, atque ita sit propriissime appetitus, ideo condistinguitur ab appetitu pure innato & metaphorico: sic enim prior divisio accipienda est. Secundum, id est actus appetendi, qui proprie dicitur appetitio, vel appetitus elicitus, nihil aliud est quam actus elicitus ab appetitu eliciente, quo[80] amat, vel desiderat bonum: & hic appetitus nunquam est innatus, saltem in nobis, de quibus in praesenti agimus: interdum vero est naturalis, ut inferius ex professo magis declarabo.

Quis elicitivus.

4. Alter igitur terminus exponendus, erat *naturaliter*: appetitus enim naturalis multipliciter dicitur, interdum enim naturale dicitur quod ab ipsa natura datum est, neque est effectum per propriam ipsius hominis, verbi gratia, actionem, seu effectionem. Et hoc modo omnis appetitus innatus, naturalis est, & ipse etiam appetitus elicitivus: non tamen appetitus seu actus elicitus, ut ex data terminorum expositione satis constat. Aliquando vero dicitur naturale quod necessario fit ex intrinseca propensione naturae, etiam si absolute & in se non sit a

Quot modis dicatur naturale.

---

80. All the early editions that I've consulted read "quo" here. Vivès reads "quod."

good, and this inclination in passive potencies is nothing other than a natural capacity for, and proportion to, their perfection, whereas in active potencies it is the natural faculty for acting itself. Thus, in all these potencies the appetite does not add something to the very nature of the thing$_r$, or to the immediate faculty by virtue of which the appetite agrees with such a thing$_r$. And in this appetite a first and second act cannot be distinguished, since to desire in this way is not to do something, but merely to have an innate propensity of the sort that heaviness has towards the center, even if it does nothing. An elicitive appetite is properly an appetite, since it is borne to the good as good, and it can desire the good through a proper act. For this reason, there are two things in this kind of appetite (we are speaking of creatures): one is the faculty of appetition, the other is the appetition itself. The first has retained the name "appetite" and is divided into sensitive and rational, and this appetite, as such, is also innate, if we speak in a general way of the innate, since it is given with the nature itself and has a natural propensity to its object and to its act. But since it is innate in such a way that it is also elicitive of actual appetition, by which it tends to the good formally and insofar as it is good, and is thus most properly appetite, it is therefore condistinguished from a purely innate and metaphorical appetite: for so is the former division to be understood. The second, that is, the act of appetition, which is properly called appetition, or elicited appetite, is nothing other than the act elicited by an eliciting appetite, by which it loves or desires the good. And this appetite is never innate, at least in us, with whom we are now dealing, but it is sometimes natural, as I shall *ex professo* make clear below.

What an elicitive appetite is.

4. The second term that must be explained is "naturally," since an appetite is called natural in many ways, for sometimes we call natural that which is given by nature itself and is not produced by (for example) a proper action or effecting of the human being herself. And in this way every innate appetite is natural, and an elicitive appetite is as well; but an elicited appetite or act is not, as is clear enough from the given explanation of terms. But sometimes we call natural that which necessarily comes about due to an intrinsic propensity of nature, even if absolutely and in itself it is not given by nature, but is produced by the thing that desires. And in this sense the appetite of hunger or thirst

In how many ways "natural" is said.

natura datum, sed ab appetente factum: & hoc modo est homini naturalis appetitus qui est fames, aut sitis, quando deficit cibus, [40b] aut potus: qua ratione appetitus elicitus, naturalis esse potest, & in appetitu sensitivo ex se semper talis est: in voluntate vero licet interdum talis appetitus sit naturalis, non tamen semper, quia libera est. Omitto, interdum sumi naturale ut a supernaturali distinguitur, quo sensu apud naturales Philosophos, seu procedendo ex solo lumine naturae, ut nunc loquimur, omnis appetitus naturalis est, nam supernaturalis appetendi modus, qui per gratiam fit, non potest naturali ratione investigari. Aliquando etiam sumitur naturale ut violento opponitur, ut est frequens in Philosophia. Atque his etiam duobus modis appetitus elicitus etiam si liber sit, naturalis tamen esse potest, ut per se constat. Imo interdum dicitur naturalis appetitus elicitus, hoc ipso quod est naturae consentaneus, & opponitur ei quod est praeternaturale tan⟨54b⟩quam naturae dissonum, etiam si violentum non sit: quo modo appetitus virtutis, naturalis est, vitii autem minime. Quo tandem fit ut multo magis naturalis dicatur appetitus ille ad quem ipsa naturae propensio necessitatem infert: & ideo appetitus necessarius, tametsi elicitus, naturalis merito vocari potest.

5. Duplex autem necessitas huius appetitus distingui solet, scilicet quoad exercitium, & quoad specificationem. Prior est quando appetitus vitalis ex necessitate elicit seu exercet actum appetendi: quae necessitas in appetitu sensitivo facile reperitur: in rationali vero non invenitur in hac vita, sed solum in beata & supernaturali, quae ad nostram considerationem non spectat. Posterior in hoc consistit quod licet voluntas non exerceat actum appetendi ex necessitate, tamen si exercet, necessario appetit, & non refugit tale obiectum, & talis actus vocatur necessarius quoad speciem, non quoad exercitium: & secundum eam necessitatem dicitur naturalis, & recedit ab actu omni ex parte libero, quoad exercitium scilicet, & specificationem: quo modo voluntas appetit bonum in communi. Ex his ergo satis clara manet illius vocis ambiguitas.

is natural to the human being when food or drink is lacking. For this reason an elicited appetite can be natural, and it is of itself always such in the case of sensitive appetite. But in the case of the will, although such an appetite is sometimes natural, still, it is not always natural, since the will is free. I leave aside the fact that, sometimes, the natural is taken insofar as it is distinguished from the supernatural, in which sense, among natural philosophers, or those proceeding only by the light of nature (as we are now), every appetite is natural, for the supernatural mode of appetition, which comes about through grace, cannot be investigated by natural reason. Also, sometimes the natural is taken insofar as it is opposed to the violent, as is often the case in philosophy. And in these two ways an elicited appetite, even if it is free, can nonetheless be natural, as is clear *per se*. In fact, sometimes an elicited appetite is called natural because it is in agreement with nature and is opposed to that which, although not violent, is preternatural because at variance with nature; in this sense the appetite for virtue is natural, but the appetite for vice is not at all so. From this it follows, finally, that that appetite upon which the very propensity of nature bestows necessity is called natural to a much higher degree; and therefore, a necessary appetite, even if elicited, can rightly be called natural.

5. The necessity of this appetite is normally distinguished into two kinds, namely, with respect to exercise and with respect to specification. The first is when a vital appetite necessarily elicits or exercises its act of appetition, and this necessity is easily found in sensitive appetite, but in rational appetite it is not found in this life, but only in the blessed and supernatural one, which is not our concern here. The second consists in this, that, although the will does not exercise the act of appetition necessarily, nevertheless, if it exercises an act, it necessarily desires, and does not flee from, an object of a certain type, and such an act is called necessary with respect to species, not with respect to exercise. And in accordance with this necessity it is called natural and falls short of an act that is in every respect free (that is, free with respect to both exercise and specification). It is in this way that the will desires the good in general. On the basis of what we've said, the ambiguity of this word is sufficiently clear.

Scientia quot modis dicatur.

6. Tertia vox est *scientia*, seu *scire*, quae ab Aristotele indefinite sumitur: & potest generatim sumi pro quacunque cognitione seu intelligentia veritatis, sed praesertim pro illa quae perfecta est, & propriam rationem scientiae habet, prout scire dicitur esse, rem per causam cognoscere cum evidentia, & certitudine. Et de scientia etiam hoc modo sumpta loqui possumus, vel indefinite, vel abstracte, vel distributive de omnibus scientiis, vel singulariter de aliqua, qui modi loquendi de scientia non parum inter se discrepant.

Omnes scientias appetit homo.

7. Incipiendo ergo ab hoc ultimo termino, certum est Aristotelem in illo generali dogmate non loqui de aliqua singulari scientia, ut patet, tum ex verbis eius, tum ex probatione, quae generalis est, tum denique ex intentione: assumit enim hoc generale principium, ut inde ad hanc scientiam in particulari descendat. Atque haec ratio ulterius concludit quod, licet Aristotelis verba indefinita sint, tamen cum sint doctrinalia, aequivalent universalibus: ita ut sensus sit omnes homines naturaliter appetere quamcunque scientiam: tum quia non ex peculiari ratione alicuius scientiae ut talis est, oritur hic appetitus, sed ex ⟨55a⟩ ratione scientiae ut sic, tum etiam quia alias [41a] non satis efficaciter procederetur in eo discursu ab indefinito sermone ad singularem. Haec est ergo mens Aristotelis: eamque sententiam in eo sensu veram esse patebit facile ex dicendis.

Appetitu innato. Scotus. Iavell. Flandria.

8. Rursus existimant multi expositores hic, praesertim Scotus & sequaces, Aristotelem loqui de appetitu innato: nec D. Tho. ab ea sententia abhorret, unde illam sequuntur Iavellus & Flandria. Neque est dubium quin eo sensu verissima sit propositio, quam variis rationibus D. Thomas confirmat. Summa earum[81] est, quia omnis res naturaliter appetit suam perfectionem, operationem, & foelicitatem: sed omnibus his modis comparatur scientia ad hominem: est enim magna perfectio eius, & operatio ipsius, & in ea eius foelicitas consistit. In qua ratione duo priora membra communia sunt omnibus scientiis, tertium vero est huius proprium, ut dicemus. Unde etiam existimo Aristotelem non ex-

---

81. Reading "earum" here with C_1, C_2, G_2, M_1, M_2, M_3, M_4, P_1, P_2, S, V_1, V_2, V_3, and V_4. The following editions have "eorum": V_5 and Vivès.

6. The third word is "knowledge" or "to know," which is taken indefinitely by Aristotle. And it can be taken in a general way for any cognition or understanding of the truth, but especially for that cognition which is perfect and has the proper nature$_r$ of knowledge, insofar as knowing is said to be cognizing a thing$_r$ through its cause with evidence and certainty. And of knowledge taken in this way also we can speak indefinitely or abstractly or distributively of all sciences, or individually of some science, and these ways of speaking about knowledge differ among themselves to no small degree.[269]

In how many ways "knowledge" is said.

7. Beginning, then, from this last term, it is certain that in this general teaching Aristotle is not speaking of some individual science, as is clear from his words, from his proof (which is general), and finally, from his aim, for he assumes this general principle in order that he might descend from there to this science in particular. And this consideration$_r$ further shows that, although Aristotle's words are indefinite, nevertheless, since they are doctrinal, his pronouncement is equivalent to a universal claim, so that the sense is that all human beings naturally desire any knowledge whatsoever, both because this appetite does not arise from the special nature$_r$ of some particular science insofar as it is such, but from the nature$_r$ of science as such, and also because otherwise he would not be proceeding in his argument in a sufficiently effective way from indefinite to singular language. This, therefore, is Aristotle's meaning. And that this opinion in this sense is true will easily be seen from the things that are to be said.

A human being desires all the sciences.

8. Further, many expositors, especially Scotus and his followers, think that here Aristotle is speaking of an innate appetite. And St. Thomas[270] does not shrink from this view, for which reason Javelli[271] and Dominic of Flanders[272] follow it. And there is no doubt that in this sense the proposition is most true, and St. Thomas confirms

By an innate appetite. Scotus. Javelli. Flanders.

269. The reader is reminded that in this translation "knowledge" and "science" render one and the same Latin word, "*scientia.*" The word "knowledge" is often used here, in part, because English lacks a verb related to "science" in the way that "*scire*" (here invariably rendered "to know") is related to "*scientia*" in Latin.

270. Thomas Aquinas, *In duodecim libros metaphysicorum Aristotelis expositio*, p. 6 (bk. I, lect. 1, ns. 2–4).

271. Giovanni Crisostomo Javelli, *Opera*, t. 1, p. 713a.

272. Dominic of Flanders, *In Duodecim Libros Metaphysicae Aristotelis*, p. 15 (bk. I, q. 2, art. 1).

clusisse hunc sensum, sed supposuisse potius. Quod autem in illo solo locutus fuerit, nec necessarium videtur, nec verum. Quod ex proprietate verborum eius colligi potest, nam ex sensuum dilectione & amore colligit scientiae appetitum: loquitur autem aperte de amore sensuum per actum elicitum: id enim proprie amor significat, & inferius similiter ait, quod sensum visus caeteris anteponimus, nimirum in elicito amore. Et quanquam dici posset verum esse Aristotelem in ea ratione loqui de actu elicito, & ex illo colligere appetitum naturalem, certe ea collectio bona non esset, nisi supponeret illum elicitum amorem esse etiam aliquo modo naturalem: quia non ex quolibet appetitu elicito colligi potest appetitus naturalis, nam interdum appetimus actu voluntatis quae ipsi naturae repugnant, ut mortem v. g. ergo si ex appetitu elicito colligit Aristoteles naturalem, supponit ipsum elicitum esse etiam naturalem: quod si amor elicitus sensuum est naturalis, multo magis amor scientiae.

Appetitu etiam elicito. 9. Dicendum est ergo hominem appetitu etiam elicito scientiam amare. Hoc probant rationes insinuatae ex D. Thoma: illae enim aeque procedunt de appetitu elicito, & de pondere naturae: quia etiam homo hoc appetitu appetit naturaliter suam perfectionem, operationem, & foelicitatem: sed scientia est perfectissima hominis operatio, & vel est foelicitas ipsa, vel ad foelici⟨55b⟩tatem, & commodum huius vitae maxime necessaria. Nam si sit contemplativa scientia, in perfectissima eius operatione foelicitas consistit, ut dicitur lib. 10. Ethic. cap. 6. aliae vero scientiae speculativae illi superiori deserviunt, & in omnibus est magna quaedam iucunditas: nam contemplari optimum est 12. Metaphysicorum, text. trigesimonono. Practicae vero scientiae ad commoda etiam huius vitae necessariae sunt, vel valde utiles.

it by means of various arguments. The best of them is: because every thing꜀ naturally desires its perfection, operation, and happiness; but knowledge is related in all these ways to the human being, since it is a great perfection and operation of the human being, and in it consists the human being's happiness. In this argument the two prior items are common to all the sciences, but the third is proper to this one, as we shall say. For this reason I think that Aristotle did not mean to exclude this sense of "appetite," but rather presupposed it. But that he spoke only in this sense seems neither necessary nor true. This can be inferred from the proper signification of his words, for he infers the appetite for knowledge from our affection for, and love of, the senses, and he speaks openly of the love of the senses by an elicited act, for love properly signifies this, and later he likewise says that we prefer the sense of sight to the other senses, undoubtedly with an elicited love. And although it could be said that it is true that Aristotle, in this argument, is speaking of an elicited act, and that from this he infers a natural appetite, certainly that inference would not be good unless he were assuming that that elicited love is also in some way natural, since a natural appetite cannot be inferred from any old elicited appetite, for sometimes we desire by an act of the will things that are incompatible with nature itself, like death, for example. Therefore, if Aristotle infers a natural appetite from an elicited one, he is assuming that the same elicited appetite is also natural. But if an elicited love of the senses is natural, much more so is the love of knowledge.

9. It must therefore be said that the human being loves knowledge with an elicited appetite as well. The arguments handed down by St. Thomas prove this, for they succeed equally regarding an elicited appetite and an inclination of nature, since the human being also naturally desires her own perfection, operation, and happiness with this appetite. But knowledge is the most perfect operation of the human being, and either it is happiness itself or it is most of all necessary for the happiness and good of this life. For if it is contemplative knowledge, happiness consists in its most perfect operation, as is said in *Ethics* X, ch. 6.[273] And the other speculative sciences serve that superior one, and in all

And also by an elicited appetite.

273. Aristotle discusses contemplation as the highest happiness in *Nic. Eth.* X, chs. 6 through 8.

Exponitur doctrina Aristotelis de visus,
aliorumque sensuum dilectione.

10. Praeterea discursus Aristotelis ex dilectione sensuum, & praesertim visus, desumptus, optimus est ad idem confirmandum. Duo autem sumit Aristoteles in eo discursu: primum est quod in dilectione sensuum visum anteponimus: secundum est, causam huius esse quia ad scientiam maxime [41b] deservit. Ex quibus infert tertium, scilicet amorem scientiae esse maiorem, magisque naturalem, quam ipsius visus, aliorumque sensuum. Quae consecutio videtur per se evidens, & fundata in eo principio, propter quod unumquodque tale, & illud magis. Prima autem propositio assumpta, in primis intelligenda est cum praecisione, ut recte fiat comparatio: tactus enim inveniri potest sine visu, non vero e contrario, quia tactus est omnium sensuum primus, aliorumque fundamentum. Unde destructo tactu non potest naturaliter visus manere: quia nec vita sine tactu conservatur, 3. de anim. cap. 12. & 13. & lib. de sensu, & sensib. cap. 1.[82] Quatenus ergo visus quodammodo includit tactum, appetibilior erit visus quam solus tactus: & in contrario sensu quatenus amissio tactus includit amissionem visus, & non e converso, praefertur tactus visui, quia potius eliget homo conservationem tactus quam visus, si ad amissionem tactus visus necessario amittendus est. Haec vero comparatio sic intellecta nullius momenti est, quia non comparantur singuli sensus inter se, sed duo ad unum qui in eis includitur: est ergo comparatio praecise facienda in eo quod singuli per se conferunt.

---

82. Reading "3. de anim. c. 12. & 13. lib. de sensu, & sensib. cap. 1." All the early editions that I've consulted read: "3 de Anim., c. 12, & lib. 13 de Sensu & sens., c. 1." However, Aristotle's *De sensu* doesn't have 13 chapters, much less 13 books. Moreover, that the life of an animal depends on the sense of touch is a point made in *De anima* III, ch. 13 (see 435b4–5).

of them there is a certain great delight, for to contemplate is the best thing, as *Metaph.* XII, text 39, says.[274] But the practical sciences are also necessary, or very useful, for the goods of this life.

Aristotle's doctrine regarding the love of
sight and the other senses is explained.

10. Moreover, Aristotle's reasoning, taken from the love of the senses, and especially from the love of sight, is best for confirming this. Aristotle assumes two things in this argument. The first is that, when it comes to the love of the senses, we prefer sight. The second is that the reason for this is that it is the most useful for knowledge. From these points he infers a third, namely, that the love of knowledge is greater and more natural than the love of sight itself and the love of the other senses. This consequence seems *per se* evident and seems to be founded on this principle: "That on account of which each thing is such is such to a greater degree." But the first assumed proposition is in the first place to be understood with a precision, in order that the comparison might rightly be made, for touch can be found without sight, but not vice versa, since touch is the first of all the senses and the foundation of the rest. For this reason, if touch is destroyed, sight cannot naturally remain, since neither is life without touch preserved, as is said in *De anima* III, chs. 12 and 13, and *On Sense*, ch. 1.[275] Therefore, insofar as sight in some way includes touch, sight will be more desirable than touch alone. And conversely, insofar as the loss of touch includes the loss of sight, but not vice versa, touch is preferred to sight, since the human being will rather choose the preservation of touch than the preservation of sight if, upon the loss of touch, sight must necessarily be lost. But this comparison, so understood, is of no importance here, since the individual senses are not being compared among themselves, but two are being compared to one which is included in them. Therefore, the comparison must be made precisely with respect to that which the individual senses supply *per se*.

<hr>

274. Aristotle, *Metaph.* XII, ch. 7, 1072b24.
275. Aristotle, *De anima* III, ch. 12, 434b8–24, ch. 13, 435b4–19, and *De sensu*, ch. 1, 436b13–15.

11. Deinde est observandum Aristotelem hic duplicem amorem sensuum indicare. Unus est ob utilitatem: alter vero propter cognitionem. Prior est per se notissimus: & sub utilitate comprehendi potest omnis commoditas corporis, pertinens vel ad conservationem eius, vel ad delectationem, vel ad alias opera⟨56a⟩tiones humanae vitae. Posterior amor est maxime proprius hominis, & in ordine ad hunc amorem praecipue comparatur hic visus cum aliis sensibus, eisque praefertur. Quod experimento probat Aristoteles, quia nihil (inquit) acturi ipsum visum aliis anteponimus. Rationem autem a priori, & quae ad rem praesentem maxime spectat, reddit in altera propositione. Circa quam est tertio notandum duos esse modos acquirendi scientiam, scilicet disciplinam, & inventionem. Ad priorem modum utilissimus est auditus, ut per se constat, quia voces sunt signa conceptuum, solus autem auditus voces percipit, & quanvis ipse non percipiat earum significationem, sed mens, satis est quod sit organum proprium, quo mediante tale signum ad mentem pervenit. Hic tamen excessus, & est per accidens, & mini-

Visus & auditus inter se comparantur.   mus. Per accidens quidem, quia modus acquirendi scientiam per disciplinam, est quasi per accidens, nam & supponit alium, loquendo secundum naturas rerum, & solum est ad supplendam imperfectionem, vel negligentiam hominum in vacando scientiis inveniendis. Minimum autem excessum appello, quia etiam visus plurimum deservit ad disciplinam: nam etiam scripturae sunt signa conceptuum, & illae percipiuntur visu: unde multo plura videntur addisci lectione, quae visu fit, quam auditione. Est tamen discrimen quod tota fere utilitas scripturae

Lege Aristotelis de sensu & sensibilibus.   potest etiam auditu percipi, non tamen e converso: ea enim energia, vis, ac claritas, quae est in voce ad exprimendos proprios conceptus, non potest scriptura sola aut visu suppleri: unde legimus nonnullos carentes visu, fuisse doctissimos, partim auditis solis scriptis aliorum, partim etiam explicationibus seu doctrinis viva voce sibi propositis: quod vero aliquis omnino surdus evaserit doctissi[42a]mus, me legisse non memini, & vix id fieri posse existimo. Non igitur comparantur hic ab Aristotele hi sensus quoad hoc munus, sed quoad modum acquirendi scientiam per inventionem. In quo dubium non est quin visus, & tactus, tam auditum, quam alios sensus superent, quod adeo notum est, ut non egeat probatione: solum de comparatione visus & tactus inter se, breviter dicendum superest.

11. Next, it must be observed that Aristotle here signals a twofold love of the senses. One is on account of utility, while the other is on account of cognition. The first is most known_n *per se*, and every bodily advantage relating to the body's preservation, to its delight, or to the other operations of human life can be comprehended under utility. The second love is most of all proper to the human being, and it is in reference to this love especially that sight is here compared to the other senses and is preferred to them. This Aristotle proves by experience, since when we are going to do nothing, he says, we prefer sight to the other senses. And he gives an *a priori* reason, which is most of all relevant to the matter at hand, in the next proposition. Concerning this proposition, it is to be noted, third, that there are two ways of acquiring knowledge, namely, instruction and discovery.[276] For the first way hearing is the most useful, as is clear *per se*, since words are signs of concepts, and only hearing perceives words. And although not hearing itself, but the mind, perceives their signification, it is enough that hearing is the proper instrument through the mediation of which such a sign reaches the mind. This preeminence, however, is both *per accidens* and insignificant. *Per accidens*, to be sure, because the way of acquiring knowledge through instruction is, as it were, *per accidens*, since it both presupposes the other way of acquiring knowledge, speaking in accordance with the natures of things_r, and is only for making good the imperfection of human beings or their negligence when it comes to devoting themselves to the discovery of the sciences. And I call this preeminence insignificant because sight also helps to a great degree for learning: for written words also are signs of concepts, and they are perceived by sight, for which reason many more things seem to be learned by reading, which occurs through sight, than by hearing. Nonetheless, there is a difference, namely, that nearly the whole benefit of writing can be had also by hearing, but not conversely, for that energy, strength, and clarity which exists in speech for expressing proper concepts cannot be made good by writing alone or by sight,

Sight and hearing are compared to each other.

See Aristotle's On Sense and Sensibles.[277]

276. The word here rendered "instruction" is "*disciplina*," which is later in this paragraph rendered "learning." I use the term "instruction" here in order to underline the fact that the learning Suárez has in mind is of the particular sort that involves instruction. We speak of researchers and discoverers as learning, too, after all.

277. Aristotle, *De sensu*, ch. 1, 436b18–437a17.

Comparatio visus cum tactu.

12. Est igitur advertendum quarto, aliud esse loqui de signo (ut ita dicam) melioris facultatis, maiorisque aptitudinis ad scientiam acquirendam: ⟨56b⟩ aliud de aptiori instrumento inveniendae scientiae: tactus enim priori ratione visum superat, quia tactus est universalis sensus ex parte subiecti: nam est per totum corpus diffusus, & est signum optimae, & temperatae complexionis; unde est illud, *Molles carnes aptae sunt ingenio,* de quo latius in 2. de anima tex. 34.[83] At visus per se, & ut instrumentum ad scientiam, multis modis tactum superat. Primo in latitudine obiecti, plures enim differentias percipit, ut hic dixit Aristoteles, & circa caelestia & terrestria vagatur, & rerum motus, actiones, & figuras perspicacius cognoscit, quam ullus alius sensus: sunt autem haec veluti prima signa, & indicia, quibus ad res cognoscendas utimur. Secundo citius quam alii sensus percipit, cum tamen ad res etiam distantissimas se se extendat, & causa est quod puriori & immaterialiori modo, & absque alteratione materiali operationem suam perficit. Tertio vehementius imprimit phantasiae quae percipit, quod experimento constat: nam tenacius inhaerent memoriae, & facilius postea occurrunt. Causa autem esse videtur, quod eius operatio sicut spiritualior est, ita maiori vi animae & conatu, & cooperatione etiam maiori ipsius phantasiae fit. Quarto experimentum visus certius esse videtur experimento tactus, per se loquendo: etsi enim Aristotel. libr. primo de histor. animal. capit. 15. dicat tactum in homine esse exquisitissimum, ibi tamen

---

83. Reading "34" here with M₁, P₁, P₂, S, V₁, and V₂. Suárez, however, seems actually to have in mind *De anima* II, text 94. The following editions read "24": C₁, C₂, G₂, M₂, M₃, M₄, V₃, V₄, V₅, and Vivès.

which is why we read that some people lacking sight were very learned, partly because they had merely heard the writings of others, and partly also because explanations or doctrines were presented to them *viva voce*. But that someone altogether deaf became very learned I do not remember having read, and I can hardly believe that this can happen. These senses, therefore, are not here compared by Aristotle with respect to this function,[278] but with respect to the way of acquiring knowledge through discovery. And in this regard there is no doubt that sight and touch surpass both hearing and the other senses, which is so well known_n that it requires no proof. It remains only to speak briefly of the comparison of sight and touch to each other.

12. It is therefore to be noticed, fourth, that it is one thing to speak of what is a sign (as it were) of both a better faculty and a greater aptitude for acquiring knowledge, and another to speak of a more suitable instrument for discovering knowledge. For touch surpasses sight as regards the former consideration_r, since touch is the universal sense on the side of the subject, for it is diffused throughout the entire body, and it is a sign of an excellent and tempered complexion. Hence the claim that "soft flesh is joined to intelligence," of which more is said in *De anima* II, text 34.[279] But sight *per se*, and as an instrument for knowledge, surpasses touch in many ways. First, with respect to the extension of its object, for it perceives more differences, as Aristotle says here, and it ranges over things heavenly and terrestrial, and it cognizes more perspicaciously than any other sense the motions, actions, and figures of things_r, and these are, as it were, the first signs and marks that we employ for cognizing things_r. Second, it perceives more quickly than the other senses do, even though it extends even to the most distant things_r, and the cause of this is that it completes its operation in a purer and more immaterial way, and without material alteration. Third, it more vehemently impresses the things that it perceives on the imagination, which is clear from experience, for they inhere more firmly in memory and thereafter more easily present themselves. The cause of this seems to be that, just as its operation is more spiritual, so it occurs with great-

Comparison of sight with touch.

278. Sc. the function of acquiring knowledge through instruction.

279. Suárez seems actually to have in mind *De anima* II, text 94 (421a18–26), and more precisely, 421a25–26.

non comparat sensus hominis inter se, & respectu ipsius hominis, sed
cum sensibus aliorum animalium: & hoc modo ait hominem superare
alia animalia in tactu & gustu, cum tamen in aliis sensibus superetur
a multis, saltem in multis conditionibus sentiendi, ut ab aquila in per-
spicacia & fortitudine visus: non tamen ait tactum hominis superare
visum in certitudine. Quin potius Sectione 31. Problem. quaestione 18.
inquit tactum aemulari visum. Itaque quilibet horum sensuum habet
suam certitudinem in ordine ad proprium adaequatum obiectum: interdum vero deficit circa communia sensibilia ex insufficiente applica-
tione: & fortasse, quia visus eminus sentit, & non tactus: ideo facilius
contingit obiectum visus indebite applicari, ac visum decipi: si tamen
caetera sint paria quoad applicationem obiecti, & dispositionem potentiae, non magis accidit deceptio in visu, quam in tactu. Et aliunde visus
ob suam immaterialitatem percipit acutius obiectum, & ex hac parte
certior est: ideoque frequentius adhiberi solet ad certitudinem de ⟨57a⟩
rebus sensibilibus accipiendam. His ergo de causis visus est simpliciter
utilior ad scientias, eamque ob rem naturaliter magis diligitur: signum
ergo est, ut Aristoteles concludit, quod & ipsa scientia naturaliter ab
homine diligitur. [42b]

er force and effort on the part of the soul, and also with greater cooperation on the part of the imagination itself. Fourth, the experience of sight seems to be more certain than the experience of touch, speaking *per se*, for even if Aristotle, *Hist. An.* I, ch. 15,[280] says that touch in the human being is the most excellent, there he is not comparing the human being's senses with each other, and in relation to the human being herself, but with the senses of other animals, and thus he says that the human being surpasses other animals with respect to touch and taste, even though, with respect to the other senses, the human being is surpassed by many animals, at least in the case of many characteristics of sensing—for instance, by the eagle, with respect to the acuity and strength of sight. But he does not say that in the human being touch surpasses sight with respect to certainty; rather, in *Problems* XXXI, q. 18, he says that touch imitates sight.[281] Thus any of these senses has its certainty in relation to its proper adequate object, but sometimes it falls short with respect to the common sensibles because of insufficient application. And perhaps because sight senses at a distance, but touch does not, it more easily happens that the object of sight is not applied as it should be and sight is deceived. But if other things are equal with respect to the application of the object and the disposition of the power, deception does not occur more in sight than in touch. And otherwise sight, on account of its immateriality, perceives its object more sharply and is in this respect more certain. And therefore, it is normally used more frequently for acquiring certainty regarding sensible things$_r$. For these reasons, therefore, sight is without qualification more useful for the sciences, and is therefore naturally more loved. This, therefore, is a sign that knowledge itself is also naturally loved by the human being, as Aristotle concludes.

---

280. Aristotle, *Hist. An.* I, ch. 15, 494b16–18.

281. See Aristotle, *Problems*, XXXI, ch. 17, 959a9–19. In this text, Aristotle raises the question why, under certain circumstances, a single line is presented to sight as double. It is after noting that a similar doubling effect takes place with respect to touch under certain circumstances that Aristotle says: "for then touch imitates [μιμεῖται] sight" (959a18–19). The claim, in other words, is that in some circumstances touch errs as sight does with respect to certain common sensibles.

De appetitu elicito scientiae.

13. Sed quo sensu intelligendum sit hominem appetere naturaliter scientiam appetitu elicito, explicandum superest. Non enim in eo sensu hoc accipi potest quod homo aut ex necessitate semper exerceat amorem vel desiderium scientiae, quoties de illa cogitat: neque quod illam spernere non possit, eamque inquirere nolle: utrumque enim contra experientiam est: non ergo potest hic appetitus elicitus esse naturalis tanquam necessarius omnino, vel quoad exercitium, vel quoad specificationem. Primum ergo certum est hunc appetitum recte dici naturalem, quod sit valde consentaneus naturae hominis, eiusque naturali inclinationi, quatenus homo est. Unde recte Cicer. 2. de Finib. *Natura* (inquit) *ingenuit homini cupiditatem veri inveniendi.* Secundo dicitur naturalis, quia est aliquo modo necessarius quoad specificationem: tum quia, licet homo possit negligere scientiam, vel nolle illam quoad appetitum efficacem quaerendi illam: id tamen solum accidere potest propter extrinsecas causas seu impedimenta quae ex accidente adiunguntur scientiae, nimirum propter laborem & difficultatem quam habet scientiae studium, aut quia impedit aliarum rerum inquisitionem, quibus homo vel indiget, vel affectus est, vel ob alias similes causas: unde rudiores ingenio minus videntur scientiam appetere ob difficultatem, quam etiam impossibilitatem vocavit Aristotel. 5.[84] Politicor. ca. ult. At vero per se se scientia non potest displicere: atque ita seclusis impedimentis, necessitate quadam amatur, saltem quoad specificationem. Atque hoc quidem maxime verum habet in scientia in communi quatenus scientia est, tamen etiam est suo modo verum de qualibet scientia in particulari, si in ea veritatis cognitio in tali materia per se spectetur: semper enim est illa perfectio per se expetibilis homini. Quod si contingit hominem unam scientiam non amare ut alteri intendat, hoc etiam reducitur ad extrinseca impedimenta, de quibus diximus: nam quia homo non potest utramque scientiam acquirere, & unius studio ab alterius perfecta in⟨57b⟩quisitione impediretur, ideo illam omittit, ut hanc obtineat. Atque hoc modo quidam homines ex individuali & propria complexione, ad unam scientiam magis afficiuntur, quam ad

Cicero.

---

84. Reading "5." here with M₁, P₁, P₂, S, V₁, and V₂. The following editions read "6" instead: C₁, C₂, G₂, M₂, M₃, M₄, V₃, V₄, V₅, and Vivès.

Regarding the elicited appetite for science.

13. But it remains to be explained in what sense the human being should be understood naturally to desire knowledge with an elicited appetite. For this cannot be understood to mean either that the human being necessarily always exercises a love or desire for knowledge whenever she thinks of it, or that she cannot spurn it or be unwilling to search after it, for both are contrary to experience. This elicited appetite cannot, therefore, be natural by being altogether necessary, either with respect to exercise or with respect to specification. In the first place, then, it is certain that this appetite is rightly called natural because it is very much in agreement with the nature of the human being, and with her natural inclination, insofar as she is a human being. For this reason, Cicero, *On Moral Ends* II, rightly says: "Nature begets in the human being a desire to discover the true."[282] Second, it is called natural by virtue of the fact that it is in some way necessary with respect to specification, because, although a human being can neglect knowledge, or can fail to want it to the point of having an efficacious appetite for seeking it, nevertheless, that can happen only on account of extrinsic causes or obstacles which are conjoined accidentally to knowledge, no doubt because of the labor and difficulty involved in the pursuit of knowledge, or because it prevents the search for other things, which the human being either needs or is drawn to, or for other similar causes. And for this reason those with a rather uncultivated intelligence seem to desire knowledge less on account of difficulty, which Aristotle, in *Pol.* V, the final chapter, even calls an impossibility.[283] But knowledge cannot be displeasing *per se*, and so, setting impediments aside, it is loved with a kind of necessity, at least as regards specification. And this indeed is most of all true of knowledge in general insofar as it is knowledge, but it is also true in its own way of any particular science, if in that science cognition of the truth regarding such a subject matter is considered *per se*, for that perfection is always *per se* desirable to the human being. And if it happens that a human being does not love one

Cicero.

---

282. Cicero, *De finibus bonorum & malorum*, II.46, in: M. Tullius Cicero, *De finibus bonorum & malorum libri quinque*, ed. L. D. Reynolds (Oxford: Clarendon Press, 1998), p. 61.
283. Aristotle, *Pol.* V, ch. 12, 1316a10–11.

aliam: per se tamen ac seclusis impedimentis, vel (quod idem est) si una alteram non impediret, omnes scientias naturaliter appeteremus,[85] nec ratione unius alteram despiceremus.

Illatio.   14. Atque hinc facile etiam constat quid sit hic appetitus in homine: si enim sit sermo de appetitu elicito, constat esse actum voluntatis, vel efficacem, vel saltem inefficacem & per simplicem complacentiam, quae maxime naturalis est, & manet etiam in his qui efficaciter non intendunt seu eligunt scientiae vacare. Si vero sit sermo de pondere naturali, illud potest considerari ut immediate terminatum ad ipsam scientiam, & sic non est aliud quam intellectus ipse & capacitas eius qua scientiam respicit ut propriam perfectionem. Sicut enim in materia prima appetitus ad formam non est aliud ab ipsa materia, & naturali eius capacitate: & similiter in omni alia potentia appetitus ad suum actum non est aliquid additum ipsi potentiae, sed naturalis constitutio & aptitudo: ita in intellectu se habet appetitus ad scientiam. [43a] At si consideretur pondus naturae ut terminatur ad scientiam medio appetitu elicito, non est aliud quam voluntas hominis, quae hoc modo naturaliter propensa est ad omnes hominis perfectiones: non enim appetit voluntas habere scientiam, appetit tamen naturaliter velle scientiam homini seu intellectui: & hoc modo dicimus hoc pondus voluntatis terminari ad scientiam medio actu elicito.

---

85. Reading "appeteremus" with C_1, C_2, G_2, M_2, M_3, M_4, P_2, V_3, V_4, V_5, and Vivès. The following editions read "appetimus": S, M_1, P_1, V_1, and V_2. But considerations of grammar seem to require the former reading.

science, in order that she might aim at another, this also is traced back to extrinsic impediments, of which we have spoken. For because the human being cannot acquire both sciences, and would be kept from the perfect acquisition of one of them by her pursuit of the other, she therefore disregards the one in order to acquire the other. And in this way certain human beings, on account of their individual and proper temperaments, are more inclined to one science than they are to another. *Per se*, however, and setting aside impediments, or (and this amounts to the same) if the one science did not get in the way of the other, we would naturally desire all the sciences, and we would not disdain one science on account of another.

14. And from this it is easily established what this appetite in the human being is, for if the discussion concerns an elicited appetite, it is clear that it is an act of the will, either an efficacious one or at any rate one that is inefficacious and of simple complacency, which[284] is most of all natural and remains even in those who do not efficaciously aim or choose to devote themselves to knowledge. But if the discussion concerns a natural inclination, that can be considered as immediately terminated in knowledge itself, and in this way it is nothing other than the intellect itself and that capacity of it by which it is related to knowledge as to its proper perfection. For just as in prime matter the appetite for form is nothing other than matter itself and its natural capacity—and similarly, in every other potency the appetite for its act is not something added to the potency itself, but its natural constitution and aptitude—so also in the case of the intellect is its appetite related to knowledge. But if the inclination of nature is regarded as terminated in knowledge through the mediation of an elicited appetite, it is none other than the will of the human being, which in this way is naturally inclined to all the perfections of the human being. For the will does not desire to have science, but naturally desires to will science for the human being or intellect. And in this way we say that this inclination of the will is terminated in knowledge through the mediation of an elicited act.

Consequence.

284. The antecedent of "which" (*quae*) here is "simple complacency" (*simplex complacentia*).

Appetitum naturalem sciendi ad speculativas scientias esse maximum.

15. Ex his ergo satis explicatum relinquitur axioma illud generale, homini innatum esse appetitum naturalem ad scientiam: sub hoc autem principio sumendum est hunc appetitum maximum esse ad scientias speculativas, quae veritatis cognoscendae gratia tantum quaeruntur. Hoc tacite videtur intendisse Aristoteles toto discursu illius capitis primi huius prooemii. Ad quod explicandum distinguit haec omnia, & ordinem eorum inter se, sensum scilicet, memoriam, experimentum, artem, scientiam, quam tacite distinguit in eam quae propter opus seu utilitatem, & eam quae propter se ipsam quaeritur, & ultimo loco adiungit sapientiam. ⟨58a⟩

Aliquot Aristotelis dicta in prooemio explicantur.

16. Dicit ergo in primis sensum a natura datum esse cunctis animantibus: non vero explicat quid sit, quia hoc non spectat ad praesens: nec etiam dicit omnem sensum communicatum esse omnibus animalibus, sed sensum indefinite: solumque intendit supponere hunc esse imperfectissimum gradum cognitionis. Secundo addit bruta animalia interdum praeter sensum habere memoriam, & quandam veluti prudentiam naturalem: & aliqua ad hoc extendi ut sint etiam disciplinabilia, parum autem vel nihil experientiae participare. Ubi adverte nomine sensus intelligere Aristotelem eam[86] cognitionem sensitivam, quae solum in praesentia obiecti fit, sive per externos[87] sensus, sive per interiorem sensum communem seu phantasiam fiat: quidquid enim ad sentiendum in praesentia obiecti necessarium est, sub nomine sensus comprehendit: est autem in omnibus necessarium aliquid phantasiae seu imaginationis ad sentiendum etiam exterius: & ideo sicut sentire, ita etiam imaginatione uti omnibus brutis commune est. Memoria autem addit vim interiorem conservandi species & utendi illis in absentia obiectorum, ut hoc modo recordari possit quis earum rerum quas sensu percepit, etiam cum illas praesentes non habet secundum externos sensus. Hanc ergo

---

86. Reading "eam" here with C_1, C_2, G_2, M_1, M_2, M_3, P_1, P_2, S, V_1, V_2, V_3, and V_4. The following editions read "etiam": M_4, V_5, and Vivès.

87. Reading "externos" with M_1, P_1, P_2, S, V_1, and V_2. The following editions read "internos" instead: C_1, C_2, G_2, M_2, M_3, M_4, V_3, V_4, V_5, and Vivès.

*The natural appetite for knowing is greatest
with respect to the speculative sciences.*

15. On the basis of these things, this general axiom—that a natural appetite for knowledge is innate to the human being—is explained. And one must understand, as something included in this principle, that this appetite is most of all for the speculative sciences, which are sought only for the sake of cognizing truth. Aristotle seems tacitly to have intended this in the entire argument of the proem's first chapter. And in order to explain this, he distinguishes all these things, and their order with respect to each other, namely, sense, memory, experience, art, and knowledge, which he tacitly distinguishes into that which is sought for the sake of work or utility and that which is sought for its own sake, and in the last place he adds wisdom.

16. He says, therefore, first, that sense is given by nature to all animals.[285] But he does not explain what it is, since this is not the concern here, nor does he say that every sense is imparted to all animals, but indefinitely that sense is imparted to all animals, and he intends only to suppose that this is the most imperfect grade of cognition. Second, he adds that brute animals sometimes have memory in addition to sense, and a sort of natural prudence, as it were, and that some are also capable of being taught, but participate little or not at all in experience.[286] Notice here that by the name "sense" Aristotle understands that sensitive cognition which comes about only in the presence of the object, whether it comes about through the external senses or through the internal common sense or imagination, for he includes under the name "sense" whatever is necessary for sensing in the presence of the object. But in all animals something belonging to phantasy or imagination is necessary for sensing even externally, and therefore, like sensing, the use of imagination is also common to all brutes. Memory, however, adds an interior power to preserve species and use them in the absence of objects, so that in this way someone can remember those things which she has perceived by sense even when she does not have them present to her external senses. Aristotle, then, says that certain animals

Some of the things said by Aristotle in the proem are explained.

285. Aristotle, *Metaph.* I, ch. 1, 980a27–28.
286. Aristotle, *Metaph.* I, ch. 1, 980a28–b27.

facultatem ait Aristoteles habere animalia quaedam, non vero omnia: non tamen declarat quaenam haec vel illa sint.

17. Communiter tamen censentur habere memoriam quae proprie ac perfecte moveri possunt de loco ad locum distantem, sive progressivo motu per terram, sive volando per aerem, sive in aqua natando: nam memoria in hunc finem data videtur animalibus, ut ad distantem locum moveri possint, vel fugiendo nociva, vel quaerendo utilia, quae aliquo modo experta sunt. Nec refert quod interdum potest brutum ad locum distantem moveri non ex aliqua memoria, ut in recens natis constat: quia vel tunc movetur ab obiecto aliquantulum distanti; [43b] vel oberrat, & quasi casu vagatur.

Muscae an habeant memoriam.

18. Quod vero de muscis ait hic Aristoteles non habere memoriam, etiam si ad loca distantia moveantur, satis incertum est: nam signum quo movetur Aristoteles ad id asserendum, scilicet, quia percussae muscae, & loco pulsae, statim redeunt importune, insufficiens est, cum potius id possit accidere ex memoria delecta⟨58b⟩tionis quam ibi capiunt, & ex vehementi appetitu, vel quia obiectum illud semper est aliquo modo praesens per visum aut olfactum; & ideo vehementius movet. De solis ergo illis animalibus imperfectis quae solo sensu tactus, aut etiam gustus potiuntur, certo affirmari potest carere memoria, quia nullum illius signum, aut effectum habent, nec utilitatem.

Qualis in brutis prudentia.

19. Quod vero Aristoteles ait, bruta quaedam cum memoria habere prudentiam, non proprie, sed per translationem intelligendum est: non enim utuntur discursu, nec habitum acquirunt quo de agendis iudicent: sed quia naturali instinctu ita saepe operantur, ut tali naturae expedit hic & nunc, & ita provident de futuris, ac si vere ratiocinarentur, ideo per metaphoram prudentia appellantur. Dices, Ergo haec prudentia brutorum nihil est aliud quam instinctus naturae: sed hunc instinctum sibi accommodatum omnia animalia habent, etiam illa quae memoria carent: cur ergo Aristoteles hoc tribuit peculiariter quibusdam brutis? Ad hoc Iavell. lib. 1. q. 7. videtur nihil distinguere inter naturalem instinctum, & prudentiam brutorum, & concedere totum quod ratio

have this faculty, but not all. However, he does not make clear which animals have it and which do not.

17. But those are commonly judged to have memory which can properly and perfectly be moved from place to distant place, whether by a progressive motion on land, by flying through the air, or by swimming in water. For memory seems to have been given to animals for this end: in order that they might be moved to a distant place, either in fleeing harmful things or in seeking useful ones that they have in some way experienced. Nor does it matter that sometimes a brute can be moved to a distant place but not because of some memory, as is clear in the newly born, for either it is then moved by an object which is somewhat distant, or it is roaming and, as it were, wandering about by chance.

18. What Aristotle says here about flies,[287] that they do not have memory, even though they are moved to distant places, is rather uncertain, since the indication by which Aristotle is moved to assert this—namely, that when flies are struck and driven from a place, they immediately and inopportunely return—is insufficient. For this might occur, rather, because of a memory of the pleasure they get there, and because of an impetuous appetite, or because that object is always in some way present to sight and smell and therefore moves the fly rather vehemently. Thus, only with respect to the imperfect animals, which possess the sense of touch alone, or also the sense of taste, can it be affirmed with certainty that they lack memory, since they have no sign or effect of it, nor any use for it. *Whether flies have memory.*

19. As for the fact that Aristotle says that certain brutes have prudence together with memory, this is to be understood not properly, but metaphorically, for they do not employ reasoning, nor do they acquire a habit by which to judge what things should be done. But because they often work by natural instinct in a way that is useful to such a nature here and now, and thus provide for the future as if they truly reasoned, they are metaphorically called prudent. You will say: therefore, this prudence of the brutes is nothing other than an instinct of nature. But all animals *Of what sort is the prudence found in brutes.*

---

287. I can find no reference to flies in Aristotle's *Metaphysics*. Pedro da Fonseca, *Commentariorum in libros Metaphysicorum Aristotelis tomus primus*, col. 43, credits the argument that Suárez mentions here to Albert the Great. See Albert's *Metaphysica*, bk. I, tract. 1, ch. 6, in: Albert the Great, *Alberti Magni opera omnia*, vol. 16, pt. 1, pp. 8–9.

facta probare videtur, esse scilicet in omnibus brutis hanc prudentiam, eamque opinionem D. Thomae ascribit. Sed licet fortasse sit quaestio de nomine, ille tamen modus loquendi alienus est a mente Aristotelis, ut ratio facta ostendit: estque praeter rationem metaphorae: nam quaedam sunt animalia ita stolida, ut nec per metaphoram possint prudentia appellari: non solum ex his omnibus quae memoria carent, sed etiam ex his fortasse quae memoria praedita sunt. Unde Aristoteles non omnia, sed quaedam dixit cum memoria habere prudentiam. Alii nimio rigore accipientes hanc metaphoram, dicunt illa tantum animalia appellari prudentia quae operantur ex memoria praeteriti, vel ad futura providenda, vel quasi ad eligendum aliquod medium. Ita tenet Fonseca hic referens alios. Sed nimia videtur haec limitatio: non est enim necessaria in metaphoris tanta proprietas. Cum enim Christus dixit, *Estote prudentes sicut serpentes,* non ob operationem cum memoria praeteriti, sed ob naturalem sagacitatem, qua serpens caput custodit, id dixit, ut Sancti exponunt. Et formica prudens censetur cum grana in hyemem congregat, etiam si sine memoria id faciat, ut cum primo ita operatur. Igitur ⟨59a⟩ prudentia haec brutorum, specialis sagacitas quorundam est, quae naturae instinctu ita reguntur ut rationem & prudentiam hominis imitari videantur, ut in genere dixit Arist. lib. 1. de hist. anim. cap. 5. & in particulari de multis lib. 9. cap. 6. & sequen. & in 7. ait hoc prudentiae genus frequentius in minori animalium genere, quam in maiori reperiri: & ibi multa commemorat, quae ad hanc prudentiam pertinere dicit: non quia ex memoria praeteritorum, sed quia ex quodam quasi naturali ingenio, quo rationem hominis imitantur, proficiscuntur. Atque in hunc modum haec prudentia naturalis non in omnibus reperitur: quae tamen bruta praedita sunt illa, semper etiam memoriam habent: non quia haec prudentia semper in me[44a]moria fundetur, sed quia haec animalia semper sunt ita perfecta, ut memoriam participent. Addere etiam possumus haec ipsamet animalia natura sua prudentia, memoria rerum quas experta sunt, prudentiora fieri. Atque hoc modo dici posset in favorem secundae sententiae, quod ipsa naturalis sagacitas tunc maxime prudentiae nomen meretur, quando rerum memoria quasi exculta est & perfecta: sed de usu vocis haec sunt satis dicta.

have this instinct suited to themselves, even those which lack memory. Why, therefore, does Aristotle attribute it to certain brutes in particular? Regarding this, Javelli, book I, q. 7,[288] seems to distinguish in no way between natural instinct and the prudence of brutes, and seems to concede all of what this argument appears to prove, namely, that this prudence is in all brutes, and he attributes this opinion to St. Thomas. However, although the dispute is perhaps over a name, nevertheless, that way of speaking is foreign to Aristotle's thought, as the argument shows, and it is at odds with the nature_ of metaphor, for there are certain animals so stupid that they cannot be called prudent even metaphorically, not only among those which lack memory, but also among those which are perhaps endowed with memory. It is for this reason that Aristotle says, not that all of them, but that certain of them, have prudence along with memory. Others, taking this metaphor too strictly, say that one calls prudent only those animals which operate on the basis of a memory of the past, either so as to provide for the future, or in order to choose some means, as it were. And this is the position of Fonseca, who here refers to others.[289] But this limitation seems excessive, for such exactitude is not necessary in metaphors. For when Christ said: "Be prudent like serpents,"[290] he said it, as the saints explain, not in consideration of an operation informed by a memory of the past, but in consideration of the natural sagacity by which the serpent guards its head. And the ant is judged prudent because it gathers grains for the winter, even if it does so without memory, as when it does so for the first time. Therefore, this prudence of the brutes is a special sagacity belonging to some of them, and these are governed by an instinct of nature in such a way that they seem to imitate the reason and prudence of the human being, as Aristotle says generally in *Hist. An.* I, ch. 5,[291] and particularly regarding many brutes in book IX, ch. 6 and following.[292] And in ch. 7 he says that this kind of prudence is more often found in the smaller genus of

---

288. Javelli does not mention prudence in this question. Suárez is thinking of book I, q. 5 ("Whether there is prudence in brutes"). See Giovanni Crisostomo Javelli, *Opera*, t. 1, pp. 714b–715a.

289. Pedro da Fonseca, *Commentariorum in libros Metaphysicorum Aristotelis tomus primus*, cols. 45–48.

290. Matthew 10:16.

291. Aristotle, *Hist. An.* I, ch. 1, 488b15.

292. Aristotle, *Hist. An.* IX, chs. 5ff.

Quae animalia disciplinabilia.

20. Subiungit Aristoteles quaedam animalia non solum memoriam habere, sed etiam esse disciplinabilia, alia vero minime. Huius posterioris generis esse dicit, quae cum memoriam habeant, auditu carent, quia auditus est sensus disciplinae: & quanvis visus etiam ad disciplinam iuvet, & interdum videamus bruta quaedam, ut catulos, signis etiam quibusdam externis doceri & instrui, tamen hoc nunquam fit sine aliqua cooperatione auditus, quo excitantur & vocantur, ut signa percipiant.

Apes an audiant.

Ponit autem Aristoteles exemplum in apibus, de quibus tamen magna controversia est an audiant, ut ipsemet Aristoteles docet lib. 9. de histor. animal. c. 40. & Plinius lib. 11. c. 20. affirmat eas audire: quod absolute videtur probabilius consideratis signis & experientiis quas ipsi autores referunt. Docent enim, apes quibusdam sonis demulceri & attrahi. Item inter se se quosdam sonos edere, quando aut fugam volunt arripere, aut a somno excitantur, aut ad dormiendum convocantur. Unde Albertus hic distinctionem quandam auditus probabilem adhibet: est enim auditus soni ut sic, vel vocis ut dearticulatus sonus est: aitque apes habere priori modo auditum, non tamen pos⟨59b⟩teriori: hunc autem modum posteriorem, esse ad disciplinam necessarium.

animals than in the larger,[293] and he there recounts many things that, he says, pertain to this prudence, not because they arise from a memory of things past, but because they proceed from a kind of natural intelligence, as it were, thanks to which they imitate reason in the human being. And this natural prudence is not in this way found in all brutes, but those brutes which are endowed with it always have memory as well, not because this prudence is always founded on memory, but because these animals are always so perfect as to have a share in memory. We can also add that these same animals, prudent by nature, are made more prudent by their memory of the things₁ they've experienced. And in this way it could be said in favor of the second opinion that this same natural sagacity is most deserving of the name "prudence" when the memory of things₁ is, as it were, cultivated and perfected. But regarding the use of this word, enough has been said.

20. Aristotle adds that certain animals not only have memory, but also admit of being taught, while others do not at all. Belonging to this second genus, he says,[294] are those which, although they have memory, lack hearing, since hearing is the sense by which one learns. And although sight also helps with learning, and we sometimes see that certain brutes, such as puppies, are taught and instructed by means of certain external signs, nevertheless, this never occurs without some cooperation on the part of hearing, by which they are roused and called in order that they might perceive the signs. And Aristotle cites bees as an example, regarding which there is, however, a great controversy over whether they hear, as Aristotle himself teaches in *Hist. An.* IX, ch. 40.[295] And Pliny, book XI, ch. 20,[296] asserts that they hear, which absolutely seems more plausible, considering the indications and experiences which the same authors relate. For they teach that bees are charmed and attracted by certain sounds, and further, that among themselves bees produce certain sounds when they want to take flight, are aroused from sleep, or are called together to sleep. For this reason, Albert here employs a certain plausible distinction about hearing, for there is the

Which animals admit of being taught.

Whether bees hear.

---

293. Aristotle, *Hist. An.* IX, ch. 7, 612b19–21.
294. Aristotle, *Metaph.* I, ch. 1, 980a27–b25.
295. Aristotle, *Hist. An.* IX, ch. 40, 627a15–19.
296. Pliny, *Natural History*, XI, ch. (20) 22, in: Pliny, *Natural History, Vol. III: Books 8–11*, trans. H. Rackham (Cambridge, Mass.: Harvard University Press, 1940), pp. 474–75.

21. De priori genere animalium, scilicet disciplinabilium, nihil notandum occurrit, nisi disciplinam hanc etiam esse metaphorice intelligendam sicut prudentiam: dicuntur enim disciplinae capacia illa animalia quae usu quodam assuescunt, vel accedere cum vocantur certo nomine, vel congregari cum talem sonum aut vocem audiunt, aut fugere cum aliud signum percipiunt. Unde quaedam docentur more humano saltare, alia loqui, & similia. Quae omnia fiunt ab his solo naturali instinctu supposita memoria & experientia talis signi aut vocis. Ait vero Aristoteles omnia animalia, quae auditum habent, disciplinabilia esse. Quod fortasse verum est, difficile tamen fuerit creditu in omnibus animalibus id experientia constare: sine experimento vero non video quomodo de omnibus, tam volatilibus, quam aquatilibus id affimari possit. Facilius dici potest omnia animalia quae disciplinabilia sunt, auditum habere, & fortasse etiam visum, memoriam, ac metaphoricam prudentiam seu sagacitatem.

22. Concludit igitur Aristoteles bruta imaginationibus, memoriaque vivere, parumque experientiae participare: indicans tres gradus, quorum posterior priorem includit: unde priores cum exclusione posteriorum intelliguntur. Animalia enim imperfecta, vivunt tantum imaginatione imperfecta, quam simul cum sensu tactus, vel etiam gustus habent: alia vero perfectiora cum imaginatione habent solam memoriam: alia vero quae his sunt disciplinae capaciora, imperfectam quandam experientiam participare dicuntur, quae usu & [44b] consuetudine assuescunt quasi experimento quodam: cur autem illa experientia imperfecta dicatur, statim amplius declarabimus. Homines vero ait arte & ratione vivere, quod in reliqua parte capitis declarat, ut ad institutum perveniat. Merito autem illas duas coniungit, quia neutra videtur sine altera sufficere, saltem ad perfectum hominis regimen: nam ratio, quae naturalis est, non sufficit nisi arte excolatur: ars vero semper indiget rationis usu, & attenta consideratione, ut ad opus applicetur.

hearing of sound as such or the hearing of an utterance, insofar as it is an articulated sound, and he says that bees have hearing in the first way, but not in the second way, and that this second sort is necessary for learning.[297]

21. Regarding the former genus of animals, namely, the genus of teachable animals, nothing presents itself to be noted except that this learning is also to be understood metaphorically, as prudence is, for those animals are said to be capable of learning which are accustomed by a kind of practice to come when called by a particular name, or to gather when they hear a particular sound or utterance, or to flee when they perceive another sign. Thus, certain animals are taught to dance in human fashion, others to speak, and the like. All these things are done by them only by natural instinct, supposing memory and experience of such a sign or utterance. But Aristotle says that all animals that have hearing admit of being taught. This is perhaps true, but it is difficult to believe that it was established by experience in the case of all animals, and without experience I do not see how this can be affirmed of all of them, both winged and aquatic. It can perhaps more certainly be said that all animals which admit of being taught have hearing and perhaps also sight, memory, and metaphorical prudence or sagacity.

22. Aristotle therefore concludes that brutes live by imagination and memory, and participate little in experience, and he mentions three grades, the later including the earlier, for which reason the earlier are understood with the exclusion of the later. For imperfect animals live only by imperfect imagination, which they have together with the sense of touch or also taste. Other, more perfect animals have only memory with imagination. But the others, which are more capable of learning than these last, are said to share in a kind of imperfect experience, and they become habituated by practice and custom, as if by a kind of experience. And we shall presently explain more clearly why that experience is called imperfect. But human beings, he says, live by art and reason, which is something that he explains in the remainder of the chapter so as to achieve his purpose. And he rightly joins these two together, since neither seems to suffice without the other, at least for the perfect direc-

---

297. Albert the Great, *Metaphysica*, bk. I, tract. 1, ch. 6, in: Albert the Great, *Alberti Magni opera omnia*, vol. 16, pt. 1, p. 9.

23. Tertio igitur ait in hominibus generari experientiam ex memoria. *Nam multae* (inquit) *eiusdem rei recordationes unius experientiae vim perficiunt.* Quo loco offerebat ⟨60a⟩ se occasio declarandi fuse quid experientia sit, & an ad sensum pertineat, vel ad intellectum: item sit ne habitus iudicativus, an apprehensivus, & quomodo gignatur, vel ad quid inclinet. Sed quia haec magis pertinent ad scientiam de anima, & obiter tantum hic ab Aristotele attinguntur, breviter advertendum est, Aristotelem hic plane docere experientiam non versari circa universale, sed circa singulare: sic enim ait, *Compertum haberi, Calliae hoc morbo laboranti hoc profuisse, itemque Socrati, atque eodem modo pluribus singulatim, experientiae esse, profuisse autem iis omnibus, qui certo morbo laborent, id iam artis esse*: & infra probat utiliorem esse ad actiones experientiam, quam solam scientiam, vel artem, quia actiones circa singularia versantur. Non ergo pertinet ad experimentum collectio universalis ex singularibus: multoque minus assensus universalis, sed solum firmum promptumque iudicium circa singularia. Potest enim experientia late sumpta dici de quacunque perceptione unius singularis, quomodo dici potest quis esse expertus vinum inebriare, etiam si semel tantum id passus sit, vel in alio viderit: quia vero, ut Hippocrates dixit, experimentum fallax est, proprie non accipitur pro unius tantum singularis cognitione, sed plurium singularium, ut dixit Aristoteles. Imo nec satis est ad propriam experientiam & perfectam, saepius eundem effectum experiri: hoc enim etiam bruta animalia possunt, de quibus Aristoteles dixit parum experientiae participare, quia solum habent simplicem memoriam eorum singularium quae sensu perceperunt: sed ad perfectam experientiam ulterius requiritur collatio quaedam eorundem singularium inter se, quae propria est hominis, & ideo dixit Aristoteles ex memoria fieri homini experientiam: quia multae eiusdem rei recordationes experientiam perficiunt. *Eiusdem rei,* dicit, non individuae & singularis, ita ut ad experientiam sufficiat saepius recordari unius & eiusdem singularis effectus sensu percepti: haec enim repetitio efficiet promptiorem memoriam talis effectus, non vero experientiam. Intelligit ergo eiusdem secundum similitudinem, &

tion of the human being. For reason, which is natural, does not suffice unless it is cultivated by art, and art always requires the use of reason and attentive consideration, in order that it might be applied to work.

23. Therefore, third, he says that in human beings experience is generated from memory. "For many memories of the same thing₁," he says, "perfect the capacity for a single experience."²⁹⁸ In this passage, the occasion presents itself to explain at length what experience is, and whether it pertains to sense or to the intellect; likewise, whether it is a judicative habit, or an apprehensive one, and how it is produced, or to what it inclines. But because these things pertain more to the science of the soul, and are touched on here only in passing by Aristotle, it is briefly to be noted that Aristotle clearly teaches here that experience is not concerned with the universal, but with the singular, for he says: "To take it as certain that this did Callias good when he had this illness, and the same for Socrates, and the same for many people one by one, pertains to experience, but to recognize that it helped all those who suffered from a particular disease, this pertains to art."²⁹⁹ And later he proves that experience is more useful for action than science or art alone, since actions have to do with singulars.³⁰⁰ The acquisition of the universal from singulars does not, therefore, pertain to experience, and much less does universal assent, but only secure and prompt judgment regarding singulars. For "experience" taken in a broad sense can be said of any perception of one singular, in the way that someone can be said to know by experience that wine intoxicates, even if he has suffered intoxication only once, or seen it in another. But since, as Hippocrates says, experience is unreliable, it is properly taken not for the cognition of one singular alone, but for the cognition of many singulars, as Aristotle says. In fact, to experience the same effect rather often is not enough for proper and perfect experience, for brute animals are capable of this also, of whom Aristotle says that they participate little in experience, since they have only a simple memory of those singulars they have perceived by sense. But for perfect experience one further requires a kind of comparison of those same singulars to each other,

298. Aristotle, *Metaph.* I, ch. 1, 980b28–981a1.
299. Aristotle, *Metaph.* I, ch. 1, 981a7–12.
300. Aristotle, *Metaph.* I, ch. 1, 981a12–24.

conuenientiam circunstantiarum: & ad hoc requiritur collatio singularium per recordationem, scilicet, quod tale medicamentum profuit
Petro laboranti hoc morbo, & Paulo similiter: nam si non sit similitudo
sufficiens, saepe videbitur esse experientia, & revera non erit. Unde
provenit, ut saepe sit ⟨60b⟩ experimentum fallax. Hoc igitur modo
propria est hominis experientia, quae licet sensu inchoetur, men[45a]
te tamen & ratione perficitur, ut declaratum est. Unde non consistit
in notitia apprehensiva, sed in iudicativa, ex qua generatur habilitas
quaedam, qua homo promptus redditur ad iudicandum hunc effectum
solere a tali causa prodire, quae habilitas fortasse nihil aliud est quam
memoria talium effectuum singularium, non utcunque, sed ut inter se
collati sunt, & similes inventi, & cum eis circunstantiis ab eadem seu
simili causa manasse dignoscuntur. Atque haec nunc pro huius loci
opportunitate de experientia sufficiant.

Experientia proprie dicta, homini peculiaris.

Experientia quantum arti, ac scientiae deserviat.

24. Quarto addit Aristoteles artem per experientiam generari,
perfectioremque cognitionem afferre quam experientiam, etiam si ad
actionem sine experientia minus sufficiens sit. Ubi primo advertere
oportet Aristotelem hic indifferenter uti nomine scientiae & artis, ut
ex contextu constat: & quia, licet alias distinctae virtutes sint, tamen
secundum quandam rationem ars, quaedam scientia est, vel saltem,
quod ad rem praesentem attinet, eadem ratio est de illa & de scientia.
Deinde oportet advertere scientiam vel artem duplicem esse: alteram

which is proper to the human being, and therefore Aristotle says that in the human being experience comes to be from memory, since many memories of the same thing$_r$ perfect experience—"of the same thing$_r$," he says, but not of the same individual and singular, as if it should suffice for experience that one and the same sensibly perceived singular effect be repeatedly remembered, for this repetition will bring about a quicker remembrance of this effect, but not experience. Therefore, he understands "of the same thing" in terms of similarity and agreement of circumstances, and for this a comparison of singulars by memory is required, for example, that a medicine of a particular sort helped Peter when he suffered from this disease, and similarly for Paul. For if the similarity is not sufficient, it will often seem to be experience, but it will not really be experience. This is why experience is often misleading. It is in this way, then, that experience is proper to the human being, for although experience takes its start from sense, still, it is perfected by the mind and reason, as has been explained. Accordingly, it does not consist in an apprehensive knowledge$_n$, but in a judicative one, from which a certain aptitude is generated, an aptitude by which the human being is made ready to judge that this effect normally proceeds from a cause of that type. And this aptitude is perhaps nothing other than the memory of such singular effects, not discerned in any way whatsoever, but as compared to each other, as found to be similar, and as having proceeded in these circumstances from the same cause or a similar one. And let these remarks regarding experience suffice in connection with the present passage.

Experience, properly so called, is peculiar to the human being.

To what degree experience serves art and science.

24. Fourth, Aristotle adds that art is generated by experience,[301] and that it provides a more perfect cognition than experience,[302] even if it suffices less for action in the absence of experience. Here it must first be noted that in this passage Aristotle indifferently makes use of the names "science" and "art," as is clear from the context, for although they are otherwise distinct virtues, nevertheless, according to a certain

301. Aristotle, *Metaph.* I, ch. 1, 981a2–7.
302. Aristotle, *Metaph.* I, ch. 1, 981a24–b9.

vocant *quia*, quae solum demonstrat hoc ita esse: alteram *propter quid*, quae reddit causam. De priori facile intelligitur, quod per experientiam generetur, quia solum ex effectibus experimento perceptis colligit rem talem esse, vel habere talem proprietatem. Sed Aristoteles hic non de hac scientia, sed de perfecta, & propter quid loquitur, ut manifeste patet: nam cum artifices sapientiores esse dixisset iis, qui experientia rerum valent, rationem reddit, *Quia illi causam sciunt, hi non item*: ergo per artem & scientiam intelligit illam quae rei causam attingit, & docet. Cumque pluribus verbis & signis declaret artifices praeferri operantibus ex sola consuetudine aut ex experientia: omnia tamen huc tendunt, quod artifices cognoscunt propter quid & causam rei. Cum ergo ait artem experientia generari, de arte architectonica & propter quid intelligit.

25. Quod tamen difficile est, quia humanum experimentum est fallax, ut ex Hippocrate dixi, & quanvis demus interdum esse certum certitudine sensus: illa tamen certitudo minor videtur quam ea quae ad scien⟨61a⟩tiam requiritur. Maxime, quia experimentum non est universale, seu de omnibus omnino singularibus: scientia autem est universalis simpliciter, & complectitur ea etiam singularia quae sub experientiam non ceciderunt. Et quanvis interdum liceat ex his quae experimur, idem colligere de singularibus, quae sub experientiam non ceciderunt: haec autem[88] collectio videtur valde infirma, & ad summum sufficiet ad scientiam quia, non vero propter quid. Rursus occurrebat hic difficultas an propositio illa Aristotelis, artem ab experientia generari, indefinita tantum sit, ut sonat, an vero sumenda sit ut doctrinalis, & universalis, ita ut nunquam contingat scientiam aut artem in nobis aliter generari.

---

88. Reading "autem" with M_1, M_2, M_3, M_4, P_1, S, V_1, V_2, V_3, and V_5. The following editions read "tamen": C_1, C_2, G_2, P_2, and Vivès. The relevant text is missing from the scan of V_4.

concept₍ᵣ₎ art is a kind of science, or at least, as far as the present issue is concerned, the concept₍ᵣ₎ is the same for it and for science. Second, one must note that science or art is twofold. One they call "*quia*," and it only demonstrates *that* something is so. The other they call "*propter quid*," and it gives the cause.[303] Regarding the former, it is easily understood that it is generated by experience, since it only concludes from effects perceived by experience that the thing₍ᵣ₎ is so, or that it has such a property. But here Aristotle is speaking not of this science, but of perfect science, that is, science *propter quid*, as is manifestly clear, for when he says that the master artisans are wiser than those who are capable by virtue of their experience of things₍ᵣ₎, he gives as a reason, "Because the former know the cause, but the latter do not."[304] Therefore, by "art" and "science" he understands that which reaches the cause of the thing₍ᵣ₎ and teaches it. And when with many words and indications he explains that master artisans are preferred to those who work only by custom or experience, all this is in the service of the conclusion that master artisans cognize the *propter quid* and cause of the thing₍ᵣ₎. When, therefore, he says that art is generated by experience, he understands that art which is architectonic and *propter quid*.

25. This, however, involves difficulties, since human experience is unreliable, as I have said by appeal to Hippocrates, and even if we grant that it is sometimes certain with a certainty of sense, still, this certainty seems to be less than that which is required for science, especially because experience is not universal, or of absolutely all singulars, whereas science is universal without qualification and also embraces those singulars which did not fall under experience. And although, on the basis of the singulars that we have experienced, we may sometimes infer the

---

303. One of the meanings of "*quia*" is "that," in the sense of "I know *that* the moon is eclipsed." A *propter quid* is a reason why or cause. Science or knowledge *propter quid*, which is science in the strict sense, is the product of a demonstration *propter quid* (τοῦ διότι), which does not merely establish *that* something is the case, but also gives the cause or reason *why* it is the case. Science or knowledge *quia*, which counts as science only in a looser sense, is the result of a demonstration *quia* (τοῦ ὅτι), which merely establishes *that* something is the case, without giving the cause or reason *why* it is the case. Note that a demonstration *quia* counts as a demonstration only in a loose sense: a demonstration, strictly speaking, always provides knowledge of something through its cause or causes. For a discussion of these two kinds of demonstration, see Aristotle, *Post. An.* I, ch. 13.

304. Aristotle, *Metaph.* I, ch. 1, 981a28.

26. Ad priorem partem respondetur argumentum concludere experientiam esse non posse propriam, [45b] & per se causam artis, seu scientiae a priori, sed esse occasionem vel conditionem quandam necessariam, qua paratur via ad scientiam acquirendam. Quod intelligetur facile, advertendo in scientia duo per se requiri, scilicet veritatem quae scitur ac demonstratur, quae conclusio dicitur; & principia, per quae scitur, ac demonstratur. Scientia ergo conclusionis per se tantum pendet ex principiis: nam, cum sit scientia a priori, ut diximus, medium ex quo per se deducitur, non est experientia, sed causa ipsius effectus quem experimur, unde si principia quae causam conclusionis continent, sciri possent vel intelligi clare sine experientia, nullo modo scientia conclusionis ab experientia penderet. Principiorum autem cognitio evidens, quae propria illorum est, non ex aliquo medio, sed ex ipso naturali lumine immediate nascitur, cognita extremorum significatione seu ratione. Agimus autem de principiis primis, & immediatis, nam si sint mediata, erunt conclusiones demonstratae, de quibus eadem erit ratio, quae de omnibus aliis veritatibus, quae a priori sciuntur. Igitur nec immediata principia per se cognoscuntur per experientiam tanquam per proprium medium: hoc enim modo non cognoscerentur ut principia, sed ut conclusiones a posteriori demonstratae, & scitae per scientiam quia: ut sic autem non possent esse sufficientia ad generandam scientiam propter quid conclusionis, quia non potest causa nobiliorem effectum producere quam ipsa sit. Relinquitur ergo experientiam solum requiri ad scientiam ut intellectus noster ⟨61b⟩ manu ducatur per eam ad intelligendas exacte rationes terminorum simplicium, quibus intellectis ipse naturali lumine suo videt clare immediatam connexionem eorum inter se, quae est prima & unica ratio assentiendi illis.

same thing about singulars of which we have no experience, neverthe-less, this inference seems to be very weak and will at best suffice for science *quia*, but not for science *propter quid*. This difficulty also presents itself: whether that proposition of Aristotle's, that art is generated from experience, is only indefinite, as it is when literally construed, or whether it is to be taken as doctrinal and universal, so that it never happens that science or art is generated in us in any other way.

26. To the first difficulty, I reply that the argument concludes that experience cannot be the proper and *per se* cause of an *a priori* art or science, but is a kind of necessary occasion or condition by which the path to the acquisition of science is prepared. This is easily understood by taking note of the fact that two things are *per se* required in a science, namely: the truth that is known and demonstrated, which is called the conclusion, and the principles through which it is known and demonstrated. Therefore, knowledge of the conclusion depends *per se* only on the principles, for, since it is an *a priori* science, as we have said, the middle term from which it is deduced *per se* is not experience, but the cause of the very effect that we experience. For this reason, if the principles which contain the cause of the conclusion could be known or understood clearly without experience, knowledge of the conclusion would in no way depend on experience. And the evident cognition of principles which is proper to them does not arise from some middle term, but immediately from the natural light itself when the significations or concepts₍ᵣ₎ of the extremes are cognized. And we are treating of first and immediate principles, for if the principles are mediate, they will be demonstrated conclusions, of which there will be the same account₍ᵣ₎ as there is of all other truths that are known *a priori*. Therefore, immediate principles are not cognized *per se* through experience as through a proper middle term, for in this way they would not be cognized as principles, but as conclusions demonstrated *a posteriori* and known through a science *quia*. As such, moreover, they could not be sufficient for generating *propter quid* knowledge of a conclusion, for a cause cannot produce an effect that is nobler than it itself is. It remains, therefore, that experience is only required for science insofar as our intellect is led by it to an exact understanding of the concepts₍ᵣ₎ of simple terms, and when these terms are understood, the intellect it-

27. Altera pars difficultatis fusior est, sed proprium habet locum in lib. 1. Poster. c. 14. & 18. & ideo breviter quod sentio, proferam. Quidam enim absolute, & sine ulla restrictione aut distinctione putant experientiam propriissime sumptam esse necessariam ad scientiam vel artem ex parte iudicii principiorum, ita ut nunquam sufficiat unius vel alterius singularis cognitio experimentalis,[89] sed necessarium sit multa experiri, & inter se conferre, & omnia uniformia & sine discrimine reperire. Nam antequam intellectus omnem hanc diligentiam adhibeat, non potest omni certitudine naturali assentire,[90] prout in primis principiis necessarium est: quia cum ipsum lumen intellectus nostri sit infirmum, & imperfectum, nisi iuvetur experientia, facile hallucinari potest: sicut e converso ipsa etiam experientia per se fallax est, nisi intellectus suo lumine invigilet ad rationes rerum, & connexionem terminorum in se ipsa intuendam. Putaturque haec sententia esse Aristotelis variis in locis, scilicet libr. 1. Prior. c. 31. & lib. 2. c. 23. & lib. 1. Poster. c. 14. & 2. Poster. c. ulti. ubi interpretes antiqui ita sentire videntur. Nihilominus si de experientia proprie dicta sit sermo, mihi videtur distinctione utendum, tam in principiis ipsis, quam in modo acquirendi scientiam. Dixi, si de experientia propria sit sermo, quia si generatim agatur de quacunque sensibili cognitione necessaria ad terminorum apprehensionem & intelligentiam, clarum est hanc esse necessariam ad cognitionem principiorum, quia omnis nostra cognitio a sensu incipit: [46a] haec autem non est proprie experientia, quae, ut ex dictis constat, in iudicio, seu habitu iudicativo consistit: & de hac sine dubio locutus est Aristoteles. De hac ergo loquendo, distinctione utendum est: principia enim non omnia aequalia sunt. Est nanque in primis unum vel alterum generalissimum & notissimum, scilicet, *Quodlibet est, vel non est. Impossibile est idem simul esse & non esse*: & ad haec cognoscenda nulla requiritur experientia, sed sola terminorum apprehensio, intelligentia

---

89. Reading "experimentalis" here with all of the early editions. Vivès has "experimentatis."

90. Reading "assentire" here with C_1, C_2, G_2, M_1, M_2, M_3, M_4, S, V_1, V_2, V_3, V_4, and V_5. The following editions read "assentiri": P_1, P_2, and Vivès.

self, by its natural light, clearly sees the immediate connection between them, which is the first and only reason for assenting to immediate principles.

27. The other difficulty is more involved, but it has its proper place in *Post. An.* I, chs. 14 and 18,[306] and therefore I shall briefly present my view. For some believe absolutely and without any restriction or distinction that experience, taken in the most proper sense, is necessary for science or art when it comes to the judgment of principles, so that experimental cognition of one or another singular never suffices, it being necessary to experience many singulars, compare them with each other, and find them all uniform and without difference. For, before the intellect applies all this care, it cannot assent with all natural certainty to the extent necessary for first principles, since, given that the very light of our intellect is weak and imperfect, unless it is aided by experience, it can easily be misled—just as, conversely, experience itself is also *per se* unreliable unless the intellect with its light applies itself to considering the natures_r of things_r and the connection between the terms in itself. And this opinion is thought to be Aristotle's in various places, namely, *Pr. An.* I, ch. 31,[307] book II, ch. 23,[308] and *Post. An.* I, ch. 14,[309] and book II, final chapter,[310] where ancient interpreters seem to interpret him in this way. Nevertheless, if the discussion concerns experience properly so-called, it seems to me that a distinction must be employed, as much regarding the principles themselves as regarding the manner of acquiring science. I say "if the discussion concerns expe-

Whether science can be generated without experience.

Fonseca, bk. I, ch. 1, q. 4.[305]

Aristotle.

305. Pedro da Fonseca, *Commentariorum in libros Metaphysicorum Aristotelis tomus primus*, cols. 85–101 ("Whether all arts and sciences are produced by experience?").

306. Suárez's *Post. An.* I, ch. 14, is our *Post. An.* I, ch. 18, and his *Post. An.* I, ch. 18, includes the very end of our *Post. An.* I, ch. 21 (82b35–36), as well as our *Post. An.* I, ch. 22. In his discussion of this issue, however, Fonseca refers us to *Post. An.* II, ch. 18, rather than to *Post. An.* I, ch. 18. See Pedro da Fonseca, *Commentariorum in libros Metaphysicorum Aristotelis tomus primus*, col. 86. According to the chapter divisions of the *Posterior Analytics* used by Suárez and Fonseca, moreover, the final chapter of *Post. An.* II was labeled chapter 18, and it stretched from 99b17 ("περὶ δὲ τῶν ἀρχῶν") to 100b17.

307. *Pr. An.* I, ch. 31, considers division as a means of obtaining definitions.

308. In some editions from Suárez's day, *Pr. An.* II, ch. 23, begins at 68b9 (with "ὅτι δ᾽οὐ μόνον"), while in others it begins at 68b15 (with "Ἐπαγωγὴ μὲν οὖν ἐστί"). In both cases, it ends where our ch. 23 ends. The chapter often bears the title "De inductione" in Latin editions.

309. Aristotle, *Post. An.* I, ch. 18.

310. Aristotle, *Post. An.* II, ch. 19, 99b17–100b17.

seu explicatio: imo vix possunt illa ⟨62a⟩ principia ad positivam experientiam reduci: nam licet de quocunque singulari possimus experiri quod sit: tamen quod tunc non careat existentia, non possumus positive experiri distincto experimento ab eo quo videtur illud esse, sed sola intelligentia id percipitur explicatis terminis. Et hoc videtur adeo per se notum, ut alia probatione non indigeat. Possumus tamen ad maiorem explicationem exemplum adhibere: nam si hominem rusticum qui ob ignorantiam terminorum nescit assentiri illis principiis, velimus inducere ad eorum assensum, nulla certe nova experientia utemur, sed solum conabimur ita terminos explicare, ut intelligat, rem, quam videt esse, non posse absolute non esse.

28. Praeter haec vero principia notissima, de quibus vix potest (ut opinor) esse controversia, quin propriam experientiam non requirant, sunt alia etiam valde universalia, & communia fere omnibus scientiis, ut, *Quaecunque sunt eadem uni tertio, sunt eadem inter se*: &, *Omne totum est maius sua parte*: &, *Si ab aequalibus aequalia demas, quae remanent sunt aequalia*. Et de his distinguere oportet, quando talium principiorum notitia inventione acquiritur, vel disciplina. Nam in hoc posteriori modo existimo non esse necessariam experientiam proprie sumptam, sed supposita illa quae ad distinctam notitiam terminorum satis sit, & explicatis sufficienter per doctrinam rationibus terminorum, absque alia experientia posse intellectum assentiri suo lumine

rience proper" because if one is treating generally of any sensible cognition that is necessary for the apprehension and intelligence of terms, it is clear that this is necessary for the cognition of principles, since all our cognition begins with sense. But this is not properly experience, which, as is clear from what has been said, consists in a judgment or judicative habit; and it is undoubtedly about this that Aristotle spoke. Speaking of this, then, one must employ a distinction, because not all principles are equal. For, in the first place, there are two that are most general and most known$_n$, namely: "Any given thing either is or is not," and "It is impossible for the same thing both to be and not to be at the same time." And in order to cognize these no experience is required, but only an apprehension, understanding, or explanation of the terms. In fact, these principles can hardly be traced back to some positive experience, for although we can experience of any given singular that it exists$_e$, nevertheless, that it does not then lack existence is something that we cannot positively experience by means of an experience distinct from that by which it is seen to exist; rather, this is perceived only by understanding once the terms have been explained. And this seems so known$_n$ *per se* that it does not require another proof. Nevertheless, we can use an example in order to give a fuller explanation: for, given an uncultivated human being who is unable to assent to these principles on account of his ignorance of the terms, if we wish to lead him to assent to them, we will certainly not make use of any new experience, but will only try to explain the terms in such a way that he understands that the thing$_r$ which he sees exists$_e$ cannot absolutely not exist$_e$.

28. But aside from these most known$_n$ principles, about which (as I reckon) there can be no question that they do not require experience proper, there are also others that are very universal and common to almost all the sciences, such as: "Whatever things are each the same as a third thing are the same as each other," and "Every whole is greater than its part," and "If you take equals from equals, the things that remain are equal." And regarding these, one must distinguish when cognition of such principles is acquired through discovery, and when it is acquired through instruction. For in the latter case, I judge that experience, properly understood, is not necessary; rather, assuming the sort of experience which is enough for a distinct knowledge$_n$ of

cum sufficiente evidentia & certitudine. Et ratio est, quia haec quae requiruntur ad huiusmodi assensum evidentem, sive sit experientia, sive quaecunque alia terminorum declaratio, non requiruntur ut formalis ratio assentiendi, neque etiam ut principium per se efficiens, seu eliciens actum assentiendi, sed ut sufficiens applicatio obiecti, ut in priori parte difficultatis declaratum est. Sed nulla est sufficiens ratio quae suadeat experientiam rigorose sumptam, prout includit multorum singularium intuitionem, & collationem, ac inductionem, esse necessariam ad sufficientem applicationem horum principiorum, per sufficientem apprehensionem terminorum, eorumque rationum intelligentiam aptamque compositionem. Cur enim non potest hoc per doctrinam suppleri, adhibito ad summum uno vel altero exemplo sensibili, quo satis penetrato per intellectum, statim apparet per se evidens veritas principii? Atque hoc ipsum confirmat experientia: ad ad⟨62b⟩mittenda enim haec principia in doctrinis, nullus expectat plurium singularium inductionem, vel experimentalem cognitionem, sed facillimo negotio rationes terminorum quisque intelligit, & statim il[46b]lorum veritatem mente intuetur, praeceptoris mediocri diligentia adhibita.

Ad scientiarum inventionem experientia principiorum regulariter necessaria.

29. At vero qui sola inventione scientias acquirunt, indigent experientia ad horum principiorum cognitionem: quia sine illa, & sine exteriori adiutorio praeceptoris & doctrinae, non possunt haec principia satis proponi, aut rationes terminorum satis cognosci, ut illis evidens praebeatur assensus. Atque hoc confirmant testimonia Aristotelis, & usus ipse satis id ipsum docet. Ratio autem est, quia nostra intellectiva cognitio valde limitata est, & imperfecta, nimiumque a sensu pendet, & ideo sine sufficiente adminiculo eius non potest cum sufficiente certitudine & firmitate procedere, & inde accidit saepe, ut qui multum de intellectu confidunt, sensum deserentes, facile in rebus naturalibus errent, ut annotavit Aristoteles 8. Physicorum capit. 3. Oportet autem hic limitationem adhibere, nimirum hoc regulariter intelligendum

the terms, and that the concepts_r of the terms have been sufficiently explained by instruction, the intellect can, by means of its light, and without any other experience, give its assent with sufficient evidence and certainty. And the reason is because the things required for this sort of evident assent, whether experience or any other clarification of terms, are not required as a formal ground_r of assent, nor as a principle *per se* effecting or eliciting the act of assent, but rather as a sufficient application of the object, as was explained in connection with the first part of the difficulty. But there is no reason sufficient to persuade one that experience, strictly understood—insofar as it involves the intuition of many singulars, a comparison, and an induction—is necessary for a sufficient application of these principles through the sufficient apprehension of terms, the understanding of their concepts_r, and their appropriate composition. For why can this not be made good through instruction, with the use of, at most, one sensible example or another, so that, once the example is sufficiently grasped by the intellect, the *per se* evident truth of the principle is immediately seen? And experience confirms this very thing, for in the context of instruction, in order to grant these principles, no one requires an induction of more singulars, or experimental cognition; rather, granted a moderate diligence on the part of the teacher, each person understands the concepts_r of the terms with the easiest of efforts and immediately beholds the truth of these principles with his mind.

29. But those who acquire the sciences only by discovery require experience for the cognition of these principles, since without it, and without the external assistance of a teacher and instruction, these principles cannot be sufficiently conceived, or the concepts_r of the terms sufficiently cognized, for evident assent to be granted to them. And the attestations of Aristotle confirm this, and practice itself sufficiently teaches the same thing. And the reason is: because our intellective cognition is very limited and imperfect, and depends overly much on sense, and therefore, without sufficient assistance from sense, one cannot advance with sufficient certainty and security, and for this reason it often happens that those who place great trust in the intellect and forsake sense easily err when it comes to natural things_r, as Aristotle notes in

For the discovery of the sciences experience of principles is normally required.

esse: nam adeo posset aliquis pollere ingenio, & tam attente ac considerate rationem totius & partis, verbi gratia, in uno tantum singulari perpendere, ut veritatem totius principii inde statim eliceret: sicut dicunt Theologi animam Christi ex sola efficacia naturalis ingenii, sine speciali adminiculo supernaturali, ex uno phantasmate elicuisse multas veritates vel principia. Quia medium experientiae non est tam per se necessarium, quin possit aliunde suppleri.

30. Alia denique sunt principia particularia & propria singularium scientiarum: & de his verisimile est necessariam esse experientiam & collationem multorum singularium ad firmum & evidentem assensum eorum, non tantum via inventionis, quod est notissimum, sed etiam via disciplinae: quia rationes terminorum in his principiis non sunt ita notae ac faciles ut sufficiat quaelibet propositio eorum, nisi is qui addiscit, eas conferat cum singularibus quae novit, & videat, cum illis, & cum omnibus quae de talibus rebus expertus est, recte consentire: nunquam item talia principia, instantiam (ut dicunt) passa esse. Denique in his tanta fere semper est difficultas, ut vix perveniatur ad assensum proprium principiorum, seu per se notum de ⟨63a⟩ illis habendum, sed in inductione,[91] & notitia a posteriori sistatur: ergo signum est ad obtinendum assensum evidentem ex ipsorum terminorum rationibus probe cognitis multam esse necessariam experientiam: maiorem quidem via inventionis, aliquam vero via disciplinae: quanvis pro ingeniorum diversitate, maior etiam, vel minor sufficiat.

Scientiae variae partitiones.   31. Quinto loco proponit tacite Aristoteles divisionem artis seu scientiae (iam enim notavimus haec nomina indifferenter hic sumi) in scientiam practicam, & speculativam, quas in eo distinguit quod practicae ad vitae usum & commoditatem: speculativae solum ad veritatis cognitionem referantur. Practicas etiam subdistinguit tacite: nam aliae ad vitae necessaria, aliae vero ad voluptatem (utique sensibilem)

91. Reading "sed in inductione," here with S, V_1, and V_2. The following editions read "sed inductione" instead: C_1, C_2, G_2, M_1, M_2, M_3, M_4, P_1, P_2, V_3, V_4, V_5, and Vivès.

Phys. VIII, ch. 3.[311] But one must add a limitation here, namely, that this must be understood to be so normally, for someone could be so powerful of mind, and so attentively and carefully consider the natures$_r$ of the whole and part (for example) in one singular alone, that he immediately infers from it the truth of the entire principle—as theologians say that the soul of Christ, merely by the force of his natural intelligence, and without any special supernatural assistance, inferred many truths or principles from a single phantasm. For experience is not so *per se* necessary a means that the lack of it cannot be made good from elsewhere.

30. Finally, there are other principles that are particular and proper to individual sciences, and regarding these, it is likely that experience and the comparison of many singulars is necessary for a firm and evident assent to them, not only by the path of discovery, which is most known$_n$, but also by the path of instruction. For the concepts$_r$ of the terms in these principles are not so known$_n$ and free of difficulty that any conception of them suffices, unless he who is learning compares them with singulars that he knows$_n$ and sees that they agree perfectly with these and with everything that he has experienced of such things$_r$, and likewise sees that such principles have never admitted of a counter-example (as they say). Finally, regarding these, the difficulty is almost always so great that one scarcely arrives at the assent proper to principles, that is, to the point of regarding them as *per se* known$_n$; rather, one stops at induction and *a posteriori* knowledge$_n$. This, therefore, is a sign that, in order to obtain an evident assent from the rightly cognized concepts$_r$ of the terms themselves, much experience is necessary—more for the path of discovery, to be sure, but some also for the path of instruction, although, because of differences with respect to intellectual ability, more or less experience will suffice.

31. In the fifth place, Aristotle tacitly presents a division of art or science (for we have already noted that these names are taken as equivalent here) into practical science and speculative science, which he distinguishes in the following way: practical sciences are directed to the advantages and conveniences of life, while the speculative are directed

Various
divisions of
science.

---

311. At several points in this chapter Aristotle rules out certain views on the grounds that they are manifestly at odds with experience.

conferunt. Prioris generis sunt vel mechanicae artes, ut sutoria, &c. vel medicina & similes: posterioris autem generis esse videntur artes quae vocantur liberales, ut musica, ars etiam pingendi, om[47a]nes denique quae ad oblectandos sensus pertinent. Ab his ergo omnibus separat scientiam speculativam, quae in contemplatione veritatis sistit, & propter eam solum est, adeo ut licet ad illam maxima voluptas consequatur, tamen secundum rectum & optimum naturae ordinem illa non propter voluptatem quaeratur, sed propter se se: voluptas autem solum ut iuvet ad fruendum ipsa veritatis consideratione & contemplatione maiori quiete ac perseverantia. Ex quo recte colligit hoc genus scientiae alteri praeferri: eosque sapientiores haberi qui contemplationem veritatis propter se ipsam intendunt. Nobilius enim est id quod est propter se, quam quod propter aliud. Item quia optimum in homine est veritatis contemplatio: haec autem eo excellentior est, quo est de rebus altioribus, & quae ad operationem non ordinantur. Hactenus Aristoteles.

Praeferuntur practicis speculativae.

Conclusio ex omnibus Aristotelis dictis iam explicatis elicita.[92]

32. Ex quibus tacite, ut dixi, concludere visus est illum appetitum quem natura homini ad sciendum dedit, maxime propendere in contemplationem veritatis propter se ipsam: quia haec est suprema hominis operatio. Et consequenter hinc concluditur quod propositum est, hunc scilicet appetitum esse magis inclinari ad speculativas scientias quam ad alias, quia illae ordinantur ad veritatem contemplandam propter se ipsam. Unde non excluditur quin appetitu ⟨63b⟩ sciendi, etiam[93] ad practicas scientias feramur, sed quod vehementius ad speculativas.

Practicae scientiae propter solam veritatis cognitionem appeti possunt.

33. Sed quaeres an practicae scientiae possint etiam appeti propter veritatis cognitionem in ea sistendo, absque usus utilitate. Quid-

92. Reading "*elicita*" here with C₁, C₂, G₂, M₁, M₂, P₁, P₂, S, V₁, and V₂. The following editions omit "*elicita*": M₄, V₅, and Vivès. The following read "*licita*" in lieu of "*elicita*": M₃, V₃, and V₄.

93. Reading "sciendi, etiam ad" here with C₁, C₂, G₂, M₁, M₂, M₃, P₁, P₂, S, V₁, V₂, V₃, and V₄. The following editions read "sciendi ad": M₄, V₅, and Vivès.

only to the cognition of truth.[312] He also tacitly distinguishes between the practical sciences, for some are necessary for life, while others are conducive to pleasure (sensible pleasure, at any rate).[313] Belonging to the former genus are the mechanical arts, such as the cobbler's art, etc., as well as medicine and the like; belonging to the latter genus, it seems, are the arts called liberal, such as music, and also the art of painting, and finally all those which pertain to the delight of the senses. From all these, therefore, he separates speculative science, which stops at the contemplation of truth and is only for the sake of that—so much so that, although the greatest pleasure ensues from this contemplation, nevertheless, according to the right and best order of nature, it is not sought for the sake of pleasure, but for its own sake; the pleasure only helps us enjoy the consideration and contemplation of truth with greater peace and constancy. From this he rightly infers that this genus of science is preferred to the other, and that those who aim at the contemplation of truth for its own sake are considered wiser. For that which is for its own sake is nobler than what is for the sake of another thing. Further, the best thing in the human being is the contemplation of truth, and this is more excellent the more it concerns things that are higher and not ordained to an operation. Thus far Aristotle.

The speculative sciences are preferred to the practical ones.

32. From all these things, as I have said, Aristotle seems tacitly to conclude that that appetite for knowledge which nature has given to the human being is inclined most of all to the contemplation of truth for its own sake, since this is the highest operation of the human being. And consequently from this he concludes what was proposed, namely, that this appetite is inclined more to the speculative sciences than it is to the other sciences, since the former are ordained to the contemplation of truth for its own sake. Thus, he does not deny that we are led by the appetite for knowledge to the practical sciences as well, but rather claims that we are drawn more strongly to the speculative sciences.

The conclusion drawn from all the things said by Aristotle, which have now been explained.

33. But you will ask whether the practical sciences can also be desired for the sake of cognizing truth, coming to a stop there, without the benefit of their employment. For some people seem generally to deny that human beings can desire the practical sciences merely for the

The practical sciences can be desired merely for the sake of cognizing truth.

312. Aristotle, *Metaph.* I, ch. 1, 981b13–25.
313. Aristotle, *Metaph.* I, ch. 1, 981b17–20.

am enim generatim negare videntur homines posse appetere scientias practicas tantum sciendi causa, sed solum propter opus. Veruntamen licet scientia practica hoc[94] differat ab speculativa, quod per se ordinatur ad opus, illa vero minime, ut suo loco dicetur: hoc tamen non excludit quin practica scientia proxime & immediate conferat alicuius veritatis cognitionem, imo id necessarium est: alioqui scientia non esset. Omnis autem cognitio veritatis est per se amabilis, etiam si aliam utilitatem non afferat: nam per se est magna perfectio naturae intellectualis. Unde angeli has artes norunt, etiam si ad suum usum illis non serviant. Et ideo scientiae practicae etiam sunt appetibiles propter cognitionem veritatis, etiam si in ea sistatur, & ad usum non ordinetur. Et confirmatur, quia alias revera non appeterentur ex vi appetitus sciendi, quia appeterentur tantum ut media: medium autem ut medium non appetitur nisi ex vi propensionis ad finem: & ita musica non appeteretur nisi ex vi appetitus voluptatis, vel lucri: & sic de aliis, non autem ex vi appetitus scientiae ut sic, cum sint verae, & in suo genere perfectae scientiae. Quod etiam experientia docet: multi enim in harum scientiarum exercitio recreantur, non propter usum, vel utilitatem, sed solum ut sciant. Regulariter autem solum propter utilitatem aliquam humanam quaeruntur: quia hoc est magis conforme institutioni & fini talium artium: & quia sensibilia commoda vel necessitates aut voluptates frequentius plus movent: & quia si scientia propter solam veritatem quaerenda esset, in aliis scientiis nobilioribus quaereretur, praesertim cum non possit homo omnibus simul vacare. Sic[95] igitur [47b] practicae scientiae appetibiles quidem sunt, multo tamen magis speculativae, si appetitus hominis, ut homo est, spectetur, & aliis humanis commodis, aut necessitatibus non impediatur.

---

94. Reading "practica hoc differat" here with C_1, C_2, G_2, M_1, M_2, M_3, M_4, P_1, P_2, S, V_1, V_2, V_3, and V_4. The following editions read "practica in hoc differat": V_5 and Vivès.

95. Reading "Sic" here with S, M_1, P_1, V_1, and V_2. The following editions read "Si" instead: C_1, C_2, G_2, M_2, M_3, M_4, P_2, V_3, V_4, V_5, and Vivès.

sake of knowing, but only for the sake of work. But in fact, although practical science differs from speculative science in being *per se* ordained to work, while the speculative is not at all so ordained, as will be said in its place, nevertheless, this does not prevent a practical science from proximately and immediately conferring cognition of some truth. In fact, this is necessary, otherwise it would not be a science. And all cognition of truth is *per se* worthy of love, even if it does not bring any additional advantage, for it is *per se* a great perfection of an intellectual nature. For this reason, angels know these arts, even if these arts do not serve a use for them. And so the practical sciences also are desirable for the sake of cognizing truth, even if one stops with the truth and does not order it to use. And this is confirmed, because otherwise they would not really be desired by the appetite for knowledge, since they would be desired only as means, and a means, as a means, is not desired except by virtue of an inclination to an end. And so music would not be desired except by virtue of the appetite for pleasure or profit, and similarly regarding the others, but not by virtue of the appetite for knowledge as such, even though they are true sciences and perfect in their own genus. And experience also teaches this, for many practice these sciences for recreation, not for the sake of use or advantage, but only in order that they might know. But normally they are sought only for the sake of some human advantage, since this is more in conformity with the establishment and end of such arts, and since sensible conveniences or necessities or pleasures more often motivate, and because, if knowledge had to be sought solely for the sake of truth, it would be sought in other, nobler sciences, especially since a human being cannot devote herself to all of them at the same time. In this way, then, the practical sciences are indeed desirable, but the speculative sciences are much more so, if the appetite of the human being, insofar as she is a human being, is considered, and it is not impeded by other human conveniences or necessities.

Totius quaestionis resolutio.

34. Ultimo concluditur ex dictis omnibus assertio intenta Metaphysicam esse maxime appetibilem ab homine ut homo est, tam appetitu naturali, quam rationali[96] optime or⟨64a⟩dinato. Probatur tacite ab Aristotele in fine eiusdem capitis, quia inter omnes speculativas scientias, haec maxime nomen sapientiae meretur: cum versetur circa primas causas, omniumque principia, quod a nobis superiori sectione satis declaratum est: si ergo scientiae speculativae inter omnes maxime appetuntur, inter quas haec est suprema: erit utique ex se maxime appetibilis. Tandem maximus hominis appetitus est ad suam naturalem foelicitatem: haec autem per hanc scientiam comparatur, vel potius in ipsius perfecta assecutione consistit. Nam ut traditur lib. 10. Ethicor. haec foelicitas in contemplatione Dei & substantiarum separatarum posita est: haec autem contemplatio proprius actus est, & praecipuus finis huius scientiae: ergo & foelicitas naturalis in actu huius scientiae consistit: est ergo hic appetitus maxime consentaneus tam naturae, quam rectae rationi. Superest ergo ut omni diligentia & studio hanc perfectissimam scientiam investigemus.

96. Reading "rationali" here with M_1, P_1, P_2, S, V_1, and V_2. The following have "rationabili": C_1, C_2, G_2, M_2, M_3, M_4, V_3, V_4, V_5, and Vivès.

Resolution of the entire question.

34. Finally, from all that has been said the assertion aimed at is inferred, namely, that metaphysics is most desirable to the human being insofar as she is a human being, as much by a natural appetite as by a rational one that is ordered in the best way. This is tacitly proved by Aristotle at the end of the same chapter, since among all of the speculative sciences this is most deserving of the name "wisdom," for it is concerned with the first causes and principles of all things, as was sufficiently explained by us in the previous section. If, therefore, among all the sciences, the speculative sciences are most of all desired, this one, which is supreme among them, will certainly be of itself the most desirable. Finally, the greatest appetite of the human being is for her own natural happiness, and this is acquired by means of this science, or rather consists in the perfect attainment of it. For, as is taught in *Ethics* X,[314] this happiness is found in the contemplation of God and the separate substances, and this contemplation is the proper act and chief end of this science. Therefore, natural happiness too consists in the act of this science. Therefore, this appetite is most in accord with both nature and right reason. It remains, therefore, for us to search after this most perfect science with all diligence and zeal.

314. Aristotle, *Nic. Eth.* X, chs. 7–8.

BIBLIOGRAPHY

First Editions of Suárez's Works

Suárez, Francisco. *Commentariorum ac Disputationum in Tertiam Partem Divi Thomae Tomus Primus. Autore P. Francisco Suarez Societatis Iesu, in Academia Complutensi sacrae Theologiae professore*. Compluti: In collegio Societatis Iesu, ex officina Typographica Petri Madrigalis, 1590. This volume is 781 double-columned pages, not including front matter and indices. Its contents are reproduced in vols. 17 and 18 of the Vivès edition.

———. *Commentariorum, ac Disputationum in Tertiam Partem Divi Thomae. Tomus Secundus. Mysteria vitae Christi, & utriusque adventus eius accurata disputatione ita complectens, ut scholasticae doctrinae studiosis, & Divini verbi concionatoribus usui esse possit. Autore Patre Francisco Suarez Societatis Iesu, in Collegio eiusdem Societatis Academiae Complutensis sacrae Theologiae professore*. Compluti: Ex Officina Ioannis Gratiani, 1592. This volume is 1204 double-columned pages, not including front matter and indices. Its contents are reproduced in vol. 19 of the Vivès edition.

———. *Commentariorum ac Disputationum in Tertiam Partem Divi Thomae Tomus Tertius. Qui est primus de Sacramentis, in quo ea continentur, quae sequens pagina indicabit. Autore P. Francisco Suarez, e Societate Iesu, in Collegio eiusdem Societatis Academiae Salmanticensis sacrae Theologiae professore*. Salmanticae: excudebat Ioannes Ferdinandus, 1595. This volume is 1328 double-columned pages, not including front matter and indices. Its contents are reproduced in vols. 20 and 21 of the Vivès edition.

———. *Metaphysicarum Disputationum, in quibus et Universa Naturalis Theologia ordinate traditur, & quaestiones omnes ad duodecim Aristotelis libros pertinentes accurate disputantur, Tomus Prior. Autore R. P. Francisco Suarez e Societate Jesu*. Salmanticae, apud Ioannem & Andream Renault fratres, 1597. This volume is 698 double-columned pages, not including front matter and indices. Its contents are reproduced in vol. 25 of the Vivès edition.

———. *Metaphysicarum Disputationum, R. P. Francisci Suarez Societatis Iesu Tomus Posterior*. Salmanticae: apud Ioannem & Andream Renaut, fratres, 1597. This volume is 728 double-columned pages, not including front matter and indices. Its contents are reproduced in vol. 26 of the Vivès edition.

———. *Doctoris Francisci Suarez Granatensis De Societate Iesu In Celebri Conimbricensi Academia Theologicae facultatis Primarii professoris. Varia Opuscula Theologica. 1. De Concursu, motione, & auxilio Dei. Lib. III. 2. De Scientia Dei futurorum contingentium. Lib. II. 3. De Auxilio efficaci. Brevis* resolutio. 4. *De Libertate divinae voluntatis. Relectio prior. 5. De Reviviscentia meritorum. Relectio altera. 6. De Iustitia Dei. Disputatio.* Matriti: Ex Typographia Regia, 1599. This volume is 574 double-columned pages, not including front matter and indices. Its contents are reproduced in vol. 11 of the Vivès edition.

————. *Commentariorum ac Disputationum, In Tertiam Partem Divi Thomae, Tomus Quartus. Expositionem quaestionum Divi Thomae, ab LXXXIIII usque ad finem: Cum Disputationibus de Virtute Poenitentiae in primis, complectens. Adduntur deinde Disputationes de Clavibus, & Sacramento Poenitentiae, de Extrema Unctione, Purgatorio, Suffragiis, & Indulgentiis. Authore P. D. Francisco Suarez Granatensi, e Societate Iesu, Sacrae Theologiae, in celebri Conimbricensi Academia, Primario Professore.* Conimbricae: Ex Officina Antonii a Mariz, per eius generum & cohaeredem Didacum Gomez Loureyro, Academiae Architypographum, 1602. This volume is 1224 double-columned pages, not including front matter and indices. Its contents are reproduced in vol. 22 of the Vivès edition.

————. *Disputationum de Censuris in Communi, Excommunicatione, Suspensione, & Interdicto, Itemque de Irregularitate. Tomus Quintus, Additus ad Tertiam Partem D. Thomae, Authore P. D. Francisco Suarez Granatensi, e Societate Iesu, Sacrae Theologiae, in celebri Conimbricensi Academia, Primario Professore.* Conimbribcae [sic]: Ex Officina Antonii a Mariz, per eius generum & cohaeredem Didacum Gomez Loureyro, Academiae Architypographum, 1603. This volume is 1235 double-columned pages, not including front matter and indices. Its contents are reproduced in vols. 23 and 23 bis of the Vivès edition.

————. *Doctoris Francisci Suarez Granatensis e Societate Iesu, in Regia Conimbricensi Academia primarii Theologiae professoris. Prima Pars Summae Theologiae de Deo Uno & Trino.* Olissipone: apud Petrum Crasbeeck Typographum, 1606. This volume is 923 double-columned pages (271 + 652), not including front matter and indices. Its contents are reproduced in vol. 1 of the Vivès edition.

————. *Opus De Virtute, et Statu Religionis. Authore P. D. Francisco Suarez Granatensi e Societate Iesu, Sacrae Theologiae, in celebri Conimbricensi academia Primario professore.* Conimbricae: Ex officina Petri Crasbeeck, 1608. This volume is 1104 double-columned pages, not including front matter and indices. Its contents are reproduced in vol. 13 of the Vivès edition.

————. *Tomus Secundus De Virtute, et Statu Religionis. Authore P. D. Francisco Suarez Granatensi e Societate Iesu Sacrae Theologiae, in celebri Conimbricensi academia Primario professore.* Conimbricae: Ex officina Petri Crasbeeck, 1609. This volume is 1284 double-columned pages, not including front matter and indices. Its contents are reproduced in vol. 14 of the Vivès edition.

————. *Tractatus De Legibus, ac Deo Legislatore In decem Libros distributus. Authore P. D. Francisco Suarez Granatensi e Societate Iesu, Sacrae Theologiae, in celebri Conimbricensi Academia Primario Professore.* Conimbricae: Apud Didacum Gomez de Loureyro, 1612. This volume is 1266 double-columned pages, not including front matter and indices. Its contents are reproduced in vols. 5 and 6 of the Vivès edition.

———. *Defensio Fidei Catholicae, et Apostolicae Adversus Anglicanae sectae errores, Cum Responsione Ad Apologiam Pro Iuramento Fidelitatis, & Praefationem monitoriam Serenissimi Iacobi Angliae Regis. Authore P. D. Francisco Suario Granatensi e Societate Iesu Sacrae Theologiae in celebri Conimbricensi Academia Primario Professore.* Conimbricae: Apud Didacum Gomez de Loureyro Academiae Typographum, 1613. This volume is 780 double-columned pages, not including front matter and indices. Its contents are reproduced in vol. 24 of the Vivès edition.

———. *Doctoris Francisci Soarii Granatensis e Societate Iesu in Regia Conimbricensi Academia olim Primarii Professoris emeriti. Operis de Divina Gratia Pars Prima. Continens Prolegomena sex, duosque priores de necessitate divinae gratiae ad honesta opera libros.* Conimbricae: apud Didacum Gomez de Loureyro, 1619. This volume is 813 double-columned pages, not including front matter and indices. Its contents are reproduced in vol. 7 of the Vivès edition.

———. *Doctoris Francisci Soarii Granatensis e Societate Iesu in Regia Conimbricensi Academia olim Primarii Theologiae Professoris emeriti, Operis de Divina Gratia Pars Tertia. Continens posteriores libros septem de habituali gratia, sanctificatione hominis ac merito.* Conimbricae: apud Didacum Gomez de Loureyro, 1619. This volume is 1032 double-columned pages, not including front matter and indices. Its contents are reproduced in vols. 9 and 10 of the Vivès edition.

———. *Doctoris Francisci Suarez Granatensis, e Societate Iesu, In Regia Conimbricensi Academia primarii Theologiae Professoris emeriti, Pars Secunda Summae theologiae de Deo rerum omnium Creatore. In tres praecipuos tractatus distributa, Quorum Primus De Angelis hoc volumine continetur.* Lugduni: Sumptibus Iacobi Cardon, & Petri Cavellat, 1620. This volume is 746 double-columned pages, not including front matter and indices. Its contents are reproduced in vol. 2 of the Vivès edition.

———. *Doctoris Francisci Suarez Granatensis, e Societate Iesu, In Regia Conimbricensi Academia primarii Theologiae Professoris emeriti, Partis secundae summae Theologiae Tomus Alter. Complectens tractatum secundum De Opere Sex Dierum, Ac tertium De Anima.* Lugduni: Sumptibus Iacobi Cardon & Petri Cavellat, 1621. This volume is 547 (310 + 237) double-columned pages, not including front matter and indices. Its contents are reproduced in vol. 3 of the Vivès edition.

———. *Doctoris Francisci Suarez Granatensis, e Societate Iesu, In Regia Conimbricensi Academia olim primarii Theologiae Professoris emeriti, Opus De Triplici Virtute Theologica, Fide, Spe, & Charitate.* Lugduni: Sumptibus Iacobi Cardon & Petri Cavellat, 1621. This volume is 498 double-columned pages, not including front matter and indices. Its contents are reproduced in vol. 12 of the Vivès edition.

———. *Operis De Religione Pars Secunda, Quae Est De Statu Religionis, ac Tomus Tertius in ordine, Complectens Tractatum Septimum De obligationibus quae Religiosum constituunt, vel ad illum disponunt. In Decem libros distributum. Auctore P. D. Francisco Suarez Granatensi e Societate Iesu, in Regia Conimbricensi Academia S. Theologiae quondam Primario, ac Emerito Professore.* Lugduni: Sumptibus Iacobi Cardon & Petri Cavellat, 1624. This volume is 660 double-columned pages, not including front matter and indices. Its contents are reproduced in vol. 15 of the Vivès edition.

———. *Operis De Religione Tomus Quartus, et Ultimus, Continens Tractatus Tres. IIX. De obligationibus Religiosorum ex regula, praelatione & subiectione regulari provenientibus, IX. De varietate Religionum, tam in genere, quam in specie, X. De Religione Societatis Iesu in particulari: Quibus totum opus completur, & absolvitur. Auctore Eximio Doctore P. Francisco Suarez Granatensi, e Societate Iesu, sacrae Theologiae, in celebri Conimbricensi Academia, Primario, ac emerito Professore.* Lugduni: Sumptibus Iacobi Cardon & Petri Cavellat, 1625. This volume is 794 double-columned pages, not including front matter and indices. Its contents are reproduced in vols. 16 and 16 bis of the Vivès edition.

———. *Eximii Doctoris P. Francisci Suarez Granatensis, e Societate Iesu, In Academia Conimbricensi Primarii atque Emeriti olim Professoris, Ad primam secundae D. Thomae Tractatus Quinque Theologici, Quorum I. De ultimo fine hominis, ac Beatitudine. II. De voluntario, & involuntario. III. De humanorum actuum bonitate, & malitia. IV. De Passionibus, & habitibus. V. De vitiis, atque peccatis.* Lugduni: Sumptibus Iacobi Cardon, 1628. This volume is 453 double-columned pages, not including front matter and indices. Its contents are reproduced in vol. 4 of the Vivès edition.

———. *Doct. Francisci Suarez Granatensis, e Societate Iesu, in Regia Conimbricensi Academia olim Primarii Theologiae Professoris emeriti; Operis De Divina Gratia Pars Secunda, Continens Libros III, IV, et V, Nimirum, De Auxiliis Gratiae, in generali; De Auxilio sufficiente; & de Auxilio efficaci Gratiae Dei.* Lugduni: Sumptibus Philippi Borde, Laurentii Arnaud, & Claudii Rigaud, 1651. This volume is 535 double-columned pages, not including front matter and indices. Its contents are reproduced in vol. 8 of the Vivès edition.

———. *Doct. Francisci Suarez Granatensis ex Societate Iesu, Tractatus Theologicus De Vera Intelligentia Auxilii Efficacis, eiusque Concordia, cum libero arbitrio.* Lugduni: Sumpt. Philip. Borde, Laur. Arnaud, & Cl. Rigaud, 1655. This volume is 408 double-columned pages, not including front matter and indices. Its contents are reproduced in vol. 10 of the Vivès edition.

———. *R. P. Francisci Suaresii Granatensis e Soc. Jesu Theologi Opuscula Sex Inedita, Nunc Primum ex Codicibus Romanus, Lugdunensibus ac Propriis Eruit et Praefationibus Instruxit Illustriss. ac Reverendiss. Dominus Joannes Baptista Malou, Episcopus Brugensis.* Bruxellis: In Aedibus Alphonsi Greuse & Parisiis: In Aedibus Joannis DeMichaelis, 1859.

Editions of Suárez's *Disputationes Metaphysicae*
cited in the Notes on the Latin Text

C_1 = Francisco Suárez, *R. Patris Francisci Suarez e Societate Iesu Metaphysicarum Disputationum Tomus Prior*. Coloniae: Excudebat Franciscus Helvidius, 1608.

C_2 = Francisco Suárez, *R. Patris Francisci Suarez e Societate Iesu Metaphysicarum Disputationum . . . Tomi Duo*. Coloniae: Excudebat Franciscus Helvidius, 1614.

G_2 = Francisco Suárez, *R. Patris Francisci Suarez e Societate Iesu Metaphysicarum Disputationum . . . Tomi Duo*. Coloniae Allobrogum [i.e., Genevae]: Apud Philippum Gamonet, 1636.

M_1 = Francisco Suárez, *R. Patris Francisci Suarez e Societate Iesu Metaphysicarum Disputationum . . . Tomi Duo*. Moguntiae: Excudebat Balthasarus Lippius, Sumptibus Arnoldi Mylii, 1600.

M_2 = Francisco Suárez, *R. Patris Francisci Suarez e Societate Iesu Metaphysicarum Disputationum . . . Tomi Duo*. Moguntiae: Excudebat Balthasarus Lippius, Sumptibus Arnoldi Mylii, 1605.

M_3 = Francisco Suárez, *R. Patris Francisci Suarez e Societate Iesu Metaphysicarum Disputationum . . . Tomi Duo*. Moguntiae: Sumptibus Hermanni Mylii Birckmanni, Excudebat Hermannus Meresius, 1614.

M_4 = Francisco Suárez, *R. Patris Francisci Suarez e Societate Iesu Metaphysicarum Disputationum . . . Tomi Duo*. Moguntiae: Sumptibus Hermanni Mylii Birckmanni, Excudebat Hermannus Meresius, 1630.

P_1 = Francisco Suárez, *R. Patris Francisci Suarez e Societate Iesu Metaphysicarum Disputationum . . . Tomi Duo*. Parisiis: Apud Michaelem Sonnium, via Iacobaea, sub scuto Basiliensi, 1605.

P_2 = Francisco Suárez, *R. Patris Francisci Suarez e Societate Iesu Metaphysicarum Disputationum . . . Tomi Duo*. Parisiis: Apud Petrum Ménier, ad portam sancti Victoris, 1619.

S = Francisco Suárez, *Metaphysicarum Disputationum . . . Tomus Prior*. Salmanticae: Apud Ioannem & Andream Renaut Fratres, 1597.

V_1 = Francisco Suárez, *Metaphysicarum Disputationum . . . Tomus Prior*. Venetiis: Apud Baretium Baretium, & Socios, 1599.

V_2 = Francisco Suárez, *Metaphysicarum Disputationum . . . Tomus Prior*. Venetiis: Apud Io. Baptistam Colosinum, 1605.

V_3 = Francisco Suárez, *Francisci Suarez e Societate Iesu, Metaphysicarum Disputationum . . . Tomi Duo*. Venetiis: Apud Haeredes Melchioris Sessae, 1610.

V_4 = Francisco Suárez, *Francisci Suarez e Societate Iesu, Metaphysicarum Disputationum . . . Tomi Duo*. Venetiis: Apud Petrum Mariam Bertanum, 1619.

V_5 = Francisco Suárez, *R. P. Francisci Suarez Granatensis e Societate Jesu, Doctoris Eximii, Metaphysicarum Disputationum . . . Pars Prima*. Venetiis: Apud Sebastianum Coleti, 1751.

Vivès = Francisco Suárez, *Opera Omnia*. Vol. 25. Paris: Vivès, 1861.

Translations of Suárez's *Disputationes Metaphysicae*

English

Francisco Suárez. *A Commentary on Aristotle's* Metaphysics, *or "A Most Ample Index to the* Metaphysics *of Aristotle."* Translated by John P. Doyle. Milwaukee: Marquette University Press, 2005.

———. *Suarez on Individuation: Metaphysical Disputation V: Individual Unity and its Principle.* Translated by Jorge J. E. Gracia. Milwaukee: Marquette University Press, 1982.

———. *On Formal and Universal Unity* [*DM* 6]. Translated by James F. Ross. Milwaukee: Marquette University Press, 1964.

———. *On the Various Kinds of Distinctions* [*DM* 7]. Translated by Cyril Vollert. Milwaukee: Marquette University Press, 1947.

———. *The Metaphysics of Good and Evil According to Suárez: Metaphysical Disputations X and XI and Selected Passages from Disputation XXIII and other Works.* Translated by Jorge J. E. Gracia and Douglas Davis. München, Hamden, & Wien: Philosophia Verlag, 1989.

———. *On the Formal Cause of Substance: Metaphysical Disputation XV.* Translated by J. Kronen and J. Reedy. Milwaukee: Marquette University Press, 2000.

———. *On Efficient Causality: Metaphysical Disputations 17, 18, and 19.* Translated by Alfred J. Freddoso. New Haven & London: Yale University Press, 1994.

———. *On Creation, Conservation, & Concurrence: Metaphysical Disputations 20–22.* Translated by A. J. Freddoso. South Bend, Ind.: St. Augustine's Press, 2002.

———. *The Metaphysical Demonstration of the Existence of God: Metaphysical Disputations 28–29.* Translated by John P. Doyle. South Bend, Ind.: St. Augustine's Press, 2004.

———. *On the Essence of Finite Being As Such, On the Existence of That Essence and Their Distinction* [*DM* 31]. Translated by Norman J. Wells. Milwaukee: Marquette University Press, 1983.

———. *On Real Relations (Disputatio Metaphysica XLVII).* Translated by John P. Doyle. Milwaukee: Marquette University Press, 2006.

———. *On Beings of Reason (De entibus rationis). Metaphysical Disputation 54.* Translated by John P. Doyle. Milwaukee: Marquette University Press, 1995.

French

Francisco Suárez. *Suárez et la refondation de la métaphysique comme ontologie: étude et traduction de l'«Index détaillé de la Métaphysique d'Aristote» de F. Suárez.* Translated by Jean-Paul Coujou. Louvain-la-Neuve & Louvain/Paris: Éditions de l'Institut supérieur de philosophie & Éditions Peeters, 1999.

———. *Disputes métaphysiques I, II, III.* Translated by Jean-Paul Coujou. Paris: Vrin, 1998.

————. *Disputes métaphysiques XXVIII–XXIX.* Translated by Jean-Paul Coujou. Grenoble: Millon, 2009.

————. *La distinction de l'étant fini et de son être: Dispute métaphysique XXXI.* Translated by Jean-Paul Coujou. Paris: Vrin, 1999.

————. *Les êtres de raison: Dispute métaphysique LIV.* Translated by Jean-Paul Coujou. Paris: Vrin, 2001.

Italian

Francisco Suárez. *Disputazioni metafisiche I–III.* 2nd. ed. Introduced and translated by Costantino Esposito. Firenze & Milano: Giunta Editore S.p.A. & Bompiani, 2017.

German

Francisco Suárez. *Über die Individualität und das Individuationsprinzip. 5. metaphys. Disputation.* Translated by Rainer Specht. Hamburg: Meiner, 1976.

Portuguese

Francisco Suárez. *As Disputações Metafísicas de Francisco Suárez: Estudos e antologia de textos* [DM 1.1, 1.5, 5.1–3, 5.5, 5.6, 7.1, 8.1–5, 31.1, 39.1]. Edited by José Francisco Meirinhos and Paula Oliveira e Silva. Porto: Faculdade de Letras da universidade do Porto, 2011.

Russian

Франсиско Суарес. Метафизические рассуждения. Т. 1. Рассуждения I–V. Пер. Г. В. Вдовиной. М.: Институт философии, теологии и истории св. Фомы, 2007.

Spanish

Francisco Suárez. *Disputaciones metafísicas.* Edited and translated by S. Rábade Romeo, Salvador Caballero Sánchez and Antonio Puigcerver Zanón. 7 vols. Madrid: Ed. Gredos, 1960–67.

Other Primary Sources

Albert the Great. *Alberti Magni opera omnia.* Vol. 16. Münster: Aschendorff, 1960.

————. *Opera omnia.* Edited by Borgnet. Vol. 5. Parisiis: Vivès, 1890.

Alexander of Aphrodisias. *Commentaria in duodecim Aristotelis libros de Prima Philosophia.* Venetiis: Apud Hieronymum Scottum, 1561.

[Ps.-] Alexander of Hales [Alexander Bonini]. *In duodecim Aristotelis Metaphysicae libros dilucidissima expositio.* Venetiis: apud Simonem Galignanum de Karera, 1572.

Al-Farabi. *Catálogo de las Ciencias.* Edited by Ángel Gonzalez Palencia. 2nd ed. Madrid: Consejo Superior de Investigaciones Científicas, 1953.

Araujo, Francisco de. *Commentariorum in Universam Aristotelis Metaphysicam Tomus Primus.* Brugis et Salmanticae: Ex Officinis Typographicis Ioannis Baptistae Varesii & Antoniae Ramirez viduae, 1617.

Aristotle. *Aristoteles Latinus III.2, Metaphysica: Translatio anonyma sive "media."* Edited by G. Vuillemin-Diem. Leiden: Brill, 1976.

———. *Aristoteles Latinus III.3.2, Metaphysica: Recensio & translatio Guillelmi de Moerbeka.* Edited by G. Vuillemin-Diem. Leiden & Köln: Brill, 1995.

———. *Aristoteles Latinus IV.1–4. Analytica Posteriora.* Edited by L. Minio-Paluello and B. G. Dod. Bruges & Paris: Desclée de Brouwer, 1968.

———. *Aristotelis Stagiritae de Prima Philosophia seu Metaphysicorum Libri XII, Ioanne Argyropylo Byzantino interprete.* Parisiis: Apud Thomam Richardum, 1548.

———. *The Complete Works of Aristotle: The Revised Oxford Translation.* 2 vols. Edited by J. Barnes. Princeton: Princeton University Press, 1984.

Averroes. *Aristotelis opera cum Averrois Commentariis.* 10 vols. in 12. Venetiis: apud Junctas, 1562.

———. *Averrois Cordubensis commentum magnum super libro De celo & mundo Aristotelis.* 2 vols. Edited by R. Arnzen, G. Endress, and F. Carmody. Leuven, Belgium: Peeters, 2003.

Avicenna. *Liber de philosophia prima, sive scientia divina I–IV.* Edited by S. Van Riet. Louvain & Leiden: Peeters & Brill, 1977.

Blasius a Conceptione. *Metaphysica in Tres Libros Divisa.* Lutetiae Parisiorum: Sumptibus Dionysii Thierry, 1640.

Buridan, John. *In Metaphysicen Aristotelis Quaestiones argutissimae.* Parisiis: Impensis Iodici Badii Acensii, 1518.

———. *Questiones Joannis buridani super decem libros ethicorum aristotelis ad nicomachum.* Paris: Ponset le Preux, 1513.

———. *Summulae de dialectica.* Translated by Gyula Klima. New Haven: Yale University Press, 2001.

Cajetan, Cardinal. See Vio, Tommaso de.

Chauvin, Stéphane. *Lexicon Philosophicum.* Leovardiae: Excudit Franciscus Halma, 1713.

Cicero, M. Tullius. *De finibus bonorum & malorum libri quinque.* Edited by L. D. Reynolds. Oxford: Clarendon Press, 1998.

———. *De officiis.* Edited by M. Winterbottom. Oxford: Oxford University Press, 2016.

———. *Rhetorica, Vol. 1: Libros de oratore tres continens.* Edited by A. S. Wilkins. Oxford: Oxford University Press, 2016.

Collegium Complutense Sancti Cyrilli [Antonio de la Madre de Dios, aka Antonio de Olivera]. *Artium Cursus sive Disputationes in Aristotelis Dialecticam, et Philosophiam naturalem.* Compluti: apud Ioannem de Orduña, 1624.

Collegium Conimbricense. *In octo libros Physicorum Aristotelis Stagiritae.* 2 vols. Lugduni: Sumptibus Ioannis Baptistae Buysson, 1594.

Dominic of Flanders. *In Duodecim Libros Metaphysicae Aristotelis.* Coloniae Agrippinae: Typis Arnoldi Kempensis, 1621.

Fonseca, Pedro da. *Commentariorum Petri Fonsecae Lusitani, Doctoris Theologi Societatis Iesu, In Libros Metaphysicorum Aristotelis Stagiritae Tomi Quatuor. Continet hic tomus primus quatuor priorum librorum explicationem.* Coloniae: Sumptibus Lazari Zetzneri Bibliopolae, 1615.

Giles of Rome. *Expositio super libros Posteriorum.* Venetiis: per Simonem de Luere, sumptibus domini Andree Torresani de Asula, 18 May 1500.

———. *Metaphysicales Quaestiones Aureae Domini Aegidii Romani.* Venetiis: Apud Octavianum Scotum D. Ama Dei, 1552.

Javelli, Giovanni Crisostomo. *Chrysostomi Iavelli Canapicii, ordinis Praedicatorum, Philosophi & Theologi nostrae aetatis eruditissimi omnia, quotquot inveniri potuerunt, Opera, quibus quicquid ad Rationalem, Naturalem, Moralem ac Divinam Philosophiam pertinet [. . .], tomus primus.* Lugduni: Apud Antonium de Harsy, 1580.

———. *Epitome Chrysostomi Iavelli Canapitii, In universam Aristotelis Philosophiam, tam naturalem, quam transnaturalem.* Venetiis: apud Ioannem Mariam Bonellum, 1555.

John Duns Scotus. *B. Ioannis Duns Scoti Opera Philosophica.* Vol. 3. St. Bonaventure, N.Y.: The Franciscan Institute and St. Bonaventure University, 1997.

———. *Joannis Duns Scoti Doctoris Subtilis Ordinis Minorum Opera Omnia.* Vol. 5. Parisiis: Apud Ludovicum Vivès, 1891.

John of St. Thomas [João Poinsot]. *Ioannis a Sancto Thoma O.P. Cursus Philosophicus Thomisticus.* Vols. 1–3. Edited by Beatus Reiser. Taurini: Marietti, 1930–37.

Mas, Diego. *Metaphysica Disputatio de Ente, et eius Proprietatibus, quae communi nomine inscribitur de Transcendentibus, in quinque libros distributa. Auctore R. P. F. Didaco Masio, Valentino Vilarealensi, ordinis Praedicatorum.* Valentiae: apud viduam Petri Huete, 1587.

Micraelius, Johannes. *Lexicon Philosophicum Terminorum Philosophis Usitatorum.* Jenae: impensis Jeremiae Mamphrasii, 1653.

Mirandulano, Antonio Bernardo. *Eversionis singularis certaminis libri XL.* Basileae: Henricum Pertri, 156–?.

Pliny. *Natural History, Vol. III: Books 8–11.* Translated by H. Rackham. Cambridge, Mass.: Harvard University Press, 1940.

Proclus. *Procli Diadochi Lycii Philosophi Platonici ac mathematici probatissimi In Primum Euclidis Elementorum librum Commentariorum ad universam mathematicam disciplinam principium eruditionis tradentium Libri IIII.* Patavii: Excudebat Gratiosus Perchacinus, 1560.

Rubio, Antonio. *Commentarii in Universam Aristotelis Dialecticam.* 2 vols. Compluti: Ex Officina Iusti Sanchez Crespo, 1603.

———. *Logica Mexicana, hoc est, commentarii breviores et maxime perspicui in universam Aristotelis dialecticam.* Lugduni: Apud Ioannem Pillohotte, 1611.

Simplicius. *Commentarii in octo Aristotelis Physicae Auscultationis libros.* Venetiis: Apud Iuntas, 1551.

Soncinas, Paul. *Pauli Soncinatis Ordinis Praedicatorum Quaestiones Metaphysicales acutissimae.* Lugdunum: apud Carolum Presnot, 1579.

Soto, Domingo de. *In Dialecticam Aristotelis Commentarii.* Salmanticae: Excudebat Andreas à Portonariis. S. C. M. Typographus, 1564.

———. *Super octo libros Physicorum Aristotelis Commentaria.* Salmanticae: ex Officina Ildefonsi à Terranova & Neyla, 1582.

———. *Super octo libros Physicorum Aristotelis Quaestiones.* Salmanticae: ex Officina Ildefonsi à Terranova [&] Neyla, 1582.

Suárez, Francisco. *De anima: Commentaria una cum quaestionibus in libros De anima.* Edited by Salvador Castellote Cubells. 3 vols. Madrid: Sociedad de Estudios y Publicaciones, 1978–91.

———. *R. P. Francisci Suarez, E Societate Jesu, Opera Omnia.* 28 vols. in 30. Parisiis: Apud Ludovicum Vivès, 1856–78.

———. "Transcripción y notas del manuscrito inédito suareciano 'De Generatione et Corruptione.'" In *Francisco Suárez: "Der ist der Mann," Apéndice Francisco Suárez,* De generatione et corruptione: *Homenaje al Prof. Salvador Castellote,* transcribed by Salvador Castellote, 435–682. Valencia: Facultad de Teología San Vicente Ferrer, 2004.

Themistius. *Themistii Peripatetici Lucidissimi Paraphrasis in Aristotelis Posteriora, & Physica. In libro[s] item de Anima, Memoria & Reminiscentia, Somno & Vigilia, Insomniis, & Divinatione per Somnum.* Venetiis: Apud Hieronymum Scotum, 1554.

Thomas Aquinas. *In duodecim libros metaphysicorum Aristotelis expositio.* Turin & Rome: Marietti, 1950.

———. *Sancti Thomae Aquinatis opera omnia.* Vol. 17. Parmae: Typis Petri Fiaccadori, 1864.

———. *Sancti Thomae Aquinatis opera omnia.* T. 4. Romae: Ex Typographia Polyglotta, S. C. De Propaganda Fide, 1888.

———. *Sancti Thomae Aquinatis opera omnia.* T. 5. Romae: Ex Typographia Polyglotta, S. C. De Propaganda Fide, 1889.

———. *Sancti Thomae Aquinatis opera omnia.* T. 6. Romae: Ex Typographia Polyglotta, S. C. De Propaganda Fide, 1891.

———. *Sancti Thomae Aquinatis opera omnia.* T. 7. Romae: Ex Typographia Polyglotta, S. C. De Propaganda Fide, 1892.

———. *Sancti Thomae Aquinatis opera omnia.* T. 8. Romae: Ex Typographia Polyglotta, S. C. De Propaganda Fide, 1895.

———. *Sancti Thomae Aquinatis opera omnia.* T. 9. Romae: Ex Typographia Polyglotta, S. C. De Propaganda Fide, 1897.

———. *Sancti Thomae Aquinatis opera omnia.* T. 10. Romae: Ex Typographia Polyglotta, S. C. De Propaganda Fide, 1899.

———. *Sancti Thomae Aquinatis opera omnia.* T. 11. Romae: Ex Typographia Polyglotta, S. C. De Propaganda Fide, 1903.

———. *Sancti Thomae Aquinatis opera omnia.* T. 12. Romae: Ex Typographia Polyglotta, S. C. De Propaganda Fide, 1906.

———. *Sancti Thomae Aquinatis opera omnia.* T. 14. Romae: Typis Riccardi Garroni, 1926.

———. *Sancti Thomae de Aquino opera omnia.* T. 45, pt. 1. Roma & Paris: Commissio Leonina & Vrin, 1984.

———. *Sancti Thomae de Aquino opera omnia.* T. 50. Rome & Paris: Commissio Leonina & Les Éditions du Cerf, 1992.

———. *Sancti Thomae de Aquino opera omnia.* T. 1*–2. Roma & Paris: Commissio Leonina & Vrin, 1989.

———. *S. Thomae Aquinatis opera omnia.* Edited by Robert Busa. 5 vols. Stuttgart-Bad Cannstatt: Frommann-Holzboog, 1980.

Toledo, Francisco de. *Commentaria una cum quaestionibus in tres libros Aristotelis De Anima.* Compluti: Apud Ioannem Gratianum, 1577.

———. *Commentaria una cum quaestionibus in universam Aristotelis logicam.* Venetiis: apud Juntas, 1580.

Vázquez, Gabriel. *Commentariorum, ac Disputationum in primam partem S. Thomae Tomus Primus.* Compluti: Ex officina Ioannis Gratiani, apud viduam, 1598.

Vio, Tommaso de, Cardinal Cajetan. *Commentaria in summam theologiae sancti Thomae Aquinatis.* In Thomas Aquinas, *Sancti Thomae Aquinatis opera omnia.* Ts. 4–12. Romae: Ex Typographia Polyglotta, S. C. De Propaganda Fide, 1888–1906.

———. *Reverendi patris fratris Thome de Vio Caietani: artium et sacre Theologie professoris. Ordinis Predicatorum Romana curia Procuratoris. in Predicabilia Porphyrii: et Aristotelis Predicamenta: ac Posteriorum analeticorum libros. Et super tractatum de ente et essentia Divi Thome Aquinatis Commentaria subtilissima. Et tractatus eiusdem de Analogia castigatissima novissime recognita cunctisque erroribus expurgata.* Venetiis: Impensis nobilis viri Luceantonii de giunta florentini, die 9 Julii 1519.

Zabarella, Jacopo. *Opera Logica.* Coloniae: Lazari Zetzneri, 1597.

Zúñiga, Diego de. *Philosophiae prima pars, qua perfecte et eleganter quatuor scientiae Metaphysica, Dialectica, Rhetorica et Physica declarantur.* Toleti: Petrus Rodriguez, 1597.

Other Resources

Dictionary of Medieval Latin from British Sources. Oxford: pub. for the British Academy by Oxford University Press, 1975–2013.

Latinitas Medii Aevi Lexicon Bohemorum. Prague: Academia, 1977–.

Secondary Sources

Note: By far the most extensive bibliography of secondary literature on Suárez is the one maintained by Sydney Penner, accessible via his website devoted to Suárez. https://www.sydneypenner.ca/suarez.shtml. Students of Suárez will find this site to be an invaluable resource.

Baciero, Francisco. "La influencia de Suárez en las universidades alemanas del siglo XVII: El caso de Leibniz." In *Filosofía hispánica y diálogo intercultural.*

Edited by Roberto Albares Albares, Antonio Heredia Soriano, and Ricardo Piñero Moral, 397–412. Salamanca: Gustavo Bueno, 2000.

Baciero González, Carlos. "Suárez y sus *Disputationes metaphysicae*. Importancia y significación histórica." *Arbor* 159, no. 628 (1998): 451–71.

Blanchette, Oliva. "Suárez and the Latent Essentialism of Heidegger's Fundamental Ontology." *The Review of Metaphysics* 53, no. 1 (1999): 3–19.

Boulnois, Olivier. *Être et représentation. Une généalogie de la métaphysique moderne à l'époque de Duns Scot. XIIIe–XIVe siècle.* Paris: PUF, 1999.

Castellote, Salvador. "Transcripción y notas del manuscrito inédito suareciano 'De Generatione et Corruptione.'" In *Francisco Suárez: "Der ist der Mann,"* 435–682.

Courtine, Jean-François. "Le projet Suarézien de la métaphysique." *Archives de Philosophie* 42, no. 2 (1979): 235–74.

———. "Ontologie ou métaphysique?" *Giornale di Metafisica* 7, no. 1 (1985): 3–24.

———. *Suárez et le système de la métaphysique.* Paris: PUF, 1990.

Coujou, Jean-Paul. "Introduction." In *Suárez et la refondation de la métaphysique comme ontologie,* *1–*67.

Darge, Rolf. "«Ens in quantum ens»: Die Erklärung des Subjekts der Metaphysik bei F. Suarez." *Recherches de théologie et de philosophie médiévales* 66, no. 2 (1999): 335–61.

———. "Suárez on the Subject of Metaphysics." In *A Companion to Francisco Suárez.* Edited by Victor M. Salas and Robert L. Fastiggi, 91–123. Leiden & Boston: Brill, 2015.

Décarie, Vianney. *L'objet de la métaphysique selon Aristote.* Paris & Montréal: Vrin & L'Institut d'Études Médiévales, 1961.

Doyle, John P. "Suárez on the Reality of the Possibles." *The Modern Schoolman* 45, no. 1 (1968): 29–48.

———. "Heidegger and Scholastic Metaphysics." *The Modern Schoolman* 49, no. 3 (1972): 201–20.

———. "Suárez on the Unity of a Scientific Habit." *The American Catholic Philosophical Quarterly* 65, no. 3 (1991): 309–31.

Duarte, Shane. "Aristotle's Theology and Its Relation to the Science of Being *qua* Being." *Apeiron* 40, no. 3 (2007): 267–318.

Elders, Leo. "Aristote et l'objet de la métaphysique." *Revue philosophique de Louvain* 60 (1962): 165–83.

Eschweiler, Karl. "Die Philosophie der spanischen Spätscholastik auf den deutschen Universitäten des siebzehnten Jahrhunderts." In *Spanische Forschungen der Görresgesellschaft, 1. Reihe: Gesammelte Aufsätze zur Kulturgeschichte Spaniens.* Edited by Heinrich Finke and Johannes Vincke, 251–325. Münster: Aschendorff, 1928.

Esposito, Costantino. "Introduzione." In Francisco Suárez, *Disputationi Metafisiche I–III,* 7–39.

Follon, Jacques. "Le concept de philosophie première dans la «Métaphysique» d'Aristote." *Revue philosophique de Louvain* 90, no. 88 (1992): 387–421.

Forlivesi, Marco. "Impure Ontology. The Nature of Metaphysics and Its Object in Francisco Suárez's Texts." *Quaestio* 5 (2005): 559–86.

————. "Approaching the Debate on the Subject of Metaphysics from the Later Middle Ages to the Early Modern Age: The Ancient and Medieval Antecedents." *Medioevo* 34 (2009): 9–59.

————. "In Search of the Roots of Suárez's Conception of Metaphysics: Aquinas, Bonino, Hervaeus Natalis, Orbellis, Trombetta." In *Suárez's Metaphysics in Its Historical and Systematic Context*. Edited by Lukáš Novák, 13–37. Berlin: De Gruyter, 2014.

Fraser, Kyle. "Demonstrative Science and the Science of Being qua Being." *Oxford Studies in Ancient Philosophy* 22 (2002): 43–82.

Frede, Michael. "The Unity of General and Special Metaphysics: Aristotle's Conception of Metaphysics." In Michael Frede, *Essays in Ancient Philosophy*, 81–95. Minneapolis: University of Minneapolis Press, 1987.

Gallego Salvadores, Jordán. "El maestro Diego Mas y su tratado de Metafísica." *Analecta sacra tarraconensia* 43 (1970): 3–92.

————. "La aparición de las primeras metafísicas sistemáticas en la España del XVI: Diego Mas (1587), Francisco Suárez y Diego de Zuñiga (1597)." *Escritos del Vedat* 3 (1973): 91–162.

Gallego Salvadores, Juan José. "El dominico valenciano Diego Mas y la primera metafísica sistemática." In *Francisco Suárez: "Der ist der Mann,"* 211–23.

Gilson, Étienne. *Being and Some Philosophers.* 2nd ed. Toronto: Pontifical Institute of Mediaeval Studies, 1952.

Grabmann, Martin. "Die Disputationes metaphysicae des Franz Suarez in ihrer methodischen Eigenart und Fortwirkung." In *P. Franz Suarez S.J.: Gedenkblätter zu seinem dreihundertjährigen Todestag (25. September 1917): Beiträge zur Philosophie des P. Suarez.* Edited by Karl Six, 29–73. Innsbruck: Tyrolia, 1917. [Reprinted in: Martin Grabmann, *Mittelalterliches Geistesleben: Abhandlungen zur Geschichte der Scholastik und Mystik*, 525–560. München: Max Hueber, 1926.]

Gracia, Jorge J. E. "Suárez's Conception of Metaphysics: A Step in the Direction of Mentalism?" *American Catholic Philosophical Quarterly* 65, no. 3 (1991): 287–309.

Heider, Daniel. "The Nature of Suárez's Metaphysics: *Disputationes Metaphysicae* and Their Main Systematic Strains." *Studia Neoaristotelica* 6, no. 1 (2009): 99–110.

————. "The Unity of Suárez's Metaphysics." *Medioevo* 34 (2009): 475–505.

Hellín, José. "Existencialismo escolástico suareciano: I. La existencia, constitutivo del ente." *Pensamiento* 12, no. 46 (1956): 157–78.

————. "Existencialismo escolástico suareciano: II. La existencia es lo principal en el ente." *Pensamiento* 13, no. 49 (1957): 21–38.

Honnefelder, Ludger. *Scientia transcendens: Die formale Bestimmung der Seiendheit und Realität in der Metafysik des Mittelalters und der Neuzeit. Duns Scotus, Suárez, Wolff, Kant, Peirce.* Hamburg: F. Meiner, 1990.

Iturrioz, Jesús. *Estudios sobre la metafísica de Francisco Suárez, S.J.* Madrid: Estudios Onienses, 1949.

Jaeger, Werner. *Aristotle: Fundamentals of the History of his Development.* 2nd ed. Translated by Richard Robinson. Oxford: Oxford University Press, 1948.

Lamanna, Marco. "Tra Fonseca e Suárez: L'ingresso della nozione di ens reale nella Schulmetaphysik." In *Francisco Suárez and his Legacy: The Impact of Suárezian Metaphysics and Epistemology on Modern Philosophy*. Edited by Marco Sgarbi, 141–68. Milano: Vita e Pensiero, 2010.

Leszl, Walter. *Aristotle's Conception of Ontology*. Padua: Editrice Antenore, 1975.

Lohr, Charles H. "Jesuit Aristotelianism and Sixteenth-Century Metaphysics." In *Paradosis: Studies in Memory of Edwin A. Quain*, 203–20. New York: Fordham University Press, 1976.

———. "Metaphysics." In *The Cambridge History of Renaissance Philosophy*. Edited by Charles B. Schmitt, Quentin Skinner, Eckhard Kessler, and Jill Kraye, 535–638. Cambridge: Cambridge University Press, 1988.

Mansion, Augustin. "L'objet de la science philosophique suprême d'après Aristote, Métaphysique, E, 1." In *Mélange de philosophie grecque offerts à Mgr. Diès par ses élèves, ses collègues et ses amis*, 151–68. Paris: Vrin, 1956.

Marion, Jean-Luc. *Sur la théologie blanche de Descartes: Analogie, création des verités éternelles et fondement*. Paris: PUF, 1981.

Maryks, Robert Aleksander. *The Jesuit Order as a Synagogue of Jews: Jesuits of Jewish Ancestry and Purity-of-Blood Laws in the Early Society of Jesus*. Leiden & Boston: Brill, 2010.

Matava, R. J. *Divine Causality and Human Free Choice: Domingo Báñez, Physical Premotion and the Controversy de Auxuliis Revisited*. Leiden & Boston: Brill, 2016.

Merlan, Philip. *From Platonism to Neoplatonism*. 2nd ed. The Hague: Martinus Nijhoff, 1960.

———. "On the Terms 'Metaphysics' and 'Being-qua-Being.'" *The Monist* 52, no. 2 (1986): 174–94.

Natorp, Paul. "Thema und Disposition der aristotelische Metaphysik." *Philosophische Monatshefte* 24 (1888): 37–65, 540–74.

Owens, Joseph. *The Doctrine of Being in the Aristotelian Metaphysics*. 3rd ed. Toronto: The Pontifical Institute of Mediaeval Studies, 1978.

Patzig, Günther. "Theology and Ontology in Aristotle's Metaphysics." In *Articles on Aristotle, Vol. 3: Metaphysics*. Edited by J. Barnes, M. Schofield, and R. Sorabji, 33–49. London: Duckworth, 1979.

Pereira, José. *Suárez: Between Scholasticism and Modernity*. Milwaukee: Marquette University Press, 2006.

Reale, Giovanni. *The Concept of First Philosophy and the Unity of the Metaphysics of Aristotle*. Translated by John Catan. Albany: SUNY Press, 1979.

Salas, Victor. "Francisco Suárez: End of the Scholastic ἐπιστήμη?" In *Francisco Suárez and his Legacy*, 9–28.

Schmutz, Jacob. "Science divine et métaphysique chez Francisco Suárez." In *Francisco Suárez: "Der ist der Mann,"* 347–79.

———. "From Theology to Philosophy: The Changing Status of the *Summa Theologiae*, 1500–2000." In *Aquinas's* Summa Theologiae: *A Critical Guide*. Edited by Jeffrey Hause, 221–41. Cambridge: Cambridge University Press, 2018.

Scorraille, Raoul de. *François Suárez de la Compagnie de Jésus*. 2 vols. Paris: P. Lethielleux, 1912–13.

Seigfried, Hans. *Wahrheit und Metaphysik bei Suarez*. Bonn: Bouvier, 1967.

Sgarbi, Marco. "Francisco Suárez and Christian Wolff: A Missed Intellectual Legacy." In *Francisco Suárez and his Legacy*, 227–41.

Shields, Christopher. "Being qua Being." In *The Oxford Handbook of Aristotle*. Edited by Christopher Shields, 343–71. Oxford: Oxford University Press, 2012.

Uscatescu Barrón, Jorge. "El concepto de metafísica en Suárez: su objeto y dominio." *Pensamiento* 51, no. 200 (1995): 215–36.

Verbeke, Gérard. "La physique d'Aristote est-elle une ontologie?" *Pensamiento* 35, nos. 138–39 (1979): 171–93.

Volpi, Franco. "Suárez et le problème de la métaphysique." *Revue de métaphysique et de morale* 98, no. 3 (1993): 395–411.

Wells, Norman J. "*Esse Cognitum* and Suárez Revisited." *American Catholic Philosophical Quarterly* 67, no. 3 (1993): 339–48.

Wolter, Allan. *The Transcendentals and Their Function in the Metaphysics of Duns Scotus*. Washington, D.C.: The Catholic University of America Press, 1946.

Also in the Early Modern Catholic Sources series

—

The Catholic Enlightenment: A Global Anthology
Edited by Ulrich L. Lehner and Shaun Blanchard

On the Motive of the Incarnation
The Salmanticenses (Discalced Carmelites of Salamanca)
Translated by Dylan Schrader

Metaphysical Disputation I: On the Nature of First Philosophy or Metaphysics was designed in Minion with Hypatia Sans display type and composed by Kachergis Book Design of Pittsboro, North Carolina. It was printed on 60-pound Maple Eggshell Cream B18 and bound by Maple Press of York, Pennsylvania.